Understanding China

The series will provide you with in-depth information on China's social, cultural and economic aspects. It covers a broad variety of topics, from economics and history to law, philosophy, cultural geography and regional politics, and offers a wealth of materials for researchers, doctoral students, and experienced practitioners.

Rixu Lan

The Financial Development of China

華中科技大學出版社
Huazhong University of Science and Technology Press

Springer

Rixu Lan
School of Economics
Central University of Finance
and Economics
Beijing, China

Translated by
Shougang Huang
Hubei University of Economics
Wuhan, China

Jue Wen
Hubei University of Economics
Wuhan, China

Yajing Wang
Hubei University of Economics
Wuhan, China

ISSN 2196-3134 ISSN 2196-3142 (electronic)
Understanding China
ISBN 978-981-97-8272-7 ISBN 978-981-97-8273-4 (eBook)
https://doi.org/10.1007/978-981-97-8273-4

Jointly published with Huazhong University of Science and Technology Press
The print edition is not for sale in China (Mainland). Customers from China (Mainland) please order the print book from: Huazhong University of Science and Technology Press.
ISBN of the Co-Publisher's edition: 978-7-5680-5408-9

This Springer imprint is published by the registered company Springer Nature Singapore Pte Ltd.
The registered company address is: 152 Beach Road, #21-01/04 Gateway East, Singapore 189721, Singapore

Contents

About the Author

Rixu Lan is a professor and doctoral advisor at the School of Economics, Central University of Finance and Economics. He serves as the director of the Department of Economic History and the Center for Comparative Economic Studies between China and Foreign Countries. He also holds positions such as a executive director of the Chinese Economic History Society, director of the National History Society, and vice president of the Chinese Business History Society. A professor Lan is dedicated to the study of financial theory and modern financial history, Sino-foreign economic relations, and business history.

He has published eight monographs, including *The Path to China's Financial Modernization*, *Research on the Changes and Performance of China's Modern Banking System*, *The Road to Economic Power: A History of China's Changing Economic Status*, *Transformation of China's Modern Banking System from the Late Qing Era to the 1930s (Vols.1 and 2)*, *The Evolution of Sino-Foreign Financial Organizations: A Perspective Based on Market-Technology-Organization*, and *Research on the Development of China's Financial Industry (1949–2019)*. A professor Lan has also edited six books and contributed to six textbooks, three of which are included in the National Social Science Fund of China's Foreign Translation Project. He has published over 100 papers, has led four projects funded by the National Social Science Fund of China, one project funded by the Ministry of Education's Philosophy and Social Science Research Fund of China, and eleven other projects, and has received four provincial and ministerial level awards.

Chapter 1
Introduction

2019 marks the 70th anniversary of the founding of the People's Republic of China.[1] The financial development of China has gone through a journey of 70 years, experiencing two distinct periods. In the 30 years before the reform and opening up, China integrated the financial systems of the old and newly liberated areas on the basis of the revolutionary war period's financial industry, establishing the financial system of China. Subsequently, to adapt to the needs of the social economic system, China quickly established a relatively single financial system with a focus on "managing funds". In the 40 years since the reform and opening up, China's financial sector has gradually shifted from "managing funds" to "regulating market", forming a multi-level financial system centered around the People's Bank of China. This system is

Lan Rixu. "Financial Changes and Characteristics in China: Based on the Perspective of Financial Function Changes", *Journal of Hebei Normal University*, 2017(6).

[1] The finance of China has always been the focus of the academic circle and in all walks of life. However, from the perspective of the changes of the finance of China in the past 70 years, the existing researches mainly focus on China's finance within 50 years and 60 years since 1949, with the latest written in 2017 (such as *50 Years of Finance of China* edited by Shang Ming, China Finance and Economics Press, 1999; Yang Xitian et al., *A General History of Chinese Finance* (Volume 6): The Period of the People's Republic of China, China Finance Publishing House, 2002; 60 Years of Finance in China, China Finance and Economics Publishing House, 2009; Li De, The Development of China's Financial Industry (Volume 1 and 2), People's Publishing House, 2015; Cao Yuanzheng, Great Power and Great Finance: 40 Years of Financial System Reform in China, 2018 edition of Guangdong Economic Publishing House, etc.) Of course, in the economic history of the People's Republic of China, there are also related to the development of the financial industry, most of the content is simple; Although there are some specialized works published in the fields of capital market, banking, the People's Bank of China, insurance, trust, etc., the contents are concentrated in relatively single and specialized fields, which is difficult to reflect the overall picture of the financial development of China, and there is no corresponding follow-up research. There are also obvious deficiencies in some fields of previous studies, and the changes are rarely analyzed from the perspective of financial functions. This book is an in-depth analysis of the 70-year history of financial development in China from this perspective.

R. Lan, *The Financial Development of China*, Understanding China,
https://doi.org/10.1007/978-981-97-8273-4_1

characterized by comprehensive functions, diverse forms, division of labor, cooperation, and complementarity. It has achieved remarkable results in utilizing macro-financial regulation to promote more than 30 years of high-speed economic growth in China, often referred to as a "miracle". In terms of current economic structural adjustments and transformations, the "Internet +" model led by internet finance has undoubtedly triggered the "Catfish Effect" in China's economic development. The financial sector has witnessed a surge of innovation, and certain branches are beginning to surpass international standards.

1.1 Financial Development Trajectory of China

Finance is the core of the modern economy. In a broad sense, it covers the money supply, which is closely related to prices, the banking and non-bank financial institutions system, the short-term money lending market, the securities market, the insurance system, and many aspects of international finance, etc.[2] Since 1949, the connotation, business and functions of various fields of finance have undergone great changes. At the same time, affected by many factors, China's financial development is quite tortuous. From the perspective of financial function changes, the financial industry has experienced a development process from diversification to simplicity and then gradually to diversification, with a clear change track, and roughly experienced four periods.

First, during the period from 1949 to 1952, the financial system with the People's Bank of China as the core was rapidly established. The origin of China's financial system can be traced back to the financial industry established in various periods of the Revolutionary War, which has been continued to provide various financial services based on collective or state capital. On December 1, 1948, the People's Bank of China was established on the basis of Beihai Bank, North China Bank and Northwest Farmers Bank, which opened the prelude to the development of China's financial industry and the establishment of a financial system. Then, in accordance with the Common Program of the Chinese People's Political Consultative Conference (hereafter referred to as the Common Program), "The People's Republic of China must abolish all privileges of the imperialist countries in China, confiscate bureaucratic capital and give it back to the state... Protect the public property of the state and the property of cooperatives, protect the economic interests of workers, peasants, petty bourgeoisie and national bourgeoisie and their private property".[3] With the People's Bank of China as the center, the different financial institutions

[2] Huang Da. *Finance—Meaning, Discipline, Situation, Method and Others*. China Finance Publishing House, 2001: 3.

[3] Documents Research Office of the CPC Central Committee: *Selected and Edited Important Documents Since the Founding of the People's Republic of China* (Volume 1), China Central Literary Publishing House, 2011: 2.

in the old liberated areas and the newly liberated areas were classified and integrated, and finally formed a relatively simple financial system in the early days of the People's Republic of China; with the first set of RMB issued by the People's Bank of China as the core, different types of currencies were gradually converted on schedule, which quickly ended the chaotic currency status quo and established a unified RMB system. The construction of China's financial system has made great contributions to the recovery of the national economy, the stabilization of serious inflation and prices in the early days of the People's Republic of China, and the balance of national fiscal revenues and expenditures.

Second, from 1953 to 1978, the function of "managing funds" was established. Learning from the Soviet Union (former USSR, now Russia), China quickly established a highly centralized and unified planned-economy. In line with this, China's financial industry has adopted a highly centralized and unified management method, with the state credit replacing commercial credit and implementing a fund management system of unified revenue, unified expenditure, unified deposit and unified lending. Financial institutions are shrinking, the Agricultural Bank of China, being abolished three times, the Bank of China and some others merged into the People's Bank of China; In 1959, the People's Insurance Company of China ceased to carry out domestic insurance business, and only engaged in very limited overseas insurance business, and the management function was transferred to the People's Bank of China.

The third is the recovery and development of the modern financial system from 1979 to 1993, but its functions experienced an obvious transition process between "managing funds" and "regulating the market". The Third Plenum of the 11th Central Committee of the Communist Party of China kicked off the reform of China's financial system. In 1979, Deng Xiaoping proposed that "banks must be really run as banks." Since then, China has established a central bank system, forming a multi-level financial organization system and diversified financial market system consisting of state-owned banks, joint-stock banks, urban commercial banks, rural credit cooperatives and foreign banks. During this period, state-owned banks were dealing with both policy business and commercial business, and there was still a big gap between them and real banks. The financial market has developed to a certain extent, but the scale is extremely small, and the gradual development is mainly driven by local governments, which has many constraints and relatively chaotic management. The goal of financial reform is fluctuating between "managing funds" and "regulating the market", during which more than a dozen modules are explored to integrate the relationship between the two, but the effect is not satisfactory, and it cannot break the cycle of "chaos when given freedom and stagnation when controlled." In November 1993, the Third Plenary Session of the 14th CPC Central Committee established the reform goal of establishing a socialist market economy, ending the debate between the functions of "managing funds" and "regulating the market" in financial reform. On December 25, The State Council made the Decision on the Reform of the financial system, clarifying that the goal of the reform of the financial system is "to establish a macro-control system of the central bank that independently implements monetary policies under the leadership of The State Council; to establish a financial organization system in which policy finance is separated from commercial finance, with state-owned commercial banks as the main body and a variety of financial institutions coexisting; to establish a unified, open, orderly competition, and strict management of the financial market system", which thus opened the curtain of China's financial deepening reform, the People's Bank of China truly turning into a central bank, state-owned specialized banks into real commercial banks, a financial market growing out of nothing, multi-department management under the leadership of local governments gradually transitioning to centralized management. The market began to play a fundamental role in resource allocation.

Fourth, since 1994, China's financial development has realized the positioning of "regulating the market", and the market has changed from a basic role to a decisive role in resource allocation, thus achieving unprecedented development of the financial industry. In the field of modern finance, the promulgation of the Law of the People's Republic of China on the People's Bank of China in 1995 clarified the responsibilities of the People's Bank of China as a central bank and strengthened the regulatory functions of the central bank. Then the central bank's goals, means, regulation and control methods have been continuously innovated and improved; We have completed the reform of integrating the RMB exchange rate into the current account and realized the convertibility of the RMB. Reform of the capital account has also been deepened. So far, 92% of all items have been fully or partially open. The separation of policy finance and commercial finance has promoted the commercialization reform of the four state-owned commercial banks, namely the Industrial and Commercial Bank of China, the Agricultural Bank of China, the Bank of China and the China Construction Bank. Through asset reorganization, introduction of strategic investors, joint-stock transformation and listing, the state-owned banks have transformed from "technical bankruptcy" to the top ten banks in the world. Among them, the Industrial and Commercial Bank of China has been the world's largest bank for many years. Bank-type financial institutions such as joint-stock banks, city commercial banks, cooperative financial institutions and other non-bank financial institutions have accelerated their reform and development. Policy banks such as the China Development Bank have clarified their positions and the relationship between commercial and policy businesses. A multi-level and multi-functional financial market has been developed and improved, and financial products have become increasingly rich and diversified. In 2003, we established and improved the separate operation and supervision system of "1 bank and 3 commissions" (The People's Republic of China, China Banking Regulatory Commission, China Securities Regulatory Commission and China Insurance Regulatory Commission). At the Fifth National Financial Work Conference in 2017, we strengthened prudential supervision, strengthened functional supervision and behavioral supervision, and established the Financial Stability and Development Committee of The State Council to guard against systemic financial risks. We vigorously promoted the development of the financial legal system and financial infrastructure, formed a multi-level and multi-channel training mechanism for financial talents, and greatly improved the level of financial services.

In the field of Internet finance,[4] the no-threshold, high-yield Internet financial products derived from Yu'e Bao and Tianhong Fund in 2013 opened the prelude to the explosive growth of pure Internet financial services in China. From its appearance in June 2013 to February 26, 2014, Yu'e Bao had 81 million users and more than 500 billion yuan in capital. In more than half a year, the number of users exceeded the number of effective users of the Shanghai and Shenzhen stock markets with more than 20 years of development history, and Tianhong Fund, which is related to Yu'e Bao, rose from a small fund company to the leader of the fund industry in more than half a year. The emergence of Yu'e Bao has rapidly triggered a "Catfish Effect" in all sectors of society. Pure Internet finance models with P2P and crowdfunding as the core have risen rapidly, and six models, including Internet payment, online lending, equity crowdfunding, Internet insurance, Internet finance and Internet consumer finance, have been fully developed. After that, the development of Internet finance that rose under the condition of "three nos" has been continuously standardized, and each model has been incorporated into the existing regulatory system of "one line and three meetings", and its strength has been enhanced. The estimated brand value and users of the four Internet finance giants centered on "BATJ" (Baidu Finance, Ant Financial, Tencent, Jingdong Finance) will or have exceeded any modern financial organization, and their cross-border operation has broken the capability boundary of modern finance, forcing modern finance to accelerate the pace of diversification. It has made Internet finance and modern finance show a trend of integrated development, promoted the construction of financial order and the improvement of financial innovation ability, and has shown a trend of leading the international level in the fields of online payment and online lending. In 2017, the four major state-owned commercial banks established close cooperation with the "BATJ" to promote the development of science and technology finance; and the four major state-owned commercial banks successively established inclusive finance departments in June 2017. The 2018 Government Work Report clearly required large and medium-sized commercial banks to set up inclusive finance departments, which greatly promoted the establishment of China's inclusive financial system, and made finance more return to the essence of serving the real economy.

In the future, China's financial industry will inevitably strengthen the construction of corporate governance mechanisms of financial institutions, promote supply side structural reform of the financial, increase the diversification of the financial market and increase the proportion of direct financing, continue to strengthen the construction of an inclusive financial system, strengthen the financial risk prevention system, so that the financial industry can truly serve the real economy.

---

[4] Lan Rixu: *Changes in Financial Organizations in China and Abroad: From the perspective of Market-Technology-Organization*, Social Sciences Academic Press, 2016: 203.

1.2 China's Financial Development Characteristics

Over the past 70 years, China's financial sector has evolved from a relatively diversified development pattern in the early days of the People's Republic of China to a single financial system with "managing funds" as the core role. After the reform and opening up, China experienced a short period of fluctuation between "managing funds" and "regulating market", and quickly established the core position of "regulating market" and developed rapidly toward diversification. In 2013, the rise of pure Internet finance changed the original development trend of China's finance, showing a transformation to inclusive finance, green finance, science and technology finance and other directions, the integration trend of modern finance and Internet finance, and the repositioning of finance and technology have greatly improved China's financial innovation ability and international competitiveness. Looking at the development process of China's finance, it obviously has the following characteristics.

First, China's financial development has shown a phased development trend. Since the establishment of the People's Bank of China on December 1, 1948, the development of China's financial industry can be basically divided into two major stages. In the 30 years before the reform and opening up, the main track of financial development was to form a single financial system under the highly centralized planned economic system, and finance acted as the cashier of financial departments around the function of "managing funds". According to the situation of this stage, the financial development can be further divided into two small stages: before 1952, the financial system of China was established; The period from 1953 to the reform and opening up was the formation and transformation of the single financial system. Since the reform and opening up, the main line of China's financial development is that under the background of the transformation and establishment of the planned economic system to the socialist market economy, a diversified financial system with the central bank as the center has been increasingly formed, and the financial function of "regulating the market" has been formed. According to the positioning of China's financial functions, it can be roughly subdivided into two stages: Before 1993, the diversified financial system with the People's Bank of China as the main body was basically formed, but its functions shifted between "managing funds" and "regulating the market"; After 1993, the diversified financial system has been comprehensively developed, the function of "regulating the market" has been fully established, and a separate management and operation system with "one bank and three commissions" as the main body has been established in the financial management system. With the establishment of the development trend of financial diversification, especially the rise of Internet finance, although China's financial industry still maintains a separate business model in the system, it has moved toward a mixed business pattern in operation, and the management system has also established a regulatory mechanism of "one committee, one bank and two commissions"[5] after the Fifth National Financial Work Conference.

Second, the path choice of China's financial development is dominated by government coercion and gradual change, and tends to be dominated by gradual change, and the function of the government is more reflected in the top-level design. Since 1949, China's financial industry has undergone great changes, but the path selection is dominated by the government, and there is a trend of both compulsory and gradual evolution under the guidance of policy. At the beginning of the People's Republic of China, according to the Common Program, the People's Bank of China classified and integrated financial organizations with different capital components, such as bureaucrats, ethnic groups, and foreign capital, to build the financial system of China. With the RMB issued by the People's Bank of China as the center, an independent and unified RMB system has been established to exchange different types of currencies within a specified time limit. After 1953, with the formation of the planned economic system, China's financial system was rapidly centralized into a unified financial system, and its functions shrank to the role of settlement and cashier of "managing funds". After the reform and opening up, the People's Bank of China was independent from the office of the Ministry of Finance, and the People's Bank of China system, banking order and necessary rules and regulations were restored. Later, the Agricultural Bank of China, Bank of China, China Construction Bank and Industrial and Commercial Bank of China were separated or established from the People's Bank of China. By 1993, China had basically completed the transformation from a single financial system to a diversified financial system, with financial markets emerging from scratch and financial services expanding and developing rapidly. At this time, the basic function of finance has gradually been restored, but it is still in the stage of transition between "managing funds" and "regulating the market", and the development of financial institutions, financial markets and financial businesses is still very irregular. In December 1993, the Decision of The State Council on the Reform of the Financial System was promulgated, which clarified the direction of China's financial reform. Since 1994, under the guidance of government policies, the independent status of the People's Bank of China as a central bank has been established, and monetary policy tools have become increasingly diversified and targeted. In banking institutions, through financial consolidation, introduction of strategic investors, joint-stock reform and listing, they have improved their own strength and corporate governance, and their business operations have become more diversified under the impact of Internet finance. The reform of non-bank institutions is deepening and their businesses are becoming more diversified. Financial markets were fully developed; In terms of financial functions, China has fully established the function of "regulating the market". In 2013, China's Internet finance rose, and the Chinese government continued the gradual approach of modern financial reform and deepening. With regard to the development of Internet finance from developed

[5] One committee: Financial Stability and Development Committee; One bank and two supervision commissions: China Banking and Insurance Regulatory Commission; People's Bank of China, China Securities Regulatory Commission.

countries in China, the government has adopted an open and inclusive policy, loosening first and then tightening, which has enabled China's Internet finance to surpass any developed country in terms of volume and scale in a short period of time and occupy a leading position in the world. The innovative behavior of Internet finance in technology, products and services has quickly formed a wave of innovation in China's finance, improved the competitiveness of China's finance, and even made China's finance achieve the goal of catching up in international competition in some fields.

Third, the relationship between China's financial development and economic development is relatively consistent. Finance is the blood of economy, and economy determines the trajectory of financial development. "It is true that economy determines finance; Financial development without the economic foundation, whether it is financial institutions, financial markets or financial macro-control, will be water without a source."[6] Finance itself is a very special industry, as it can penetrate other sectors of the economy. "In contemporary times, finance is a special industrial sector, operating money, securities, financial derivatives and other financial commodities, is a relatively independent system in the national economy, with its own unique operating mechanism and trajectory." The relationship between finance and economy permeates and integrates with each other, which has long gone beyond the subordinate and passive position of traditional finance to the economy. Finance is not only in the dominant position in the economy, but also separated from the economy, showing a trend of independent development. Therefore, to discuss the separation of finance and economy does not mean that the economy cannot determine finance, nor does it emphasize that finance has a negative effect on the economy, but that the existence, activities, development and evolution of finance itself are not based on the real economy, and have their own specific forms and laws."[7] By combing and analyzing the financial development process of China, we clearly see that although financial development is quite tortuous, the relationship between financial development and economic development is relatively consistent. In the stage of shrinking financial functions, China's economic development level is low and the industry is single. This is reflected in the relationship between finance and economic development before the reform and opening up. At the beginning of the People's Republic of China, in order to quickly restore the national economy and quell hyperinflation, China's financial development focused on the unification of the financial system into the financial business with the People's Bank of China as the main body, and on the end of the chaotic monetary system and the establishment of a unified RMB system. After that, with the establishment of the development strategy of heavy industry, it is necessary to establish a highly centralized financial system to match it and mobilize all funds to support the implementation of the national economic development plan in China, which is highly short of funds. However, this period was deeply disturbed by various political movements so that the financial function could not play, and

[6] Li Yang et al.: *60 Years of Financial Development in China*, China Finance and Economic Press, 2009, Preface.

[7] Zhang Xiaojun, Ma Yue. *Understanding Chinese Finance*, Chemical Industry Press, 2016: 155.

the economy also encountered great ups and downs, with the exploration for a good financial system difficult and tortuous.

In the period of better financial development, China's economy has shown a rapid development trend. This can be evidenced by the changes in the relationship between finance and economic development since the reform and opening up. From 1979 to 1993, China clearly established a planned socialist commodity economy, and there was a huge debate on the relationship between plan-oriented economy and market-oriented economy, which was reflected in the financial development. Although China established a diversified modern financial system with the People's Bank of China as the core, the financial function fluctuated between "managing funds" and "regulating the market". This also leads to a certain degree of divergence between financial and economic development, leading to problems such as overheating of the economy and lagging financial reform. With the adoption of the Decision of the Central Committee of the Communist Party of China on Several Issues Concerning the Establishment of a Socialist Market Economy by the Third Plenary Session of the 14th CPC Central Committee in November 1993, China has clearly defined the goal of establishing a socialist market economy. Subsequently, the Decision of The State Council on the Reform of the Financial System was published, which clarified the goals of financial development, established the independent status of the central bank and the reform of financial commercialization. In this way, in the positioning of financial functions, China has completely turned to and established the goal of "adjusting the market", thus creating good conditions for social and economic development.

Since 2013, China's economic development has been faced with difficulties such as insufficient domestic demand and excess production capacity, and the tendency of capital flow to "avoid real economy" has aggravated the "Macmillan gap" of small and medium-sized enterprises and the financing and financial management difficulties of middle and lower-class people. In addition, the long-term rapid economic growth has significantly increased the income level of the general public and increased the demand for financial services. Under the condition of information asymmetry and uncertainty, the existing financial suppression phenomenon cannot meet the ever-expanding diversified financial needs. In this context, the rise of pure Internet finance with P2P and crowdfunding as the main body, in the spirit of openness, inclusiveness, collaboration, and sharing of the Internet, has partially made up for the shortcomings of existing financial services, covered the original financial service blind spot in terms of time, space, people, and enterprises, and partially alleviated the problem of "financing difficulties". At the same time, the development of Internet finance has stirred the wave of innovation in technology, products and services in the entire financial field, and promoted many aspects of China's financial field to gradually lead the international level. In many practices such as imitation and innovation, market and government relations, it also provides a useful mirror for the economic restructuring since China's economy entered the new normal.[8]

[8] Lan Rixu: *The Reflection of the Development of Internet Finance Industry on the Adjustment of China's Industrial Structure*, Industrial and Technological History Research, Volume 2, 2017.

Fourth, the development of the financial industry has a strong administrative color, but the degree of marketization has been deepening. During the period from 1949 to the reform and opening up, China's financial sector fully realized the transformation from a diversified financial structure to a single financial system under the guidance of government policies, and financial functions were increasingly concentrated in the field of "capital management" with settlement, cashier and cash management as the connotation, so as to meet the needs of the highly centralized planned economic system. At the beginning of the reform and opening up, although the commercial function of the People's Bank of China was constantly stripped away and corresponding financial institutions were set up, the newly established institutions still shoulder the policy task and bear the commercial duty. The development of the financial market is dominated by local governments, and it is extremely administrative in multi-department management. "To some extent, the scope of the Chinese government's intervention in the securities market has exceeded the scope of market failure, and the tangible hand of the government has become a 'restless hand' to a certain extent, even at the cost of sacrificing the efficiency of the entire market to regulate the market",[9] so that in China's financial field, there is a "chaos when given freedom and stagnation when controlled" crux. Since 1994, with the separation of policy and commercial functions, the degree of marketization of financial functions in the development of diversified and multi-level financial system has been deepening. In the financial market, the multi-department management system led by the local government is gradually changing to the unified and centralized management of the central government. So far, the degree of administrative intervention has gradually decreased, and the market has increasingly become the decisive means of resource allocation in China's financial field. In 2012, the report to the 18th CPC National Congress made clear the decisive position of the market in resource allocation. In 2017, the Chinese government further established the decisive role of the market in the allocation of financial resources at the Fifth National Financial Work Conference, and the government should play a more important role. The 19th National Congress of the Communist Party of China was held on October 18, 2017, and Chinese president Xi Jingping once again pointed out in his report that "the market should play a decisive role in resource allocation".

In addition, in the long-term development of China's finance, China's direct financing has achieved rapid development, and the development of Internet finance has increasingly blurred the boundary between the market and institutions, showing a cross-border business trend, but indirect financing with banks as the main body still occupies an absolute advantage. At the same time, China's financial development is basically synchronized with policy changes and has a downward spiral development trend under policy guidance, which has become a distinctive feature of China's financial development in this period.

[9] Hu Ruyin: *The Development and Changes of China's Capital Market*, Gezhi Publishing House, Shanghai People's Publishing House, 2008: 230.

1.3 Experiences of China's Financial Transition

In the 70 years of financial development and change, although China's financial industry has experienced a complicated and tortuous process, it has provided a lot of useful experience for the further modernization of the financial industry and the powerful promotion of social and economic development in the future. One is the financial development to deal with the relationship between market and government. Since 1949, China's financial changes have experienced an obvious process of "marketization—non-marketization—transition between market and government function—marketization". When the relationship between the government and the market is moderately balanced, China's financial development is relatively smooth. To be specific, before the reform and opening up, China implemented a highly unified financial management system and replaced the market with government means. Although it was beneficial for the government to concentrate limited funds to realize the development strategy of heavy industry under the condition of shortage of funds, long-term government intervention could not give full play to the basic role of the market in resource allocation. It leads to the complete distortion of financial functions, low operating efficiency, and difficult to achieve the best allocation of funds. In this context, once the government intervenes excessively or policy measures deviate, it will inevitably lead to the failure of finance to meet the needs of economic development, resulting in a high degree of disorder in financial development under the "political leadership". From the reform and opening up in 1978 to 1993, the financial development fluctuated between the market and the government, with government intervention as the core of "managing funds" at one time and market functions as the core of "regulating the market" at the other. Although China tried to adopt various models to achieve the balance between the two, the effect was not satisfactory. This has also led to various disorders and perplexities in China's financial development. Since 1994, with the establishment of the socialist market economy system, government intervention in financial development has been significantly reduced, and market functions have gradually been established. In 1997, the first National Financial Work Conference was held, and thereafter it was held every five years, which greatly changed the practice of "crossing the river by feeling the stones" in the previous financial reform. The Party and the government increasingly highlighted their top-level design ideas in the financial reform and development, and clarified the development direction of the financial industry in the following period of time, as shown in Table 1.1.

During this period, China effectively handled the relationship between the government and the market, and China's finance entered a stage of rapid development. In 2013, the rise of China's Internet finance, the government in the "visible hand" and "invisible hand" appropriate balance, giving them sufficient space for innovation and development. This is not only expressed in the reports of the two sessions at the central and local levels, but also expressed very clearly in the "Guiding Opinions on Promoting the healthy Development of Internet Finance" jointly issued by the People's Bank of China and other ten ministries and commissions on July 18, 2015,

Table 1.1 Top-level design of China's financial reform

Reform timeline	Important meeting	Top-level design idea
1993	Market economy orientation was set in The Third Plenary Session of the 14th CPC Central Committee	Decision of The State Council on reform of the financial system
1997	1st National Financial Work Conference	Strengthen financial supervision and banking reform, and comprehensively clean up rural cooperative foundations
2002	2nd National Financial Work Conference	Strengthen financial supervision, banking reform, and reform of rural credit cooperatives
2007	3rd National Financial Work Conference	Strengthen financial supervision, banking reform, and management of foreign exchange reserves
2012	4th National Financia Work Conference	Strengthen and improve financial regulation, specify the general requirements and main principles for financial work, increase financial services to the real economy, and ensure that capital flows to the real economy; Resolutely restrain the economy from "turning from real to virtual", clarify the direction of reform in the allocation of resources by the market, clarify the boundaries and scope of the role of the government, and expand the opening up of the financial sector
2017	The Fifth National Financial Work Conference and the 19th CPC National Congress and the Third Plenary Session of the 19th CPC Central Committee	Strengthen financial supervision, clarify the four principles and three tasks for the development of the financial sector, emphasize the strength of financial support for the real economy, and strengthen the Party's leadership over financial work. The report of the 19th National Congress of the Communist Party of China says to hold the bottom-line of no systematic financial crisis. The third Plenary Session of the 19th CPC Central Committee decides on the reform of government institutions, so as to clarify the direction for the reform of financial management institutions

"Internet finance is a new thing and an emerging business form, and it is necessary to develop moderately loose regulatory policies so as to leave room and space for Internet financial innovation." After a long period of exploration, the People's Bank of China, together with relevant ministries and commissions, incorporated various modes of Internet finance into the relevant bodies of the original financial management system, formulated and introduced relevant management rules, and set aside certain adjustment time for the development of Internet finance. The proper balance between the government and the market has undoubtedly played a huge role in promoting the rise of Internet finance, which has narrowed the gap between China and developed countries in financial development level in a very short period of time, and even surpassed developed countries in some aspects, ahead of the international level, and enhanced the international competitiveness of China's financial field.

Second, the relationship between economy and finance has been effectively handled in the course of financial development. As mentioned above, economy determines finance, and finance reacts on economy. When the relationship between the two is effectively handled, China's financial development and economic growth will inevitably complement each other. Financial viability enables economic viability and financial stability, economic stability. When the relationship between economy and finance is smooth, China's economy is bound to develop rapidly. "History since 1949 has proved that when the position and role of finance in the socialist economy is more correctly understood, the development of finance will be more healthy and smooth, and the greater its achievements in supporting and promoting the development of the national economy."[10] Before the reform and opening up, although financial changes complied with the reform of the social and economic system, the financial function was suppressed for a long time, and the allocation of resources in the financial market was not effectively used, but was artificially impacted in various political movements, which led to the lack of the role of finance on the economy, and the economy also fluctuated greatly under the impact of various political factors. The economic structure is severely distorted. Since the reform and opening up, the Chinese government has gradually recognized the importance of a good relationship between finance and economy through the gradual reform of the earlier economic system. As a result, the relationship between finance and economy has changed from passive obedience to active adaptation over the past 40 years, resulting in finance increasingly returning to the essence of serving the real economy. In the report of the 19th National Congress of the Communist Party of China, it was clearly pointed out that "strengthening the ability of financial services to serve the real economy".

The third is the effective balance between supervision and innovation in financial development. Crisis and finance go hand in hand, and financial crisis is an important source of social and economic fluctuations. "Finance is the lifeblood of the real economy and plays a subordinate role. Independent development of finance divorced from the real economy will lead to asset price bubbles, financial crises and jeopardize financial security." While promoting financial development and enhancing financial competitiveness, if financial regulation and innovation can be effectively balanced, the financial sector will surely achieve rapid development. If there is no effective balance, there may be a dilemma at the beginning of reform and opening up that "chaos when given freedom and stagnation when controlled"; Or, as before the reform and opening up, the financial function was completely suppressed, unable to play a role in promoting economic development, and finance was only a vassal of finance, acting as a single role of "managing funds" mainly based on settlement and cashier. Or let the development of finance, resulting in a virtual bubble, capital "dodging the reality", the accumulation of financial risks, may lead to regional or systemic financial waves. From the perspective of the financial change process since 1949,

---

[10] Yang Xitian et al. *China's Financial History (Volume 6): The Period of the People's Republic of China*, China Finance Publishing House, 2002, Introduction, p. 5.

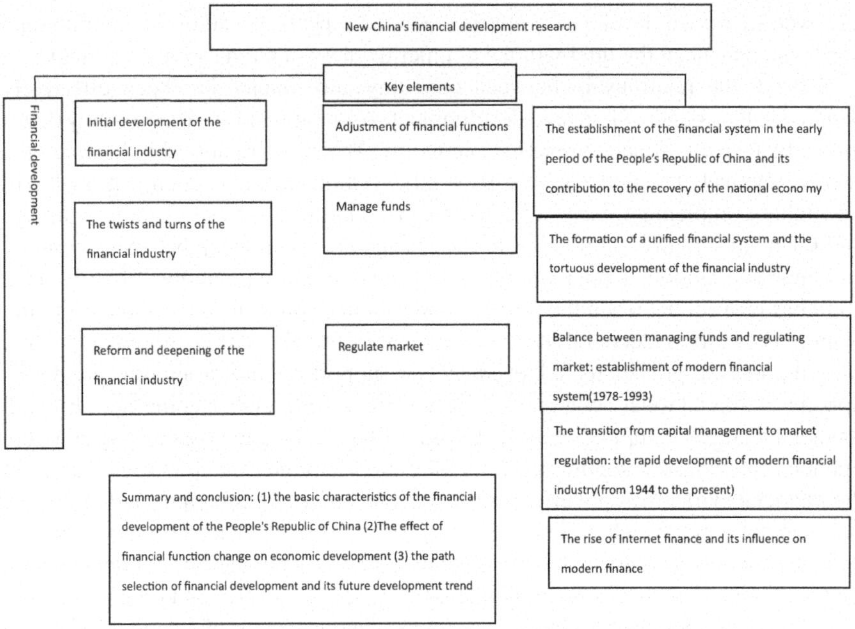

Fig. 1.1 Research framework of financial development of China

we must effectively play the role of financial resource allocation, give finance a certain space for innovation, but at the same time, we must also moderately supervise the development of finance, improve the financial supervision system, and hold the bottom line of no systemic financial risks.[11]

1.4 The Structure of the Book

From the perspective of changes in financial functions, this book focuses on the main line of resource allocation in each period under the premise of economic changes, and reviews thoroughly and systematically the 70-year history of financial development in China. The research content and structure are shown in Fig. 1.1.

This book takes the change of core elements as the standard, divides China's financial development into four parts and ten chapters, plus an introduction and a conclusion. The introduction part, a brief review of the development process of China's finance in the past 70 years, summarizes the characteristics and experiences of the development and change of China's finance in the past 70 years, and provides

[11] Xi Jinping: "Secure a Decisive Victory in Building a Moderately Prosperous Society in All Respects and Strive for the Great Success of Socialism with Chinese Characteristics for a New Era—Report at the 19th National Congress of the Communist Party of China.".

some useful references for the development of China's financial industry in the future. At the same time, make a brief explanation of the structure and style of the book. After that, it focuses on the four parts of the financial development of China, and gives a brief introduction to the social economy of the relevant period before each part, which lays the foundation for the socio-economic background of the financial development in the subsequent part.

The first part is the initial development period of our country's financial industry. According to the difference of financial functions, it is divided into two chapters. The first chapter mainly introduces the origin of the financial system of China and how to build the financial system of China around the establishment of the financial institution system and the unification of RMB. On the surface, the new Chinese financial system originated from the People's Bank of China established in December 1948 and the RMB issued by it, but in fact, its roots can be traced back to the State Bank of the Chinese Soviet Republic established during the Great Revolution, and after several institutional evolution, it eventually evolved into the Northwest Farmers Bank, an important part of the People's Bank of China. The banks, which had been established during the first Revolutionary Civil War, raised funds by using collective assets and issuing money to promote production, stabilize prices, support the war, and care for people's lives, which became the common experience of the financial industry in all subsequent periods. After the founding of the People's Bank of China, China centered on it and finally established the financial institution system in the early stage of China by merging financial institutions in liberated areas, accepting bureaucratic capital financial institutions, reforming national capital financial institutions, and stopping the privilege of foreign financial institutions. At the same time, a unified RMB system was realized through the conversion of the currencies issued by the liberated areas, the suspension of the use of the national government-issued currencies such as legal coins, and the prohibition of the circulation of gold, silver and foreign currencies; the foreign-controlled foreign exchange system was transformed into an independent foreign exchange management system. With the increasing simplification of China's financial organizations, financial functions have also been transformed from complex to relatively simple, which is more conducive to the centralized management and control of the government. The third chapter explains that during the construction of China's financial system, the Chinese government has made important contributions to the recovery of national economy and the suppression of inflation by means of credit policy, interest rate lever and other tools. Later, with the initial formation of the organizational structure of the People's Bank of China, under its leadership, insurance, foreign exchange and other businesses were smoothly developed, and the relationship between finance and economy gradually entered into a good cycle.

The second part explores the development of the financial industry during the period of twists and turns in the planned economy. Based on the changes in financial functions, it is divided into Chaps. 4 and 5. Chapter 4 focuses on the formation of a highly centralized and unified financial management system. After 1953, through further nationalization of financial organizations and simplification of institutions, China rapidly established a highly centralized and unified national banking system. Bank credit replaced commercial credit, with all credit concentrated in the People's

Bank of China. In terms of operational management, the People's Bank of China exercised both monetary issuance and financial regulatory functions, as well as engaged in commercial banking activities such as lending, savings, settlement, and foreign exchange. Under this highly centralized financial system, the functions of finance almost shrunk to the core tasks of cash management, settlement, and fund management. Subsequently, influenced by adjustments in the planned economic management system and changes in the social, political, and economic environment, the highly centralized financial management system experienced fluctuations and underwent partial improvements. However, its unified structure and fund management function continued until the beginning of the reform and opening up. Chapter 5 introduces the tortuous development process of China's financial industry during the planned economy period. According to the three stages of the "First Five-Year Plan", the Great Leap Forward and the period of rectification, detailed and systematic analysis is conducted on China's financial system, monetary system, and contents such as "centralized deposits" and "centralized loans". It points out that China's financial industry has experienced twists and turns and fluctuations, although there have been adjustments and rectification, the overall trend of financial functions and business has shown a decline. The third part is the development period of financial industry towards market economy. In line with the transformation of financial function from "managing funds" to "regulating the market", and finally the status of "regulating the market" being established, the financial body has changed from a single system of the People's Bank of China to a multi-function financial organization and financial market. According to the perspective of the evolution of financial bodies, this part is divided into five chapters: Chaps. 6, 7, 8, and 9. Chapter 6 is a systematic introduction to the separation of the People's Bank of China from the Ministry of Finance, its commercial functions being stripped, the establishment of independent functions of the central bank, improve its management and currency control functions being improved, thus a relatively independent central bank system was in the making.

Chapter 7 systematically reviews the process of recovery, establishment and reform of China's banking institutions since the reform and opening up, and points out that China has formed a macro banking system composed of state-owned commercial banks, joint-stock commercial banks, city commercial banks, foreign banks and diversified rural financial institutions. In the transformation and positioning of financial functions to "regulating market", China's experience is reflected in the expansion of asset scale, improved capital quality, enhanced ability to serve the real economy, improved operational efficiency, and accelerated internationalization. Chapter 8 analyzes the emergence, development and expansion of non-bank financial institutions in China since the reform and opening up, indicating that the development of non-bank financial institutions is a process of continuous adaptation to social and economic development; Chapter 9 details and summarizes the process of China's capital market and money market from the beginning of reform and opening up, gradually expanding and expanding, and becoming an extremely important part of China's financial industry. During this period, although it has experienced a relatively tortuous development process, after 40 years of development, the market scale has greatly expanded and the degree of internationalization has been increasing day by day. To our country's social and economic development has played the obvious promotion role; Chapter 10 briefly analyzes the changes of China's RMB exchange rate management system and the formation and development process of the foreign exchange market. After long-term government intervention, the degree of marketization continues to grow.

The fourth part is on the rise of Internet finance and its impact on the existing financial system, that is, Chap. 11. This chapter systematically reviews the emergence and development process of China's Internet finance. After decades of slow development, Internet finance burst out in 2013, and after a short period of rapid development under the condition of zero-basis, it gradually entered the stage of standardized development in July 2015. The rapid development of Internet finance in China has brought a huge impact on existing financial organizations and presented a new trend of development in various fields of existing finance. Up to now, a trend of integration has been formed between the two, which jointly use information technology to blur the boundary between financial institutions and financial markets and move towards inclusive, green and technological finance. To a certain extent, it has changed the status quo of "difficult financing" and "expensive financing" in China, narrowed the gap with developed countries in the financial field, and even in the Internet payment, online lending and other fields have been ahead of developed countries, with international competitiveness. Finally, on the basis of the above, for future development in our country finance need to put special emphasis on the six aspects of made a briefly summary, as the conclusion of the book.

Finally, based on the above, the author makes a brief summary of six aspects that need to be paid special attention to in the future development of Chinese finance, as the conclusion of the book.

1.5 Supplementary Specifications

First, in terms of time, this book mainly focuses on the period from the establishment of the People's Bank of China to 2019. However, in order to clarify the origins of the new Chinese financial system, it traces back to the revolutionary base banks established during the domestic revolutionary period. Between the establishment of Xiaoshan Yaqian Credit Cooperative in 1924 and the establishment of the National Bank of the Chinese Soviet Republic in 1932, although nearly ten revolutionary base red financial institutions were established, they did not directly continue as components of the new Chinese financial system. However, their practices of raising funds and issuing currency to serve the people and the war have been continued. Based on this consideration, the research timeframe briefly extends to the revolutionary base banks established during the first domestic revolutionary war, and the lower limit extends to the 70th anniversary of the establishment of the People's Republic of China (2019).

Second, in terms of structure, there are differences between the third part and other parts due to the constraints of the development level of financial business and the complexity of content. In the first and second parts, the development of China's financial industry and the simplification of financial institutions, where financial contraction became the sole function of "managing funds," to meet the needs of a highly centralized planned economic system. Thus, in terms of chapter layout, it mainly analyzes and describes the changes from the overall perspective of the financial industry. In the third part, with the increasingly diversified demand for finance in the socio-economy, a diversified financial system gradually formed and developed, and the financial industry achieved comprehensive development with increasingly complex content. Obviously, it is difficult to describe, sort out, and summarize the structure as in the first two parts. Based on this, this part is divided and studied according to the importance of the various components in China's financial sector, including the establishment and improvement of the central bank's status, the development and changes of different types of banks, the development of non-banking financial institutions, the development of financial markets, and the transformation of the foreign exchange market, in order to align with the diversified demands of the socio-economy. The fourth part then returns to the perspective of the entire financial industry to analyze the development of internet finance, the formation of new financial formats, and their impact on existing financial organizations.

Thirdly, the content of the book is organized according to the changes of financial functions. This book discusses the changes in the financial development of China in chronological order, taking the changes in the functions of "managing funds" and "regulating the market" as clues. Therefore, the financial development of China naturally experienced four periods, although there is a certain degree of connection and overlap between each period, but the positioning of financial functions in each period is still very clear.

Fourth, it is the definition of "managing funds" and "regulating market". "Managing funds" primarily refers to the gradual trend of financial institutions towards singularity, with financial functions increasingly shrinking to unified deposit-taking and lending, with bank credit replacing commercial credit. The role of interest rates, exchange rates, and other adjustments is reduced, gradually becoming subordinate to fiscal policies, with funds allocated based on instructions and fulfilling the functions of cashier, settlement, and cash management. On the other hand, "regulating market" entails the gradual establishment of an independent and market-oriented diversified financial system separate from fiscal policies. Financial institutions progressively transform into modern enterprises that bear their own profits and risks, and the allocation of financial resources relies more on market forces rather than administrative directive planning.

Part I
The Development of Finance in the Early Period of the People's Republic of China

Chapter 2
The Establishment of China's Financial System

At the beginning of the People's Republic of China, China's financial industry was quite chaotic, and the primary task facing the central government was to establish a unified RMB system, and effectively integrate financial organizations in the old and new liberated areas on the basis of the People's Bank of China to establish a new Chinese financial system, unify the currency, stabilize prices and promote the rapid recovery of the national economy.

2.1 The Origin of China's Financial System

The financial system of China was not established directly on the basis of the nationalization of the original financial organizations after taking the political power, but the crystallization of the classification and integration of different financial organizations and financial market businesses under the conditions of the establishment of a large number of banks and financial market businesses in the process of the new-democratic revolution. Obviously, the financial system of China grew directly out of the State Bank of the Soviet Republic of China, established during the Second Revolutionary Civil War, and gradually developed with the victory of the Chinese revolution through various historical institutions such as the Bank of the anti-Japanese revolutionary base areas and the Bank of the liberated areas. The establishment of the People's Bank of China and the issuance of the Renminbi (Chinese yuan) on December 1, 1948 marked the beginning of the construction of China's financial system.

R. Lan, *The Financial Development of China*, Understanding China,
https://doi.org/10.1007/978-981-97-8273-4_2

2.1.1 Financial Industry During the Revolutionary War

The financial industry in the period of the New Democratic Revolution of China originated in the period of the first Revolutionary Civil War.

At that time, in order to resist the exploitation of usurers, improve the lives of the general public, develop production and support the war, under the leadership of local peasant associations, nearly ten Farmers Banks of China, Civilian Banks of China and Credit Cooperatives were established successively from 1924, when the first financial institution in the revolutionary base area—the credit cooperative was established in Yaqian Village, Xiaoshan District, Zhejiang Province, to the end of the first Domestic Revolutionary War. See Table 2.1.

The banks established during the First Revolutionary Civil War were small in size and operated in a limited territory. Their funds are basically from the rural

Table 2.1 The main revolution-regime banks established during the first revolutionary civil war

Bank name	Founding Time	Bank address	Bank Officer	Business Sphere
Xiaoshan Yaqian Credit Cooperative	1924	Yaqian Village Xiaoshan District	Jin Lutao	Deposit-services
No.1 Farmers Bank of Caishanzhou Special District, Hengshan County	Apr, 1926	Caishanzhou District, Hengshan County	Wen Hainan Xia Zhaomei	Currency issue& Deposit-services
No. 2 Farmers Bank of Caishanzhou Special District, Hengshan County	Feb, Mar, 1927	Youmatian Village, Hengshan County	Xiao Yucheng Liu Jinsheng	Currency issue& Deposit-services
Civilian Bank of Liuyang East	Jan, 1927	Liuyang City	LiMingxuan Tang Youxian	Currency issue& Deposit-services
Local Bank of Liling	Jan, 1927	Liling City	–	Currency issue& Deposit-services
Wenjiashi Production Cooperative of South Liuyang	Mar, 1927	Wenjiashi Town, Liuyang city	You Xianfeng Wu Xianjing	Currency issue
Jinggang Town Depository of Public Property of Liuyang City	Feb, 1927	Jinggang Town, Liuyang City	He Wenyuan	Currency issue
Industrial and Rural Bank of Liling	Mar, 1927	Liling City	Tang Boxian	Currency issue
The Farmer Credit Association of Huanggang County	Feb, 1927	Huanggang County	Cao Liudie	Currency issue Deposit-services

Source Jiang Hongye, *History of Local Banks in China*, Hunan Publishing House, 1991, p. 640. Adjusted

association, the amount is small, so they provide corresponding financial services mainly through the issuance of currency for the members of the rural association in the locality. YaQian Credit Cooperative of Xiaoshan is the only bank that focuses on deposit business, while the others basically issue currency or concurrently engage in deposit business on the basis of currency issuance, and three of them simply issue currency to provide financial services. The first farmers Bank in the Chashanzhou Special area of Hengshan county is the first bank in the revolution-base area of our country to issue currency, after the establishment of the bank issued a denomination of one-yuan cloth note. Because of its good reputation after the issuance of that note, its experience was soon adopted by the revolution-base area banks that were subsequently established. During this period, a total of nine banking institutions issued currency.

Of course, the banks in the revolution-base areas established during the first Revolutionary War were basically established for the purpose of economic self-rescue, recovery of production, and support for the war under the severe situation of tight blockade. In a strict sense, they did not have the real functions of banks, and were basically limited to the scope of credit cooperation, with poor independence. They existed for a short time, with a limited scope of activities and single function of service, but their exploration in the financial field played a big role in promoting the development of the farmers associations and revolutionary activities, meanwhile The experience they have accumulated in their financial practices in the form of collective funds and the issuance of currency provided obvious reference for the development of financial business of various financial institutions in China since the Second Civil Revolutionary War.

After the counterrevolutionary coup of 12th April 1927, The Communist Party of China swiftly shifted its armed forces from urban to rural areas. In October 1927, under the leadership of Mao Zedong, the armed forces established the first rural revolutionary base at Jinggangshan. Subsequently, more than ten rural revolutionary bases were established across the country. These bases were mainly located at the borders of provinces, characterized by economic backwardness, and were surrounded and economically blocked by the Kuomintang regime. In order to raise funds, support the war, break the blockade, regulate finances, stimulate the market, and meet the needs of the local population, the governments of these revolutionary bases successively established more than fifty Soviet banks and issued over two hundred types of currency, as shown in Table 2.2.

In order to carry out the Agrarian Revolution, defend the achievements of the revolution, break the economic blockade, promote production and invigorate economy, the economic departments and labor banks were first established in Leiyang and Haifeng in 1928. They adopted the practice of the banks in the revolutionary base areas during the First Revolutionary Civil War, and carried out various financial services such as production and making loans by issuing currency or withdrawing part of the funds from the confiscated assets of landlords and despotic forces. In May 1928, the Hunan-Jiangxi border Soviet government set up the Shangjing Red Army Mint in Shangjing Village in Jinggangshan, casting silver dollars with various silver products obtained in the war and resolving the plight of the general public who lacked

Table 2.2 Financial organizations of major revolutionary regimes established during the second revolutionary civil war

Bank name	Founding time	Bank address	Bank officer	Business scope
Economical department of Soviet Government Leiyang County	Feb, 1928	Leiyang	Tan Chucai	Currency issue Treasury agency
Hai Lufeng Labor Bank	Feb, 1928	Haifeng	Chen Ziqi	Currency issue
Shangjing Mintage ofJinggangshan	May, 1928	Shangjing Village of Jinggangshan	Wang Zuo	Currency issue
Civilian Bank of Donggu	Aug, 1928	Donggu Village of Ji'an	Huang Qishou	Currency issue Deposit business
Donggu Bank (Former Donggu Civilian Bank)	Mar, 1930	Donggu Village of Ji'an	Huang Qishou	Currency issue Deposit business
Industrial and Agricultural Bank of West Fujian	Nov, 1930	Longyan, Hugang, Baisha, Changting	Ruan Shan	Currency issue Deposit business
Industrial and Agricultural Bank of Jiangxi	Oct, 1930	Ji'an, Yongfeng,Wan'an,Xingguo, Ruijing	Yan Da	Currency issue
State Bank of the Soviet Republic of China	Feb, 1932	Ruijing	Mao Zeming	Currency issue Deposit business
Fujian Branch of the State Bank of the Chinese Soviet Republic	Apr, 1932	Changting	Li Liuru	Dealing with the work assigned by general bank
Jiangxi Branch of the State Bank of the Soviet Republic of China	Feb, 1933	Bosheng county (former Ningdu county)	Zhong Shenghu	Dealing with the work assigned by general bank
Shishou Agricultural Bank	1930	Shishou	–	Currency issue

(continued)

Table 2.2 (continued)

Bank name	Founding time	Bank address	Bank officer	Business scope
Farmers Bank of West Hubei	Apr, 1930	Shishou	Dai Butian	Currency issue Deposit, loan and exchange businesses
National Bank of the Soviet Republic of China Hunan and Hubei Special Zone Branch	Nov, 1931	Shishou, Jianli,Honghu	Cui Qi	Currency issue Deposit, loan and exchange businesses
Farmers Bank of North Hubei	July, 1931	Fangxian	Wang Shouxun	Currency issue Deposit, loan and exchange businesses
Hefeng Soviet Bank	1931	Hefeng	Yuan Jianzhang	Currency issue
Hubei-Henan-Anhui Special Zone Soviet Bank	Oct, 1930	Qiliping town of Huang'an County, Xingji County	Zheng Weisan	Currency issue Deposit, loan and exchange businesses
Soviet Bank of Northwest Anhui Special Zone	May, 1931	Jingjiazai County, Mabu town	Wu Baocai	Currency issue Deposit, loan and exchange businesses
Hubei-Henan-Anhui Provincial Soviet Bank	1932	Xingji	Zheng Yizai	Currency issue Deposit, loan and exchange businesses
Civilian Bank of Northeast Jiangxi Special Zone	Oct, 1930	Fajiadun village of Geyang county, Hengfeng County	Zhang Qide	Currency issue Deposit and loan businesses

(continued)

Table 2.2 (continued)

Bank name	Founding time	Bank address	Bank officer	Business scope
Northeast Jiangxi Provincial Soviet Bank	Nov, 1931	Fengshuwu of Hengfeng county	Zhang Qide	Currency issue Deposit and loan businesses
Northeast Jiangxi Provincial Soviet Bank Minbei Branch	1931, winter	Da'an street of Chong'an county	Xu Fuyuan, etc	Currency issue Deposit and loan businesses
Fujian, Zhejiang and Jiangxi Provincial Soviet Bank	Dec, 1932	Fengshuwu of Hengfeng county	Zhang Qide	Currency issue Deposit and loan businesses
Fujian-Zhejiang-Jiangxi Provincial Soviet Bank Minbei branch	Dec, 1932	Da'an street of Chong'an county	Xu Fuyuan,etc	Currency issue Deposit and loan businesses
Industrial and Agricultural Bank of Pingjiang Ciunty	Nov, 1930	Pingjiang	Huang Qinghuai	Currency issue Deposit and loan businesses
Gongnongbing Bank of Liuyang	Jan, 1931	Liuyang	Huang Ren, Li Dao	Currency issue Deposit and loan businesses
Gongnongbing Bank of Wanzai County	Jan, 1931	Wanzai	Zhong Xuekui (Gan Yunong)	Currency issue Deposit and loan businesses
Gongnongbing Bank of Yichun	July, 1931	Yichun	OuYang Bo	Currency issue Deposit and loan businesses
Gongnongbing Bank of XiushuiCounty	May, 1931	Xiushui	Zhang Wen (GanZuowu)	Currency issue
Gongnongbing Bank of Tonggu County	Jan, 1931	Tonggu	Liu Xianchang	Currency issue

(continued)

Table 2.2 (continued)

Bank name	Founding time	Bank address	Bank officer	Business scope
Farmers Bank of East Hubei	Sept, 1930	Jinglong Distrit of Yangxin	Cao Junbai	Currency issue
Fufeng Distrcit Farmers Bank of Yangxin	1930	Fufeng Distrcit of Yangxin	–	Currency issue
Longyan District Farmers Bank of Yangxin County	1930	Longyan District of Yangxin	–	Currency issue
Dafeng District Farmers Bank of Yangxin County	1930	Dafeng District of Yangxin	–	Currency issue
Yanhe District Farmers Bank of Yangxin County	1930	Yanhe District of Yangxin	–	Currency issue
Workers-farmers-soldiers Bank of Southeast Hubei	Feb, 1931	Longgang town of Yangxin	Liu Jieyun Chen Diguang	Currency issue
Industrial and agricultural Bank of East Hubei	Mar, 1932	Longgang town of Yangxin	–	Currency issue
Industrial and agricultural Bank of Southeastern Hubei	May, 1932	Longgang town of Yangxin Tongshan	–	Currency issue
Workers Farmers Soldiers' Bank of Wu Ning County	Nov, 1931	Wu Ning	Cheng Ruizhi	Currency issue
Workers Farmers Soldiers' Bank of Rui Cang County	1932	Ruicang	–	Currency issue
Workers Farmers Soldiers' Bank of Daye County	1931	Daye	Chen Yumen	Currency issue Deposit and loan businesses
No.5 Distrct Workers Farmers Soldiers' Bank of Daye	1930	No.5 district of Daye	–	Currency issue
Workers Farmers Soldiers' Bank of Tongcheng County	July, 1931	Tongcheng	–	Currency issue
Workers Farmers Soldiers' Bank of Tongshan County (Agency)	Oct. 1930	Tongshan	Huang Kexiao	Currency issue Deposit and loan businesses

(continued)

Table 2.2 (continued)

Bank name	Founding time	Bank address	Bank officer	Business scope
Industrial and Agricultural Bank of Xiang-E-Gan Provinces	Nov, 1931	Xiushu Wanzai Pingjiang	Li Guohua Liu Wenchu Tu Zhengkun Cheng Gong	Currency issue Deposit and loan businesses
Industrial and Agricultural State Bank of Hunan&Hubei Provinces of Chinese Soviet Republic	Jan, 1932	Yongxin	Hu Xiang	Currency issue Deposit, loan and exchange businesses
State Bank of Chinese Soviet Republic Hunan&Hubei Provincial Branch	Jan, 1933	Yongxin Taihe	Hu Xiang	Currency issue Deposit, loan and exchange businesses
Industrial and Agricultural Bank of Sichuan-Shanxi Provinces of Soviet Government	Dec, 1933	Tongjiang	Zheng Yizai	Currency issue Deposit, loan and exchange businesses
Industrial and Agricultural Bank of Sichuan-Shanxi Provinces of Chinese Soviet Republic	Dec, 1933	Tongjiang	Zheng Yizai	Currency issue Deposit, loan and exchange businesses
Industrial and Agricultural Bank of Sichuan-Shanxi Provinces of Chinese Soviet Republic	Dec, 1933	Tongjiang	Zheng Yizai	Currency issue Deposit, loan and exchange businesses
Farmers Cooperative Bank of Shaanxi-Gansu Border Areas	Nov, 1934	Nanliang town of Huachi city	–	Currency issue
Soviet Bank of Shanxi-Gansu Provinces	Spring, 1935	Nanliang town of Huachi city	Yang Yuting	Currency issue
Soviet Bank of Shanxi-Gansu-Thansi Provincs	June, 1935	Yongding Anping Wa Yaobao	Ai Chu-nan Li Qingping	Currency issue

(continued)

Table 2.2 (continued)

Bank name	Founding time	Bank address	Bank officer	Business scope
Resisting-Japan People's Revolutionary Committee Bank of North Shanxi Shenfu Special Area	Apr, 1936	Shenmu Fugu	–	Currency issue
Northwest Branch of State Bank of the Soviet Republic of China	Nov, 1935	Wayaobao Bao'an Yan'an	Lin Boqu Cao Juru	Currency issue Deposit, loan and exchange businesses, running domestic and Foreign trade

Source Jiang Hongye, *The History of Local Banks in China*, Hunan Publishing House, 1991, pp. 640–646. Adjusted

money. With the continuous establishment and expansion of the rural revolutionary base areas, the financial industry in the base areas achieved great development, and almost every base area set up its own bank and issued currency. In February 1932, the State Bank of the Soviet Republic of China was established in Ruijin of the Central Soviet Area, with Mao Zemin as the president. National bank notes were issued in July. After that, the State Bank promulgated the provisional charter of the State Bank of the Soviet Republic of China, which clarified the responsibilities of the State Bank and improved its organizational structure. In accordance with the charter of the bank, the bank management committee formulated the banking regulations and detailed rules of operation. After the establishment of the State Bank of the Soviet Republic of China, although its name has undergone many changes and its institutions have undergone many mergers, its institutional organization, management personnel, business operations, etc., have always survived, and later became an important part of the People's Bank of China (see Fig. 2.1). The establishment of the State Bank of the Chinese Soviet Republic marked the emergence of the embryonic financial system in China.

With the establishment of the State Bank of the Soviet Republic of China, the banks originally established in the various base areas were restructured and successively transformed into branches of the State Bank. Later, affected by the failure of the fifth Anti-Encircle Wars, the State Bank of the Chinese Soviet Republic was incorporated into the 15th Party of the column directly under the Central Military Commission, and worked with the Central Military Commission on the Long March to ensure various funding during the Long March. In November 1935, the main force of the Long March arrived at Wayaobo and worked with the Shan-Gan-Jin Soviet Bank, which was part of the Soviet Government of Northern Shaanxi Province. In the same month,

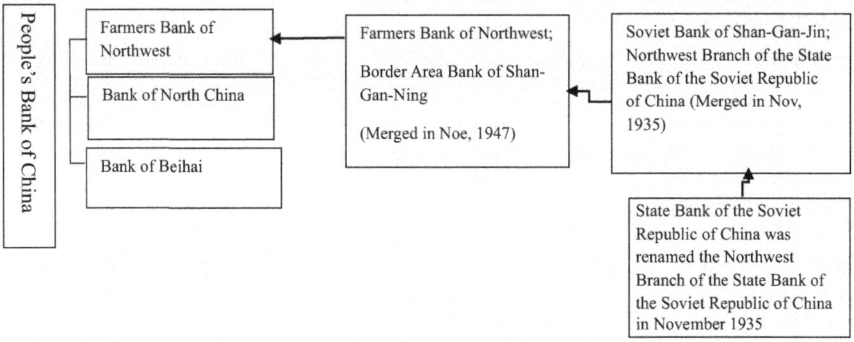

Fig. 2.1 Evolution diagram of State Bank of the Soviet Republic of China

the State Bank of the Soviet Republic of China was renamed the Northwest Branch of the State Bank of the Soviet Republic of China, and the assets and institutions of the Shan-Gan-Jin Soviet Bank were merged into the Northwest Branch of the State Bank of the Soviet Republic of China, and began to issue banknotes of the Northwest Branch of the State Bank of the Soviet Republic of China, offering various financial services.

2.1.2 Financial Industry in Resisting-Japanese Base Areas

After the July 7 Incident of 1937, the Central Committee of the Communist Party of China led the Resisting-Japanese armed forces to go deep behind enemy lines, recapturing large areas of lost territory in war, and successively established 19 Resisting-Japanese base areas. In order to support the Resisting-Japanese War, develop the economy, stabilize prices and facilitate people's everyday lives, the Central Committee of the Communist Party of China implemented the policy of National United Front of Resistance against Japan, renamed the Northwest Branch of the National Bank of the Soviet Republic of China to the Bank of the Shan-Gan-Ning Border Area, withdrew the Soviet paper money issued, and adopted the legal currency issued in the area under control. At the same time, banks in other base areas had been gradually changed into border banks in the corresponding regions. In the newly opened Resisting-Japanese base areas, a number of new revolutionary base area banks were built in accordance with the situation, as shown in Table 2.3.

In October 1937, the Northwest branch of the State Bank of the Soviet Republic of China was reorganized into Border Area Bank of Shanxi-Gansu- Ningxia Provinces, which opened the prelude to the reorganization of the Resisting-Japanese base areas and the construction of new banks. In order to secure military supplies, support the war, carry out economic construction in the border areas, and wage a struggle against the enemy's pseudo currency, the resisting-Japanese armed forces under the leadership of the Communist Party of China continuously established banks

Table 2.3 The main banks of the revolutionary government reorganized and established during the war of resistance against Japan

Bank name	Founding time	Bank address	Bank officer	Businesses	Currency name
Border Area Bank of Shaan-Gan-Ning	Oct, 1937	Yan'an	Cao Juru, Zhu Lizhi, Huang Yaguang	Currency issue Deposit Loan and exchange businesses concurrently trade businesses within the boader area and beyond	Currency of boader area Voucher Currency-note
Border Area Bank of Jin-Cha-Ji	Feb, 1938	Wutai County Zhangjiakou Shijiazhuang	Guan Xuewen, He Songting	Currency issue Deposit Loan and exchange businesses	Currency of boader area, currency-note
Bank of Beihai	Aug, 1938	Yexian (now Laizhou city), Linyi	Ai Chunan ChenMu Chen Wenqi Sa Haiqiu	Currency issue Deposit Loan and exchange businesses	Beihai dollar
Bank of Shangdang	Oct, 1938	Qinxian	Bo Yibo	Currency issue	Bank of Shangdang dollar
Bank of South Hebei	Dec, 1939	Licheng Shexian Wu'an Handan Shimen city	Gao Jiecheng Lai Qin HuJingyun Chen Xiyu	Currency issue Deposit and loan businesses	South Hebei dollar
Bank of West Shandong	May, 1940	Dongping	Lvlin Zhang Lianfang LinHaiyun	Currency issue	Shandong dollar, currency-note
Farmers Bank of Northwest	May, 1940	Xingxian	Liu Shaobai Yu Jie	Currency issue Operation of banking, finance and trade	Xinong dollar
Bank of Jianghuai	Sparing, 1941	Yancheng, Rudong County	Zhu Yi Li Renjun Luo Gengmo	Currency Issue Deposit Loan and exchange businesses	Jianghuai dollar, currency-note, voucher
Bank of Yanfu	Apr, 1942	Yancheng	Luo Gengmo	Currency issue Deposit Loan and exchange businesses	Yanfu dollar

(continued)

Table 2.3 (continued)

Bank name	Founding time	Bank address	Bank officer	Businesses	Currency name
Provincial Bank of Huaibei	June, 1942	Kunxin of north Anhui	Chen Xing Zi Feng	Currency issue Deposit Loan and exchange businesses	Kang dollar
Bank of South Anhui	Feb, 1942	Yutai	Gong Yinong Yu Songyue Dong Xiaochuan	Currency issue Deposit and loan businesses	Huainan dollar
Provincial Bank of Huaihai	Sept, 1941	Lianshui		Currency issue	Huaihai dollar
Bank of Dajiang	July, 1943	Wuwei	Yejinming JingGuanyi Xu Deming	Currency issue	Dajiang dollar
Bank of Huinong	Oct, 1942	Yanling of Danyang		Currency issue	Huinong dollar
Bank of Jiangnan	June, 1945	Guangde	Fan Xingzhi Guan Hantao	Currency issue	Jiangnan dollar
Bank of East Zhenjiang	Apr, 1945	Yu Yao Liangnong	Wu Shanmin Lu Muyun Wang Haifeng	Currency issue Deposit and loan businesses	Kang dollar, token
Construction Bank of Henan-Hubei Border Area	Apr, 1941	Jiangshan Dawushan	Zuo Zhongxiu Zhuang Guo	Currency issue Deposit and loan businesses	Border-area dollar, token
Bank of Central China	Aug, 1945	Yutai Huanyin Shandong Jiangsu-Aihui area	Chen Mu Xu Xuehai Gong Yinong Deng Kesheng Sun Gengtuo	Currency issue Deposit and loan businesses	Central China dollar

Source Jiang Hongye, *History of Local Banks in China*, Hunan Publishing House, 1991, pp. 739–740; Jiang Hongye, *The General History of Chinese Finance (Volume 5): the Base Area Period of the New Democratic Revolution*, China Finance Press, 2004. Adjusted and issued currency in the newly opened base areas. During the period from the July 7 Incident to the final victory of the war of resistance against Japan, banks were established and currencies were issued in each counter-Japanese base area. According to statistics, the banks in each resisting-Japanese base area issued 53 kinds of regional standard coins, including 27 kinds of toponym voucher. There were 199 kinds of local currency once in circulation in these regions, and 252 kinds of the two types of currency combined.[1] The banks and the issue of currency in these revolutionary bases of the counter-Japan political power effectively guaranteed the supply of war, resisted the invasion of the pseudo currencies from the enemy, and played a positive role in the economic construction of the counter-Japanese base areas; At the same time, we had trained a large number of talents in the financial industry and accumulated a lot of useful financial work experience.

2.1.3 Finance During the Liberation War

After the victory of the war of resistance against Japan, the Central Committee of the Communist Party of China complied with the public opinion and took the initiative to cede the counter-Japanese base areas of Guangdong, Zhejiang, Southern Jiangsu, southern Anhui, central Anhui, Hunan, Hubei, Henan (not including Northern Henan) in the "Double Tenth Agreement". The banks established in these areas also adapted to the situation and were integrated into the banks in other base areas. The banks in the remaining revolutionary base areas continued to exist. When the nationalist government provoked a full-scale civil war and broke the agreement, the Central Committee of the Communist Party of China adopted a tit-for-tat strategy, reorganizing the armed forces in the anti-Japanese base areas into the Chinese People's Liberation Army, and the banks in the original base areas were also adjusted accordingly. After the merger of Shaanxi-Gansu-Ningxia Liberated Area and Jin-Sui Liberated Area. In October 1947, Bank of Shaanxi-Gansu-Ningxia Border Area and Northwest Farmers Bank of Jin-Sui Border Area merged into Northwest Farmers Bank; When the liberated area of Shanxi-Cha-Hebei and the liberated Area of Shanxi-Hebei-Shandong-Henan joined together, the Bank of Shanxi-Cha-Hebei Border Area and the Bank of Jinan became Bank of North China in July 1948, thus laying the foundation of the People's Bank of China.

With the continuous opening up and expansion of the newly liberated areas, the army and people in the liberated areas set up a number of new banks in these areas, as shown in Table 2.4.

With the expansion and gradual integration of the liberated areas, banking institutions continued to merge, and the main body of currency issuance continued to decrease. From August 1945 to 1949, the number of currency issuing institutions (excluding the nation-wide RMB) in the base areas of the liberated areas was

[1] Xu Shuxin. *Outline of the Monetary History of Chinese Revolutionary Base Areas*, China Finance Press, 2008: 5.

Table 2.4 Banks of revolutionary political power established during the war of liberation

Bank name	Founding time	Bank address	Bank officer	Businesses	Currency name
Bank of Northeast	Nov, 1945	Haerbing Shengyang	Ye Lizhuang, Cao Juru, Zhu Lizhi, Wang Qizhi	Currency issuance, deposit, loan and exchange businesses	Local currency note
Bank of Hejiang	Jan, 1946	Jiamusi	Ma Zhong, Meng Qinghui	Currency issuance	Local currency note
Industrial Bank of Mudanjiang	Jan, 1946	Mudanjiang	–	Currency issuance, concurrently enterprise investment	Local currency note
Bank of Jilin Province	Mar, 1946	Panshi county, Jilin, Tumen, Yanji	–	Currency issuance, deposit and loan businesses	Local currency note
Bank of East Jilin	Apr, 1946	Yanji	–	Currency issuance	Local currency note
Provincial Bank of Nengjiang	Apr, 1946	Qiqihaer	Can Genquan	Currency issuance, treasury agency	Local currency note
Bank of Guandong	Apr, 1947	Dalian	Zhou Ziyang, Yiqintang	Currency issuance, deposit and loan businesses	–
Provincial Bank of Rehe	1946	Chengde	–	Currency issuance	Local currency note
Bank of the Great Wall	Feb, 1948	Linxi, Chengde	Shi Lide, Shen Yujie	Currency issuance	Local currency note
Bank of Dongmeng	Mar, 1946	Wulanhaote	XiaoShun'a, Yang Yingui, Liu Fengchi	Currency issuance	Temporary currency note
Bank of Inner Mongolia Bank	Jun, 1947	Wulanhaote	Hu Zishou, Yang Yingui, Liu Fengchi	Currency issuance	Inner mongolia dollar
People's Bank of Inner Mongolia	Jun, 1948	Wulanhaote	Hu Zishou, JingMoyan, Liu Fengchi, Cui Yanxu	Currency issuance	New inner Mongolia dollar
Farmers Bank of Zhongzhou	June, 1948	Baofeng Zhengzhou, Wuhan	Chen Xiyu	Currency issuance, deposit loan and exchange businesses	Zhongzhou dollar

(continued)

Table 2.4 (continued)

Bank name	Founding time	Bank address	Bank officer	Businesses	Currency name
Bank of Yuming	The end of 1948	Dabeishan District	Liu Huanan, Huang Runze	Currency issuance	Currency note
Bank of Xinlu	Apr, 1949	Lufeng	Zheng Dazhong, Mai Youjian	Currency issuance	Currency note
People's Bank of the South	July, 1949	Jiexi, Hepo	Cai Fusheng, Zhao Yuanhao	Currency issuance, deposit loan and exchange businesses	Bank note of the South
Bank of North China	Apr, 1948	Shijiazhuang	Nan Hanchen, Hu Jinyun, Zheng Xuewen	Businesses of Bank of the former Bank of South Hebei and Bank of Shanxi-Chahar-Hebei border Area	South Hebei dollar, border area dollar
People's Bank of China	Dec.1, 1948	Shijiangzhuang, Beijing	Nan Hanchen, Hu Jinyun, Zheng Xuewen	Currency issuance, deposit loan and exchange businesses	Old RMB

Source Jiang Hongye. *History of Local Banks in China.* Hunan Publishing House, 1991, pp. 740–741. Adjusted

compressed from 198 into 97, and the number of currency types was reduced from 252 to 111.[2] With the successive victories of the War of Liberation, the Central Committee of the Communist Party of China launched the work of unifying finance and economics while setting up a national political power. In the spring of 1947, Financial and Economic Office of North China was established; In October, the Financial and Economic Office of North China proposed to the Central Committee of the Communist Party of China the unified issuance of currency and the establishment of a central bank. Subsequently, the North Financial Office of China set up the Preparatory Office of the People's Bank of China. In October 1948, the Central Committee of the Communist Party of China issued clear instructions for the People's Bank of China to issue RMB. On December 1, the People's Government of North China issued a notice on the establishment of the People's Bank of China and the issuance of Renminbi, deciding to establish the People's Bank of China on the basis of the Bank of North China, the Bank of North Sea and the Farmers Bank of Northwest, and to issue a unified RMB. The establishment of the People's Bank of China and the issuance of the renminbi opened a new chapter in the establishment of China's financial system.

[2] Xu Shuxin. *Outline of the Monetary History of Chinese Revolutionary Base Areas*, China Finance Press, 2008: 58.

On the whole, the financial organizations in the base areas during the revolutionary period not only laid the foundation of financial organizations, talents and technology for the financial system of China, but also provided experience for the development of China's financial industry in the following aspects: first, serving economy. Whether during the Soviet period (1931–1937), the War of Resistance against Japanese Aggression, or the War of Liberation, the main tasks of various financial organizations were to serve the social and economic activities of the communist base areas, restore production, promote commercial circulation, and meet the needs of daily life and revolutionary activities. Second, stabilizing economic activity. During each period of the Revolutionary War, the revolutionary district was hindered by various obstacles, the economy was blocked, and many monetary struggles were launched on the currency. The primary task of the various financial organizations established under these conditions is to stabilize the economic activities in the revolutionary district, facilitate rational monetary struggle, stabilize prices, issue loans, enrich materials, and achieve sustainable economic development in the revolutionary district. Third, collective or state-owned funds are used as the capital of financial organizations, and currency is issued to enlarge credit funds and make up for the shortage of loan business caused by the instability resulting from the war. Fourth, establishing and developing financial organizations independently.

In the different stages of the revolutionary war, as long as we adhere to independent financial activities that conform to the revolutionary cause, the financial business will certainly be welcomed by all sectors of society and achieve rapid development. Even if they encounter temporary setbacks, they can develop again under new conditions.

2.2 The Establishment of China's Financial System

On December 1, 1948, the People's Bank of China was established on the basis of the Bank of North China, the Bank of North Sea and the Farmers Bank of Northwest, which opened the prelude to the construction of the new Chinese financial system. The Common Program made it clear that the financial sector should be strictly managed by the state, and the right to issue currency belongs to the state. Under the guidance of this programmatic document, the People's Bank of China on the one hand, with the idea of "taking over while setting up banks", establish or replenish different levels of branches of People's Bank of China and at the same time rectify and reform different types of financial institutions. On the other hand, issuance of RMB and differentiated measures in different regions for currency exchange ended the chaotic domestic monetary system and gradually established an independent and unified RMB system.

2.2.1 The Unification of the RMB System

At the beginning of the People's Republic of China, China's monetary system was quite chaotic. On the one hand, though with the issuance of RMB, the type of currency issued in the liberated areas has decreased, but there are still more than 100 types.

The comprehensive monetary statistics in the liberation area during liberation-war period as shown in Table 2.5.

On the other hand, in newly liberated areas and areas that have not yet completed liberation, fiat currency (gold certificates), gold and silver, and foreign currency are mixed and circulated, and the problem of speculation is serious. Such a disordered monetary system has seriously affected the recovery of the national economy and the lives of the vast majority of the people. Therefore, the people's government made a decision to implement differentiated measures for the currency types of different issuers, and quickly established an independent and unified RMB system, as follows.

The first measure is to gradually withdraw the currencies issued by different liberated areas. On December 1, 1948, along with the issuance of RMB, the People's Government of North China issued a notice that "the Government of Shandong Province and the regional governments of Shaanxi-Gansu-Ning-Shansi-Sui agreed to unify circulation and the currencies of North China, East China and Northwest

Table 2.5 Comprehensive currency statistics of liberated areas during the war of liberation (1945–1951) (unit: type)

Name of liberation area	Currency type	Regional standard currency type	Local currency type	Denomination type	Number of editions
North China	10	4(1)	6	9	42
Northwest	4	2	2	14	24
East China	8	4	4	19	116
Notheast	30	6(3)	24	17	156
Inner Mongolia	16	2	14	13	40
Central Plains	18	4(3)	14	14	46
South China	25	1	24	17	103
Total by liberation areas	111	23(7)	88[b]	103[b]	527
All over China((RMB)	2	1	1	12	65
Total	113	24(7)	89[b]	115[b]	592

[a] The data in the regional currency column includes the number of local currency types within parentheses, and the Chinese yuan is also counted as a regional currency. The data at [b] contains a total calculation error, which has been corrected. *Source* XU Shuxin: *Outline of Chinese Revolutionary Base Currency History*, Chinese Financial Publishing House, 2008, p. 94

Table 2.6 Exchange ratio between RMB and currencies issued in different liberated areas

Exchange of RMB with currencies in different liberated areas	Exchange rate
With Zhongzhou Bank notes	1:3
With Jinan Bank notes, Beihai Bank notes, Central China Bank notes	1:100
With Great Wall Bank notes	1:200
With the Jin-Cha-Ji Border Area Bank notes, Rehe bank notes	1:1000
With the bank notes of Farmers Bank of Northwest, with Shaanxi-Gansu-Ningxia Border trading company coupon	1:2000
With the currency of Border Area Bank of Shaanxi-Gansu-Ningxia, with the price circulation coupon of Guanghua store in Yan 'an	1:40,000
With the boader area currency of Ji-Re-Liao	1:5000
With local circulation notes of Bank of Notheast and bank of Inner Mongolia[a]	1:9. 5

Note [a]The exchange rate between RMB and local circulation notes of Northeast Bank and Inner Mongolia Bank was set in April 1951

China…. All public and private payments and all transactions are denominated in RMB. After the issuance of RMB, Hebei dollar (Including west Shandong dollar), border region dollar, Beihai dollar, Xinong dollar (hereinafter referred to as old currency were gradually withdrawn".[3] At the time of the issuance of the RMB, the people's government indicated its determination to gradually unify the currency under the premise of protecting the interests of the people, "The people's government is not only responsible for the new currency of the People's Bank, but also responsible for the local currency issued by all the banks in the liberated areas in the past."[4] In the future, when we withdrew the local currency, we shall exchange it at the rate now fixed, until the last note." After that, in accordance with the policy of "fixed parity, mixed circulation, gradual withdrawal, and responsibility to the end", the currencies issued by different liberated areas were gradually withdrawn in a planned way. In January 1949, the People's Government of North China stipulated the exchange rate of RMB against the currencies of different liberated areas, as shown in Table 2.6.

Through the efforts of the People's Bank of China and its branches, by April 1950, the old currencies withdrawn were equivalent to 23.95 billion yuan, accounting for 82.95% of the total number of old currencies issued.[5] In 1951, the Government Administration Council issued an order on the purchase and exchange of local circulation bonds in Northeast China and Inner Mongolia. In this way, by November 1951, except for Tibet and Taiwan, the unified exchange of RMB was basically completed.

---

[3] Shang Ming. *Financial Undertakings in Contemporary China.* China Social Sciences Press, 1989, p. 31.

[4] "People's Bank of China General Manager Nan Hanchen Speech New currency issuance is extremely supported by the people Some people's doubts have been answered in detail", *People's Daily*, January 13, 1949, 1st edition.

[5] Dai Xianglong. *Fifty Years of the People's Bank of China: The Development of the Central Banking System.* China Finance Press, 1998: 41.

In Tibet, it was not until August 10, 1959 that the circulation of silver dollars and Tibetan coins was stopped, all replaced by RMB.

The second is to eliminate the currency issued by the national government. Since the National Government issued the fiat currency in November 1935, the fiat currency has witnessed hyperinflation and the purchasing power has almost dropped to zero. In the period from June 1937 to May 1949 alone, under the rule of the National government, the inflation rate of fiat currency reached 140 billion times, and prices increased by more than 8.5 billion times. For this reason, an American journalist made an analogy:

In 1937, with 100 yuan in fiat people could buy 2 cows; in 1945, people could buy 2 eggs, 1/6 bar of soap in 1946, one coal in 1947, 1/10000 kilos of rice in 1948 and 1/100billion kilos of rice in 1949.

In August 1948, the gold-yuan notes (paper money issued by Kuomingtang) was issued, and in less than 10 months, the circulation increased by 340,000 times. Facing such severe inflation, every time the people's government liberated a region, it took resolute measures to eliminate fiat currency, gold-yuan notes and other currencies, and took RMB as the only legal currency. At the same time, in order to protect the interests of the general public, the people's government has implemented measures to exchange the money issued by the Guomingtang government within a time limit. A shorter time limit, a lower price ratio, and a wider range of exchange sites helped reduce the losses caused by the increasingly serious inflation.

The third is to prohibit foreign currency from circulating in the domestic market. Before 1949, the western powers issued currency in our country one after another by virtue of their privilege in China. By 1949, US $300 million of US dollar notes were in circulation in Shanghai, Tianjin, Peiping (Peking) and other places, and about HK $580 million were in circulation in Guangzhou and its adjacent areas.[6] In order to maintain independent RMB system, the people's government resolutely banned foreign currencies issued in China and controlled the right to operate foreign exchange in China, exchanged foreign currencies such as the US dollar and the British pound at reasonable prices, and prohibited their circulation in the domestic market and private trading.

Fourth, it is strictly prohibited to price and circulate gold and silver and to buy and sell them without official permission. During the rule of the Guomingtang government, hyperinflation caused the sharp depreciation of fiat currency and gold-yuan notes. People used gold and silver to price and circulate to avoid losses, and gold and silver gradually became the main currency in market circulation. Amid sharp price fluctuations, gold and silver speculation was rampant. In order to stabilize the value of the RMB, the central government explicitly prohibited the circulation of gold and silver, and cracked down on gold and silver speculation. The People's Bank of China exercised unified control over the sale, exchange and allocation of gold and silver; Gold and silver ornaments in gold and silver shops could be bought and sold, but the raw materials should be uniformly allocated and sold by the State.

---

[6] Yang Xitian et al. *General History of China's Financial (Volume 6): Law of the People's Republic of China period.* China Finance Publishing House, 2002: 29.

2.2.2 *The Establishment of China's Financial System*

After the establishment of the People's Bank of China, although it had the status of a state bank, the composition of the financial organizations is extremely complicated. In the old liberated areas, there were a dozen banks of the revolutionary political power; In the newly liberated areas and the areas not yet liberated, there were banks of bureaucratic capital of Guomingtang government, banks of foreign capital, private banks dominated by national capital, insurance, stock exchanges and other forms of financial organizations. Faced with such a large number of financial organizations, after 1949, differentiated measures were taken to integrate them according to different financial components, thus forming the financial system in the early days of China.

The first measure was to transform the banks of revolutionary political power in the liberated areas into the branches of the People's Bank of China. After the People's Bank of China moved from Shijiazhuang to Beijing, it successively reorganized the banks established in the liberated areas in accordance with the four-tier system: headquarter—district bank—branch bank—sub-branch. On this basis, it set up offices, office branches and savings banks in the cities and business offices in the rural towns. By 1951, with the reorganization of Bank of Northeast, The People's Bank of Inner Mongolia and Bank of Xinjiang into The District Bank of Northeast of The People's Bank of China, The Inner Mongolia Autonomous Region Branch of The People's Bank of China and The Xinjiang Uygur Autonomous Region Branch of The People's Bank of China respectively, the reorganization of the existing banks of revolutionary political power was completed, and The People's Bank of China had established corresponding branches except for Tibet and Taiwan. In this way, China initially formed a relatively complete organizational framework of the People's Bank of China composed of four levels, which provided a powerful leading organ of financial organizations for the later recovery and development of the national economy.

The second was to take over the job of transformation of financial institutions of bureaucratic capital. After the establishment of Nanjing Guomingtang Government in 1927, it used the military and political privileges to carry out the strategy of government-run finance. By the mid-1930s, a financial system of bureaucratic capital was formed with "four banks, two bureaus and one treasury" (The Central Bank, Bank of China, The Bank of Communications, The Farmers Bank of China, The Central Trust Bureau, The Postal Savings Bureau and The Central Cooperative Treasury) as the main body, including provincial, municipal and county banks and government-commercial joint banks. In accordance with the provisions of the Common Program on the confiscation of bureaucratic capital and to the people's state ownership, and depending on the different properties of the financial institutions of bureaucratic capital, the central government and local governments at various levels adopted differentiated strategies. The Central Bank, The Farmers Bank of China, Postal Savings and Exchange Administration and other provincial and municipal banks shall be suspended for liquidation, and their institutions and personnel shall be gradually transformed into the relevant business departments of the People's Bank of China after being taken over; For Bank of China and the Bank of Communications, under the policy of "retaining the original name, the original organization, the original business, steady transformation, and to resume business as soon as possible", they were respectively transformed into professional banks operating foreign exchange business and long-term credit business of industrial, mining and transportation business under the leadership of The People's Bank of China. In December 1949, the headquarter of the Bank of China moved from Shanghai to Beijing, and in 1950, it was put under the leadership of The People's Bank of China. In October 1953, the Regulations of the Bank of China were promulgated, officially confirming the Bank of China as the chartered specialized foreign exchange bank in China. Xinghua Trust and Savings Bank, The National Industrial Bank of China, the Siming Commercial Reserve Bank and The Commercial Bank of China will be transformed into a public–private joint bank. In addition, it took over Bureaucrat Capital Insurance Company and liquidated all but the China Insurance Company and China Aviation Association Insurance Company, which were still in business at the time; The stock institutions in Shanghai and Tianjin were successively taken over, cleaned up and abolished by July 1952.

Third, the privileges of foreign banks in China would be abolished. Since the British Oriental Bank set up a branch in China in 1845, Western powers, relying on their political and economic privileges, opened financial institutions in China, issued currency, monopolized the listing rights of foreign exchange, manipulated financial markets, wantonly plundered China's assets, and brought huge negative impacts on social and economic development. Therefore, the Central Government of People revoked their privileges in China, allowed them to continue to operate in accordance with our laws and regulations, protected their legitimate rights and interests, and designated the Bank of China as the full-time manager of foreign banks. As foreign financial institutions lost their privileges in China, the high monopoly benefits they used to rely on also lost, so a large number of foreign banks successively applied for closure, by the late 1950s, in addition to Hong Kong, Macao and Taiwan, in the mainland only two British banks HSBC and Macquarie Bank (also known as Standard Chartered Bank) were still in business.

At the same time, Chinese governments at all levels had recalibrated the foreign insurance industry, revoked their privileges in China, and allowed them to continue to operate related businesses in accordance with unified regulations after they deposit a certain amount of earnest money according to the type of business. Of course, affected by the loss of monopoly benefits, these foreign insurance companies soon withdrew from the Chinese insurance market.

The fourth was to rectify and reform the national financial industry. At the beginning of the People's Republic of China, there were 1032 national capital banks, old-style Chinese private bank, trust companies and their branches in China. However, due to the long-term war and hyperinflation, their capital had been greatly weakened, and they had basically fallen into the decline and speculation of businesses. In this context, the central government and local governments at all levels carried out phased rectification and transformation of the above-mentioned national financial industry, as shown in Table 2.7.

Table 2.7 Reorganization and transformation of the national financial industry at the beginning of the People's Republic of China

Time	Reorganization stage	Reorganization content
Before June 1950	Preliminary stage	Business facilitation and strict management
From June to December 1950	Second stage	Adjustment of the public–private relationship of the national financial industry
From January to December 1951	Third stage	Further the reorganization of the national financial industry, organize joint management and united management
1952	Fourth stage	Complete the socialist transformation of the national financial industry

Through the reorganization and transformation of the above four stages, the national financial organization eventually formed a unified public–private joint bank. Later, under the unified leadership of the People's Bank of China, it transformed into a professional bank for private industry and commerce to handle deposit and loan business, which marked the completion of the reorganization of the national banking industry by the Chinese government and realized the unification of the banking industry.

In terms of the insurance companies of national capital, Chinese governments at all levels had taken similar measures to the reorganization and transformation of the above-mentioned banking industry of national capital. On the basis of re-registration and business management, the number of the insurance companies of national capital had shrunk substantially. In October 1949, China established Ming'an Insurance Company in Hong Kong, and set up its branch company in Macao in 1966. In July 1951, the remaining insurance companies in the mainland were merged into two public–private joint insurance companies: Taiping and Xinfeng.

The fifth was to set up rural credit cooperatives on a trial basis. Before1949, a large number of credit cooperatives had been established in rural areas, more than 800. Affected by war damage and inflation, most credit cooperatives were in trouble. After 1949, in order to restore agriculture and revive the rural economy, the vast rural areas were in urgent need of financial support. "Credit cooperatives are 'the bridge between the national bank and people'. It is impossible for the national bank to contact the masses of people door to door. It is necessary to extensively develop credit cooperation and establish a broad rural financial network."[7] In 1951, the People's Bank of China put forward the policy of "actively developing credit cooperation" and tried to promote it gradually on the basis of pilot projects. Subsequently, in the new and old liberated areas, the People's Bank of China selected some economically developed rural areas for trial operation. After more than two years of practice, credit

[7] Xu Tangling. *History of Rural Finance in China*. China Finance Publishing House, 1996: 280.

cooperatives had achieved initial development. By 1953, there were more than 9400 credit cooperatives, more than 20,000 mutual assistance credit groups, and more than 3000 credit departments within the supply-marketing cooperatives. More than 60 million farmer households were share-holders, absorbing more than 12 million yuan for share capital, more than 74 million yuan in deposits, and more than 77 million yuan in loans.[8] The establishment of rural credit cooperatives not only promoted the development of rural credit undertakings, effectively cracked down on the usury exploitation activities prevalent in rural areas at that time, but also laid the necessary foundation for the recovery of rural economy and the active rural market.

Through the above diversified measures, under the extremely severe conditions at home and abroad, China soon built a new financial system with the People's Bank of China as the center, the Bank of China, the Bank of Communications and other specialized banks and rural credit cooperatives as components.

2.2.3 The Establishment of Foreign Exchange System

Before 1949, Western powers controlled China's foreign exchange business for a long time by virtue of their privileges in China, especially HSBC, which monopolized China's foreign exchange listing rights. According to statistics, in 1948, foreign banks accounted for 53.7% of the foreign exchange business in Tianjin; China's banks of bureaucratic capital and banks of national capital accounted for 36.4% and 9.9% respectively.[8] Foreign banks manipulate China's foreign exchange market, which seriously affected China's foreign trade and social and economic stability.

After 1949, the People's Bank of China quickly formulated the Interim Regulations on Exchange Control, which for the first time set the requirements for banking institutions to participate in China's foreign exchange business: Any bank that can abide by the laws and regulations of the Chinese government, has a certain amount of foreign exchange funds, has branches and agent banks abroad, and has a good reputation and the ability to handle foreign exchange business may apply to the People's Bank of China for designation as a bank dealing in foreign exchange. According to this requirement, the People's Bank of China selected and approved 53 banks nationwide to operate the foreign exchange business of the People's Republic of China. Among them, there are 35 Chinese banks such as Shanghai Commercial Savings Bank, Bank of Xinhua, Bank of Jincheng, Bank of Guohua, Industrial Bank of China, Industrial Bank of Zhejiang, Bank of Zhongnan and Bank of Juxingcheng, and 3 overseas China-funded banks such as Bank of East Asia, OCBC Bank and Bank of Jiyou. There are 15 foreign banks, including HSBC, Calyon Bank, Bank of Macquarie, Generale Belgian Bank, Woori Bank and ABN Amro Bank.

Second, the People's Bank of China gradually unified the country's foreign exchange prices. In the early days of Tianjin's liberation, the People's Bank of China

---

[8] Yang Xitian et al. *China's Financial History (Volume 6): The Period of the People's Republic of China.* China Finance Publishing House, 2002: 29.

took the lead in formulating Tianjin's foreign exchange quotation based on factors such as local foreign exchange supply and demand conditions. On January 19, 1949, the Tianjin foreign exchange rate was announced to be 800 yuan per US dollar. With the liberation of Shanghai, Guangzhou and other places, the regional bank of the People's Bank of China issued the relevant RMB exchange rate in these areas. On this basis, the People's Bank of China has set up foreign exchanges in Tianjin, Shanghai, Guangzhou and other places, where banks with foreign exchange operations act as dealers to buy and sell foreign exchange on behalf of clients.

Banks dealing in foreign exchange shall, on the basis of the daily quoted rates of RMB exchange rates published by the head office of the People's Bank of China and its regional banks, conduct transactions freely through negotiation in accordance with the supply and demand of foreign exchange. Later, due to changes in the foreign exchange management system, import and export must be approved in advance, foreign exchange trading is subject to planning constraints, and there is little room for free bargaining. In this way, the bargaining system was abolished in April 1950 and changed to a unified listing of the People's Bank of China for flexible adjustment. After the unification of foreign exchange prices, the function of foreign exchanges that originally established was lost, and this institution was also abolished. On July 8, 1950, the People's Bank of China unified the country's foreign exchange quotations, which was published by the head office to the whole country.

Third, an independent management system of foreign exchange was established. In the foreign exchange management, China gradually implemented the system of the supply and settlement of foreign exchange. According to the Interim Regulations for the Allocation and Use of Foreign Exchange, the foreign exchange of all localities in the country shall be uniformly controlled by the central government.

Foreign exchange allocation was realized through the principle of "central first, then local; First industry, then commerce; First public and then private".

No department shall have the right to use foreign exchange without application and obtaining approval in accordance with regulations. All foreign exchange earned from export, business and labor services and foreign exchange imported by overseas Chinese and foreigners must be sold to or deposited in the Bank of China. Later, the Government Administration Council issued the "Regulations of the People's Republic of China to Prohibit the entry and exit of National Currency" and the "Interim Regulations of the People's Republic of China to prohibit the entry and exit of National Currency Bills and Securities", which clearly stipulates: Bills of exchange, promissory notes, cheques, certificates of deposit and passbooks paid in the domestic currency, bonds, stocks, corporate bonds and other securities issued in the domestic currency, and all other documents for payment in the domestic currency, unless the People's Bank of China (PBC) or the Bank of China entrusted by PBC (hereinafter referred to as the Bank) approve to carry or send those local currency notes into or out of the country, certificates issued by the bank are required, and application to the Customs is required for inspection and release;

It is prohibited to carry or send RMB remittances and approval letters approved by the bank into or out of the country unless they are released after customs inspection. If you carry foreign currency, payment certificates of foreign currency, securities of foreign currency out of the country, you must obtain the approval of the People's Bank of China and then an "approval card" issued by the bank. Through these regulations, China fully realized unified foreign exchange management and established a comprehensive border control system for foreign currencies. At the same time, since 1949, governments at all levels attached great importance to the work of overseas Chinese remittances to protect the interests of overseas Chinese and their relatives. In order to protect them from the loss of foreign currency depreciation, the RMB remittance business was launched in November 1950.

Finally, a new international settlement system was established. In the early days of the People's Republic of China, the western capitalist countries led by the United States adopted a strict economic blockade and embargo policy against China. Under the pressure of the United States, some countries refused to accept letters of credit issued by the Bank of China, and had to use the banks of these countries to issue letters of credit and pay a full deposit according to the purchase requirements. In response to this unfair practice, China took tit-for-tat measures based on its own economic conditions. The first was to completely stop using the US dollar, gradually shifted to the socialist countries dominated by the Soviet Union in terms of trade objects, and implemented the settlement system of agreement accounting; Second, according to the trade needs of both sides, China gradually adopted the direct payment of trade with some countries in Asia, Africa and Latin America; The third was to adopted the method of payment on delivery and delivery and payment on export, and at the same time, the method of barter for import and export was not used for some specific goods.

Chapter 3
China's Financial Contribution to National Economic Recovery

With the process of building an independent financial system and unifying the RMB system in the early days of the People's Republic of China, financial organizations with the People's Bank of China as the main body gave full play to their functions, laying a good foundation for the recovery of the national economy. It has taken less than three years for our country to reach the highest level of national economic development before 1949. At the same time, the combination of political and economic measures has quickly calmed the persistent high prices and inflation. Under these conditions, China's financial industry has achieved rapid development.

3.1 The Appeasement of Inflation

After 1949, large-scale military activities continued, and a large number of personnel of the old government had to be accepted and resettled. Fiscal expenditure ballooned, and financial work such as taxation was not unified. The resulting fiscal deficit could only be made up by the inertial mode of currency issuance by the banks in the revolutionary base areas, which led to a rapid rise in prices.

3.1.1 The Cause of Inflation in the Early Years of the People's Republic of China

In the early days of the People's Republic of China, affected by historical inertia and military activities that had not yet ended, four large-scale price hikes occurred in the country in April, July, October 1949 and February 1950. The soaring prices seriously threatened the lives of the broad masses of the people, destroyed the normal operation of the whole national economy, and intensified the financial and economic

R. Lan, *The Financial Development of China*, Understanding China,
https://doi.org/10.1007/978-981-97-8273-4_3

difficulties of the new regime. There are various factors that have led to multiple price surges and severe inflation which can be broadly summarized as follows.

Firstly, price surges caused by historical inertia. Since the outbreak of the full-scale Anti-Japanese War in 1937, factors such as the deepening of Japanese aggression, gradual isolation from the outside world, escalating military expenditures, lack of external assistance, and the division of fiscal revenues and taxes have led the Nationalist Government to rely on issuing fiat currency to make up for fiscal deficits. After the victory of the Anti-Japanese War in 1945, Kuomingtang Government quickly initiated a civil war, intensifying the already tight financial situation and resulting in a significant increase in deficits. As a result, there was a further reliance on increased issuance of banknotes to cover the fiscal deficits, thereby exacerbating inflation. Subsequently, with the expansion of the domestic war, inflation became increasingly severe. This gradually gave rise to a large number of speculative merchants across the country who sought to profit and manipulate the market. They took advantage of the country's financial difficulties and tight urban supply to hoard goods, drive up prices, and make huge profits. They led with price hikes in rice, followed by cotton cloth, exacerbating inflation. This led to the popular saying, "Merchants are better off than workers, hoarding is better than being a merchant, and speculation is better than hoarding." A large group of speculators ignited a speculative frenzy in major cities such as Tianjin, Shanghai, Wuhan, and Guangzhou, while bureaucratic capital relied on privileges to profit from it, and idle social funds chased after profits. In larger cities, bulk transactions were often conducted using gold, silver dollars, or bartering. The situation of speculative trading in gold, US dollars, and silver dollars was also very serious, resulting in a sharp increase in gold and silver prices. The surge in gold and silver prices, in turn, fueled the rise in general prices. Meanwhile, although the first set of Renminbi issued on December 1, 1948, quickly achieved the task of unifying and stabilizing the chaotic monetary system after the establishment of the People's Republic of China, it still bore the characteristics of inflation and the wartime environment. In daily production and commodity circulation, it was usually priced and settled in billions, tens of billions, or even hundreds of billions, further driving up prices.

Secondly, there was a decline in production, transportation blockages, and a lack of supplies. By the time the People's Republic of China was declared in 1949, the national economy had reached a state of complete bankruptcy. In 1949, compared to the highest historical annual output, industrial output decreased by 51.6% in coal production, 13.9% in iron production, 17.1% in steel production, and 73.5% in cotton production. In agriculture, the grain production in 1949 dropped by nearly one-fourth compared to the highest historical annual output, and cotton production dropped by nearly half. Agricultural tools were severely damaged, and there were significant losses in water resources, resulting in consecutive years of disasters. In 1949, the total affected agricultural area in the country was 120 million mu, with more than 40 million affected people, of which the severely affected areas accounted for 28 million mu, with 7 million affected people in urgent need of relief. Additionally, production stagnation and paralyzed domestic transportation led to a bottleneck in the exchange of goods between urban and rural areas, further driving up prices.

Thirdly, the national finances were in extreme difficulty and had to rely on issuing currency to make up for it. 1949 was the year when the Chinese People's Liberation War achieved decisive victory nationwide, but it was also the most financially challenging year. At that time, the national fiscal revenue was only equivalent to 30.3 billion jin (half a kilo) of rice, while fiscal expenditures reached 57 billion jin. The newly established People's Government had not yet implemented a unified tax policy and tax system, and all liberated areas were not fully connected. Each liberated area had its own fiscal revenue and expenditure policies, and issued their own currency, which further exacerbated the fiscal disorder. This led to increasingly difficult financial conditions for the government, with two-thirds of the fiscal deficit having to be filled by increasing the issuance of paper currency. By the end of June 1949, the total amount of Renminbi in circulation was only 280 billion yuan, but by the end of November 1949, it had increased to 1.6 trillion yuan.[1] While this satisfied the needs of the fiscal deficits, it inevitably intensified the rise in prices.

Fourthly, there was a sharp increase in expenditures, including military expenses. At the establishment of the People's Republic of China, except for coastal islands like Taiwan, there were still parts of the country that had not been completely liberated. The reactionary forces of the Kuomintang still had over one million troops, occupying the entire provinces of Guangdong, Guangxi, Sichuan, Guizhou, Yunnan, Xikang, as well as parts of Shaanxi, Hubei, Hunan, Fujian, and other provinces. The People's Revolutionary War was still ongoing, and military expenditures remained a significant part of the fiscal budget (around half in 1949). At the same time, the new government had to take full responsibility for the millions of military and political personnel left behind by the Nationalist government. Including our own military and political personnel, there were approximately over 9 million people. Additionally, transportation and industrial enterprises needed priority restoration, and a large number of unemployed people urgently required relief. The combined effect of these factors eventually led to multiple significant price surges at the outset of the establishment of the People's Republic of China.

3.1.2 Governance of Inflation

The continuously soaring prices and rapid inflation posed a severe challenge to the governing capacity of the Communist Party of China (CPC) Central Committee, which was in the process of seizing power. In response, the CPC Central Committee quickly made decisions and emphasized the need to curb inflation. At the Second Plenary Session of the 7th CPC Central Committee, it was decided to establish the Central Finance and Economic Committee (later referred to as the CFEC), and transferred Chen Yun from the northeast to the central government to uniformly lead the financial and economic work of the whole country. After that, the Central Financial

[1] Yang Xitian et al., *General History of Finance in China (Vol. 6): Period of the People's Republic of China*, China Finance Press, 2002, p. 40.

and Economic Commission held multiple meetings and established a stable monetary policy, opposing the previous practice of excessive currency issuance leading to inflation. "There is no alchemy in the world, nor a money tree. Yet we have to feed 9 million people. So, there are only two options: printing money and raising taxes. We cannot choose the path of printing money. The prudent approach is to find more ways to increase tax revenue and come up with ideas." After all, "comparing between tax collection and currency issuance, in the best possible circumstances, collecting a little more tax is less harmful than printing more money. By doing so, although the burden on the industrial and commercial sector may be slightly heavier, the prices remain stable, which benefits legitimate businesses. Conversely, if prices fluctuate greatly, no one would be willing to invest in the industrial and commercial sector, and funds would be hoarded in goods or remain idle at home, causing a lack of employment opportunities for workers. This will inevitably result in wastage of funds and labor, severely impacting production. … Issuing less currency and collecting more taxes might increase the burden, but it ensures price stability and gradual economic development, making it a progressive approach".[2] Under Chen Yun's leadership, the CPC Central Committee formulated policies to curb inflation. Firstly, it vigorously cracked down on speculative hoarding activities. In response to speculation during the financial and economic difficulties, such as hoarding, price manipulation, and speculation in gold and silver, the governments at all levels in China implemented strong economic measures and necessary administrative measures, engaging in a powerful struggle. The first step was to combat the black market for silver yuan. Under the unified deployment of the People's Bank of China and the Ministry of Public Security, operations were launched to inspect underground money shops and arrest speculators in major cities such as Shanghai, Wuhan, and Guangzhou. In Shanghai, the People's Bank of China simultaneously exchanged and redeemed silver yuan while promoting deposits with tangible assets. The Trade Department also sold rice, coal, salt, oil, and used renminbi (Chinese yuan) to purchase industrial products. Additionally, the government proposed five measures to crack down on silver yuan speculation. Chen Yun drafted the "Directive of the CPC Central Committee on Seizing the Position with Renminbi by Suppressing Silver Yuan", and the Shanghai Stock Exchange building was sealed off, leading to the rectification of the currency market and capital market. Through unified deployment and actions, illegal activities of speculating on silver yuan were effectively curbed nationwide, curbing price fluctuations caused by the rise in silver yuan.

Furthermore, efforts were made to suppress the rise in prices of grain and cotton yarn. Dissatisfied with the failure of silver yuan speculation, speculators turned to grain and cotton yarn as new targets for speculation, triggering another wave of price

[2] Bo Yibo. *A Review of Some Major Decisions and Events (Part I)*, Party School of the CPC Central Committee Press, 1991, p. 92.

increases in the market. Under Chen Yun's unified deployment, "a purposeful, organized, and systematic battle to curb skyrocketing prices and crack down on speculators was immediately launched nationwide".[3] The Central Financial and Economic Commission swiftly made decisions, mobilizing the forces of state-owned trading companies, finance, and banks to combat illegal activities in grain and cotton. In terms of specific measures, trading companies released supplies and temporarily reduced purchases; the finance department strengthened taxation and raised public debt; and banking institutions absorbed deposits and called in loans. As a result, speculators were constrained by the actions of supply release and reduced purchases, leading to their financial difficulties within less than half a month. They suffered significant losses, went bankrupt one after another, and ultimately ended in failure. This initially stabilized financial prices and greatly enhanced the credibility of the Communist Party of China and the People's Government among the people.

The second measure was the implementation of real-value savings and the issuance of real-value government bonds. In order to alleviate public concerns about inflation and support the efforts of the Central Financial and Economic Commission to combat speculative activities, the People's Bank of China, in addition to actively cooperating with the aforementioned actions of the Commission, started real-value savings in cities such as Tianjin, Shijiazhuang, and Beijing since April 1949. Real-value savings involved converting currency into a unit of measurement based on tangible goods, known as the "real-value unit price", for deposit and withdrawal purposes. The specific goods included in the real-value unit varied by location. Generally, one real-value unit included one market liter of polished rice, one market two taels of cooking oil, one market foot of high-quality white cloth, and one market jin (half a kilo) of coal. When people deposited their savings, they converted the currency into the relatively stable "real-value unit" based on the daily "real-value unit price". When making withdrawals, they exchanged the "real-value unit" back into currency according to the same daily "real-value unit price". People did not have to worry about price fluctuations when saving money, making real-value savings highly popular among the general public. This initiative began in Tianjin, and by the end of 1949, there were 194,698 savings accounts with a total balance of 2.5 million "real-value units". During a significant price fluctuation in Shanghai on November 16, 1949, the amount of real-value savings reached 11.2 million units, which increased to 46.61 million units by February 28 of the following year. Meanwhile, the value of one real-value unit increased from 1855 (old currency) to 6546 (old currency).[4]

At the same time, the People's Bank of China also collaborated with the Ministry of Finance to issue 100 million "fen" (0.01Chinese yuan) worth of 'People's Victory Real-Value Government Bonds' in December 1949. The value of one "fen" in the real-value government bonds was calculated based on the average wholesale prices of 6 market jin (half a kilo) of rice (millet in Tianjin), 1.5 market jin of flour, 4 market feet of white cloth, and 16 market jin of coal in six cities including Shanghai,

[3] Literature Research Office of the CPC Central Committee. *Chen Yun Biography (Part I)*, Central Academic Press, 2005, p. 645.

[4] Yao Sui, *The Financial History of China*, Higher Education Press, 2007, p. 427.

Tianjin, Hankou, Xi'an, Guangzhou, and Chongqing.[5] Through this measure, the purchasing power of the subscribers' currency was safeguarded. The bonds were issued starting from January 5, 1950, and the first-phase issuance plan was quickly oversubscribed. The issuance of government bonds significantly reduced reliance on monetary issuance to cover fiscal deficits and effectively stabilized financial prices.

The third measure was the unification of the country's financial and economic work. Despite the temporary control of the initial surge in prices under the leadership of the Central Financial and Economic Commission, the nation's financial and economic work remained disorganized and lacked unity due to the impact of the war. Without unified financial and economic work, it would be difficult to achieve a balance in fiscal revenue and expenditure, thus leaving room for potential fluctuations in prices that had just stabilized. In this context, on March 3rd, following the National Financial and Economic Conference held in February 1950 under the guidance of the Central Financial and Economic Commission, the State Council issued the "Decision on the Unification of National Financial and Economic Work", which clarified the objectives of unifying the country's financial and economic work. Around this goal, the central government established a unified national finance through the "three unifications" approach. The "three unifications" refer to: (1) unifying national financial work to achieve a balance in fiscal revenue and expenditure nationwide. In terms of fiscal revenue, it was specified that the revenue from public grain, taxes, stockpiled goods, and profits from state-owned enterprises would be pooled into the national treasury and uniformly allocated by the Ministry of Finance. As for fiscal expenditure, strict adherence to prescribed budgeting and supply standards was mandated to achieve a balance in fiscal revenue and expenditure, eliminating the practice of relying on currency issuance to cover fiscal deficits. (2) unifying national state-owned trade work to achieve a balance in the allocation of national goods. The Ministry of Commerce was responsible for the operations and allocation of goods for state-owned trade units nationwide. At the same time, it was stipulated that the military and government agencies were not allowed to engage in commercial activities, in order to facilitate supply–demand balance. (3) Unifying national financial work to achieve a balance in cash inflow and outflow nationwide. The People's Bank of China acted as an agent for the national treasury, serving as the central authority for cash and foreign exchange management.

In order to ensure nationwide cash management, the People's Bank of China convened the First National Financial Conference in March 1950 and formulated specific guidelines for unifying national financial work. "These guidelines focused on efficient management, organizing deposits, treasury management, flexible allocation, expanding and consolidating the position of the Chinese currency, controlling foreign exchange and commodities, and improving systems. The first step was to transform the central bank into a cash center and effectively organize clearing and credit operations, laying the foundation for further development and gradually

[5] Yang Xitian et al., *General History of Finance in China (Vol. 6): Period of the People's Republic of China*, China Finance Press, 2002, p. 45.

advancing the bank towards becoming a center for cash, clearing, and credit."[6] Based on this deployment, the People's Bank of China established the direction of "building treasury, collecting deposits, and flexible allocation." Building the treasury meant consolidating national fiscal revenue from all regions into the national treasury to ensure unified use of national income. In March 1950, the State Council issued the "Central Treasury Regulations", which specified that the national financial treasury was divided into four levels: central, regional, provincial or autonomous region, and county (city) treasury, with the heads of each level's treasury serving concurrently as officials of the People's Bank of China. At the same time, the People's Bank of China also negotiated with the Ministry of Commerce to establish a "trade treasury", requiring state-owned trade companies to deposit daily sales cash into the treasury for remittance and settlement. The practice of the Ministry of Commerce gradually extended to various industries and departments, including the Ministry of Railways, Ministry of Fuel Industry, Ministry of Heavy Industry, and others. Collecting deposits involved implementing a cash management system to centralize funds and ensure unified use. On April 7th, 1950, the State Council issued the "Decision on Cash Management of State Institutions", which required the People's Bank of China to centrally manage cash dispersed in state-owned enterprises, institutions, troops, and cooperatives. Flexible allocation, on the other hand, involved consolidating the cash and funds dispersed in various units nationwide into the treasuries and then flexibly allocating them within the country. Clearly, in the process of "building treasury, collecting deposits, and flexible allocation", the People's Bank of China formed the functions of "credit, settlement, and cash centers". Thus, based on the principle of credit concentration in the national bank, a vertical credit distribution system was established, achieving the goal of a unified national financial and economic management system, curbing inflation, and gradually transforming the financial functions into a single function of serving the fiscal sector. This laid the foundation for the emergence of a rudimentary form of "fund management".

The fourth measure was to regulate currency circulation. In the process of unifying national financial and economic work, although funds were centralized and uniformly allocated nationwide, the excessive concentration of funds caused market position tensions and shortages, leading to market downturn, difficulties in private enterprise operations, and unemployment, among other negative impacts on the socio-economic situation. In response, the Central Financial and Economic Commission proposed four measures and two defense lines based on the principle of balancing public and private interests, aiming to alleviate unemployment, maintain the development of private industry and commerce, and prevent the escalation of social conflicts. The four measures were as follows: firstly, ensuring an adequate supply of cotton fabrics and strengthening the capacity for increased fabric purchases, including procuring cotton for processing by private fabric mills to help them overcome difficulties and reduce unemployment; secondly, expanding the circulation scope and range of the Chinese currency; thirdly, encouraging the acceptance of fixed-term deposits; and

[6] Yang Xitian et al., *General History of Finance in China (Vol. 6): Period of the People's Republic of China*, China Finance Press, 2002, p. 46.

fourthly, if necessary, delaying the disbursement of military and government funds, temporarily freezing a significant portion of deposits from government agencies, state-owned enterprises, and cooperatives or restricting their withdrawal. These four measures formed the first defense line, while the last measure served as the second defense line. Through these measures, the negative effects of unifying the national financial and financial work were basically resolved, and the effect of activating the market was received. However, due to the outbreak of the Korean War and the United States to China's economic blockade, restrictions and frozen funds and other adverse factors, China's just stable prices were facing new uncertainties. For this reason, the central government quickly formulated a new financial and economic work policy known as the "Three-Pronged Approach of Defense, Stability, and Development", with a primary focus on consolidating national defense, stabilizing the market, and addressing other priorities. Based on this policy, the Central Financial and Economic Commission issued the "Instructions on Freezing Cash and Stabilizing Prices", which aimed to temporarily freeze public deposits in bank accounts, strengthen cash management, tighten credit, promote savings, and counter the blockade, restrictions, and freezing of funds imposed by the United States.[7] Later, in view of the market problems in rural areas, the People's Bank of China, based on the actual situation at that time, expanded the amount of money invested in the rural market, and clarified the circulation pattern of money between different regions and units, which made the market increasingly active and basically solved the new problems in the social economy. In this process, the central government also adopted many policies and measures to gradually establish a system of planned adjustment of currency circulation, thus consolidating the ultimate goal of stabilizing prices and quelling inflation.

3.2 Financial Function in Recovery of National Economy

Under the destruction of the long war and hyperinflation, China's economy was deeply trapped in the pattern of industrial decline, agricultural decay, and material shortage. In its efforts to build a financial system, the central government had actively used financial functions to boost the recovery of the national economy. In less than three years, the national economy had recovered to the highest level before 1949, and surpassed the past in many fields.

[7] Yang Xitian et al., General History of Finance in China (Vol. 6): Period of the People's Republic of China, China Finance Press, 2002, p. 50.

3.2.1 *The Adjustment of Credit Policy to Promote the Recovery of National Economy*

Since the establishment of the People's Republic of China, the People's Bank of China has always prioritized bank credit work in supporting the recovery and development of the national economy. During the first and second National Financial Conferences held in February 1950 and early 1951, the People's Bank of China further emphasized the importance of vigorously promoting private businesses such as savings, insurance, lending, and foreign exchange in order to attract deposits, accumulate funds, support the recovery of industrial and agricultural production, and facilitate the exchange of goods between urban and rural areas. In terms of RMB credit from financial institutions, total deposits increased from 149 million yuan in 1949 to 9.33 billion yuan, and total loans increased from 104 million yuan in 1949 to 180 million yuan in 1952.[8] Specifically, the bank's credit policy in promoting the recovery and development of the national economy was mainly manifested in the following three aspects.

Firstly, pooling funds to support the development of state-owned and cooperative economies. The "Common Program" clearly stipulated that "state-owned economy is a socialist economy. All matters related to the national economy and those capable of manipulating the livelihood of the people should be centrally operated by the state", and "cooperative economy is a semi-socialist economy and an important part of the entire national economy. The people's government should support its development and provide preferential treatment". Based on this concept, the People's Bank of China first supported the development and growth of state-owned and cooperative economies through its credit policies. From 1950 to 1952, loans to state-owned industries increased threefold, and loans to state-owned commercial sectors increased 5.5 times.[9] Currently, although the central government has established a credit support strategy of "industry first, commerce later", data shows that the People's Bank of China provides more support to the state-owned economy in the commercial sector. Firstly, to curb speculative activities such as hoarding and profiteering, the People's Bank of China fully supports the funding needs of state-owned wholesale enterprises, aiming to gradually replace privately-owned wholesale businesses and cut off credit to them by reclaiming previously issued loans, thereby interrupting their supply chain. Secondly, it comprehensively supports state-owned businesses in expanding their processing, ordering, centralized purchasing, and marketing services to private industrial and commercial enterprises, strengthening their reliance on state-owned businesses. Thirdly, the People's Bank of China increases loan demand for state-owned businesses and cooperatives to acquire agricultural and sideline products, specialty products, and export commodities, among others, while lowering loan interest rates. This is done to enhance the role of state-owned businesses in the exchange of goods between urban and rural areas. Consequently, with prioritized

[8] Su Ning. *China Financial Statistics (1949–2005)*, China Financial Press, 2007, p. 1059.

[9] The People's Bank of China. *Sixty Years of the People's Bank of China (1948–2008)*, China Financial Press, 2008, p. 49.

Table 3.1 Five major adjustments of credit policy of private industry and commerce (May, 1949–the end of 1952)

Time	Contents
May 1949–August 1949	Supported state trade in expanding processing, ordering, purchasing and marketing of private enterprises, and increase loans to support them in fulfilling their tasks on schedule
August 1949–February 1950	Raised interest rates on deposits and loans for private companies and cooperated with authorities to crack down on their speculative behavior
March 1950–the end of 1950	Reinvigorated the private sector by increasing loans to private enterprises, lowering interest rates on loans and conducting negotiation transactions
1951	Catered to the policy for financial and economic work: national defense first, price stability second and other third and adjusted credit policies flexibly
1952	Cooperated with "Three Antis movement"(battle of anti-corruption, anti-waste and anti-bureaucracy among government officials) and "Five Antis movement"(anti-bribery, anti- "tax-evasion", anti- "cheating of state property", anti- "cutting corners" and anti- "theft of national economic information among private industry and commerce"), and strengthened credit management for private industry and commerce

support from banking credit policies, the state-owned economy experiences rapid development.

By the end of 1952, there were over 9,500 national state-owned industrial enterprises with more than 25.1 million employees. The proportion of state-owned industrial output in the overall industrial output reached 41.5%... The share of socialist commerce in the total sales revenue increased from 19.4% in 1950 to 51.9%.[10]

The second aspect is implementing the principle of "balancing public and private interests" and utilizing, restricting, and transforming private industrial and commercial enterprises. The "Common Program" explicitly states that "the people's government should encourage the initiative and support the development of private economic activities that are beneficial to the national economy and people's livelihood". Based on this principle, the People's Bank of China adopts differentiated credit policies for different industries and entities within the private industrial and commercial sector. On one hand, it encourages deposit-taking and foreign exchange business to provide necessary financial services for private industrial and commercial enterprises. On the other hand, it appropriately adjusts its loan measures, adopting a flexible approach depending on the socio-economic situation at different times. From before the establishment of the People's Republic of China to the end of 1952, the People's Bank of China made five major adjustments to its credit policies for private industrial and commercial enterprises, as shown in Table 3.1.

[10] Yang Xitian et al., *General History of Finance in China (Vol. 6): Period of the People's Republic of China*, China Finance Press, 2002, p. 50.

After the credit adjustments made by the People's Bank of China in the five phases mentioned above, the Chinese government not only guided the majority of the private industrial and commercial enterprises onto the path of primary state capitalism, significantly increasing the proportion of public–private joint venture industries in the overall industrial output value but also restored and developed the private industrial and commercial sector. This laid the foundation for the subsequent complete transformation of all private industrial and commercial enterprises into public–private joint ventures.

The third aspect involves coordinating with land reform and supporting the recovery and development of agricultural production. The "Common Program" clearly states the requirements for land reform and the development of agriculture, forestry, animal husbandry, and fisheries: "Land reform is a necessary condition for the development of productive forces and the industrialization of the country. In areas where land reform has been implemented, the ownership of land obtained by farmers must be protected. In areas where land reform has not yet been implemented, farmers must be mobilized, farmer organizations established, and steps taken to eliminate bandits, reduce rents and interest, and distribute land, thereby ensuring that those who work the land own it." Regarding agriculture, forestry, animal husbandry, and fisheries: "In all areas where land reform has been thoroughly implemented, the people's government should organize farmers and all labor forces engaged in agriculture to prioritize the development of agricultural production and related industries. Farmers should be gradually guided to form various forms of labor cooperation and production cooperation based on voluntary and mutually beneficial principles. In the newly liberated areas, every step of land reform should be combined with the restoration and development of agricultural production. The people's government should strive to restore and surpass the pre-war levels of grain production, industrial raw materials, and exports within a short period of time, based on national plans and the needs of the people's livelihood. Attention should be given to water conservancy construction, flood and drought prevention, restoration and development of animal power, increasing fertilizer usage, improving agricultural tools and seeds, preventing diseases and pests, providing relief during disasters, and implementing planned immigration and land reclamation.' In accordance with these requirements, the People's Bank of China actively supported the financial needs of land reform and the recovery of agricultural production in various regions. At the Second National Financial Conference held in early 1951, the focus of rural financial work was clearly defined: "Provincial branches of the People's Bank should take the lead in organizing and leading rural financial work, with 80% of their efforts dedicated to rural financial work. Bank institutions should be decentralized by one level, establishing branches at the district level, while simultaneously developing credit cooperatives".[11] The People's Bank of China and its branches at all levels were tasked with organizing rural funds, providing agricultural loans, and actively supporting the commercial

[11] Yang Xitian et al., *General History of Finance in China (Vol. 6): Period of the People's Republic of China*, China Finance Press, 2002, p. 60.

sector in acquiring agricultural and sideline products to alleviate the financial difficulties faced by agriculture and farmers. As a result, by the winter of 1952, land reform was essentially completed, the total agricultural production value witnessed a significant increase, growing by 48.5% compared to 1949, and the initial recovery and development of agricultural production were achieved.

3.2.2 Flexible Use of Interest Rate Leverage

In addition to vigorously adjusting credit methods to support the recovery and development of the national economy, the People's Bank of China has also flexibly applied interest rate leverage to boost the national economy. Interest rate is an important means to regulate the supply and demand of funds. From May 1949 to June 1952, the People's Bank of China comprehensively adjusted the deposit interest rate for many times to meet the needs of different economic situations, organize social funds to support production and expand the power of the state-owned economy. The adjustment of interest rates by the People's Bank of China during this period is shown in Table 3.2.

The interest rate adjustments made by the People's Bank of China in response to changes in the socio-economic situation greatly meet the needs of economic recovery and development. In this process, the People's Bank of China gradually established a diversified and multi-level interest rate management system based on the needs of the initial stage of social and economic development. For the management of deposit interest rates for industrial and commercial enterprises, the People's Bank of China clearly stated that the limits of interest rate fluctuations were controlled by regional banks and branch banks before June 1952. As for the management of interest rates in private banking and money industry, the People's Bank of China would not impose any other restrictions, but would gradually reduce interest rates as required by the interest rate committee composed of the People's Bank of China and local financial industry. Regarding the management of credit cooperatives and private lending rates, the People's Bank of China explicitly stipulated that the interest rate on credit cooperatives' deposits transferred to banks should not exceed 10% of private deposits, and the fluctuation range of interest rates for credit cooperatives borrowing from banks should not exceed 10% of the bank's interest rate on private loans. On June 21, 1952, while adjusting the national interest rates, the People's Bank of China started to unify the interest rates nationwide (excluding the Northeast region), swiftly ending the aforementioned diversified and multi-level interest rate management system, thus preparing the necessary conditions for the subsequent nationwide interest rate unification and gradual elimination of commercial credit activities.

In addition, the central government and the Central Finance Committee made full use of the insurance organizations established in the early days of the People's Republic of China, determining their business principles as "protecting national assets, ensuring production safety, promoting commodity exchange, and enhancing

Table 3.2 The adjustment of interest rates by the People's Bank of China before and after 1949 (September 1998–September 1999)

Adjustment time	Reason for adjustment	Degree of rate adjustment
May 12, 1949	Restrained speculative activities caused by increasing prices	Demand deposits: 30–60‰ (per month, the same below); time deposits for three months: 85‰; for six months:150‰; public industrial lending: 60–120‰; public commercial lending: 75–150‰; private industrial lending: 75–150‰; private commercial lending:90–210‰; agricultural and sideline monetary lending: 75–150‰
June 27, 1950	Depositors were reluctant to discount their deposits while borrowers demanded to discount their loans because of fallen price	Demand deposits (personal deposits): 9‰; time deposits (personal deposits) for three months: 18‰; for six months: 21‰; public industrial lending: 21‰; public agricultural lending: 20‰; private industrial lending: 30‰; private commercial lending: 39‰
February 9, 1951	In response to the requirements of "three balances"(balance between government revenue and expenditure; balance between credit payments; balance between supply and demand for materials) and the tendency of price stabilization	Interest rate of demand deposit for corporate were 3‰ and 12‰ for one-year time deposit. Lending rates were 15% for mortgage lending and 16.5% for credit lending for three months and over. The rate cap for private lending and private bank lending from National Bank was 39‰ for one month and 42‰ for two months or more. The one-year interest rate for capital guaranteed and inflation-proof bank savings was 20‰. The interest rate for agricultural loans was 10‰ to 18‰
July and September 1951	To reduce business costs and facilitate the mobilization of capital	Maximum monthly interest rate of deposits was 20‰; of lending was 30‰ (divided into two phases)
June 21, 1952	In response to the requirements of the "Three Anti" and "Five Anti" campaigns as well as the stability of prices	The interest rate of demand deposits was 2.4‰ for public accounts and 4.5‰ for private accounts. The rate of time deposits was 4.5‰, of demand deposits was 10.5‰ for six months and 12‰ for one or more than more year. For business loans, the interest rate of commercial sector was 11.1‰ for three months, 11.4‰ for six months and 12‰ for a year; the interest rate of industrial sector was 6‰ for three months and 9‰ for a year. For private loans, the rate of industry was 10.5‰ to 15‰, of business was 13.5‰ to 19.5‰, of agriculture was 10‰ to 15‰ and of water conservation was 7.5‰ to 9‰

people's welfare". Subsequently, insurance organizations at all levels continuously improved insurance terms, reduced insurance rates, piloted agricultural insurance and various foreign-related insurance businesses, and implemented mandatory insurance for state institutions, state-owned enterprises, cooperative properties, ships, and railway vehicles based on actual needs. These measures greatly promoted the recovery and development of China's national economy.

3.3 Smooth Development of Foreign Exchange and Insurance Business

3.3.1 The Development of Insurance Business

The initial development of insurance business in China was, to some extent, built upon the aforementioned cancellation of privileges of foreign insurance companies, the restructuring of national capital insurance companies, and the confiscation of bureaucratic capital insurance companies. The establishment of the People's Insurance Company of China (PICC) then marked the beginning of rapid development in China's insurance business.

With the establishment of the financial system in China and the progress of economic recovery, the organizational structure of the People's Bank of China began to take shape. Under its leadership, insurance and foreign exchange businesses were smoothly carried out, and the relationship between finance and the economy gradually entered a virtuous cycle.

Firstly, the establishment of the People's Insurance Company of China allowed for the construction of its organizational structure. Prior to 1949, in accordance with the requirements of the National Finance and Economics Conference, the People's Bank of China had already begun preparations for the establishment of a national state-owned insurance company. On September 25, 1949, the first national insurance work conference was held by the People's Bank of China, setting the direction for the development of insurance business in China. Subsequently, the proposal to establish a unified national insurance company was approved by the Central Committee of the Communist Party of China. On October 20, 1949, the People's Insurance Company of China was established. Afterward, the People's Insurance Company of China gradually established a relatively complete organizational structure throughout the country. By the end of 1952, the company had reached 4,416 branches at various levels, with a workforce of over 34,000 employees.

Secondly, various insurance businesses were gradually launched. Before the establishment of the People's Insurance Company of China, the People's Bank of China actively utilized the National Capital Insurance Company to carry out insurance operations in accordance with the deployment of the central government. In May 1949, the People's Bank of China attempted to conduct property insurance and trial agricultural insurance in the recently liberated Pingjin area, using the China Property Insurance Company as the target, accumulating experience for the development of insurance business in China. After the establishment of the People's Insurance Company of China, the China Insurance Company was immediately set up in Shanghai to specialize in foreign-related insurance business. The People's Insurance

Company of China continuously established branches throughout the country, and in areas without branches, agencies of the People's Bank of China were entrusted to handle the business. This allowed the scope of insurance business in China to rapidly expand. In urban areas, property, transportation, fire, and personal insurance businesses were established, while in rural areas, starting with trial livestock insurance, coverage gradually expanded to important crops such as cotton, wheat, rice, tobacco, sugarcane, grapes, and their harvests. In February 1951, the State Council issued the "Decision on Implementing Mandatory Insurance for State Institutions, State-Owned Enterprises, Cooperative Properties, and Mandatory Passenger Insurance", and in April, the "Regulations on Mandatory Insurance for Railway Vehicles" and "Regulations on Mandatory Insurance for Ships" were promulgated. These regulations stipulated that the aforementioned institutions were required to mandatorily insure with the People's Insurance Company of China. As a result, insurance business in China gradually covered all important sectors.

At last, we have strengthened the processing of overseas insurance operations and the connection with overseas insurance businesses. During the old era of China, the overseas insurance industry was mainly dominated by foreign insurance companies. Bureaucratic capital insurance companies established institutions in some important cities overseas and partially participated in related businesses. After canceling the privileges of foreign insurance companies and taking over bureaucratic capital insurance companies, the overseas insurance operations of China experienced a period of decline. The establishment of the People's Insurance Company of China (PICC) has enhanced the development of international insurance business. To meet the needs of trade, shipping, and other industries, PICC started offering war insurance for ships, crew, and cargo transportation. In order to support international insurance business, PICC highly valued reinsurance operations on one hand and gradually maintained and established good reinsurance relationships with places like London, leveraging the overseas relationships of previous Chinese insurance companies on the other hand. As China's overseas trade shifted towards the Soviet Union, Eastern Europe, and other socialist countries, PICC actively established multi-channel reinsurance relationships with insurance companies from the Soviet Union, Poland, Czechoslovakia, North Korea, and other socialist countries to promote the development of foreign trade. Through various efforts mentioned above, the development of China's insurance business with overseas countries and the connection with their insurance companies have been greatly promoted, ensuring the smooth operation of our international insurance business.

3.3.2 The Development of Foreign Exchange Business

The People's Bank of China (PBOC), under the conditions of gradually establishing China's foreign exchange management system and unifying the announcement of the national renminbi(Chinese yuan) exchange rate, completely changed the pattern of foreign banks monopolizing foreign exchange rates and manipulating the foreign exchange market before 1949. This laid a necessary institutional foundation for the development of China's foreign exchange business and promoted its growth.

Firstly, it centralized the national foreign exchange allocation under the unified configuration of the central government. In response to the phenomenon of foreign exchange speculation in the early stages of the People's Republic of China, the PBOC gradually centralized the scattered foreign exchange earnings from different industries and units nationwide to the head office. Under the management of the Bank of China, foreign exchange was used in a unified manner based on the sequence of allocation, thereby initially reversing the dilemma of the widening gap between the scarcity of foreign exchange and its demand in China, and directing limited foreign exchange to areas and sectors in urgent need.

The second aspect is the development of foreign exchange business with the socialist camp. At the time when the United States imposed economic sanctions on China and triggered the Korean War, the existing foreign exchange settlement rules that China had formed in its foreign trade faced unprecedented challenges from abroad. In response, based on its own reality, China, on one hand, engaged in a confrontational struggle with countries like the United States, refusing to use the US dollar and adopting third-party transaction mechanisms with countries in Asia, Africa, and others. On the other hand, China transformed the form of foreign trade and shifted its focus predominantly towards socialist countries such as the Soviet Union and Eastern Europe, changing the method of trade payment. Additionally, China actively established agency relationships and conducted foreign exchange business with countries in regions like Japan and Western Europe.

The third aspect is to effectively handle overseas remittances and increase foreign exchange income. At the beginning, our foreign trade experienced a significant decline, resulting in a shortage of foreign exchange. To change this situation, the People's Bank of China attached great importance to overseas remittances and instructed the Bank of China to strengthen the protection of remittances from overseas Chinese. Based on the prevailing circumstances, the Bank of China quickly established a set of measures to "serve overseas Chinese and facilitate remittances." Firstly, it widely publicized and implemented the government's policy of protecting overseas remittances, particularly focusing on safeguarding the interests of individuals involved in remittances. Secondly, it established efficient remittance channels and a wide network of payout locations to facilitate remittances from overseas Chinese. In addition to establishing direct remittance channels through the Bank of China, strategies such as "maintaining protection and long-term utilization" and "foreign exchange benefiting the public, profits benefiting individuals" were adopted for existing private remittance bureaus or remittance offices to fully leverage their advantages. Utilizing the convenience of remittance agents (commonly known as "shuǐkè") to collect remittances from overseas Chinese in remote areas and bring them back to the country, the funds were converted into domestic currency through banks and delivered to their families. The Bank of China also established remittance business agency relationships with correspondent banks in the United States, Canada, Western Europe, Southeast Asia, and other regions, allowing overseas Chinese to apply for remittances through these foreign banks to send money back home. While actively

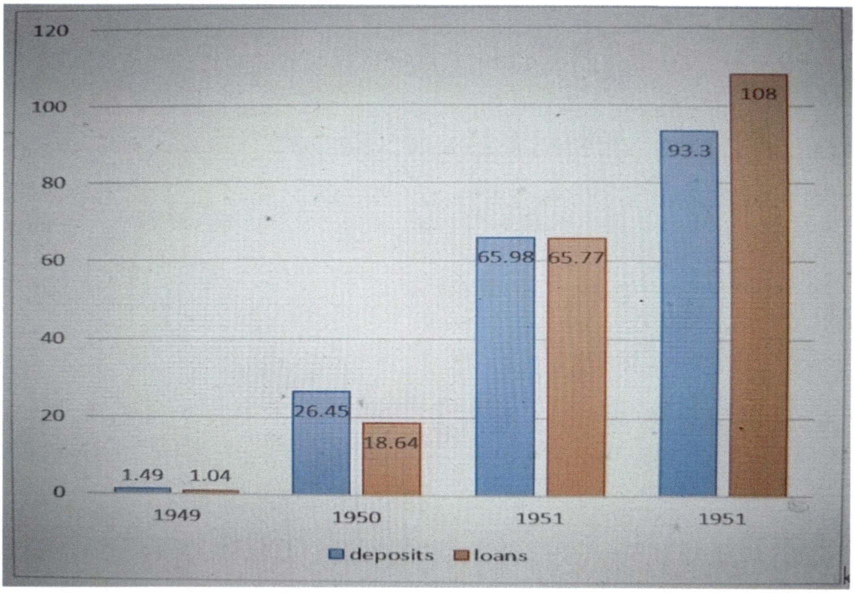

Fig. 3.1 Statistical chart of RMB credit balance from 1949 to 1951

establishing communication channels for remittances, the bank also strengthened the payout process for remittances.[12]

In this way, through the aforementioned measures and the proactive efforts of the Bank of China, the foreign exchange management and business of China quickly achieved results. From 1950 to 1952, the national foreign exchange income greatly increased, initially reversing the long-term deficit in foreign exchange receipts and payments from 1864 to 1949 (except for a surplus from 1872 to 1876 and 1948). This also corroborated the development of China's foreign exchange business and the effectiveness of foreign exchange work. Additionally, the banking and rural credit cooperative sectors in China also experienced rapid development, with branches established throughout the country and significant growth in deposit and loan business. The statistics on RMB credit receipts and payments from 1949 to 1951 are shown in Fig. 3.1.[13] The rapid expansion of credit business laid a necessary financial foundation for the recovery and development of the national economy, allowing the economy to rapidly recover and reach its highest level before 1949 in a very short period of time. This also demonstrates the essence of finance serving the real economy and embodies the true meaning of "vibrant finance, vibrant economy".

[12] Yang Xitian et al. *A General History of Chinese Finance (Volume 6): The Period of the People's Republic of China*, China Finance Press, 2002, p. 75.

[13] Su Ning. *Chinese Financial Statistics (1949–2005)*. China Finance Press, 2007, p. 1059.

Part II
The Tortuous Development of the Financial Industry in the Period of Planned Economy

Chapter 4
The Formation and Development of "Unified" Financial System

With the establishment of the highly centralized planned economic management system, China also established a financial management system that was adapted to this system. The People's Bank of China was practically the only financial institution at that time, with commercial credit concentrated in the national bank. The People's Bank of China undertook both commercial banking operations such as deposit-taking and loan granting, as well as performing the central banking functions of regulating currency circulation and credit allocation. During this process, the functions of finance became increasingly simplified, focusing on core tasks such as cash management, settlement, and treasury management.

4.1 Establishment of a Highly Centralized and Unified Financial Institutional System

In the process of constructing the financial system in China, after stages like acquisition, consolidation, and transformation, our country's financial organizations have been significantly streamlined. In order to adapt to the highly centralized planned economic management system and achieve the goal of modernization centered around heavy industry, financial organizations were further nationalized and financial institutions were simplified. Ultimately, there was only the People's Bank of China at the national level, and rural credit cooperatives under the leadership of the People's Bank of China were dispersed in rural areas. Financial functions were highly centralized within the realms of credit, settlement, and cash management.

R. Lan, *The Financial Development of China*, Understanding China,
https://doi.org/10.1007/978-981-97-8273-4_4

4.1.1 Integration of the Banking System

Alongside the establishment of the planned economic management system, the financial sector in China began to establish a highly centralized management financial system. In terms of ideology, it was widely recognized that the construction and realization of socialism required large banks, which must be nationalized and controlled by the proletariat. Through the ownership of national capital and the exclusive monopolistic power of the national bank, credit would be concentrated in the hands of the state.[1]

In practice, based largely on the experience of the Soviet Union in building socialism, banks were transformed into national accounting agencies and planning bodies for the production and distribution of national products in the process of constructing a socialist country. This can be considered as a backbone of a socialist society, as socialism cannot be achieved without large banks. After the Second World War, various socialist countries established a socialist banking system gradually through the nationalization of banks after the victory of revolution. They organized and regulated the national economic activities through socialist banking. Based on this understanding, China further promoted the nationalization process of banks after completing the socialist transformation of the private financial industry in 1953 and ultimately established the leadership position of the People's Bank of China. One aspect was the incorporation of joint public–private banks into the People's Bank of China. By the end of 1952, the joint public–private banks that had been established had already demonstrated the initial formation of a highly unified national banking system in our country. In March 1953, the report titled "Basic Completion of the Socialist Transformation of the Private Financial Industry" submitted by the People's Bank of China to the Central Committee of the Communist Party of China clearly stated: "The policy of the central government towards the private financial industry is very clear: 'The financial industry should be strictly managed by the state'... The national bank takes over the financial position for strengthening the state's leadership over private industry and commerce, and manages the financial industry that is capable of manipulating the national economy and people's livelihoods. It mainly wields two weapons: administrative management and business competition, and has implemented the policy of unified state management of the financial industry through three stages".[2]

As the socialist transformation of the private industry and commerce continued to progress, the financial operations of the joint public–private banks responsible for the private industry and commerce experienced a significant decline, forcing them to turn to the People's Bank of China for savings services. In February 1955, the branches of the joint public–private banks located in cities such as Shanghai, Beijing, Tianjin, Nanjing, Guangzhou, Xiamen, Hankou, Chongqing, Kunming, Suzhou, Changsha, Wuxi, Nantong, and Qingdao first merged their offices with the savings departments of the People's Bank of China. In July 1956, the central administration of the joint

[1] Marx and Engels. *The Communist Manifesto*, People's Publishing House, 2009.

[2] *Selected Works of Lenin (Volume 3)*. People's Publishing House, 2012, p. 311.

public–private banks merged their offices with the private business management bureau of the head office of the People's Bank of China. In this way, within less than four years, the joint public–private banks were fully integrated into the system of the People's Bank of China, achieving the complete nationalization goal of the private financial industry.

The second aspect is the simplification of the organizational structure of the People's Bank of China. The head office, district branches, regional branches, and sub-branches constituted the four-tier organizational structure established by the People's Bank of China in the early days of the establishment of the People's Republic of China. However, with the abolition of the regional level government agencies in June 1954, the administrative foundation of the regional branches ceased to exist. Consequently, the People's Bank of China abolished the regional branches, and the head office directly led the provincial branches, autonomous region branches, and municipalities directly under the central government branches. The four-tier organizational structure was simplified into a three-tier structure consisting of the head office, sub-branches, and sub-branches (see Fig. 4.1). The previous vertical management system transformed into a vertical management system, further strengthening the leadership of the head office of the People's Bank of China over the financial activities nationwide.

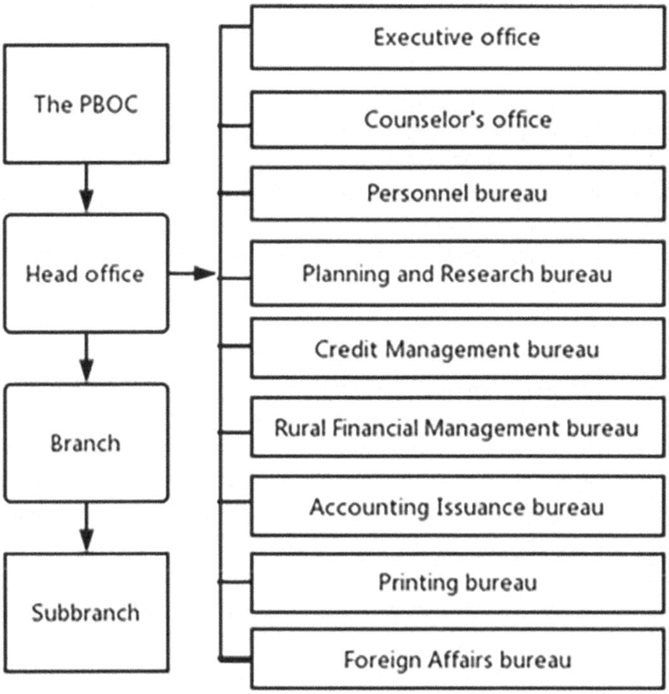

Fig. 4.1 Organizational framework diagram of the PBOC in 1956

After the abolition of regional branches, the management authority of the People's Bank of China became increasingly centralized in the head office, which facilitated the adaptation of the planned economic management system.

The third aspect is the establishment and abolition of the Agricultural Bank of China through the "three establishments and three abolitions" policy. During the period of economic recovery, China had previously established and abolished the Chinese Agricultural Cooperative Bank once. In 1953, with large-scale economic construction activities and the implementation of the First Five-Year Plan, the urban and rural economies in our country experienced rapid development, leading to an increasing demand for funds. The existing banking institutions faced heavy tasks of raising funds and regulating the currency. In order to promote the socialist transformation of agriculture and support agricultural production, the head office of the People's Bank of China proposed in the report reviewing the work of the past four years and the work suggestions for 1954, submitted to the Central Finance and Economic Committee at the end of 1953, the consideration of establishing an Agricultural Bank to strengthen the leadership over rural financial work.[3] In October 1954, the People's Bank of China submitted a request to the State Council in a report titled "Request for the Establishment of the Agricultural Bank of China", proposing that, following the Soviet experience, China must establish a specialized agricultural bank to unify national agricultural loans, lead credit cooperative organizations, support the agricultural cooperative movement, combat usury, and ensure the smooth progress of agricultural production. In March 1955, the State Council approved the proposal of the People's Bank of China and officially established the Agricultural Bank of China as a directly administered branch of the head office of the People's Bank of China. In accordance with this proposal, the Agricultural Bank of China was formally established on March 25th.

After the establishment of the Agricultural Bank of China, it carried out a significant amount of work in areas such as providing loans for poor farmers' cooperative funds and supporting agricultural cooperativization. However, due to the low level of development of the rural commodity economy in China and the relatively small volume of financial transactions, the operational structure of the Agricultural Bank of China overlapped with the operational departments of the People's Bank of China set up in rural areas. This created many inconveniences in handling agricultural funding work and added additional steps in fund circulation. In light of this, in February 1957, the head office of the People's Bank of China submitted a request to the State Council in a report titled "Request for the Re-merger of the Agricultural Bank with the People's Bank". On April 12th of the same year, the State Council approved the notice from the head office of the People's Bank of China regarding the abolition of the Agricultural Bank of China, agreeing to merge the various levels of institutions of the Agricultural Bank of China with the corresponding level institutions of the People's Bank of China. In August of the same year, the Agricultural Bank of China was abolished, and the operations previously handled by the Agricultural Bank of

[3] Li De. The Development History of China's Financial Industry (Vol. 1), People's Publishing House, 2015, p. 88.

Table 4.1 The "three establishments and three withdrawals" of the ABC before the reform and opening-up

Name	Establishing time	Withdrawing time
The Agricultural Cooperative Bank of China	July 1951	July 1952, withdrawn, rural finance was managed by the PBOC
The Agriculture Bank of China	March 1955	August 1957, merged into the PBOC
The Agriculture Bank of China	November 1965	November 1967, merged into the PBOC

China were taken over by the Rural Financial Management Bureau established by the head office of the People's Bank of China and the agricultural credit departments set up by various levels of institutions of the People's Bank of China. After the "adjustment, consolidation, enrichment, and improvement" of the national economy, the Agricultural Bank of China was reestablished in 1965. However, two years later, it merged with the People's Bank of China again, and agricultural credit continued to be handled by various levels of branches of the People's Bank of China. The "three establishments and three abolitions" of the Agricultural Bank of China before the reform and opening up are shown in Table 4.1.

The fourth is the establishment of China Construction Bank by the Chinese people. With the implementation of the "First Five-Year Plan", the focus of infrastructure development shifted to the forefront of the entire investment sector. During the period of national economic recovery, it became apparent that the situation, where the construction investment allocation was handled by the Bank of Communications, which also managed the financial management of public–private joint ventures and the clearance of government-owned equity, could no longer meet the demands of large-scale economic development. Against this backdrop, the Ministry of Finance submitted a report to the Financial and Economic Commission in May 1954, proposing the establishment of a specialized bank to handle the supervision of construction investment allocation based on the existing institutions and personnel of the Bank of Communications. In order to expedite fund accumulation and allocation and accelerate the socialist industrialization, the Financial and Economic Commission agreed to the Ministry of Finance's proposal to establish and lead the China Construction Bank. In September 1954, the State Council approved the "Decision on the Establishment of China Construction Bank", which clarified its main tasks: (1) supervising the allocation of budget appropriations for national infrastructure construction and self-raised funds for enterprises and institutions; (2) providing short-term loans to state-owned and local state-owned subcontractors in accordance with approved credit plans; (3) handling settlement operations for construction investment allocations; (4) supervising the designated use of funds for infrastructure construction and inspecting the utilization of funds, financial management, cost accounting, and completion of investment plans by construction units and subcontractors.[4] In the

[4] Yang Xitian et al., *General History of The Finance of China (Vol. 6): Period of the People's Republic of China*, China Financial Press, 2002: 87.

same year, in October, China Construction Bank was formally established under the leadership of the Ministry of Finance, and it was responsible for the supervision of financial construction investment allocations.

Through the nationalization of banking institutions and further integration of organizations, the core leadership position of the People's Bank of China (PBOC) became clear, which essentially reflected the viewpoint expressed by Vice Premier Li Xiannian at the time, stating that "banks are a mirror reflecting the economic situation, the national accountant, and a lever for implementing economic accounting in state-owned enterprises".[5] This emphasized the role of finance in managing funds.

4.1.2 The Adjustment to the Rural Financial System

During the period of national economic recovery, China initially formed a rural financial system under the leadership of the PBOC, consisting of rural credit cooperatives, grassroots institutions of the PBOC, and the Agricultural Cooperative Bank of China. Due to significant overlap in agricultural credit business and other aspects with the grassroots institutions of the PBOC, both the Agricultural Cooperative Bank of China and later the establishment of the Agricultural Bank of China were gradually merged and integrated. As a result, the rural financial system was left with rural credit cooperatives and the grassroots institutions of the PBOC.

After 1953, in order to support the agricultural cooperation movement, rural credit cooperatives received significant attention from the central government. In February 1954, the People's Bank of China held the first national credit cooperative conference in Beijing, clarifying the development goals for credit cooperatives. By the end of 1954, the aim was to have 30,000 to 40,000 credit societies and achieve one credit society per township by 1957, essentially realizing credit cooperation.[6] Subsequently, rural credit cooperatives experienced rapid development. By 1955, there were already 160,000 credit cooperatives established, covering 85% of all townships in the country. By the end of 1956, 97.5% of townships nationwide had established credit cooperatives, essentially achieving the goals set in 1954 and creating a miracle in the development of rural financial organizations in China.

The widespread establishment of rural credit cooperatives greatly promoted the agricultural cooperation movement in our country. Under the leadership of the People's Bank of China, rural credit cooperatives served as a powerful assistant to the national bank in supporting production and combating usury. They not only had a

[5] Shang Ming, Chen Li, Wang Chengming. *The Financial Events of the People's Republic of China*, China Financial Press, 1993: 115.

[6] Yang Xitian et al., *General History of The Finance of China (Vol. 6): Period of the People's Republic of China*, China Financial Press, 2002: 87.

necessary existence for a considerable period but also played an increasingly significant role.[7] The popularization of rural credit cooperatives also established a financial system that covered the entire country from top to bottom. To a certain extent, credit cooperatives became the extended arms of the People's Bank of China reaching out to the vast rural areas nationwide, further consolidating the highly centralized and unified financial system centered around the People's Bank of China. This facilitated the penetration of financial organizations into the grass-roots level and greatly enhanced the ability of the People's Bank of China to absorb surplus capital from society.

4.1.3 The Transformation of the Insurance System

During the period of national economic recovery, with the establishment and development of the People's Insurance Company of China, as well as the takeover, reorganization, and reform of the insurance system in our country, the insurance business experienced rapid growth. However, in rural areas, due to low levels of economic development and insufficient understanding of agricultural insurance and related services, there were instances of forced insurance, which led to dissatisfaction among some people. Against this backdrop, the head office of the People's Bank of China and the People's Insurance Company of China issued a joint directive in June 1953 to their affiliated institutions titled "Joint Instructions Regarding the Termination of Agency Relationships in Rural Insurance Operations", which decided to discontinue rural insurance operations. However, this "one-size-fits-all" approach deeply affected the progress of the agricultural cooperation movement. Therefore, starting from 1954, the People's Insurance Company of China gradually resumed agricultural insurance. In June 1956, the company issued the "Draft Measures for Rural Property Resource Insurance", which required farmers to pay their own insurance premiums for property insurance. In the industrial and commercial sector, as the socialist transformation of private industry and commerce progressed smoothly, the People's Insurance Company of China discontinued property insurance for systems such as railways, grain, postal and telecommunications, geology, water conservancy, and transportation nationwide in 1955, as well as compulsory insurance for railway vehicles and ships. At the same time, the People's Insurance Company of China intensified its development efforts in foreign insurance and vigorously carried out independent international reinsurance operations.

Under the influence of the "leftist" erroneous ideology, it was generally believed in various sectors of society that insurance had lost its role in socialist economic construction. In October 1958, the Ministry of Finance pointed out in the "Report on the Issue of Insurance Work After the Establishment of People's Communes (Draft)" that "...there is no longer a need to continue handling various types of

[7] Shang Ming, Chen Li, Wang Chengming. *The Financial Events of the People's Republic of China*, China Financial Press, 1993: 115.

insurance in rural areas, and it should be gradually discontinued."[8] On December 29, in the "Report on the Post-Closure Cleanup of Domestic Insurance Business and the Transfer of Foreign Insurance Business to the People's Bank of China" jointly issued by the Ministry of Finance and the People's Bank of China, it was proposed that "the role of insurance work has disappeared after the establishment of people's communes. Apart from the necessary continuation of foreign insurance business, domestic insurance business should be immediately discontinued.[9] In 1959, except for Shanghai and Harbin, domestic insurance business was completely discontinued nationwide. As a result, the People's Insurance Company of China became a specialized institution for handling foreign insurance business only at certain coastal ports, with its management transferred from the Ministry of Finance to the Overseas Business Bureau of the People's Bank of China. During the "Cultural Revolution", except for the existing foreign insurance business, which had continuity and was constrained by international conventions, all other foreign insurance business was completely terminated.

In this regard, it can be seen that after 1959, there was effectively no insurance business in China. The existing institutions were completely incorporated into a highly centralized and unified financial system, with only banking institutions remaining in the entire financial system. Except for the People's Construction Bank of China, all banking institutions were under the centralized leadership of the People's Bank of China, performing planned functions related to credit allocation, settlement, and cash management. However, even the People's Construction Bank of China was abolished in 1958 after the start of the "Great Leap Forward". As a result, the country's financial organizations were essentially reduced to the People's Bank of China and the rural credit cooperatives under its leadership.

4.2 Establishment of a Highly Centralized and Unified Financial Management System

With the increasing simplification of the financial institutional system and the concentration of institutions under the control of the People's Bank of China, the functions of financial management became increasingly singular. Banks gradually assumed the role of the nation's central accountant, serving as the cash center for credit, settlement, and cash management. The function of "managing funds" became more prominent.

---

[8] Chinese Academy of Social Sciences, Central Archives. *1958–1965 Economic Archives of the People's Republic of China: Finance Volume*, China Financial and Economic Press, 2011: 11.

[9] Chinese Academy of Social Sciences, Central Archives. *1958–1965 Economic Archives of the People's Republic of China: Finance Volume*. China Financial and Economic Press, 2011: 420.

4.2.1 *Formation of the Unified Deposit and Loan System*

With the gradual establishment of a highly centralized and unified planned economic management system, the People's Bank of China strengthened the construction of the credit management system centered around the unified deposit and loan system to adapt to this system. In September 1952, the People's Bank of China held a banking planning work conference, emphasizing the implementation of a unified plan to implement the central government's policy guidelines. The conference adopted "Provisional Measures for the Compilation of Comprehensive Credit Plans by the People's Bank of China (draft)", which fully defined the basis, content, management system, authority allocation, approval procedures, inspection systems, and other practices for credit plan compilation. This practice was implemented starting from 1953, with its core content being "all levels of banks should pool the deposits they absorb to the head office of the People's Bank of China, which will have unified control over them, while loans will be uniformly authorized by the head office of the People's Bank of China. The deposits and loans of various levels of banks are not linked, and loan quotas cannot be transferred between them. The loan plans of various enterprises are to be compiled by the relevant enterprise authorities and reported level by level, and then approved by the higher-level supervisory authorities in conjunction with the corresponding level of the People's Bank of China, and finally implemented step by step with the consent of the national supervisory authority and the head office of the People's Bank of China".[10] As a result, a vertically integrated credit and fund management system centered around the unified deposit and loan system was initially formed, with the People's Bank of China almost being the sole banking institution controlling the majority of financial resources. "The People's Bank of China, as both a central bank and a commercial bank, held 93% of the total financial assets, and it also received cash held by urban residents and credit held by state-owned enterprises. Settlements between state-owned departments were also conducted through the People's Bank of China."[11] Despite some changes and adjustments afterwards, this practice's core content remained throughout the entire planned economy period.

As for the relationship between bank credit plans and fiscal budgets, as well as credit plans and cash plans, the People's Bank of China specifically discussed this issue at the National Planning Conference held in 1954. The comprehensive credit plan of banks was incorporated into the national economic plan, serving as the fundamental means for the state to allocate credit funds, reflecting and guiding the redistribution of short-term credit funds in the national economy. In this way, the credit function of the People's Bank of China cooperated with fiscal actions, providing impetus for economic development. Subsequently, the People's Bank of China made several revisions to address issues during the implementation of credit management plans, enabling it to control the quantity and scale of money issuance

---

[10] The People's Bank of China. *Sixty Years of the People's Bank of China (1948–2008)*. China Finance Press, 2008: 53.

[11] Li Zhihui. *The Development and Change of China's Banking Industry*. Gezhi Press, Shanghai People's Publishing House, 2008: 15.

through credit plans, reflecting the guiding role of credit policies in the national economy.

4.2.2 Bank Credit Replacing Commercial Credit

During the period of national economic recovery, commercial credit was already abolished between the military, government agencies, state-owned enterprises, organizations, and cooperatives. Funds between units were settled through allocation and liquidation. However, due to the diverse social-economic components at that time, commercial credit could not be completely eliminated.

With the launch of large-scale planned economic construction activities in 1953, commercial credit dissociated from the planned economic management system, disrupting centralized and unified management and distribution of funds. The People's Bank of China was unable to exercise necessary supervision over enterprise funds. Against this backdrop, the People's Bank of China adopted policies of utilization and restriction towards non-state-owned economic commercial credit. For state-owned commerce, the People's Bank of China, in collaboration with the Ministry of Commerce, issued specific regulations on the "Interim Measures for the People's Bank of China to Handle Short-term Loans for State-owned Commerce", whereby, except for certain special circumstances, the settlement of funds within state-owned commercial units as well as between enterprises was handled by the People's Bank of China.

Subsequently, with the smooth progress of the socialist transformation of private industry and commerce, the People's Bank of China and the Ministry of Finance jointly passed the "Report on Abolishing Commercial Credit between State-owned Industries and between State-owned Industries and Other State-owned Enterprises and Replacing it with Bank Settlement". The report stated that "all transaction payments between state-owned industries, as well as between other state-owned enterprises and their internal hierarchies, should be settled through banks, and advance payments, prepayments, deferred payments, and arrears of payments should be abolished. State-owned commercial departments should promptly settle the sales of state-owned industrial products within the plan, and for those outside the plan, the plan should be revised in a timely manner while resolving their funding sources to achieve timely liquidation. Prepayments made by state-owned industries for import payments, prepayments made by private capitalist enterprises for processing orders, and prepayments made by entrusted supply and marketing cooperatives to purchase agricultural products or industrial raw materials from farmers are not included in the scope of abolishing commercial credit due to their broader involvement".[12] The State Council quickly approved this report, abolishing commercial credit that was detrimental to the implementation of planned economic management. The People's Bank of China subsequently abolished commercial credit and mandated that all

[12] Yao Sui, *The Financial History of China*, Higher Education Press, 2007: 453–454.

enterprises settle transactions through the People's Bank of China. In terms of settlement methods, China gradually adopted eight settlement methods used by the Soviet Union, including collection and payment, telecommunication settlement, letters of credit, special accounts, checks, guaranteed payment settlements, collection without payment, and planned settlements. As a result, by the later stages of the First Five-Year Plan, China had basically achieved the substitution of bank credit for commercial credit, with all credit concentrated in the People's Bank of China. The People's Bank of China also achieved a high degree of centralized and unified management of national funds, successfully transitioning into the role of "capital management" for the national economy.

Although the form of the People's Bank of China's "capital management" has undergone changes in the subsequent social, political, and economic environment, its core function of cash management, settlement, and cash management has been maintained until after the reform and opening-up.

4.2.3 The Establishment of the Cash Management System for Monetary Withdrawal and Return

Constrained by factors such as market size and regional dispersion, the People's Bank of China established a cash management system to ensure the smooth operation of the highly centralized planned economic system. Under this system, monetary circulation is strictly divided into two parts: transfers and cash. The production, distribution, exchange, and consumption of means of production strictly follow the directive plan and are settled through transfers. Funds transfer between enterprises is conducted through bank transfers. Cash is primarily concentrated in consumer goods transactions, and cash payments are only required for salary payments, purchase of agricultural and sideline products, personal withdrawals, and miscellaneous expenses in daily economic activities. It is evident that the People's Bank of China aims to control the issuance of cash by maintaining the circulation of cash in line with the demand for and circulation of consumer goods, thus successfully achieving the objectives of monetary and credit policies.

In order to implement the cash income and expenditure plan, the People's Bank of China formulated the "Draft Measures for Cash Teller Planning" in October 1952 to promote planned injection and withdrawal of money. The Financial and Economic Committee issued the "Instructions on Strengthening the Work of Cash Teller Planning" in September 1953, requiring unified management of cash teller planning nationwide. Based on this instruction, the People's Bank of China began to formulate cash teller plans and implemented them uniformly nationwide. In July 1954, with the assistance and advice of Soviet experts, the People's Bank of China formulated and implemented the "Interim Measures for Bank Cash Allocation" to further strengthen the centralized management of currency issuance. In January 1960, "China decided to implement supervision over the wage fund, with banks cooperating with relevant departments to supervise the overall wage expenditures of government agencies, organizations, and state-owned enterprises, in order to control the increase in employment and the excessive growth of wage expenditures".[13] After that, the People's Bank of China implemented the cash income and expenditure plan through various means to ensure currency stability. However, after the Great Leap Forward, the function of fund management was severely distorted due to various political and economic events. As for the relationship between bank credit plans and cash plans, the People's Bank of China explicitly stated that "both plans are arranged based on production plans, commodity circulation plans, and financial plans. Credit plans directly affect commodity production and circulation, as well as directly influence the amount of currency in circulation; cash plans serve as a tool to regulate currency circulation, directly impacting prices and also to some extent affecting credit plans".[14] The People's Bank of China has maintained this relationship with credit plans throughout the implementation of the cash teller plan, until the reform of the planned economic management system.

4.2.4 The Establishment of a Highly Centralized Interest Rate and Exchange Rate Management System

In order to complement the implementation of highly centralized financial management functions, the People's Bank of China also formulated a highly centralized management mechanism in the field of interest rates and exchange rates.

In the field of interest rates, a gradually established highly centralized interest rate management system was implemented. As mentioned earlier, during the period of national economic recovery, the People's Bank of China adopted a tiered management system for interest rates. The specific approach was that the Head Office of the People's Bank of China periodically announced a range of interest rates, while regional branches and local branches in various provinces and cities determined the specific interest rate levels based on local conditions. To avoid significant fluctuations in interest rates, the People's Bank of China conducted seven major adjustments to interest rates between 1950 and 1952. In 1953, with the implementation of the planned economic management system, the People's Bank of China centralized the authority for setting interest rates to the Head Office, which unified the national interest rates to be uniformly implemented across regions. By September 1956, the People's Bank of China had unified the deposit and loan interest rates and obtained approval from the State Council for nationwide implementation. During the "First Five-Year Plan" period, interest rates underwent four major adjustments, with the types and levels of interest rates gradually unified and simplified, as shown in Table 4.2.

[13] The People's Bank of China. *Sixty Years of the People's Bank of China (1948–2008)*, China Finance Press, 2008: 54.

[14] Yang Xitian et al., *General History of The Finance of China (Vol. 6): Period of the People's Republic of China*, China Financial Press, 2002: 87.

Table 4.2 The four adjustments of the rates in 1953–1957

Time	Extent
October, 1953	The monthly interest rate for state-owned commercial loans was adjusted from 10–12 to 6.9‰. The monthly interest rate for state-owned industrial loans was adjusted from 6–6.9 to 6.3‰ of the quota, the one of exceeding the quota is 4.8‰, and the rate regardless of quota and excess quota was 4.65‰ The monthly interest rate of loans to supply and marketing cooperatives was transferred from 9–10.8 to 6.3‰ The monthly interest rate for industrial production cooperatives was adjusted to 4.2‰ from 5.4 to 10.5‰
October, 1955	Deposit rate: The annual interest rate of one-year savings deposit was reduced from 14.4% to 7.92%, and the three-year term savings interest rate was 8. 5% and the five-year annual interest rate was 9% Lending Rate: State-owned industry was no longer divided into quotas and excess quotas, with a monthly interest rate of 4.8‰. The monthly interest rate for state-run commercial loans was decreased from 6. 9‰ to 6‰. The monthly interest rate of supply and marketing cooperatives was 6‰. The monthly interest rate of agricultural production cooperatives was reduced from 7.5‰ to 6‰
February, 1956	The interest rates on loans to agricultural cooperatives, farmers and handicrafts were transferred to 7. 2‰ per month
November, 1957	Deposit rate: The monthly interest rates of savings deposits for urban and rural residents were 6.6‰ Lending rate: The interest rates for state-own industrial and commercial loans were 6‰ per month. The monthly interest rate of rural credit cooperatives was 5.1‰

However, the interest rates of rural credit cooperatives were not included in this adjustment range, as their rates were determined independently by the cooperatives based on market fluctuations. In the specific implementation process, the interest rates of rural credit cooperatives were generally slightly lower than market interest rates but slightly higher than bank interest rates. Subsequently, the People's Bank of China gradually narrowed the range within which rural credit cooperatives could set their own interest rates. By 1959, it was stipulated that the interest rates of rural credit cooperatives should be aligned with bank interest rates, and they were no longer allowed to set their own deposit interest rates. By 1965, the interest rates of rural credit cooperatives were fully aligned with bank interest rates, both of which were uniformly determined by the People's Bank of China and implemented nationwide upon approval from the State Council. The establishment and uniformity of the interest rate management system clearly deviated from the function of interest rates as a monetary policy intermediary. They were not primarily used to regulate the money supply or measure the price of funds supply and demand. Instead, they were used to monitor the extent of price increases to stabilize deposits and restrict enterprises' demand for funds, aiming to control inflation.

In the field of exchange rates, a highly centralized and unified foreign exchange management system gradually took shape. With the nationalization of private financial institutions and the socialist transformation of private import–export businesses, the previously implemented foreign exchange management system, which focused on private financial institutions and private import–export businesses, could no longer meet the needs of the new situation. In order to adapt to the planned economic management system, it was necessary to establish a highly centralized foreign exchange management system.

In June 1953, the People's Bank of China submitted a special report on foreign exchange management and a draft of the Interim Measures for the People's Republic of China on Foreign Exchange Management to the Party Central Committee, clarifying that both foreign exchange management and foreign exchange business operations should be unified and conducted by the People's Bank of China. The report was approved by the Party Central Committee, marking the beginning of constructing a highly centralized foreign exchange management system based on administrative measures. After the work during the "First Five-Year Plan" period, China had established a unified foreign exchange management system. The foreign exchange management system primarily included the following issues. Foreign exchange revenues and expenditures are subject to comprehensive mandatory planning and management. All foreign exchange income must be sold to the Bank of China, with unified collection and disbursement. The allocation of foreign exchange is determined by the state according to the plan, and it is not allowed to buy, sell, or transfer foreign exchange among individuals. The National Development and Reform Commission is responsible for the overall planning and comprehensive balance of the national foreign exchange revenues and expenditures, and vertical distribution is carried out with the approval of the State Council. The Ministry of Foreign Trade and Economic Cooperation, the Ministry of Finance, and the People's Bank of China jointly assume the responsibility for foreign exchange management within the authorized scope of the State Council. The RMB funds required for foreign exchange revenues and expenditures are managed separately, with the People's Bank of China managing the RMB funds and the Bank of China managing the foreign exchange funds. Strict management and control measures are implemented for foreign exchange rates, using administrative means to balance foreign exchange revenues and expenditures.[15]

Under a highly centralized and unified foreign exchange management system, China has made two adjustments to the Renminbi (RMB) exchange rate during the planned economy era. The first adjustment took place in 1953, where, apart from certain capitalist countries' currencies, the fixed exchange rate system was largely maintained. The second adjustment occurred in 1973 when capitalist countries, led by the United States, abandoned the fixed exchange rate system and adopted a floating exchange rate system. China then changed the principle of determining the RMB exchange rate from the "comparison of prices" to a calculation based on the changes in the international currency market rates using a "basket of currencies" approach for real-time adjustments. From then until 1984, China carried out seven adjustments to

[15] Li Yang et al., *60 Years of Finance in China*, China Finance and Economic Press, 2009, p. 44.

Table 4.3 One US dollar for CNY from 1973 to 1984

Year	One US dollar for CNY/yuan
1973	2.0202
1974	1.8397
1975	1.9663
1976	1.8803
1977	1.7300
1978	1.5771
1979	1.4962
1980	1.5303
1981	1.7051
1982	1.8926
1983	1.9757
1984	2.3270

the RMB exchange rate. However, the fluctuation range between the RMB and the US dollar was relatively small, as shown in Table 4.3.

As demonstrated in the table, the fluctuation range of 1 US dollar to RMB does not reflect the degree of societal demand for foreign exchange but rather exhibits the closed nature of foreign exchange control.

Chapter 5
The Tortuous Development of the Financial Industry During the Planned Economy Period

With the formation of China's highly centralized and unified financial management system, the functions of finance gradually shrank to the scope of "managing funds". However, it played a significant role in the early completion of the three major socialist transformations in China and the smooth implementation of "the First Five-Year Plan". Subsequently, influenced by changes in social, political, and economic environments, China's financial industry experienced a series of twists and turns, frequent adjustments, but overall presented a declining trend in financial functions and business.

5.1 The Financial Industry During "The First Five-Year Plan Period

During "the First Five-Year Plan" period, China gradually established a highly centralized financial management system that was compatible with the planned economic management system. This system played a positive role in the early completion of the three major socialist transformations and the smooth implementation and completion of the First Five-Year Plan. It basically met the conditions proposed by Alexander Gerschenkron for backward countries to achieve industrialization through advantage substitution for disadvantage. However, during the process of plan implementation, the disadvantages of excessive management and strict control became increasingly prominent, which drew high attention from the central government and prompted some targeted adjustments to streamline the relationship between various links and subjects in the function of "managing funds". At the same time, the financial industry achieved significant development in the areas of "unified storage" and "unified lending" around the single function of "fund management".

R. Lan, *The Financial Development of China*, Understanding China,
https://doi.org/10.1007/978-981-97-8273-4_5

5.1.1 Adjustment of Financial Management System

The highly centralized and unified planned economic management system established following the Soviet model, while playing a positive role in large-scale economic construction, also exposed many shortcomings in practice. In the financial field alone, the highly centralized credit funds were "unified storage and lending", with high authority, some plans detached from local realities, making execution difficult. Deposits were handed over, and branches of the People's Bank of China scattered across the country had no authority to control them. Credit quotas could only be applied for from the head office, leading to a disconnect between credit plans and local production and circulation plans. There was excessive control over cash plans, resulting in mechanical restrictions such as "in the bank remittance method, money for buying vinegar cannot be used to buy soy sauce, and funds remitted to one place cannot be used in another place",[1] which seriously affected the enthusiasm of localities and the people. In response to this, while the Central Committee of CPC endeavored to adjust the shortcomings of the planned economic management system, the PBOC also made some adjustments to the deficiencies in the financial system.

In terms of settlement and cash management methods, the entire society's fund circulation is concentrated on two methods: cash and transfers, with cash accounting for only about 5% of the total.[2] Adjustments have been made to the scope of cash management in settlement methods to adapt to the limited scope of cash usage. In terms of credit fund management, the PBOC has made significant adjustments: "First, agricultural loans are allocated by the head office with two indicators of the highest balance and year-end balance. Within these two indicators, localities can arrange quarterly plans on their own to adapt to the seasonal needs of agricultural loans. Second, for the four types of loans for local state-owned industries, joint ventures, joint businesses, and handicraft industries, under the annual plan indicators allocated by the head office, localities can arrange quarterly plans on their own and can be mutually adjusted and used. Third, sufficient funds are provided for the purchase of important agricultural and sideline products, without being restricted by planned indicators. Fourth, the head office of the PBOC allocates a portion of reserve indicators to branches in various places, mainly used to solve the shortage of annual intermediate loan indicators for state-owned industrial and commercial enterprises. Excess portions of urban savings deposits over the planned completion can be used to increase the indicators for local state-owned industries and the four types of loans or increase reserve loan indicators."[3]

[1] Zhang Bangju. "A Study on Bank Transfer Settlement in China (Part II)". Journal of Shaanxi Institute of Finance and Economics.1982. Issue 1, p. 84–97.

[2] Zhang Bangju. "A Study on Bank Transfer Settlement in China". Contemporary Social and Economic Science.1982. Issue 4, p. 72–79.

[3] Yang Xitian et al. *A General History of Chinese Finance (Volume Six: The Period of the People's Republic of China).* China Financial Publishing House. 2002.

Through the above adjustments, the highly centralized financial management system is more in line with the goals of planned economic management, promoting the rapid development of the national economy.

5.1.2 Improvement and Adjustment of the RMB System

During the period of recovery of the national economy, our country's chaotic monetary system was unified in a short period of time, laying a solid foundation for monetary stability in supporting state-owned businesses to replenish commodity inventories and supporting the "centralized purchasing and sales" of grain, oil, and cotton. However, the first set of RMB issued in December 1948 encountered many problems in actual operation: First, there were 12 denominations of RMB, with the largest denomination being 50,000 yuan and the smallest being 1 yuan. Although the denominations seemed large, the unit value was actually very low, leaving traces of severe inflation from the past. Although the RMB is nominally in "yuan" units in the market, there are no goods priced at 1 yuan in daily transactions. The circulation of goods by enterprises and the daily consumption of the people are often valued and calculated in billions, tens of billions, or even hundreds of billions of yuan, indicating that high-denomination currencies have difficulty meeting the economic needs of the general public. Second, there are 62 versions of RMB, making it difficult for the masses to identify, and the paper quality is poor, prone to damage, and easily exploited by counterfeiters and those who seek to undermine the RMB system, greatly affecting the stability of the RMB. Third, except for a few printed in Mongolian and Uighur, most RMB only have Chinese characters, making circulation extremely inconvenient in many ethnic minority areas. The improvement of the national economy and the balance of fiscal revenue and expenditure have laid a good foundation for the improvement of the RMB. Therefore, the replacement of the old RMB with the new RMB and the improvement of the RMB system have become urgent issues for the Central Committee of the Communist Party of China and the State Council to address.

In fact, shortly after the first set of RMB was introduced, China began preparations to issue new currency. In early 1950, the PBOC proposed a plan to print new currency, but due to the prevailing conditions at the time, it was not implemented. Subsequently, after preparation, the Central Financial Committee formally submitted a proposal report to the Central Committee of the Communist Party of China in August 1953, recommending the reform of the Renminbi system. In November, they submitted a "Request Report on the Issuance of New Currency", pointing out that "due to the result of past inflation, the existing currency denominations are very large, while the unit value is very low. The value of every 100 yuan is less than four cents before the Anti-Japanese War. Although it is nominally in yuan, the value of one yuan has completely lost its function in calculations. ... It is necessary to issue a new currency with a higher unit value to withdraw the existing Renminbi, to organize chips, reduce denominations, and it is imperative."[4] After more than a year of thorough preparation, the State Council issued the "Order on the Issuance of New RMB and the Withdrawal of Existing RMB" in February 1955, ordering the PBOC to issue new Renminbi (new currency, the second set of Renminbi) from March 1, 1955, to withdraw the existing Renminbi (old currency, the first set of Renminbi). The new currency denominations include main denominations of 1 yuan, 2 yuan, 3 yuan, 5 yuan, and 10 yuan, and subsidiary denominations of 1 Fen, 2 Fen, 5 Fen, 1 Jiao, 2 Jiao, and 5 Jiao. Each denomination is printed with four languages: Chinese, Tibetan, Mongolian, and Uighur. The exchange ratio between the new and old currencies is set as 1 yuan of the new currency equals 10,000 yuan of the old currency. From the date of the issuance of the new currency, all transactions, pricing, contracts, agreements, documents, vouchers, bookkeeping, and international settlements of government agencies, organizations, enterprises, and individuals are conducted in the new currency as the unit of account. All debts and obligations before the issuance of the new currency, including national bonds, are also converted and settled in the new currency according to the statutory ratio from the same date. Due to sufficient preparation and extensive publicity, after the issuance of the second set of Renminbi, the PBOC established currency exchange points and mobile exchange teams nationwide, and entrusted state-owned enterprises, supply and marketing cooperatives, and credit cooperatives to exchange old currency. As a result, the task of exchanging old currency was completed in less than 100 days, achieving 98.06% of the exchange task, realizing the transition between old and new currency, completely eliminating the remnants of inflation, and ensuring the smooth issuance of the second set of RMB.

In the process of promoting the second set of RMB, China implemented policies such as equivalent exchange and non-discriminatory exchange between old and new currencies, gaining the support of the vast majority of the people, which created a stable pattern for China's monetary system and provided favorable conditions for the rapid development of the national economy, socialist transformation, and the early completion of the First Five-Year Plan. However, there was one drawback with the second set of Renminbi, namely, that the 3 yuan, 5 yuan, and 10 yuan notes were printed by the Soviet Union. In the mid-1950s, as Sino-Soviet relations deteriorated, the Soviet Union often used these three denominations to disrupt and sabotage China's economic development, causing inconvenience to the daily lives of the general public. Therefore, the People's Bank of China issued the "Notice on the Deadline for the Withdrawal of Three Types of RMB Notes" on April 14, 1964, requiring the withdrawal of the above-mentioned three types of notes within 30 days, thereby safeguarding the independent and autonomous status of the Renminbi system.

Of course, shortly after the issuance of the second set of Renminbi, influenced by the anti-rightist conservative ideology, there emerged a trend of "one large and two excessive" in economic work, characterized by a rash and impetuous approach. "One large" refers to the excessively large scale of infrastructure construction, which

[4] Chen Yun. *Four Essays on Finance and Economy (March or April 1944)—July 1956*, Party Literature, Issue 3, 2005.

increased by 62% in 1956 compared to the previous year, leading to a fiscal deficit of about 1.8 billion yuan. "Two excessive" refers to excessive increases in the number of workers, with 1.46 million more workers added throughout the year than planned; excessive issuance of agricultural loans and loans to handicraft industries, with agricultural loans alone increasing by 80% compared to 1955. Excessive lending beyond the plan led to the loss of control over the three channels of cash injection into infrastructure, wage payments, and agricultural loans, resulting in a 42% increase in cash circulation in the market compared to the end of 1955. "Currency is the chip of commodities, and the issuance of currency must be backed by equivalent commodities. In terms of the quantity of commodities, there was an increase in 1956 compared to 1955, but a phenomenon of supply shortage occurred, because the fiscal and credit sectors overspent nearly 3 billion yuan."[5] This situation drew high attention from the Central Committee of the Communist Party of China and the State Council. At the Eighth Plenary Session of the 2th Central Committee of the Communist Party of China held in November 1956, Zhou Enlai pointed out the need to appropriately scale down infrastructure construction and adjust the proportionate relationship between various economic sectors to adapt to the country's financial and material resources. In January 1957, Chen Yun explicitly stated that measures should be taken to resolve the problem of "rashness" in economic and financial work in 1957. Specifically, this involved launching campaigns to increase production and save resources through the channels of cash injection, appropriately reducing the scale of infrastructure investment, and planning to control the growth rate of social purchasing power. Based on this, Chen Yun summarized the comprehensive balance relationship between finance, credit, and goods: "Fiscal revenue and expenditure and bank credit must be balanced, and there should be a slight surplus. As long as fiscal revenue and expenditure and credit are balanced, the balance between social purchasing power and commodity supply will also be balanced overall."[6] Subsequently, the PBOC convened a national conference of branch directors to summarize the problems encountered in financial work in 1956. "Some people at the meeting doubted whether there were too many market tickets. It should be affirmed that there were indeed too many. The main sign of excessive tickets is the shortage of commodity supply, poor purchase of agricultural products, and some farmers have both stored goods and money."[7] It was determined that in 1957, there must be contractionary arrangements for bank credit and currency issuance.

Through targeted measures such as these, investment scale, fiscal expenditure, currency issuance, and other areas were effectively controlled, and the relationship between market currency circulation and production and commodity circulation was roughly aligned.

---

[5] Central Compilation and Translation Bureau of the CPC Central Committee: *Collected Works of Chen Yun (Volume Three)*. Central Compilation and Translation Press. 2005:50.

[6] Central Compilation and Translation Bureau of the CPC Central Committee: *Collected Works of Chen Yun (Volume Three)*. Central Compilation and Translation Press. 2005:52–53.

[7] Financial Research Institute of the People's Bank of China: *Collected Works of Cao Jurong*. China Financial Publishing House. 1983:144.

5.1.3 Development and Regulation of Financial Business

Alongside the formation of a highly centralized and unified financial management system, the development of financial business gradually shifted its focus to the field of "managing funds" such as credit and cash management. During the First Five-Year Plan period, financial institutions, after undergoing the aforementioned processes of nationalization and simplification, had become highly centralized under the control of the People's Bank of China, as well as rural credit cooperatives managed by it. Although the China Construction Bank was under the leadership of the Ministry of Finance, it had a short existence, and its main business was to allocate funds for infrastructure projects and supervise management, without involvement in the field of credit fund raising and cash management.

From the perspective of "unified storage", the main sources of funds were concentrated in various types of deposits and credit funds allocated by government departments. Regarding credit funds, the Ministry of Finance allocated funds to the People's Bank of China annually as credit funds, which were included in the bank's sources of funds to balance credit inflows and outflows. Provinces, autonomous regions, and municipalities also allocated a certain amount of credit funds to local banks each year. During the First Five-Year Plan period, the credit funds were relatively stable, but the overall trend of credit funds showed an upward trajectory. The changes in bank credit funds from 1953 to 1978 are shown in Table 5.1."[8]

The credit funds allocated by various levels of government to banks effectively act as the banks' capital, playing a role in balancing income and expenditure and coordinating the relationship between fiscal appropriations and bank credit.

As for deposits, it is a central task of the PBOC and the rural credit cooperatives it manages. In order to strengthen the sources of deposits and fund management, the People's Bank of China, following the principle of "unified storage", requires government agencies, organizations, enterprises, and institutions to deposit surplus cash above a certain limit into banks. By using bank credit instead of commercial credit, it actively promotes urban and rural savings, and concentrates the deposits absorbed by various levels of institutions to the central bank for unified allocation. During the "First Five-Year Plan" period, the amount of deposits showed a significant increase, as shown in Table 5.2.

During the "First Five-Year Plan" period, bank deposits increased significantly. Looking at the composition of deposits during this time, influenced by the highly centralized and unified financial management system, fiscal deposits and enterprise deposits accounted for the vast majority, while urban and rural deposits accounted for a relatively small proportion. However, the proportion of the latter showed an upward trend later on. During this period, Chinese banks also raised foreign exchange funds from various channels to expand their sources of funds. Measures were taken

---

[8] To comprehensively reflect the changes during this period and to avoid re-listing corresponding tables in the following text, some tables in the entire book cover a slightly longer time span. The situation of multiple tables later in the book is similar and will not be noted again.

Table 5.1 Changes in bank credit funds from 1953 to 1978

Year	Credit funds (in 100 million yuan)	Percentage of total deposits (%)
1953	15.9	14.8
1954	21.0	13.8
1955	25.9	18.3
1956	38.1	28.4
1957	54.3	32.8
1958	96.9	32.8
1959	293.8	73.7
1960	369.9	80.4
1961	183.3	37.5
1962	201.3	49.1
1963	229.7	55.5
1964	102.7	23.4
1965	106.5	22.1
1966	124.3	22.5
1967	145.4	25.3
1968	166.6	26.7
1969	193.1	30.1
1970	220.3	31.3
1971	152.3	19.8
1972	138.9	17.9
1973	183.1	21.2
1974	222.6	24.8
1975	258.1	26.5
1976	303.0	31.0
1977	359.9	33.8
1978	421.9	37.2

Information Source "Forty years of endeavor (1949–1989)" by the national bureau of statistics, China Statistics Press, 1989 edition

to protect the interests of overseas Chinese and their dependents, promoting the development of remittances from overseas Chinese.

From the perspective of "unified storage," banks utilized their "managing funds" function to formulate differentiated credit policies, focusing on supporting the development of state-owned economy and promoting the socialist transformation of capitalist industry, agriculture, and handicraft industry. In terms of the state-owned economy, the PBOC prioritized support for state-owned commerce and supply and marketing cooperatives, with bank loans to them increasing from 9.38 billion yuan in 1952 to 21.64 billion yuan in 1957 during the "First Five-Year Plan" period, nearly

Table 5.2 Changes in the growth rate and structure of bank deposits nationwide from 1952 to 1978

Year	Total deposits at year end	Fiscal deposits		Enterprise deposits		Urban savings deposits		Rural deposits	
		Amount (100 million yuan)	Percentage of total (%)	Amount (100 million yuan)	Percentage of total (%)	Amount (100 million yuan)	Percentage of total (%)	Amount (100 million yuan)	Percentage of total (%)
1952	93.3	47.6	51.0	33.0	35.4	8.6	9.2	–	–
1957	165.5	80.0	48.3	39.7	24.0	27.9	16.9	17.9	10.8
1962	409.6	194.3	47.4	152.3	37.2	31.4	7.7	31.6	7.7
1965	481.0	196.7	40.9	181.9	37.8	52.3	10.9	50.1	10.4
1970	704.3	330.4	46.9	226.1	32.1	64.5	9.2	83.3	11.8
1975	975.1	360.9	37.0	362.7	37.2	114.6	11.8	136.9	14.0
1978	1134.5	456.8	40.2	368.4	32.5	154.9	13.7	154.4	13.6

Information Source "Forty Years of Endeavor (1949–1989)" by the National Bureau of Statistics, China Statistics Press, 1989 edition

doubling.[9] State-owned industry was ranked second in terms of bank lending, with funds allocated in accordance with the actual needs of production, supply, sales, and financial revenues and expenditures approved by the state. Following the policy of prioritizing the development of heavy industry, banks particularly emphasized loans to heavy industry, which accounted for 44–60% of the bank's industrial credit, effectively promoting the construction of heavy industry.

In promoting the socialist transformation of capitalist industry, the People's Bank of China formulated specific credit support measures. Firstly, it implemented the principle of "setting credit based on deposits" to strengthen the organization and supervision of funds from public to private. Secondly, it adopted differentiated credit policies. In terms of credit recipients, private industry was favored over private commerce. However, strict control was imposed on loans to large-scale private wholesalers from the second half of 1953 onwards, ceasing loans to wholesalers identified by the state for nationalization. Thirdly, it strengthened credit management for private industry and commerce. In the financial market, restrictions were imposed on the establishment of accounts and check activities for private industry and commerce from 1954 onwards. Their idle funds were strictly regulated, and commercial entrusted payment and collection transactions were stopped. Fourthly, full support was provided for the public–private joint ventures, clarifying their demonstrative effect. Under the differentiated credit principles of the PBOC, the process of socialist transformation of capitalist industry and commerce was accelerated.

In terms of the socialist transformation of agriculture, the PBOC actively supported rural cooperative construction, disbursed various types of agricultural loans, and vigorously promoted the development of rural credit cooperatives. This assistance aimed to help impoverished farmers overcome production and living difficulties, combat usurious activities in rural areas, and advance the process of agricultural cooperation. Additionally, the PBOC provided the necessary funds for the cooperative process of handicraft industries, addressing their capital needs for expanded production post-transformation. In 1956 alone, the PBOC increased funding threefold compared to the previous year to support the transformation and expansion of production in the handicraft industry.

5.2 Financial Industry During the "Great Leap Forward" Period

During the "Great Leap Forward" period, influenced by many mistakes in the exploration of the planned economic management system, problems such as excessive delegation of management authority and serious disruption of financial regulations and systems emerged in the financial field, leading to excessive credit expansion and chaos in lending within the banking system in the national economy. In response, the

[9] Hong Jiaguan. *History of Chinese Finance*. Southwest University of Finance and Economics Press.2001:474.

Central Committee of the Communist Party of China made appropriate adjustments and formulated effective measures such as the "Six Principles of Bank Work" and the "Six Principles of Fiscal Work," allowing the almost out-of-control financial order to be restored and the financial management system to return to the track of centralized and unified management. In aspects such as "unified storage" and "unified lending," the financial industry encountered serious setbacks.

5.2.1 Errors and Corrections in the Financial Management System

With the completion of socialist transformation and the early realization of the "First Five-Year Plan," some contradictions in the highly centralized and unified planned economic management system began to surface, especially in the economic management authority between the central and local levels, and the contradiction between accumulation and consumption. In response, the Central Committee of the Communist Party of China and the State Council began to improve the economic management system in 1954, proposing to gradually delegate management authority, adjust the relationship between the central and local governments, and between the state and enterprises, to resolve contradictions in the national economic development and streamline the relationships between various economic entities. Against this backdrop, corresponding adjustments were made to China's highly centralized and unified financial management system. This adjustment mainly manifested in the following three aspects.

First, the delegation of financial management authority. In November 1958, at the National Bank Branch Managers Conference convened by the People's Bank of China in Wuhan, the issue of delegating banking credit management authority was extensively discussed. In 1959, the People's Bank of China redefined the central and local credit management authority in accordance with the spirit of the conference, and established the management principle of "delegated deposits and loans, planned package responsibility, differential management, unified scheduling." Specifically, agricultural loan management authority was delegated, with loan quotas arranged by local authorities and used under collective responsibility; industrial loan authority was delegated, with management authority devolved by the PBOC headquarters based on methods such as "delegating institutions, delegating personnel," "unified policies, unified plans, unified management of circulating funds," and "inclusive of fiscal tasks"; apart from deposits managed by the central finance, the military, central enterprises, and government agencies, all other bank deposits were allocated to local governments as their credit income; except for loans required by centrally managed enterprises, all other bank loans were allocated to local governments for management, and the deposit-loan gap was used collectively by local authorities; the PBOC fully supplied funds needed by enterprises to expand production and circulation to adapt to the situation of the "Great Leap Forward." However, the excessive delegation of financial management authority led to uncontrolled credit, resulting in a rapid upward trend in prices.

Second, Severe Weakening of Financial Functions. During the "Great Leap Forward" period, the prevalence of the "communist atmosphere, exaggerated atmosphere, command atmosphere, special cadres atmosphere, blind command atmosphere" led to a severe weakening of the functions of the People's Bank of China (PBOC), with key banking personnel being massively transferred out. The staff of the PBOC headquarters decreased sharply from 2088 at the end of 1956 to 820 at the end of 1959, with only 9 internal institutions retained.[10] Nationwide, nearly 100,000 bank employees were reduced, and grassroots business backbone personnel were basically transferred out. The delegation of rural credit authority led to the establishment of credit departments in people's communes managed by them. Consequently, the basic business system and fund management system of the PBOC suffered severe blows, weakening its macro-management and regulation of credit and currency circulation. Credit, in particular, was almost entirely out of control, resulting in staggering losses and waste, exacerbating the difficulty of the socio-economic situation.

Third, Serious Damage to Financial Regulations and Systems. Since the establishment of the People's Republic of China, an effective set of financial regulations and systems has been established. However, during the "Great Leap Forward" process, behaviors such as "great destruction and great establishment," and "destruction before establishment" caused these standardized systems to be abolished as something that hindered the economic construction of the broad masses. Consequently, China's financial sector lacked necessary institutional constraints, leading to a chaotic state of affairs where there were no rules to follow. Practices like "off-book accounting," "physical deposits," and "substituting vouchers for accounts" became rampant, resulting in the nationwide loss of control over credit funds and currency issuance, and an increasing number of errors in bank accounts and funds.

The financial adjustments during this period, along with the disorder in the function of "managing funds" and the transfer of staff, led to financial work errors, causing the country's monetary and credit system to spiral out of control, with all types of loans experiencing significant increases. In 1960, bank credit funds amounted to as much as 95.44 billion yuan, an increase of 2.35 times compared to 1957. Industrial loans increased by 10.9 times, commercial loans by 1.3 times, state agricultural loans by 2.1 times, and rural cooperative loans by 0.8 times.[11] Blind lending without necessary personnel guidance and institutional constraints not only led to low economic efficiency but also caused serious fiscal deficits, significant increases in retail commodity prices, and the entrenchment of the national economy in difficulties. Faced with this situation, the State Council took a series of measures to restore a highly centralized and unified financial management system to strengthen the function of "managing funds". The various erroneous behaviors caused by the delegation

---

[10] People's Bank of China. *Sixty Years of the People's Bank of China (1948–2008)*. China Financial Publishing House. 2008:51.

[11] Zhou Taihe. *Economic System Reform in Contemporary China*. China Social Sciences Press.1984:76.

of banking management authority prompted the Central Committee and the State Council to clearly recognize the importance of reclaiming delegated management authority. It was stated that "power should not be overly decentralized, and the credit management authority delegated to specialized counties should be quickly recovered. Banks should plan and account, and departments such as planning, statistics, accounting, and cashiering in banks should not be weakened. Reasonable regulations and systems are tools for national economic planning, and the reform of regulations and systems must adopt a pragmatic and cautious approach."[12] In September 1960, the State Council forwarded the PBOC's "Report on Strict Implementation of Cash Management System," emphasizing strict cash management. In April 1961, the PBOC issued the "Notice on Changing the Credit Management System," strengthening quarterly credit plan management. Subsequently, the Central Committee of the Communist Party of China further established the practice of centralized management in the financial sector at the "Seven Thousand People Conference" in January 1962 and the "Xilou Meeting" in February 1962. In March 1962, the "Decision of the Central Committee of the Communist Party of China and the State Council on Strengthening the Centralized and Unified Management of Bank Work and Strictly Controlling Currency Issuance" was issued, known as the "Six Principles of Bank Work."

In the "Six Principles on Banking Work," the central government clearly stated that "decisive measures must be taken to implement the highly centralized and unified management of banking work, truly concentrate the power of currency issuance in the central government, and tightly control the national currency. Moreover, during a certain period, it must be managed more strictly and tightly than during the unified financial management in 1950 in order to be conducive to the adjustment and development of the national economy." Specifically, the following six regulations were stipulated:

(1) Reiteration: All powers delegated in recent years regarding banking work must be withdrawn, and banking operations must be thoroughly and completely vertically led. The various branches of the People's Bank of China are still subject to the leadership of local Party committees and people's committees in party and administrative work. However, in matters related to business planning, systems, and cash management, they must be under the vertical leadership of the People's Bank of China headquarters.

(2) Strict Credit Management, Strengthening the Planning of Credit: Without the approval of the People's Bank of China headquarters, no localities, departments, enterprises, or institutions shall increase loans beyond the planned amount. Party and government organs at all levels shall not compel banks to increase loans. Within the approved plan, all departments and regions must exercise control and responsibility layer by layer, without deviation. The loan quotas for enterprises under various central departments shall be issued by the competent departments and the People's Bank of China headquarters to the banks in the locations of

[12] Shang Ming, Chen Li, Wang Chengming. *Chronicle of Financial Events in the People's Republic of China*. China Financial Publishing House. 1993:183–184.

the enterprises, and the local banks shall examine and verify each loan within the quota, and strictly control them.

(3) Clear Division between Bank Credit Funds and Fiscal Funds, Prohibition of Using Bank Loans for Fiscal Expenditures: Bank credit is different from fiscal revenue and expenditure. Banks must ensure that loans are repayable on time. All non-repayable expenditures must use fiscal budget funds according to fiscal regulations, and must not embezzle or occupy bank loans.
(4) Strengthen Cash Management, Strict Settlement Discipline: All units, groups, enterprises, institutions, schools, and troops must strictly implement the cash management system. Excess cash stocks exceeding the prescribed limit must be deposited in the People's Bank of China at any time. Transactions above a certain amount must be settled through the People's Bank of China's transfer settlement system and must not be paid in cash directly.
(5) All levels of the People's Bank of China must regularly report to local Party committees and people's committees on the situation of currency issuance, withdrawal, and circulation; report on the increase, decrease, and repayment of industrial and commercial loans; report on the payment of wage funds; report on the financial compensation for enterprise losses; report on cases of using bank loans for fiscal expenditures in violation of regulations and other important matters.
(6) While strengthening banking work, fiscal management must also be strictly enforced. Both fiscal and banking operations must follow the plan. Expenditures must be arranged by the responsible parties, and deficiencies must be rectified. Fiscal revenue must be in accordance with policies, and expenditures must follow the budget, with additional appropriations following procedures. Fiscal revenue and expenditures must be implemented to prevent any false phenomena and truly achieve a balance between the budget and credit.[13]

In April 1962, the "Decision of the Central Committee of the Communist Party of China and the State Council on Strict Control of Fiscal Management" was issued, further clarifying the relationship between banking work and fiscal work. "By plugging the loopholes in bank credit and fiscal expenditures, it is conducive to the adjustment of the national economy, the promotion of enterprise restructuring, the reduction of personnel, the exploration of potential, and the improvement of management."[14] Through these measures, the adverse consequences caused by the previous delegation of authority were basically adjusted, and the centralized and unified leadership of banking work was restored, allowing the delegated bank officials to return. The functions and status of the People's Bank of China were further clarified, bad debts were written off, and credit management was strengthened. "The total amount of rural debts exempted by the State Council before 1961 amounted to 9.1 billion yuan, including: 4.5 billion yuan for agricultural loans from banks, 1 billion yuan for

[13] "Decision of the CPC Central Committee and the State Council on Strengthening the Centralized and Unified Banking Work, and Strictly Controlling Currency Issuance," (http://www.china.com.cn/guoqing/2012-09/12/content_26747202.htm).

[14] "Decision of the CPC Central Committee and the State Council on Strictly Controlling Fiscal Management," (http://www.china.com.cn/guoqing/2012-09/12/content_26747195.htm).

credit cooperatives, and 3.6 billion yuan for commercial departments' credit sales, prepayments, and deposits."[15] Through these efforts, the chaotic financial order was restored, and it returned to normal operation.

5.2.2 *Monetary Imbalance and Governance*

The issue of monetary imbalance originated from the "Great Leap Forward" and the movement of people's communes in 1958, which brought serious impacts to the financial work of our country. Starting from March 1958, the PBOC convened several meetings successively, demanding that the financial system closely follow the situation of the "Great Leap Forward" and boldly support and fully supply the flowing funds needed for enterprises to expand production and circulation. This led to prevalent phenomena of blind command and exaggeration in the financial sector, causing the loss of control over credit quotas and currency issuance. At this time, various levels of fiscal departments exhibited the phenomenon of "squeezing banks." "Because the government can say it has no money, but banks cannot; spending government money is distressing, but spending bank money is not. The government can squeeze banks, but banks have nowhere to squeeze and can only expand credit scale and issue more currency, leading to inflation."[16] The fiscal squeezing of bank funds further aggravated the loss of control over currency issuance, resulting in serious problems of nationwide monetary imbalance and loss of control over cash management.

To address the issue of monetary imbalance, the Central Committee of the Communist Party of China and the State Council continuously issued effective measures in response to changes in the socio-economic situation. In the second half of 1960, the Central Committee of the Communist Party of China decided to compress construction projects, strengthen agricultural production, and abolish the practice of maintaining two sets of accounts in the national economic plan to avoid any deficits. When implementing the policy of "adjustment, consolidation, enrichment, and improvement" in the development of the national economy in 1961, there was insufficient understanding of financial difficulties and the execution effect was not ideal. Therefore, in August 1961, Deng Xiaoping further clarified adjustments to the national economic plan, including resolutely reducing investment in infrastructure, streamlining the workforce, and reducing urban population. In order to achieve fiscal and credit balance, the Central Committee of the Communist Party of China and the State Council attached great importance to the role of finance and banking and adopted various effective measures, such as continuing to freeze the deposits of government agencies and organizations in banks, clearing overdue accounts, turning

[15] People's Bank of China. *Sixty Years of the People's Bank of China (1948–2008).* China Financial Publishing House. 2008:51.

[16] Yang Xitian et al. *General History of Chinese Finance (Volume VI: The Period of the People's Republic of China).* China Financial Publishing House. 2002:132.

around loss-making enterprises, saving non-productive expenses, and compressing the purchasing power of social groups. At the same time, the PBOC needed to further strengthen cash management, supervise wage funds, in order to reduce and control currency issuance. In February 1962, in response to significant inflationary pressure, Chen Yun clearly proposed at the "Xilou Meeting" to "strictly manage cash, save cash expenditures; increase production of daily necessities for the people as much as possible; increase the supply of high-priced goods, with fewer varieties, and retrieve more currency; persist in combating speculation and profiteering activities..."[17] In March of the same year, the CPC Central Committee and the State Council issued the "Six Regulations on Banking Work" mentioned above, centralizing the authority of currency issuance to the central government and strictly controlling credit issuance and cash scale. In April, in order to prevent fiscal squeezing behaviors, the "Six Regulations on Fiscal Work" were issued.

In addition to adopting the above-mentioned financial and economic policy measures, the CPC Central Committee and the State Council also implemented special measures such as supplying goods with vouchers and supplying goods at high prices in the practical process, in order to retrieve currency and ensure the production and living needs of the people. For essential daily necessities, voucher supply was adopted, while for non-essential daily necessities, high-price supply was implemented. In terms of voucher-supplied goods, the types of goods showed a trend of continuous increase with changes in the socio-economic situation, but gradually decreased after 1964 following the improvement of the economic situation, in order to ensure the minimum basic living needs of the people, stabilize prices, and alleviate the harm caused by inflation to the people. In terms of high-price supplied goods, the basic approach was similar to that of voucher-supplied goods, with the types of goods first increasing and then gradually withdrawing according to the improvement of the socio-economic situation. "High prices are a temporary measure with side effects...a slightly higher price can facilitate sales...it's better to have goods available than to have money but nothing to buy. From the actual results, it does not harm the fundamental interests of the people, allows those with more money to improve their living conditions somewhat, allows the country to retrieve more currency, and has certain benefits in alleviating inflation."[18]

Through the above-mentioned measures for monetary governance, our country achieved fiscal balance with a slight surplus in 1962, and in 1964, banks also achieved a surplus of credit over expenditure, leading to a slight retrieval of currency. In this way, prices became increasingly stable, and inflation was effectively controlled.

---

[17] Bo Yibo. *Review of Several Major Decisions and Events (Part II)*. CCP Party History Publishing House. P. 1050.

[18] *On Fiscal, Financial, and Trade Issues by Li Xiannian (1950–1991) (Volume II)*. China Finance and Economics Press. P. 11.

5.2.3 *Changes and Adjustments in the Financial Industry*

During the "First Five-Year Plan" period, a highly centralized and unified system for "managing funds", with a single institution and highly concentrated credit, was established. However, the "Great Leap Forward" in 1958 began the decentralization of financial management authority, causing significant adverse impacts on the development of the financial system and industry. It was only after subsequent adjustments that the financial sector gradually returned to a normal development track.

In the area of "unified storage," during the "First Five-Year Plan" period, credit funds allocated by various levels of government were mostly retained and managed separately. However, during the "Great Leap Forward" period, this approach changed, with the management authority for credit funds being decentralized to local governments, leading to the phenomenon of fiscal encroachment on banks and triggering uncontrolled currency issuance. Regarding bank deposits, influenced by trends such as arbitrary command and exaggeration, the deposit business suffered severe setbacks. Firstly, there was a prevalence of practices such as banks in many places dismantling counters and merging institutions, while in some places banks did not keep accounts or manage deposits, leading to unattended savings. Secondly, urban and rural savings work pursued high targets, resulting in the phenomenon of virtual increase in deposits, which in turn led to a significant apparent increase in urban and rural savings in China during this period, as shown in Table 5.3.

During the "Great Leap Forward" period, there was a significant increase in urban and rural savings deposits in China. However, under the "political mobilization," the promotion of savings business led to the prevalence of "communist atmosphere." In some areas, phenomena such as canceling savings interest rates and units not keeping accounts emerged, leading to distortions and rigidities in interest rate policies, which affected the enthusiasm of people to deposit money. Therefore, after the consolidation and adjustment of financial management authority, savings deposits experienced a significant decline.

Table 5.3 National urban and rural savings deposits from 1958 to 1965

Year	Amount (in 100 million yuan)	Growth rate (%)
1958	55.2	56.8
1959	68.3	23.7
1960	66.3	− 2.9
1961	55.4	− 16.4
1962	41.1	− 25.8
1963	45.7	11.2
1964	55.5	21.4
1965	65.2	17.5

Data Source "Forty years of endeavor (1949–1989)" by the national bureau of statistics, published by China Statistics Press in 1989

In the field of "unified lending," in 1958, the PBOC implemented "full-amount credit" management for the working capital of state-owned enterprises, changing the principle of separate supply by finance and banks implemented in state-owned industrial and commercial enterprises' working capital in 1955. Under this principle, finance allocated funds up to a certain quota, while funds exceeding the quota needed to be supported by bank loans. In January 1959, the "full-amount credit" system was implemented nationwide, and the working capital of state-owned enterprises was unified managed by the People's Bank of China until the management authority was withdrawn in 1963. The "full-amount credit" management system was then abolished, and banks continued to retain the credit funds allocated by finance, while the credit funds allocated by state-owned enterprises were redistributed to individual enterprises.

In terms of transfers and cash management, the transfer settlement system was arbitrarily abolished. Practices such as "using checks as cash, exchanging payments for checks at the door, abolishing the endorsement of the payee on checks, not reviewing reasons for dishonored payments, and allowing intercity collections without verification for commodity transactions" were implemented. In terms of interregional settlement methods, there was "unilateral emphasis on service, abandonment of supervision, blind pursuit of targets, and acceleration of fund turnover, resulting in banks advancing large amounts of funds, fostering fraudulent activities, and seriously disrupting the normal order of settlement work."[19] After three years of adjustment, the damaged environment for financial development was restored.

5.3 "The Cultural Revolution" and the Period of Rectification After the Turmoil

Starting in May 1966, the "Cultural Revolution" led to widespread "leftwards" struggles by "revolutionary mass organizations" across the country, severely affecting the social and economic order. Despite the State Council's strict orders to maintain banking order and preserve the integrity of the banking system, financial institutions were downsized, staff were relocated, and various regulations were disrupted under the impact of "revolutionary mass organizations." Financial functions were negated, leading to significant confusion in financial work, business policies, fund management, and organizational structure. During this period, there were two brief opportunities for adjustment after the September 13th Incident, when Premier Zhou Enlai and later Deng Xiaoping, during his tenure leading the Central Committee and the State Council in 1975, attempted brief adjustments. However, the disruptions caused by the "Gang of Four" hindered financial work again. After the fall of the "Gang of Four" in 1976 and before the convening of The Third Plenary Session of the

[19] Yao Sui. *History of Chinese Finance*. Higher Education Press. 2007: 465.

11th Central Committee of the Communist Party of China, the country began rectifying the "leftwards" errors, laying the necessary groundwork for the transformation of financial functions after 1978.

5.3.1 *Impact on Financial Management System*

The "Cultural Revolution" launched in May 1966, under the "Great Criticism" movement, promoted the "upgrading" of ownership and vigorously pursued the "elimination of capitalist remnants." The recently restored financial management system suffered severe setbacks and destruction. The centralized and unified banking work was denounced as "dictatorial," credit principles were criticized as "ignoring people and only focusing on money," and financial rules and regulations were regarded as tools of "control, obstruction, and pressure." Branches of banks at all levels were impacted by "mass movements," financial functions were criticized, and the business command system was severely weakened. In response, the central government sent military representatives to various levels of the PBOC to implement military control and provide comprehensive leadership over banking operations.

As the domestic socio-economic situation deteriorated, in 1969, a major restructuring of the organization of the head office of the People's Bank of China was conducted, with the previous nine bureaus reduced to only two departments: Political Work and Business (see Fig. 5.1). Except for 87 individuals barely responsible for business work, all other personnel were sent to labor at the "May Seventh Cadre School". At various levels of local institutions of the PBOC, under the goal of political establishment, institutions shrank, personnel were relocated, and numerous regulations were abolished. In July of the same year, the head office of the PBOC shared office space with the Ministry of Finance, while branches of the PBOC at various levels were decided upon by provinces, autonomous regions, and municipalities directly under the central government. At the provincial level, some banks merged with the finance department to form financial bureaus, some banks were directly merged into the finance department, retaining only some banking business management functions, while a few maintained relatively independent banking and financial settings. At the regional and county levels, the operational autonomy of branches of the PBOC was largely maintained.

Following the organizational and functional changes, the PBOC basically lost the ability to independently execute financial functions. The previously relatively complete organizational system became fragmented, and the lack of a unified mechanism between upper and lower organizational structures completely eliminated the comprehensive balancing role between finance and the economy. The disorder artificially created in the financial system had a serious impact on the development of the national economy. After the emergence of the above situation, the Central Committee of the Communist Party of China and the State Council carried out two major rectifications and improvements to the problems in the financial management system, marking a significant turning point in the financial management system.

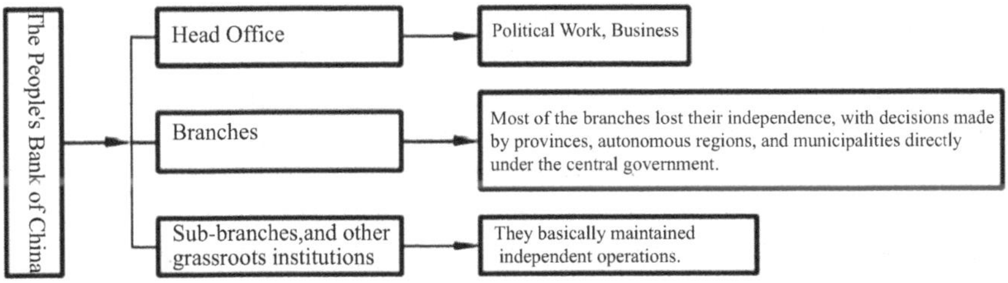

Fig. 5.1 Organizational structure of the people's bank of China in 1969

Firstly, after the September 13th Incident, under the leadership of Premier Zhou Enlai of the State Council, several measures were taken to strengthen bank credit management. In early 1972, the State Council requested the PBOC to strengthen credit management. In September of the same year, the PBOC convened a national banking work conference. At the meeting, Vice Premier Li Xiannian and others emphasized the need for the PBOC to correctly understand the role of banking functions, strengthen the independence of banking work, unify the allocation of national credit funds, unify cash settlement, and unify the management of national foreign exchange and gold and silver, correcting the aforementioned problems in banking management work. Subsequently, the PBOC issued the "Trial Measures for Credit and Cash Planning Management," further clarifying the principles of cash and credit planning management, improving the credit planning management system, and restoring the cash planning system that had been disrupted. Through a series of effective corrective measures by the Central Committee of the Communist Party of China and the State Council, the disrupted financial system and financial management functions gradually recovered, returning to the track of a highly centralized and unified financial management system, and there was a turning point in the socio-economic development. However, subsequent political movements such as the "Criticism of Lin Biao and Confucius" once again disrupted the just-restored financial order, plunging the financial system and financial work into chaos once more.

The second initiative was the financial restructuring during Deng Xiaoping's leadership of the Central Committee of the Communist Party of China and the State Council in 1975. In accordance with Chairman Mao Zedong's instructions to boost the national economy, the State Council convened several planning conferences starting from June 1975, explicitly emphasizing the importance of fiscal and financial work. In response, the Ministry of Finance and the PBOC held multiple meetings in Shanghai, Beijing, and other places to strive for fiscal balance without increasing or minimizing currency issuance. Under these requirements, the PBOC and the Ministry of Finance submitted a "Outline for Reporting on Financial and Monetary Affairs" to the State Council. Subsequently, in accordance with the State Council's directives, they drafted "Several Issues Regarding the Rectification of Finance", known as the "Ten Financial and Monetary Measures," as well as a comprehensive set of rectification plans concerning banking system, currency circulation, fund management, lending methods, cash management, settlement systems, and supervision of wage fund payments. These plans were discussed at the National Conference on Finance and Trade in October of the same year. With the implementation of these robust measures, the People's Bank of China's centralized and unified guidelines were clarified, which significantly promoted the recovery of financial work. The role of financial functions was greatly strengthened, currency circulation improved, the efficiency of credit fund utilization enhanced, and the distorted "managing funds" function was transformed. However, this period of progress was short-lived. In 1976, during the nationwide campaign of "Criticism of Deng Xiaoping and Counterattack against Rightwards Reversals," the financial order and financial system once again suffered severe shocks, plunging the slightly improved financial work back into dire straits.

5.3.2 The Impact and Rectification of Monetary Stability

"The Cultural Revolution", which lasted for a decade starting from May 1966, had a significant impact on the socio-economic landscape. In 1967, economic pragmatism swept across the nation, followed by waves of violence and chaos. Under this backdrop, financial and economic activities suffered severe disruptions. Within just two years, in 1967 and 1968, "fiscal deficits occurred, bank credit exceeded receipts, excessive currency issuance amounted to an additional 25.6 billion yuan, and the ratio of cash circulation to retail sales of commodities dropped to around 1:6, exacerbating the problem of shortages in the supply of goods."[20] Subsequently, the scale of infrastructure construction continued to expand, leading to the "Three Breakthroughs" by the end of 1971, namely, the sudden surge in the number of state-owned enterprise employees to over 50 million, total wages exceeding 30 billion yuan, and grain sales surpassing 4 million tons, resulting in market turmoil, currency mismanagement, and price fluctuations.

In response to the uncontrolled issues of monetary credit, the Central Committee of the Communist Party of China (CPC) and the State Council adopted corresponding measures at different times. However, overall, the effectiveness of measures such as dispatching military representatives to protect banks was not satisfactory. Instead, the two brief adjustments mentioned earlier had more practical effects.

Firstly, in 1972, under the leadership of Premier Zhou Enlai, corrective measures were taken. Addressing the uncontrollable credit and monetary issues caused by the "Three Breakthroughs," measures were implemented to reduce infrastructure investment plans, strengthen infrastructure management systems, strictly control the increase in new employees, enhance wage fund management, strengthen economic accounting in state-owned enterprises, implement a highly centralized grain management system, and restore and strengthen bank credit and cash management. Meanwhile, the PBOC enhanced the independence of bank operations and corrected the

[20] Yang Xitian et al. *A Comprehensive History of Chinese Finance (Volume Six): The People's Republic of China Era*. China Financial Publishing House. 2002: 138.

situation of loose credit. With these favorable measures, the uncontrollable situation of currency and credit was effectively brought under control, leading to currency stability and a positive trend in the market. However, subsequent political movements such as the "Criticism of Lin Biao and Confucius" once again severely impacted the just-stabilized credit and currency, resulting in a dire situation of excessive currency and tightening commodity supply in the market.

Secondly, in 1975, during Deng Xiaoping's leadership of the Central Committee of the Communist Party of China and the State Council, corrective measures were taken. Deng Xiaoping, by excluding the interference of the "Gang of Four," convened several virtual meetings and emphasized consolidation. The PBOC and the Ministry of Finance submitted a "Outline for Reporting on Financial and Monetary Affairs" to the State Council, implementing strict measures to control currency issuance and balance credit receipts and disbursements. With the strong push from the State Council and the banking and financial functional departments, issues such as currency mismanagement were corrected to a certain extent, and the socio-economic situation showed signs of improvement. However, in 1976, under the influence of the "Criticism of Deng Xiaoping and Counterattack against Rightwards Reversals," urban areas began to criticize "bourgeois rights," and rural areas vigorously pursued the "elimination of capitalist vestiges." Against this backdrop, the previously improved financial situation once again collapsed. Banks increased currency issuance, credit expansion, and issues such as excessive currency circulation and rising prices resurfaced in the market.

5.3.3 The Impact and Changes in Financial Operations

During the "Cultural Revolution," under the slogan of "class struggle as the key link" and the implementation of "proletarian dictatorship over the bourgeoisie," China's financial business suffered severe impacts due to the assault by "revolutionary mass organizations."

Firstly, the already limited number of financial institutions were forced to close. As mentioned earlier, after the nationalization of financial organizations, China established a highly centralized and unified financial institution system, with essentially only the PBOC remaining as the organizational structure. Other financial organizations, even if they existed in some form, were revoked or merged into the PBOC after the outbreak of the "Cultural Revolution," as shown in Table 5.4.

Although the Bank of China was retained, it only functioned as the foreign exchange department of the PBOC, responsible for managing foreign exchange operations. While rural credit cooperatives experienced some degree of development, their management authority was delegated by the PBOC to the grassroots level, implementing the "Yanzhuang Experience" of managing the poor and lower-middle peasants. The funds of credit cooperatives were uniformly allocated and used by people's communes, providing loans to members and production teams, until this

Table 5.4 Changes in financial institutions during the "cultural revolution"

Organization name	Establishment or restoration date	Dissolution or merger date
Overseas Chinese Investment Company	Established in 1957	Dissolved in 1970
People's Construction Bank of China	Restored in 1962	Merged into the PBOC in 1970
Agricultural Bank of China	Restored in 1965	Merged into the PBOC in 1967

grassroots management authority was transferred back to the PBOC and its various branches in 1974.

The second aspect is the contraction of financial services. In the insurance sector, in June 1968, the PBOC issued a notice "Regarding Not Insuring Strike Insurance for Export Transport" while the well-functioning "Insurance for Foreign Aid Equipment and Exhibition Goods" was discontinued. Reinsurance business with overseas insurance companies suffered a severe blow. Consequently, the number of countries with reinsurance relationships with China decreased from 32 to 17, the number of foreign companies with business dealings dropped from 67 to 20, and the number of business contracts decreased from 219 to 49. In the banking sector, savings services suffered severe damage. Savings interest was considered bourgeois exploitation. Some banks introduced interest-free deposits and cash custody services, and even mobilized the masses to "voluntarily contribute" personal savings deposits. During the "Great Leap Forward," after undergoing rectification, the development of savings services that had just returned to normal became difficult. "Fixed-term savings" was retained for periods of over six months and over one year, consolidating interest rates into three tiers for loans to state-owned, collective, and individual industrial, commercial, and agricultural enterprises, and consolidating loan interest rates for credit cooperatives into two tiers. Meanwhile, interest on deposits for institutions, groups, schools, and others was abolished, and the provision of interest on overdue enterprise loans was canceled. Some suggested that savings interest was exploitative income. In some places, bank savings departments set up two windows for "interest-bearing deposits" and "interest-free deposits," indirectly exerting political pressure on depositors, causing some depositors to refrain from collecting interest upon maturity.[21] Subsequently, after the aforementioned two adjustments by the Central Committee of the Communist Party of China and the State Council, savings services gradually resumed. However, throughout the entire "Cultural Revolution" period, savings deposit services underwent twists and turns, with the amount of deposits showing some degree of growth, as shown in Fig. 5.2.[22]

In the composition of bank funding sources, fiscal deposits and deposits from state-owned enterprises far exceeded urban and rural savings deposits, ranking first

21 Yao Sui. *A History of Chinese Finance*. Higher Education Press. 2007: 489.

22 National Bureau of Statistics. *Forty Years of Endeavor (1949–1989)*. China Statistics Press. 1989: 459.

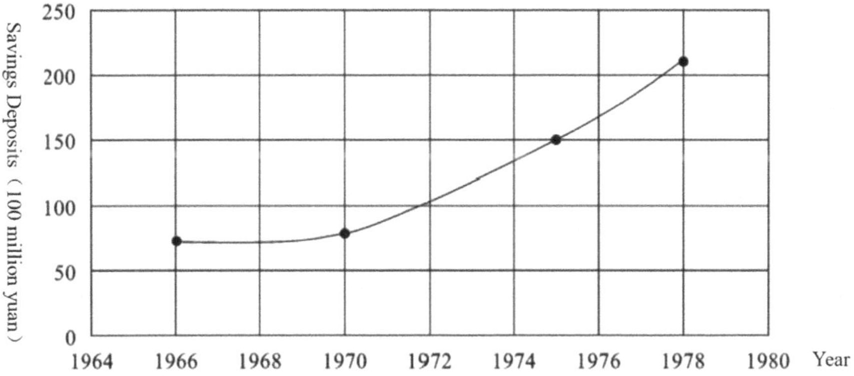

Fig. 5.2 Savings deposits in urban and rural areas nationwide from 1966 to 1978

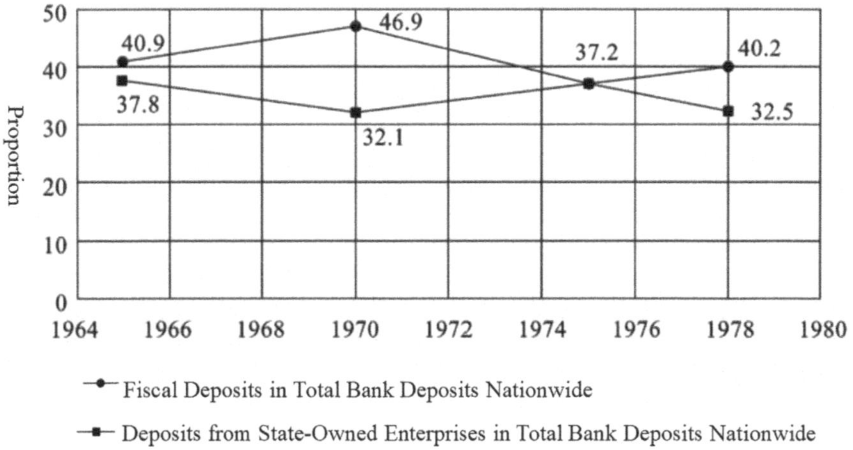

Fig. 5.3 Proportion of fiscal deposits and deposits from state-owned enterprises in total bank deposits nationwide, 1965–1978

and second, respectively. The combined total of the two accounted for over 75% of the national deposit total, as shown in Fig. 5.3.[23]

Since the establishment of the People's Republic of China, foreign exchange business has always been highly valued by the central government. However, due to fluctuations in the international environment and domestic political and economic factors, the state's foreign exchange business has experienced significant fluctuations. Regarding remittances from overseas Chinese, before the "Cultural Revolution", all levels of government attached great importance to this aspect, ensuring the protection of the legitimate rights and interests of overseas Chinese and their families. However,

[23] National Bureau of Statistics. *Forty Years of Endeavor (1949–1989)*. China Statistics Press. 1989: 430.

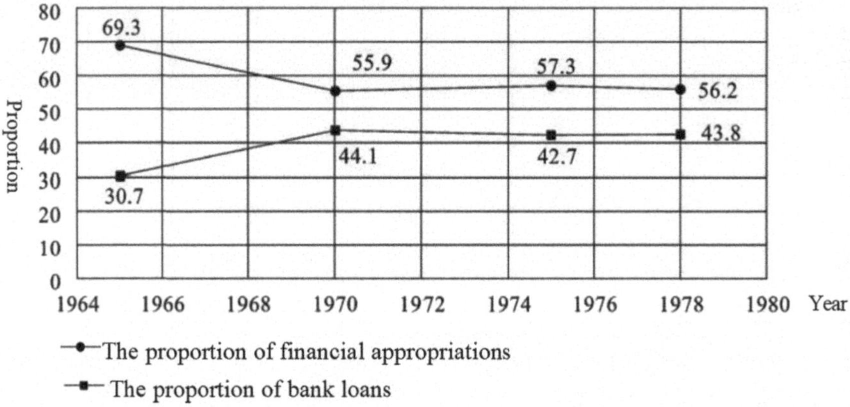

Fig. 5.4 Utilization of working capital in state-owned industry, 1965—1978

since the outbreak of the "Cultural Revolution", remittance services were severely impacted, with the handling of remittances being labeled as "serving foreign capitalists" and even accused of being "funds for espionage activities," leading to calls for the suspension of remittance services. The previously thriving private remittance business was forcibly shut down." Before 1966, there were 318 private remittance businesses nationwide, accounting for about 40% of the country's total remittances. At the beginning of the "Cultural Revolution", some regions abolished this industry, and their business was taken over by banks. On May 8, 1972, the 'private remittance business' was completely abolished..."[24] Under the influence of abnormal political and economic factors, the foreign exchange business experienced a significant contraction trend.

In terms of lending and cash management, credit management was criticized as "control, restriction, and pressure," and effective credit management systems were abandoned, leading to ideological confusion. Reforms in urban and rural commercial loans and settlements allowed grassroots supply and marketing cooperatives to open accounts in both urban and rural areas, facilitating loans and repayments on both ends. This approach, known as the "four localities" method (local procurement, local lending, local sales, and local repayment), weakened credit management supervision.[25] Regarding loans to state-owned enterprises, the practice largely continued, with the finance department responsible for fixed quotas of circulating funds, while banks handled excess funds. During the "Cultural Revolution", instances of fiscal encroachment on banks occurred, resulting in increased lending to state-owned enterprises. This can be observed in Fig. 5.4.[26]

---

[24] Yao Sui. *A History of Chinese Finance*. Higher Education Press. 2007: 485.

[25] Yang Xitian et al. *A General History of Chinese Finance (Volume VI: The People's Republic of China Period)*. China Financial Publishing House. 2002: 186.

[26] Compiled based on data from the annual "China Statistical Yearbook" for relevant years.

For loans to state-owned commercial enterprises' circulating funds, the majority came from banks. The resulting phenomenon of uncontrolled credit significantly impacted price stability, leading to inflationary tendencies. Despite undergoing two short-term adjustments and rectifications, their effects did not last long, as they were soon disrupted by new "political movements," plunging back into chaos and loss of control.

Thirdly, the role of money was negated. As early as the "Great Leap Forward" period, some individuals attempted premature entry into communism while trying to prematurely eliminate commodity production and exchange, as well as denying the positive roles of commodities, value, money, and prices. This erroneous thinking was later denounced by the Central Committee of the Communist Party of China and the State Council. Since the outbreak of the "Cultural Revolution", a nationwide campaign against "revisionism" and "preventing capitalist restoration" was launched. At that time, in theory, the commodity economy, monetary exchange, distribution according to labor, and the law of value were all criticized as the economic basis of capitalism. In practice, the law of value was largely ignored, and the role of money was greatly restricted. This negation of commodity money directly affected the credit activities of the PBOC. Actions such as internal and external borrowing for economic construction, originally aimed at raising construction funds, were directly opposed to the notion of "independence, self-reliance," and were negated. Mechanisms such as interest and interest rates in deposit and loan activities were strictly limited, with decreasing interest differentials and fewer tiers. As a result, the leverage effect was significantly weakened, if not entirely lost. This trend gradually led to the loss of the "three major centers" of credit, settlement, and cash within the highly centralized and unified financial management function, with banks only being loosely connected to simple functions such as accounting and cashiers, no longer fulfilling their true banking roles.

5.3.4 Rectification of the Financial Sector During the Period of Rectifying Mistaken Practices and Restoring Order

The overthrow of the "Gang of Four" in 1976 cleared political obstacles for the rectification and development of the national economy. However, underestimating the serious consequences of the "Cultural Revolution" and failing to thoroughly repudiate the leftist errors led to the proposal of unrealistic high targets and the blind introduction of advanced foreign technology and equipment in practice. Consequently, in the financial field, this led to the serious consequences of excessive and rapid issuance of currency and the severe loss of control over bank credit scale. In this context, the Central Committee of the Communist Party of China and the State Council launched actions to rectify the financial industry and clarify the functions of "managing funds."

Firstly, the rectification of the financial functions and institutional setup of the People's Bank of China (PBC). In October 1976, the PBC convened a national banking work conference in Shenyang, establishing three principles for reforming the banking credit management system: centralization of currency issuance authority, national unified planning and comprehensive balance, and separate management of fiscal and credit funds. In December 1977, the State Council decided that the head office of the PBC would be established as a department-level unit under the State Council, with branches of the PBC to be established in various regions in accordance with the Ministry of Finance. Thus, the system of the PBC's work being primarily led by the head office with dual leadership from the head office and the local government was initially formed. This strengthened the financial management system and centralized the banking work, laying a solid foundation for the development of financial organizations after the reform and opening up.

Secondly, strengthening the rectification of cash management and the transfer settlement system. In October 1976, the Central Committee of the Communist Party of China issued an "Urgent Notice on Freezing Deposits of Various Units" and, as required by the State Council, recalled excessive currency in 1977 to achieve fiscal balance. In 1977, the State Council, the People's Bank of China, and other institutions issued a series of documents on rectifying cash management and the transfer settlement system, as shown in Table 5.5.

Through these documents, China strengthened the rectification of cash management and transfer settlement system, achieved stable currency issuance, and standardized the transfer and settlement system, laying the necessary foundation for later reforms.

Furthermore, efforts were made to strengthen the management of credit and cashiers. In March 1977, the Ministry of Finance emphasized the need to strengthen commercial credit management in the financial sector and reduce the level of industrial enterprises' use of working capital. Subsequently, the People's Bank of China reiterated the policy boundaries and principles of loans, emphasizing strict implementation of nationally unified systems for credit management and working capital management. Meanwhile, the People's Bank of China issued documents such as "Opinions on Further Strengthening Cash Management Work" and "Opinions on

Table 5.5 Important documents on rectifying cash management and transfer settlement system issued in 1977

Date	Issuing unit	Document title
July 30	Ministry of finance, people's bank of China	"Report on achieving the recall of some currency this year"
October 28	People's bank of China	"Settlement measures of the people's bank of China"
November 28	State council	"Several provisions on rectifying and strengthening banking work" and reissued "decision on implementing cash management"

Conducting Clearing of Funds, Accounts, and Finances" to enhance the quality of cashier and accounting work in the financial industry.

Lastly, efforts were made to strengthen financial business operations. Through rectification work in the financial field, it was gradually recognized that organizing deposits and aggregating funds were the primary tasks of the People's Bank of China. Therefore, besides strengthening cash management, the People's Bank of China also emphasized the importance of developing urban and rural savings. By correcting the erroneous practices of the "Cultural Revolution" period, the People's Bank of China clarified the implementation of savings policies, safeguarded the interests of depositors, reaffirmed that individual legitimate income deposited in banks belongs to individuals permanently and is permanently protected by national law. Meanwhile, the People's Bank of China and the rural credit cooperatives under its leadership also strengthened their lending business to promote the development of industry and agriculture.

Economic and Social Development Research Monograph of the People's Republic of China

1949—2018

Part III
Development of the Financial Industry in the Transition to a Market Economy Period

Chapter 6
Establishment and Improvement of the Central Banking System

After the dismantling of the "Gang of Four," accompanied by the rectification of the economic sector, the financial domain also began to adjust and streamline. The Third Plenary Session of the 11th Central Committee of the Communist Party of China made the decision to shift the focus of work to the economic sector, initiating financial system reforms around the idea of "truly turning banks into banks."[1] The People's Bank of China (PBOC) gradually transformed from its dual functions before the era of reform and opening up, strengthening its role as the central bank. In 1984, with the establishment of the Industrial and Commercial Bank of China (ICBC), PBOC preliminarily confirmed its position as the central bank. From then until 1993, PBOC underwent a transformation towards exclusively exercising the functions of the central bank. Since 1994, in line with the establishment of a socialist market economy system, PBOC has ultimately solidified its position as the central bank in terms of institutions and functions, constructing a modern central banking system. During this process, the functions of PBOC gradually shifted from the "managing funds" domain to the areas of macroeconomic regulation, maintaining financial stability, and expanding into the realm of "regulating market".

6.1 The Establishment of the Central Bank's Position

Since the beginning of the reform and opening-up, PBOC has gone through three distinct phases in establishing its position as the central bank. Before 1984, PBOC continuously strengthened its central banking functions while retaining dual roles. From 1984 to 1993, the commercial banking functions of PBOC were gradually stripped away, and it began to exclusively exercise the functions of the central bank. From 1994 to the present, PBOC has fully confirmed its status as the central bank,

[1] Deng Xiaoping. *Deng Xiaoping Selected Works (Volume 2)*, People's Publishing House, 2008: 200.

R. Lan, *The Financial Development of China*, Understanding China,
https://doi.org/10.1007/978-981-97-8273-4_6

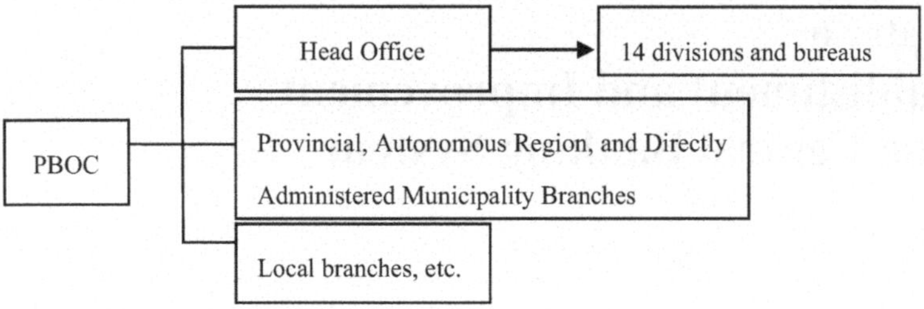

Fig. 6.1 Organizational structure of PBOC (1978)

ultimately constructing and refining a modern central banking system. Since 2018, the "super central bank" status of PBOC has been increasingly reinforced.

6.1.1 Formation of the Central Banking System

During the period of "managing funds", PBOC had dual functions. After the initiation of reform and opening-up, guided by the idea of "truly turning banks into banks," there was a gradual shift towards transforming PBOC into a dedicated central bank. This process involved a dynamic adaptation to the ongoing socioeconomic system reforms, rather than an immediate and complete transition.

Firstly, PBOC restructured its organizational system. In January 1978, PBOC officially separated from the Ministry of Finance, reinstating organizational structures that had been previously dismantled. Subsequently, at the local level, various branches of PBOC were established independently from local finance departments, forming a relatively comprehensive organizational framework, as illustrated in Fig. 6.1.

Through the separation from the Ministry of Finance, PBOC reestablished a top-down vertical leadership system, reinforcing the principle of centralized leadership in financial management. With the restoration and improvement of organizational structures, previously decentralized staff at various levels gradually returned to their respective positions, leading to a reversal of the chaotic financial order. By the end of 1979, PBOC had a total of over 330,000 cadres and employees, with more than 15,000 institutions. This included 29 provincial branches, 148 municipal branches, 220 central branches, 2277 county branches, 886 urban offices, 2042 sub-branches, 6790 savings institutions, and 2883 county-managed offices.[2] In this way, within a short span of two years, the previously fragmented organizational structure was reestablished, laying the organizational foundation for PBOC to exercise its central banking functions.

Secondly, PBOC continuously weakened the functions of commercial banks. Under the highly centralized and unified financial management system, PBOC not

[2] Yang Peixin. *China's finance*. People's Publishing House, 1982: 19.

only performed central banking functions but also engaged in commercial banking operations. As the reform of the planned economic system unfolded, this dual-function approach, where central banking and commercial banking functions coexisted, became inadequate to meet the needs of social and economic development. PBOC timely advanced reforms to weaken the functions of commercial banks, separating commercial functions that were originally concentrated in PBOC and assigning them to newly restored and established state-owned financial institutions. The widespread implementation of the Household Responsibility System in rural areas marked the beginning of rapid socioeconomic development in China, giving rise to a substantial demand for financial services. In order to promote agricultural development and effectively manage funds for supporting agriculture, PBOC first proposed the restoration of the Agricultural Bank of China and the development of rural credit cooperatives to the State Council. In March 1979, the Agricultural Bank of China (ABC) was restored, and under its leadership, rural credit cooperatives experienced rapid growth. To meet the demands of opening up to the outside world, large-scale infrastructure construction, insurance, and other aspects, entities such as the Bank of China (BOC), China Construction Bank (CCB), and People's Insurance Company of China (PICC) were gradually established. Concurrently, non-banking financial institutions such as trust and investment companies and financial leasing companies emerged to address the demands of socioeconomic development. By 1983, the financial system had evolved from the initial situation where only PBOC existed to a diversified financial landscape. Correspondingly, the highly centralized financial management functions gradually dispersed to different financial organizations. This led to a progressive weakening of the commercial functions previously held by PBOC, as illustrated in Fig. 6.2.

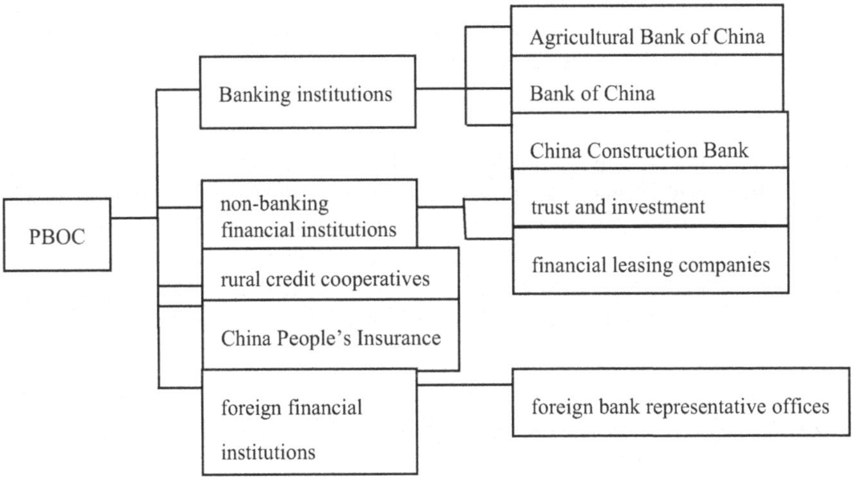

Fig. 6.2. 1983 framework of China's financial system

Furthermore, PBOC strengthened its central banking functions. While weakening the functions of commercial banks, PBOC continuously enhanced its central banking functions in response to the needs of the socioeconomic and financial system reforms.

Firstly, it reinforced the role of "the bank for banks." As increasingly restored and newly established financial organizations took on their commercial functions, PBOC gradually shifted towards regulating and providing corresponding services to these entities. "The establishment of commercial financial institutions is the premise and main step in the reform of the central bank. The independence of commercial financial institutions directly determines the independence of the central bank. The healthy development of commercial banks, in turn, requires the central bank to fully play its own functions…"[3] During this period, PBOC initiated exploration in financial legal construction, actively promoted cross-region entrusted collection and settlement, as well as quota settlement methods. It gradually established a new financial institution system with PBOC at the center, specialized banks as the main entities, and a variety of financial institutions coexisting.

Secondly, in coordination with the reform of the fiscal and taxation system, it strengthened the national treasury institutions, bolstered personnel, and gradually standardized the functions of managing the national treasury. In 1979, the national treasury implemented a pilot project of "tax-for-profit reform" and introduced a budget management system of "divided revenue and expenditure, tiered responsibility" To adapt to this trend in fiscal and taxation system reform, PBOC restored independent accounting, normal financial statement systems, and increasingly strengthened its role as "the bank of the nation."

Thirdly, it gradually strengthened the management of the issuance and circulation of the RMB, enhancing the functions of "the issuer's bank." As market-oriented reforms advanced, the role of the price mechanism became increasingly prominent, leading to the continuous development of the monetary system as a framework of the price mechanism. This was notably reflected in the increase in the money supply from 1978 to 1984, as shown in Fig. 6.3.[4]

Lastly, PBOC specifically exercises central banking functions. With the restoration and establishment of other financial organizations, the functions of PBOC gradually transitioned towards the exclusive exercise of central banking functions. In January 1981, Vice Premier Yao Yilin emphasized, "The head office of the People's Bank should actively play the role of the central bank, and the branches of the People's Bank in provinces, cities, and autonomous regions should also play this role under the leadership of the head office."[5] The State Council issued the "Decision on Strictly Controlling Credit Management and Currency Issuance," explicitly

---

[3] Li Zhihui. *The Development and Changes of China's Banking Industry*. Truth & Wisdom Press, Shanghai People's Publishing House. 2008: 33.

[4] Compiled based on data from relevant years on the official website of the National Bureau of Statistics.

[5] Yang Xitian et al. *General History of Chinese Finance (Volume 6): The Period of the People's Republic of China*, China Finance Publishing House, 2002: 216.

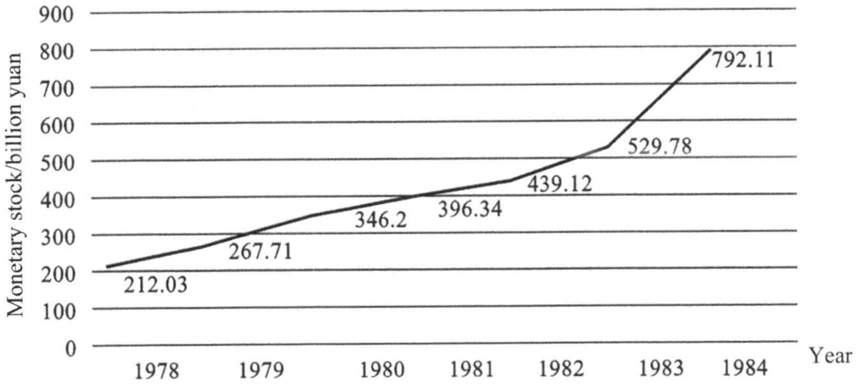

Fig. 6.3 Inflation changes in China from 1978 to 1984

stating that PBOC should conscientiously carry out its central banking responsibilities. In July 1982, the State Council clearly stated, "PBOC is the central bank of our country and is a national institution for the unified management of the country's finances under the leadership of the State Council."[6] Subsequently, in response to differing opinions regarding whether PBOC should maintain the existing highly centralized and unified financial management system or specialize in performing central banking functions, after multiple rounds of deliberation, the State Council finally promulgated the "Decision of the State Council on the People's Bank of China Exclusively Exercising Central Banking Functions" on September 17, 1983. This decision clearly defined the specialized role of PBOC in performing central banking functions. The decision outlined the main functions of PBOC, including formulating policies, regulations, basic systems, and legislation for financial work, organizing and executing them upon approval; controlling currency issuance and regulating the circulation of market currency; unifying management of RMB deposit and lending rates and exchange rates; formulating national credit plans and centrally managing credit funds; managing national foreign exchange, gold and silver, national foreign exchange reserves, and gold reserves; acting as the agent for the national treasury; approving the establishment, consolidation, or closure of financial institutions; coordinating and auditing the business operations of various financial institutions; managing financial markets; and representing the government in relevant international financial activities. Simultaneously, the establishment of the Industrial and Commercial Bank of China (ICBC) took place, taking over the industrial and commercial credit and savings operations previously handled by the People's Bank. In January 1984, PBOC established a council to strengthen its leadership and decision-making status. The formation of ICBC and its branches allowed PBOC to specialize in central banking functions, marking a departure from the unified banking system and implementing a central banking system adapted to the planned

[6] People's Bank of China. *Sixty Years of the People's Bank of China (1948–2008)*, China Finance Publishing House, 2008: 57–58.

commodity economy. In February 1994, PBOC issued the "Interim Measures for the Management of Credit Funds," establishing a mechanism for controlling the total quantity of monetary credit. Subsequent revisions and adjustments to financial regulations shifted the focus of PBOC towards macroeconomic control and financial supervision.

6.1.2 Further Strengthening of the Central Banking System

From January 1984, when PBOC officially began exclusively exercising central banking functions, until the period of transition leading up to the establishment of the "Decision of the Central Committee of the Communist Party of China on Certain Issues Concerning the Establishment of a Socialist Market Economic System" at the Third Plenary Session of the 14th CPC Central Committee in 1993, China remained in a transitional stage. During this time, it did not fully relinquish its financial management functions, oscillating between "managing funds" and "regulating market". The control of credit scale and cash issuance remains the central bank's primary policy tools; various regions and departments, based on their economic needs, exert varying degrees of intervention in the financial sector, making it challenging for PBOC to achieve effective macroeconomic financial regulation. At the same time, PBOC also undertook some specialized lending tasks, and its branches operated some financing entities."[7] Although PBOC faced certain constraints in fulfilling its central banking functions, its role as a central bank was strengthened to a certain extent."

In 1984, following the "Decision of the Central Committee of the Communist Party of China on Economic System Reform," the State Council established a financial system reform research group with Liu Hongru as the head. At that time, the research group proposed several reform suggestions, including the separation of government functions from enterprise operations, the commercialization of banks, granting financial institutions the authority to determine loan amounts, interest rates, and other service charges within the scope allowed by the central bank's credit and interest rate policies, allowing financial institutions to decide investment methods independently without government intervention, and operating specialized banks through a three-tiered system of head office, branch, and central branch. The reforms also advocated for the liberalization of commercial credit, the introduction of commercial credit bills, permission for enterprises to directly raise funds through issuing stocks and bonds, and the establishment of securities exchanges. The proposal called for the creation of various financial institutions and the improvement of the central bank's macroeconomic control system, utilizing tools such as money supply, leveraging interest rates, reserve requirements, and notice loans.[8] In

---

[7] People's Bank of China. *Sixty Years of the People's Bank of China (1948–2008)*, China Finance Publishing House, 2008: 59.

[8] Liu Hongru. *Breakthrough—The Development Path of China's Capital Market (Volume 1)*, China Finance Publishing House, 2008: 30–32.

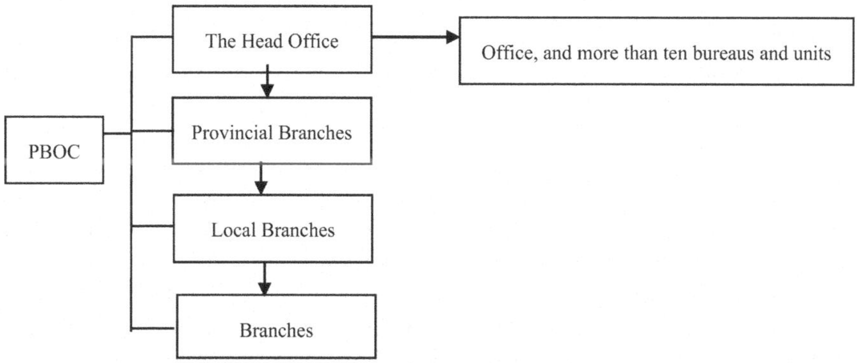

Fig. 6.4 Organizational structure of PBOC (1985)

June 1985, PBOC abolished the practice implemented in 1984, where county-level and municipal-level branches were no longer established in regions below the prefectural level (except for a few economically and financially developed areas). Instead, all branches were reinstated, leading PBOC to once again establish a comprehensive system covering central, provincial, municipal, and county levels. This restructuring significantly reinforced PBOC's top-down vertical leadership structure, as illustrated in Fig. 6.4.

In January 1986, the State Council promulgated the "Interim Regulations of the People's Republic of China on Banking Supervision," reaffirming PBOC as the central bank of the country. In Chap. 2, Part V, the document explicitly outlined twelve responsibilities of PBOC:

(1) Research and formulate the national financial work guidelines and policies, organize and implement them upon approval.
(2) Draft financial regulations.
(3) Formulate basic regulations for financial operations.
(4) Control currency issuance, regulate currency circulation, and maintain currency stability.
(5) Manage deposit and loan interest rates, determine the exchange rates of the Renminbi against foreign currencies.
(6) Develop national credit plans, centrally manage credit funds, and unify the management of working capital for state-owned enterprises.
(7) Manage foreign exchange, gold, silver, national foreign exchange reserves, and gold reserves.
(8) Approve the establishment or consolidation of specialized banks and other financial institutions.
(9) Lead, manage, coordinate, supervise, and audit the business operations of specialized banks and other financial institutions.
(10) Manage the national treasury, act as an agent for issuing government bonds.
(11) Manage corporate stocks, bonds, and other securities, and oversee financial markets.

(12) Represent the government in relevant international financial activities.

The regulations also systemically institutionalized activities such as specialized banks, other financial institutions, and currency issuance. In December of the same year, Deng Xiaoping emphasized once again the need to "truly turn banks into banks," stating that "the previous banks were currency issuance companies and treasuries, not genuine banks."[9] Based on this advice, PBOC proposed goals for establishing a new financial system and reforms in 1987. "These goals included establishing a financial control and regulation system with indirect control as the main feature, a credit system with bank credit as the main component, a socialist financial system led by the central bank with various banks and financial institutions coexisting and collaborating, and a modernized management system for financial institutions."[10] Following these reform objectives, the functions of PBOC were further strengthened.

In October 1992, the 14th National Congress of the Communist Party of China (CPC) established the goal of establishing a socialist market economy system. In November 1993, the Third Plenary Session of the 14th Central Committee of the Communist Party of China passed the "Decision of the Central Committee of the Communist Party of China on Establishing a Socialist Market Economy System," aligning with this goal. In response to these developments, the State Council expedited the establishment of a financial system that would be compatible with the requirements of a socialist market economy. In December of the same year, the "Decision of the State Council on Financial System Reform" was issued. This decision explicitly outlined the deepening of financial system reform, with the primary task being to transform PBOC into a genuine central bank. The main functions of PBOC were specified as formulating and implementing monetary policy to ensure currency stability and exercising strict supervision over financial institutions to guarantee the safe and effective operation of the financial system. In light of this, the State Council established the goals of financial system reform, including the establishment of an independent central bank macroeconomic control system under the leadership of the State Council, the separation of policy-based and commercial financial functions, the dominance of state-owned commercial banks with multiple financial institutions coexisting, and the creation of a unified, open, orderly competitive, and rigorously managed financial market system. The decision on financial system reform marked the beginning of a rapid transformation of PBOC towards a modern central banking system.

---

[9] Deng Xiaoping. *Selected Works of Deng Xiaoping (Volume 3)*, People's Publishing House, 2008: 193.

[10] Li De. *The Development Course of China's Financial Industry (Volume 1)*, People's Publishing House, 2015: 147.

6.1.3 Formation of the Modern Central Banking System

After the State Council established the goals of financial system reform at the end of 1993, PBOC, following a legal and standardized direction, focused on improving macroeconomic regulation and strengthening financial supervision. A systematic reform and adjustment were carried out on the organization structure, functions, and operations of PBOC. In January 1994, PBOC officially issued the "Opinions on the Transformation of Functions of PBOC Branches," comprehensively transforming the functions of its branches, primarily exercising functions such as financial supervision, investigation and statistical analysis, lateral position adjustment, managing the national treasury, cash allocation, foreign exchange management, and interbank clearing. Simultaneously, the PBOC headquarters improved the central bank's functions in the following aspects: (1) enhancing macroeconomic regulation functions to maintain centralized management of monetary credit and strengthen the uniformity of monetary policy; (2) abolishing the profit retention system and implementing an independent financial budget management system; (3) clarifying the relationship between monetary policy and fiscal policy by stopping overdrafts from the Ministry of Finance to the PBOC from 1994 and ceasing borrowing from the Ministry of Finance to PBOC from 1995; (4) establishing a standardized financial organizational system to strengthen the supervision of different types of financial organizations; (5) streamlining the relationship between monetary policy and investment policy; (6) establishing three policy banks—the China Development Bank (CDB), the Export–Import Bank of China (EIBC), and the Agricultural Development Bank of China (ADBC)—to take over policy-related business that the PBOC had previously undertaken.[11]

On March 18, 1995, the Third Session of the Eighth National People's Congress officially passed the "Law of the People's Republic of China on the People's Bank of China" (hereinafter referred to as the "PBOC Law"). The first article of the law clearly outlines the purpose of formulating this law: to establish the status and responsibilities of PBOC, ensure the correct formulation and execution of the country's monetary policy, to establish and improve the macroeconomic regulation system of the central bank, and to strengthen the supervision and management of the financial industry. The "PBOC Law" provides explicit regulations on the nature, status, functions, organizational structure, monetary policy, and financial supervision of PBOC. This is China's central bank law, the first comprehensive financial law since 1949, marking the formal establishment of PBOC as the central bank of China through national legislation. This also signifies the entry of China's financial sector into a legal and standardized track.[12] According to the "PBOC Law," PBOC established the Monetary Policy Committee. According to the regulations of the State Council, its responsibilities, composition, and working procedures are determined, clarifying the

---

[11] People's Bank of China. *Sixty Years of the People's Bank of China (1948–2008)*, China Finance Publishing House, 2008: 59–60.

[12] Yang Xitian et al. *General History of Chinese Finance (Volume 6): The Period of the People's Republic of China*, China Finance Publishing House, 2002: 222.

regulatory system for segmented supervision in the financial sector. In April 1997, the State Council issued the "Regulations on the Monetary Policy Committee of PBOC," defining it as an advisory and deliberative body for PBOC. Its responsibilities include discussing and providing recommendations on various monetary policy issues based on a comprehensive analysis of the macroeconomic situation, macroeconomic control goals, and coordination of monetary policy with other macroeconomic policies. In July of the same year, PBOC released the "Procedures for the Meetings of the Monetary Policy Committee of the People's Bank of China." To fulfill the responsibilities of the Monetary Policy Committee, regular meetings are held in the first half of each quarter to determine the direction of monetary policy.

With the gradual establishment of the socialist market economy system in China, the organizational structure of PBOC, initially based on administrative divisions, could no longer meet the needs of socio-economic development. Therefore, in November 1997, during the first National Financial Work Conference convened by the State Council, efforts were made to transform the PBOC into a true central bank, deepening financial system reform. In 1998, in accordance with the State Council's proposal for financial system reform, the PBOC advanced organizational restructuring. The reform aimed to "strengthen the vertical leadership of the central bank, establish branch offices across administrative regions, abolish provincial branch offices, enhance the independence of the PBOC in implementing monetary policy; strengthen supervisory functions over various financial institutions, including commercial banks and cooperative financial institutions, emphasize the use of financial electronic information means, establish financial risk monitoring and warning systems; monitor, analyze the flow and direction of funds, and financial activities across society, enhance the management level of the PBOC, and provide more accurate, secure, and efficient financial services such as payment and settlement for the financial system and society."[13] In line with these key reform requirements, the PBOC proposed the plan to abolish provincial branch offices and establish cross-province (autonomous region, direct-administered municipality) branch offices in June 1998. On October 17, the State Council approved this reform plan. On November 18, the Shanghai branch was the first to be established, and by December 18, all nine cross-province branches of the PBOC were set up. Simultaneously, 31 provincial branch offices were abolished, and the functions of the existing sub-branches were adjusted. Following this reform, the PBOC's headquarter now has 9 branches and 2 operational management departments, 326 central sub-branches, and 1827 county (city) sub-branches, as illustrated in Fig. 6.5. The significant adjustment in the organizational structure of the PBOC expanded the authority of its head office further centralized financial macro-control functions, and unified the decision-making and implementation of monetary policy, ensuring the central bank's independent and impartial fulfillment of financial regulatory responsibilities.

In October 2003, the Third Plenary Session of the 16th Central Committee of the Communist Party of China made the "Decision of the Central Committee of

[13] People's Bank of China. *Sixty Years of the People's Bank of China (1948–2008)*, China Finance Publishing House, 2008: 60.

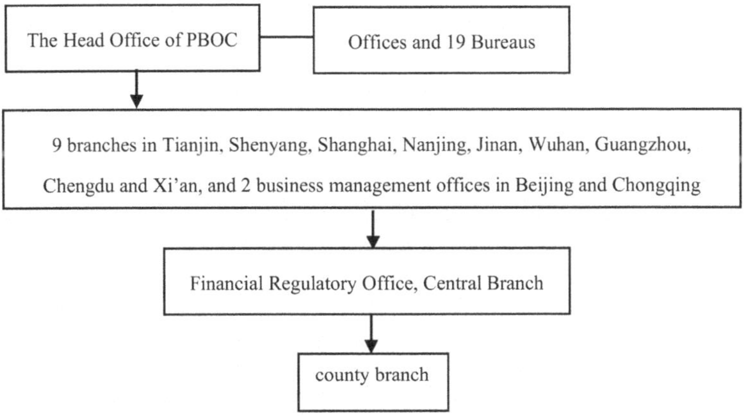

Fig. 6.5 Organizational structure of PBOC (1998)[14]

the Communist Party of China on Some Issues Concerning the Improvement of the Socialist Market Economic System," continuing to advance the construction of the socialist market economy system and institutional innovation. In line with this, China strengthened the construction of the central bank, promoted financial reform, openness, and development, improved financial macro-control, and maintained the stability of the financial system. On one hand, the State Council separated the regulatory functions of PBOC over banking and financial institutions from its other functions. These regulatory functions were integrated with the relevant functions of the Central Financial Work Commission established in 1998, leading to the establishment of the China Banking Regulatory Commission (CBRC). On the other hand, it was decided to revise laws and regulations such as the "Law of the People's Republic of China on the People's Bank" issued in 1995. The "Law of the People's Republic of China on Banking Supervision and Regulation" was passed to institutionalize the achievements of financial system reform. The revised "Law of the People's Republic of China on the People's Bank" took effect on February 1, 2004.

The revised "Law of the People's Republic of China on the People's Bank" maintains the legislative purpose, similar to that in 1995, aiming "to establish the position of PBOC, clarify its responsibilities, ensure the correct formulation and execution of the national monetary policy, establish and improve the macroeconomic regulation and control system of the central bank, and maintain financial stability." The functions are now more explicitly defined as "formulating and implementing monetary policy, preventing and mitigating financial risks, and maintaining financial stability."

[14] The Tianjin branch has jurisdiction over Tianjin, Hebei, Shanxi, and Inner Mongolia; the Shenyang branch has jurisdiction over Heilongjiang, Jilin, and Liaoning; the Shanghai branch has jurisdiction over Shanghai, Zhejiang, and Fujian; the Nanjing branch has jurisdiction over Jiangsu and Anhui; the Jinan branch has jurisdiction over Shandong and Henan; the Wuhan branch has jurisdiction over Jiangxi, Hunan, and Hubei; the Guangzhou branch has jurisdiction over Guangdong, Guangxi, and Hainan; the Chengdu branch has jurisdiction over Sichuan, Guizhou, Yunnan, and Tibet; the Xi'an branch has jurisdiction over Xinjiang, Gansu, Qinghai, Ningxia, and Shaanxi.

To better fulfill the central banking functions of PBOC, the amendments to the law are characterized by "strengthening, transforming, and adding." The "strengthening" aspect involves enhancing PBOC's authority in formulating and implementing monetary policy, changing the previous status where the PBOC Monetary Policy Committee was merely a consultative body. Its responsibilities have been significantly strengthened and expanded, with "the committee playing a crucial role in national macroeconomic regulation and monetary policy formulation and adjustment." The "transformation" involves adapting to the financial regulatory system by converting the direct supervisory functions, such as approval of the establishment of banking and financial institutions, approval of business operations, qualification examination of senior management personnel, and routine supervision and management, into indirect control responsibilities related to financial macroeconomic regulation, prevention and mitigation of financial risks, and maintaining financial stability. The "adding" aspect includes the addition of two functions: anti-money laundering and the management of credit reporting agencies. Clearly, the revised "Law of the People's Republic of China on the People's Bank" provides a more precise definition of the central banking functions of PBOC, solidifying its status as a modern central bank.

In order to adapt to the new functional positioning of PBOC and enhance the clear delineation of functions among its branches, PBOC underwent organizational changes in 2003. The Financial Stability Bureau was established to strengthen the prevention, monitoring, and assessment of financial risks. In 2004, PBOC restored the administrative level of Fuzhou, Hangzhou, Shijiazhuang, Zhengzhou, and Shenzhen branches to be consistent with the nine major branches. However, personnel authority remained under the jurisdiction of the respective branches. In August 2005, the Shanghai branch was dissolved, and the PBOC Shanghai Head office was established to increase the influence of the Shanghai financial market and promote the construction of the Shanghai International Financial Center. Simultaneously, PBOC initiated modern corporate system reforms for its directly affiliated enterprises, reinforcing the support role of relevant affiliated units in fulfilling the central banking functions of PBOC. In 2008, responding to the global financial crisis, PBOC further improved the monetary policy system, strengthened the financial regulatory coordination mechanism, and made corresponding adjustments to its responsibilities. Subsequently, to address the challenges of mixed-ownership and fragmented regulation, PBOC, with the approval of the State Council, established the Financial Supervision Coordination Inter-Ministerial Joint Conference system in 2013, led by PBOC, to enhance coordination of regulatory policies among the "one bank, three commissions." In 2017, the State Council set up the Financial Stability and Development Committee, and within PBOC, the Office of the Financial Stability and Development Committee was established. By 2017, the organizational structure of the PBOC had undergone some changes, as illustrated in Fig. 6.6.

In February 2018, the Third Plenary Session of the 19th Central Committee of the Communist Party of China made a clear decision on institutional reforms. In March, during the two sessions (National People's Congress and Chinese People's Political Consultative Conference), a resolution on institutional reform was passed.

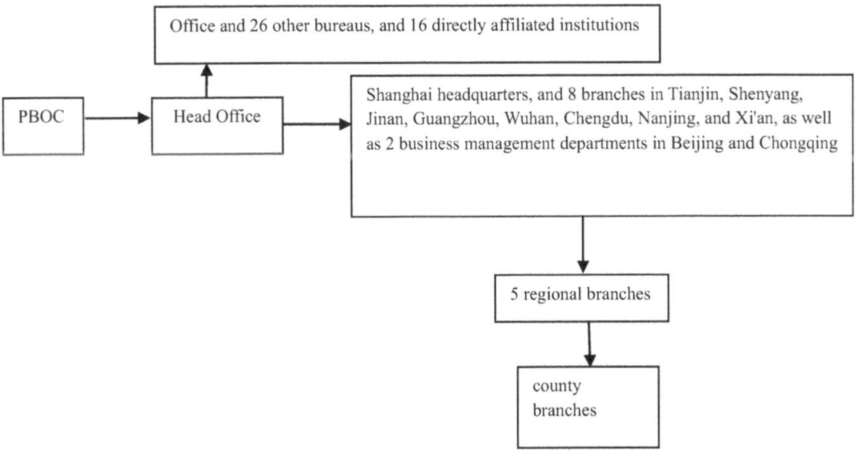

Fig. 6.6 Organizational structure of PBOC (2017)

China Banking and Insurance Regulatory Commission (CBIRC) was established by merging China Banking Regulatory Commission (CBRC) and China Insurance Regulatory Commission (CIRC). The regulatory powers that were previously under CBRC and CIRC, such as formulating regulations, were transferred to PBOC. The chairman of CBIRC concurrently serves as the secretary of the CPC Committee of PBOC, forming a preliminary pattern of the "mega central bank." This move further strengthened the authority of the central bank. In terms of financial regulatory agencies, a supervisory and management structure of "one commission, one bank, two committees" was established, enhancing financial risk management and achieving the goal of the financial sector returning to serve the real economy.

To align with the strengthening central banking functions of PBOC, the changes in organizational structure, and the increasingly diverse needs of the socio-economic landscape, PBOC has placed significant emphasis on the training of financial talents and the development of its cadre team since 1978. In terms of talent development, PBOC has not only established numerous higher education institutions dedicated to cultivating financial talents but has also continuously increased the proportion of undergraduate, master's, and doctoral talents. Concerning the cadre team, in 2008, PBOC introduced the concept of a cadre team with "five types": learning-oriented, research-oriented, expert-oriented, pragmatic, and innovative. It set the goal of "creating a learning organization and fostering a workforce with knowledge-based skills." This significantly advanced the construction of the personnel system for financial talents, promoting the development of employees' macro awareness, global perspective, and research capabilities. In May 2010, PBOC convened a special talent work conference, deploying the "talent-driven" strategy and accelerating the development of the "five-type" cadre and talent team goals at PBOC. In January 2011, PBOC, together with CBRC, CIRC, and China Securities Regulatory Commission (CSRC), jointly issued the "Medium and Long-Term Plan for the Development of Financial

Talents (2010—2020)." This plan outlined the strategic goals for the development of financial talents over the next decade. Examining the profiles of previous PBOC governors, the transition to an "expert" type of talent has been achieved, as indicated in Table 6.1.

Table 6.1 Introduction to the governors of PBOC since the reform and opening-up

Name	Tenure	Educational background	Key experiences before assuming the position of Governor of the People's Bank of China
LI Baohua	1978–1982	College diploma	Deputy Minister of Water Resources
LV Peijian	1982–1985	College diploma	Deputy Minister of Finance, Deputy Secretary of the Party Group
CHEN Muhua	1985–1988	High school	State Councilor, Minister of the Ministry of Foreign Economic and Trade
LI Guixian	1988–1993	Bachelor's degree	Secretary of the Liaoning Provincial Committee, Secretary of the Anhui Provincial Committee
ZHU Rongji	1993–1995	Bachelor's degree	Deputy Director of the National Development and Reform Commission, Mayor of Shanghai, Vice Premier of the State Council
DAI Xianglong	1995–2002	Bachelor's degree	Vice President of Agricultural Bank of China, General Manager and Deputy Chairman of China Merchants Bank, Chairman of China Pacific Insurance Company, Vice President of PBOC
ZHOU Xiaochuan	2002–2018	Doctorate (Ph.D.)	Director of the State Administration of Foreign Exchange, Vice President of PBOC, President of China Construction Bank, Chairman of the China Securities Regulatory Commission
YI Gang	Since 2018	Doctorate (Ph.D.)	Professor at Peking University, Director and Party Secretary of the State Administration of Foreign Exchange, Deputy Secretary of the Party Committee and Vice President of PBOC

To more effectively leverage the overall efficiency of monetary and credit policies with other economic measures, PBOC has endeavored to enhance scientific decision-making and execution capabilities, continually elevating the efficiency and standards of financial services. In 2013, with the rise of internet finance, PBOC initiated comprehensive research efforts, strengthening collaboration with CBRC, CSRC, and CIRC. It formulated and implemented numerous measures aimed at guiding and regulating financial innovation, ensuring the stable development of the financial sector.

Through long-term enhancements and adjustments in the central banking functions, as well as improvements in organizational structures, PBOC, as a modern central bank, has solidified its institutional framework. It has established macroeconomic regulatory functions at the core of the "regulating market" with the key roles of being the "national bank," the "bank for banks," and the "currency issuer." This represents a complete departure from the highly centralized financial management system before the era of economic reform. With the changing landscape of the socio-economic situation, the central banking system of PBOC is expected to undergo further improvements and refinements.

6.2 Evolution of Central Bank Functions

With the independent exercise of the central banking functions by PBOC, the system's formation, development, and maturation have led to continuous adjustments and developments in its central banking functions. To date, its traditional central banking functions have been strengthened, the macroeconomic control system is gradually improving, and significant achievements have been made in international cooperation and the prevention of financial risks.

6.2.1 Adjustments to the Functions of the Central Bank

PBOC, as the central bank of China, has undergone significant changes in its functions from the period of Reform and Opening up to the present. The evolution can be broadly categorized into several adjustment stages.

Before 1978, PBOC engaged in both commercial banking activities and performed central banking functions. Its dual functions, under a highly centralized financial management system, essentially served as the treasury for the government, with "funds management" being its sole function. After the economic reforms, with the gradual formation of a diversified financial system, the function of "managing funds" became inadequate to meet the rapidly developing social economy and the increasingly complex demands of the financial sector. In response, the State Council adapted to the trend of financial development in China and, before 1984, continuously delegated commercial business to re-established or newly established state-owned financial institutions. This way, PBOC significantly strengthened its central banking functions in formulating and executing monetary policy, managing the national treasury, issuing and managing the currency, and supervising the financial industry. However, it still retained some commercial banking functions. It is evident that the undefined positioning of PBOC brought inconvenience to its normal operation and the exertion of its macroeconomic regulatory functions.

From 1984 to 1993, PBOC began to specialize in executing central banking functions, but due to constraints such as the reform of the social and economic system, it remained in a transitional stage toward a modern central banking system. During this period, PBOC significantly strengthened its central banking functions in areas such as formulating and executing monetary policy, preventing financial risks, supervising the financial industry, and issuing and managing the currency. It no longer handled credit transactions for enterprises and individuals but continued to undertake policy loans and provide borrowing and overdraft services for the fiscal department. In financial management, it adhered to the traditional fund allocation method, regulating the total amount and flow of funds and oscillating noticeably between the functions of "managing funds" and "regulating market."

From 1994 to 2002, PBOC moved toward transforming into a modern central bank. Firstly, the bank separated policy-related businesses it used to undertake and assigned them to policy financial institutions such as China Development Bank (CDB), the Export–Import Bank of China (CEXIM), and Agricultural Development Bank of China (ADBC). Simultaneously, it gradually ceased the overdraft and borrowing services for the fiscal department. Secondly, PBOC accelerated the pace of legal and normative construction. The "Law of the People's Republic of China on the People's Bank of China," promulgated in 1995, explicitly positioned the functions of PBOC as formulating and implementing monetary policy and supervising and managing the financial industry, gradually clarifying the system of industry supervision. It outlined specific functions, totaling 11, as shown in Fig. 6.7.

From the composition of these eleven functions, its roles had shifted towards "the country's bank," "the bank's bank," and "the issuer's bank." However, influenced by the mixed operation pattern in the financial sector during this period, PBOC not only

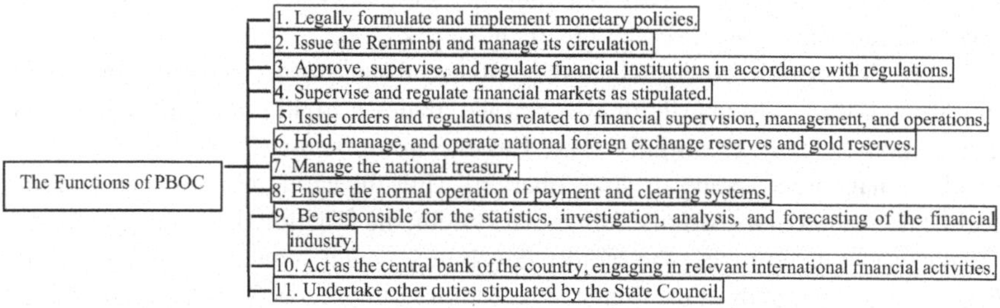

Fig. 6.7 The functions of PBOC (1995)

needed to supervise and manage various financial markets but also had to oversee various financial institutions. This mixed function, coupled with significant overlaps with other financial regulatory bodies like the Central Financial Work Committee, made it challenging to achieve effective supervision, resulting in the dilemma of "chaos when given freedom and stagnation when controlled" in financial supervision during this period.

From 2003 to the present, PBOC has completed the transformation of its functions into that of a modern central bank, and the central banking system has been fully established and formalized. The amended "Law of the People's Republic of China on the People's Bank of China" in 2003 adjusted the functions of PBOC into three aspects: formulating and implementing monetary policy, maintaining financial stability, and providing financial services. Compared to 1995, the functions of PBOC have undergone significant changes. In line with the separation of financial business operations and industry supervision, the regulatory functions of PBOC in the financial industry were delegated to CBRC, CSRC, and CIRC. This highlighted the functions of implementing monetary policy, preventing financial risks, maintaining financial stability, and providing financial services. Accompanying this trend, there have been some changes in the functions of PBOC, as shown in Fig. 6.8.

With the transition to a sectoral regulatory system, PBOC has clearly strengthened the functions of the central bank, reduced unrelated regulatory business, and enhanced functions related to formulating and executing monetary policy and maintaining financial stability. In 2014, the "Deposit Insurance Regulations" were passed, and as of January 1, 2015, it specified that the deposit insurance fund would be deposited with PBOC. The deposit insurance managing funds organization participated in the financial supervision and management coordination mechanism and established an information-sharing mechanism with PBOC and other financial regulatory departments to strengthen the stable development of finance. Subsequently, PBOC has continuously adapted to the needs of social and economic development, strengthening and perfecting the traditional functions of "the country's bank," "the

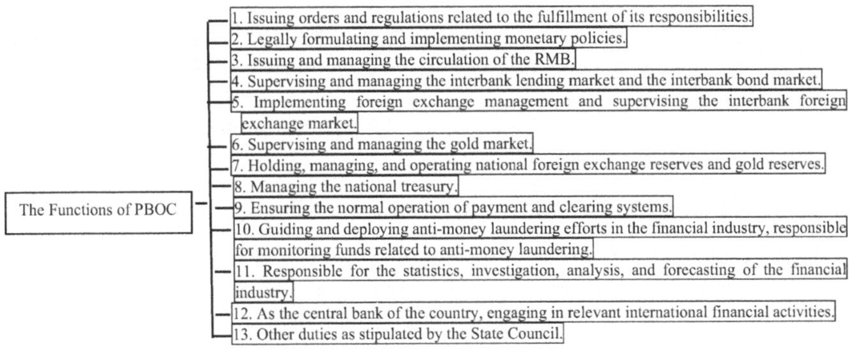

Fig. 6.8 The functions of PBOC (2003)

bank's bank," and "the issuer's bank," with an emphasis on the macroeconomic regulatory function centered around monetary policy. As of June 2019, the functions of PBOC have become more specialized, as shown in Table 6.2.

Clearly, PBOC has fully adhered to the system of sectoral regulation. While strengthening the functions of formulating and executing monetary policy and maintaining financial stability, it has paid more attention to improving financial service functions. With the reform of financial regulatory agencies in 2018, the functions of PBOC are expected to undergo significant adjustments, emphasizing the formulation of financial regulations and the role of monetary policy to meet the goals of preventing financial risks, promoting financial innovation, and serving the development of the real economy.

Looking back on the evolution of the functions of PBOC since the reform and opening-up, its phased changes are entirely consistent with the reform of China's social and economic system and the changing domestic and international economic situation.

6.2.2 Improvement of the Macroeconomic Regulation System

In the process of the phased changes in the functions of PBOC, the objectives of macroeconomic regulation have become more explicit, and the tools of regulation have become more diversified. The focus has increasingly shifted towards achieving the overall goal of promoting socio-economic development on the basis of currency stability, making the role of "regulating market" more apparent. This has, in turn, laid the necessary groundwork for the sustained, stable, and rapid development of China's economy since the reform and opening-up.

A. Changes in Monetary Policy Objectives

Before Reform and Opening-up, China's monetary policy aimed to use credit, interest rates, and administrative measures to maintain the comprehensive balance between fiscal revenue and expenditure, commodity production and sales, and bank credit. The goal was to achieve economic development and price stability. Since Reform and Opening-up, after multiple changes in practice, the monetary policy objectives gradually clarified to focus on "maintaining the stability of the currency value and promoting economic growth based on this."

(a) Changes in the Ultimate Objective of Monetary Policy

At the beginning of Reform and Opening-up, PBOC had not yet separated from its dual functions. At that time, monetary policy was still influenced by historical inertia, with the ultimate goal being economic development and price stability. Subsequently, as the diversified financial organizational system gradually took shape, the ultimate goal of monetary policy formulated by PBOC gradually moved away from the original dual functional system of "funds management," as shown in Table 6.3.

Table 6.2 The functions of PBOC (June 2019)

The main functions of PBOC	Formulating strategies and plans for the reform and development of the financial industry, undertaking comprehensive research, and coordinating the resolution of significant issues in financial operations. Bearing the responsibility to promote the coordinated and healthy development of the financial industry, participating in the assessment of the impact of major financial mergers and acquisitions on national financial security, and providing policy recommendations. Facilitating the orderly opening-up of the financial industry
	Drafting relevant laws and administrative regulations, refining operational rules for financial institutions, and issuing and implementing orders and regulations related to its responsibilities
	Legally formulating and implementing monetary policies, as well as developing and implementing macro-prudential guidance policies
	Improving the financial macro-control system, being responsible for preventing and resolving systemic financial risks, and maintaining the stability and security of the national financial system
	Responsible for formulating and implementing RMB exchange rate policies, continuously improving the exchange rate formation mechanism, maintaining international balance of payments, implementing foreign exchange management, monitoring and issuing risk warnings for the international financial market, monitoring and managing cross-border capital flows, holding, managing, and operating national foreign exchange reserves, as well as gold reserves
	Supervising and managing the interbank lending market, interbank bond market, interbank bill market, interbank foreign exchange market, gold market, and related derivative transactions in the aforementioned markets
The main functions of PBOC	Responsible for collaborating with financial regulatory authorities to formulate regulatory rules for financial holding companies and standards and norms for cross-sector financial businesses. Also responsible for monitoring financial holding companies and cross-sector financial instruments
	Undertaking the responsibility of the ultimate lender, responsible for inspecting and supervising the actions of financial institutions using central bank funds for resolving financial risks
	Formulating and organizing the implementation of a comprehensive statistical system for the financial industry, responsible for data compilation, macroeconomic analysis and forecasting. Also responsible for the unified compilation of national financial statistics, reports, and their public disclosure in accordance with relevant national regulations
	Organizing the formulation of development plans for the informatization of the financial industry, responsible for organizing, managing, and coordinating financial standardization work, and providing guidance on information security in the financial industry
	Issuing the Renminbi and managing its circulation

(continued)

Table 6.2 (continued)

	Formulating a national payment system development plan, coordinating and overseeing the construction of the national payment system, collaborating with relevant departments to establish payment and settlement rules, and ensuring the normal operation of the national payment and clearing systems
The main functions of PBOC	Manage the national treasury
	Undertaking the responsibility for organizing, coordinating, and supervising the national anti-money laundering efforts, responsible for monitoring funds suspected of money laundering and terrorist activities
	Managing the credit reporting industry and promoting the establishment of a social credit system
	Engaging in international financial activities related to the business of PBOC
	Engaging in financial business activities in accordance with relevant regulations
	Handling other matters assigned by the State Council

Table 6.3 Evolution of China's monetary policy ultimate objectives since the opening-up and reform

Time	Policies	Implications of ultimate objectives
1986	"Provisional Regulations of the People's Republic of China on Banking Supervision"	Promoting economic development, stabilizing currency, and improving economic efficiency
December 1993	"Decision of the State Council on Financial System Reform"	Maintaining the stability of the currency to promote economic growth
March 1995	"The Law of the People's Republic of China on PBOC"	Maintaining the stability of the currency value to promote economic growth

In 1986, according to the "Interim Regulations of the People's Republic of China on Banking Management," the ultimate goal of PBOC was defined as "economic development, currency stability, and improved economic efficiency." This multi-target formulation was evidently very rough, and the various goals were filled with contradictions. Soon, the multi-target approach shifted to the dual goals of "currency stability and economic development." This goal lacked sequentially and was difficult to achieve in practice. Thus, by 1993, China explicitly stated in the "State Council's Decision on Financial System Reform" that "maintaining currency stability and promoting economic growth" was the ultimate goal of monetary policy. Subsequently, this goal was confirmed in the "People's Bank of China Law" of 1995 and 2003. From the perspective of this goal composition, it clearly distinguished the relationship between currency stability and economic development, specifying that promoting economic growth is based on the premise of currency stability. This resolved the contradictions between various goals, laying a solid foundation for fully leveraging the role of monetary policy in macroeconomic regulation.

(b) Changes in Intermediate Targets of Monetary Policy

Monetary policy tools, when applied to ultimate goals, often result in a relatively long policy lag. Central banks typically establish intermediate targets to mitigate the impact of lags. In practice, central bank monetary policy intermediate targets fall into two categories: quantity indicators and price indicators. Quantity indicators mainly include money supply, base money, reserve requirements, credit scale, etc., while price indicators include interest rates, exchange rates, etc.

Before 1978, the intermediate target of PBOC's monetary policy was to achieve currency stability through the balance of finance, credit, and material in the overall national economic plan. Clearly, the balance between fiscal revenue and expenditure, material production and sales, and bank credit played the role of intermediate targets for currency stability and economic development. The functions of PBOC were essentially to "adhere to the plan and control the outlets," artificially controlling the transmission of monetary policy, with simple and relatively stable intermediate indicators, resulting in limited effectiveness. From 1978 to 1984, with the establishment of various financial organizations, PBOC began to prioritize the setting of intermediate targets for monetary policy, focusing on cash control. After PBOC specialized in performing central bank functions, intermediate targets of monetary policy expanded to include credit scale and cash supply. However, before 1993, the intermediate targets of PBOC's monetary policy were not very clear. At that time, PBOC mainly disclosed its monetary policy through leadership speeches, and the public speculated based on this information to form expectations, promoting the formation and implementation of intermediate targets for monetary policy. In 1993, PBOC began to publicly announce money supply indicators to the society and gradually narrowed the scope of credit scale control, introducing open market operations in foreign exchange. In 1996, PBOC officially adopted money supply as the intermediate target of China's monetary policy. Subsequently, PBOC published the actual growth rates of M0, M1, and M2[15] in mid-month each month, along with monthly financial statistics data such as short-term loans, medium-to-long-term loans, corporate loans, savings deposits, and foreign exchange reserves of financial institutions. However, from a practical perspective, there is a certain degree of disparity between China's announced money supply targets and the actual implementation results, as shown in Table 6.4.

In 1998, as PBOC shifted its monetary policy towards indirect regulation, the corresponding control over the loan scale of state-owned commercial banks was abolished, and the formal planning of base money was established. In terms of intermediate indicators of monetary policy, PBOC no longer considered the volume of

[15] M0 refers to the currency in circulation; M1 is M0 plus demand deposits, bank checks, and other deposits that can be easily converted to cash; M2 is M1 plus the balance of money market mutual funds, savings deposits, and small time deposits.

Table 6.4 Target values and actual values of the annual growth rates for china's money supply M1 and M2 from 1996 to 2006

	Unit %			
Year	M1 annual growth rate		M2 annual growth rate	
	Goals	Actual	Goals	Actual
1996	18	18.9	25	25.3
1997	18	16.5	23	17.3
1998	17	11.9	17	15.3
1999	14	17.7	14.5	14.7
2000	14	16	14	12.3
2001	15.5	12.7	13.5	14.4
2002	13	16.8	13	16.8
2003	16	18.7	16	19.6
2004	17	13.6	17	14.6
2005	15	11.8	15	17.6
2006	14	17.5	16	16.9

Data Source Compiled based on information from relevant years of China Financial Yearbook, Monetary Policy Implementation Reports, and the Statistical Communiqués of the People's Republic of China on National Economic and Social Development

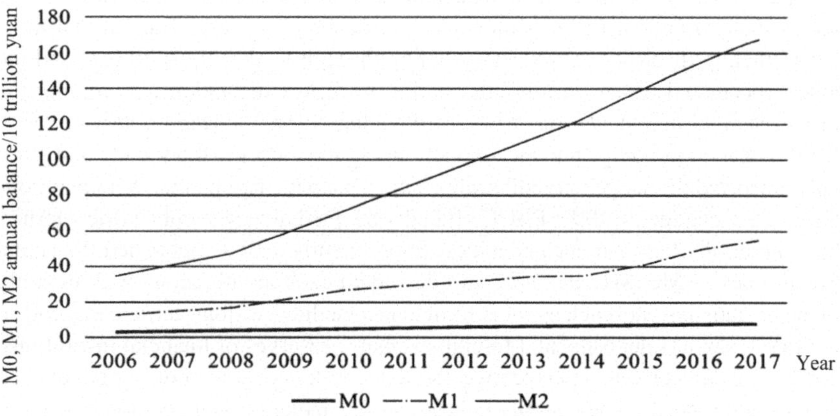

Fig. 6.9 Annual changes in China's M0, M1, and M2 balances since 2006[16]

cash issuance as a control indicator for monetary credit and fully shifted to money supply. The annual balance changes are illustrated in Fig. 6.9.

As of 2017, China's broad money supply increased rapidly, reaching 167.7 trillion yuan, making it the central bank with the largest currency issuance in the world. Since

[16] Compiled based on relevant data from the "Quarterly Monetary Policy Implementation Reports for Each Year Since 2006".

2018, PBOC has continuously adjusted the money supply in response to changes in the domestic and international economic environment. Just in July 2018, PBOC released money supply twice using measures such as targeted reserve requirement reductions in April and June.

Meanwhile, PBOC has also included price indicators such as interest rates and exchange rates in the range of intermediate targets. Although PBOC has occasionally adjusted intermediate targets and indicators based on the needs of monetary policy since then, there has been no fundamental change in its overall intermediate targets. Since 2013, the rise and rapid development of internet finance have, to some extent, changed the practice of using the money supply as an intermediate indicator of monetary policy by PBOC. In the future, interest rates and other indicators are likely to play a more significant role as intermediate indicators.

B. Evolution of Monetary Policy Tools

Since the establishment of the People's Republic of China, the tools employed by PBOC in implementing monetary policy have not remained constant. They have evolved with the development of the socio-economic landscape and the continuous refinement of the central bank's functions, showing an increasing diversity, as illustrated in Table 6.5.

Table 6.5 Evolution of the main monetary policy tools in China since 1949

Time	Monetary policy tools
Before reform and opening up (before 1978)	Credit planning and cash planning Credit policy Interest rate policy Administrative measures
1979–1997	Credit planning and cash planning Refinancing Interest rate policy Reserve requirements Credit policy Rediscounting Open market operations "Window guidance" Special deposits
Since 1998	Refinancing Interest rate policy Reserve requirements Credit policy Rediscounting Open market operations "Window guidance" Special deposits Standing lending facility (established in 2013), etc.

Before 1978, monetary policy tools were extremely simple and gradually simplified due to the constraints of the "managing funds" function. In the early stages of Reform and Opening up, monetary policy tools became more diverse. However, before the financial reforms in 1993, PBOC primarily utilized rediscount and credit quota policies. Subsequently, as financial reforms deepened, in addition to continuing to use existing monetary policy tools, new tools such as rediscounting, open market operations, interest rate policies, "window guidance," standing lending facilities, targeted reserve requirement reductions, and others were gradually introduced.

(a) Reform of Credit Management System

In response to the deepening reforms of the socio-economic system, China's credit management system has undergone multiple changes, as shown in Table 6.6.

Before 1978, in line with the highly centralized planned economic system, PBOC implemented a monetary policy tool of "unified storage, unified lending, unified collection, and unified disbursement." In 1979, in response to the needs of the reform of the socio-economic system, PBOC began to reform the credit management system, fundamentally changing the past practice of purely administrative methods and the nationwide banks sharing resources.

In 1981, PBOC implemented a credit management method nationwide, characterized by "unified planning, hierarchical management, linking deposits with loans, and lump-sum allocation of differences." The "lump-sum allocation of differences" changed the long-standing practice of focusing more on lending than on deposits, motivating banks to actively attract deposits. "However, due to the lack of a reserve requirement system at that time and the difficulty of controlling the derivative effect of deposits within a reasonable range, there was a lack of an effective mechanism

Table 6.6 Evolutionary process of credit management system reform in China

Time	Significance of the reform of credit management system
Before 1978	Unified deposits and unified loans, unified revenue collection and unified expenditure allocation
1979	The reform solely relies on administrative intervention and the nationwide practice of "eating from the same big pot" in the banking sector
1981	Unified planning, hierarchical management, linking of deposits and loans, fixed quotas with balance retained
1985	Unified planning, allocation of funds, real lending and real deposits, mutual interconnection
September 1988	Restore quota management for loans to financial institutions, abolish the practice of "more deposits, more loans" for working capital loans, and concentrate the authority for loan quotas at the head office of PBOC
1994	Asset-liability ratio management and asset risk management system
1998	Planning guidance, comparative management, self-balancing, and indirect regulation

to restrain the total amount of loans, posing challenges to macroeconomic regulation."[17] Subsequently, the credit management system underwent several reforms until 1998 when PBOC abolished the loan quota management for state-owned commercial banks and shifted to indirect credit control measures. Nevertheless, in practice, influenced by the asymmetric impact of money supply during different economic cycles, PBOC did not completely abandon credit control measures. During periods of high inflation and investment growth, PBOC tended to focus more on controlling bank credit.

(b) Open Market Operations

Open market operations are a primary monetary policy tool through which a central bank controls the base money and regulates market liquidity. China's open market operations include operations in the RMB market and the foreign exchange market. Foreign exchange open market operations were formally introduced into the realm of monetary policy tools in March 1994, while RMB open market operations started in 1996. Due to factors such as the small size of the bond market and the unreasonable maturity structure of government bonds, PBOC did not conduct open market operations until 1997. In 1998, PBOC abandoned credit control measures and officially resumed open market operations trading on May 26. The scale gradually expanded. Since 1999, open market operations in China have rapidly developed and, as of December 2018, have become one of the main tools in the daily operations of PBOC's monetary policy. They play an active role in adjusting the liquidity level of the banking system, guiding the trend of money market interest rates, and promoting the reasonable growth of money supply.

In 1998, PBOC began to establish the first-level market-maker system for open market operations. Initially, only 40 deposit-type financial institutions participated. Since then, the ranks of market makers have continued to expand, including banks, securities firms, insurance companies, and other entities in various financial markets. In terms of transaction methods, PBOC's open market operations include repurchase transactions, spot transactions, and the issuance of central bank bills. In terms of transaction types, open market operations involve government bonds, central bank bills, and policy financial bonds. Starting from June 2002, PBOC began conducting reverse repurchase operations in the open market to stabilize the growth rate of the base money. In September of the same year, constrained by insufficient bonds, PBOC converted outstanding reverse repurchase varieties into central bank bills. In January 2013, PBOC introduced "short-term liquidity adjustment tools" (SLO) as a necessary supplementary tool for regular open market operations. Of course, according to the needs of China's monetary control and financial environment, PBOC continuously innovates open market operations, such as issuing forward central bank bills and targeted bills, to enhance the efficiency and effectiveness of open market operations in monetary policy. While open market operations were introduced relatively late as a monetary policy tool in China, they have become one of the important tools in

[17] People's Bank of China. *Sixty Years of the People's Bank of China (1948–2008)*, China Finance Publishing House, 2008: 63.

China's monetary policy, playing an increasingly significant role in macroeconomic regulation.

(c) Reserve Requirement System

Reserve requirements refer to the funds that financial institutions set aside to ensure the withdrawal of deposits and fund clearing. The ratio of the reserve required by financial institutions to their total deposits is called the statutory reserve ratio. Before the establishment of the People's Republic of China, reserve requirements were dispersed among different banks, such as the Bank of China and Bank of Communications. After 1949, under the highly centralized financial management system, all funds were collected by PBOC, and there was no such thing as a reserve requirement. Since Reform and Opening up, the variety of banking institutions has increased, and China's reserve requirement system was established in 1984. At that time, reserve ratios varied by deposit type: 25% for rural deposits, 40% for savings deposits, and 20% for enterprise deposits. In 1985, PBOC unified the reserve requirement ratio to 10%. Over the next two years, PBOC raised the reserve requirement ratio to 12% and 13%, respectively, to suppress excessively high inflation rates. In 1998, PBOC conducted a major reform of the reserve requirement system. The reforms included seven main points: (1) merging "reserve deposit" and "prepaid deposit"[18] accounts into a unified "reserve deposit" account; (2) lowering the statutory reserve ratio from 13 to 8%, with excess reserves to be determined by each bank; (3) assessing statutory reserve requirements uniformly on legal entities of various financial institutions; (4) assessing statutory reserve requirements as ten days; (5) depositing the statutory reserve requirement of 8% of the previous ten days ending general deposit balance with PBOC and imposing penalty interest on any shortfall at a daily rate of 0.006%; (6) setting the deposit interest rate for reserves held by PBOC at 5.22%; and (7) adjusting the scope of general deposits of financial institutions. During this period, China implemented a point-in-time method to assess the reserve requirement of financial institutions, requiring the reserve requirement to be met daily based on statutory requirements. Specifically, reserve requirements were deposited with PBOC on the 5th, 15th, and 25th of each month, and banks were subject to the principle of excess withdrawal and shortfall replenishment based on the month-end, 10th, and 25th deposit bases. On April 25, 2004, PBOC implemented a differential reserve requirement ratio system, linking the reserve requirement ratio to various indicators such as the capital adequacy ratio and asset quality of different financial institutions. This aimed to encourage and promote the healthy and sustained development of financial institutions. On September 15, 2015, PBOC reformed the reserve requirement assessment system, changing from a point-in-time method to an average method. Under the average method, during the maintenance period, the arithmetic average ratio of reserve deposits to statutory reserve assessment bases

[18] Deposit reserve is the funds set aside by financial institutions to restrict credit expansion, ensure customer withdrawals, and meet the clearing needs of funds. Reserve fund refers to the amount of funds that commercial banks, in addition to the statutory reserve deposited with the central bank based on a certain percentage of their deposits, need to store in the central bank to meet the requirements for daily business transactions, commonly known as excess reserves.

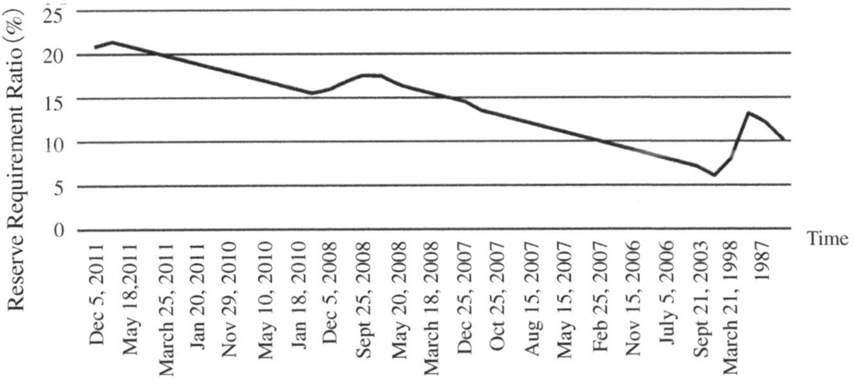

Fig. 6.10 Chart of changes in reserve requirement ratio from 1985 to March 25, 2011

must not be lower than the statutory reserve ratio. Since July 15, 2016, the assessment base for the RMB reserve requirement has been adjusted from the end-of-period general deposit balance to the arithmetic average of the end-of-day general deposit balance during the assessment period. This adjustment aims to enhance the flexibility of liquidity management for financial institutions and smooth out fluctuations in the money market.

Following the comprehensive reform in 1998, the reserve requirement system has become one of the frequently used tools in the monetary policy arsenal of China's central bank. The changes in the reserve requirement ratio from 1985 to March 25, 2011, are illustrated in Fig. 6.10.

In the first six months of 2011, the reserve requirement ratio was increased once every month, reaching 21.50% by June. Starting from November 30, 2011, the reserve requirement ratio began to enter a downward trend, and by February 29, 2016, it had been lowered nine times, reaching 16.50%. This highlights the significance of the reserve requirement system in China's monetary policy toolkit. Subsequently, PBOC expanded and optimized this system, introducing the targeted reserve requirement policy, allowing for the implementation of targeted reserve requirement policies on commercial banks that meet specific criteria for a particular purpose. In 2014, the targeted reserve requirement policy was launched, implemented three times in April and June 2014, and once in June 2015. On September 30, 2017, PBOC implemented targeted reserve requirement policies for commercial banks meeting the criteria to support the State Council's goal of promoting inclusive finance. In March, April, June, and October 2018, targeted reserve requirements were implemented four times, and in January, May, and September 2019, additional targeted reserve requirement measures were adopted. The changes in the reserve requirement system have significantly enhanced PBOC's control over monetary policy, allowing for more precise implementation of corresponding monetary policy measures to achieve specific macroeconomic goals.

(d) Refinance

Refinance is PBOC's provision of loans to financial institutions, and it used to be one of the most important channels for the PBOC to regulate the basic money supply. The PBOC adjusts the amount and interest rates of rediscounting timely, regulates the basic money supply, achieves the goal of controlling the overall volume of monetary credit, and reasonably guides the flow of funds and credit direction. Since PBOC assumed the specific functions of a central bank in 1984, rediscounting has become a crucial monetary policy tool. Before 1994, the PBOC primarily achieved the expansion or contraction of monetary policy goals by directly increasing or decreasing rediscounts for commercial banks. After the reform of the foreign exchange management system in 1994, due to constraints on the composition of the base currency put into circulation by the foreign exchange deposit channel, the PBOC's ability to regulate the base currency through adjustments in rediscounting became weaker. In this context, the PBOC supplemented the diminishing function of rediscounting in regulating the base currency by introducing tools such as issuing central bank bills and adjusting reserve requirements, while refinance measures were increasingly used to maintain financial stability.

On March 25, 2004, the PBOC implemented the floating interest rate system for refinancing within the authorized scope of the State Council. This system allowed the PBOC to determine and publicly announce the extent to which it would add interest rates to the benchmark rediscount rate based on the macroeconomic and financial situation. The introduction of this system clarified the interest rate relationship between the central bank and borrowers, enhancing the PBOC's ability to guide market interest rates. Subsequently, the role of refinance in maintaining financial stability became more prominent. The PBOC could provide liquidity support to financial institutions through refinance, and at the same time, express its approach to the operation of the financial market.

(e) Rediscounting

Rediscounting is the practice whereby a central bank discounts commercial bills held by financial institutions before their maturity, addressing issues related to insufficient reserves and poor liquidity in banking institutions. Rediscounting serves as a vital monetary policy tool for central banks, playing a significant role in refining the transmission mechanism of monetary policy, facilitating adjustments in credit structures, guiding the expansion of financing for small and medium-sized enterprises, and promoting the development of the bill market. To some extent, it embodies the central bank's role as the lender of last resort. In 1986, PBOCintroduced the "Trial Measures of Rediscounting of the People's Bank of China," initiating a pilot program for rediscounting operations in ten cities, including Beijing, Tianjin, and Shanghai. By the end of 1995, the PBOC standardized rediscounting operations, incorporating rediscounting as a crucial component of the monetary policy toolkit. The focus shifted towards using rediscounting to transmit signals of monetary policy, leveraging the "announcement effect" to convey the central bank's policy intentions and influence the expectations of banks and the public. In 1998, the PBOC formulated a series of policies to enhance the management of commercial bills and rediscounting. Reforms in the rediscount and discount rate generation mechanism made the rediscount rate an independent benchmark rate for the central bank, preparing the conditions for the rediscount rate to effectively signal monetary policy. In 2008, the PBOC further refined rediscounting management by appropriately increasing the rediscount transfer authorization window, facilitating financial institutions, especially local small and medium-sized financial institutions, to apply for and handle rediscounting. The scope of eligible institutions for rediscounting was expanded to include rural credit cooperatives, deposit-taking foreign financial institutions, deposit-taking new-type rural financial institutions, and non-banking financial institutions such as corporate group financial companies. The use of commercial acceptance bills was broadened to promote the securitization of commercial credit. The PBOC explicitly identified key financial institutions supported by rediscounting, giving priority to the rediscounting of bills related to agriculture, county-level enterprises, and small and medium-sized financial institutions. Furthermore, it clarified that rediscounting could be conducted through repurchase agreements and outright purchases, enhancing operational efficiency.

(f) Special Deposits

Special deposits refer to a specific method employed by central banks to channel a certain amount of funds in a concentrated manner to financial institutions based on the credit fund situation, cash conditions, and fund scheduling needs. As a crucial tool in the central bank's monetary policy toolkit, PBOC utilized special deposits in 1987 and 1988 by providing 50 billion yuan each to Rural Credit Cooperatives (RCC) and the Guangdong Branch of the PBOC. This initiative aimed to adjust the credit structure. On December 27, 2007, the PBOC once again introduced special deposits to financial institutions such as Rural Credit Cooperatives and urban commercial banks, with terms of 3 months and 1 year and annual interest rates of 3.37% and 3.99%, respectively. Through special deposits, the PBOC significantly strengthened the functionality of monetary policy tools for withdrawing liquidity, allowing for more flexible coordination with its open market operations.

(g) Window Guidance

Window guidance refers to a monetary policy tool used by PBOC to influence the lending behavior of commercial banks through advice and recommendations based on industrial policies, financial conditions, and trends in the financial market. As an optional instrument in monetary policy, window guidance is a suggestive and guiding measure. In 1987, the PBOC established a relatively stable system of joint meetings and consultations with state-owned specialized banks. During these meetings, state-owned specialized banks reported their current credit progress to the central bank, while the PBOC shared its views on the economic and financial situation and communicated the intentions of monetary policy to improve the management of credit business and adjust credit allocation.

Although window guidance lacks legal effect, financial institutions typically accept these suggestions or recommendations. Window guidance has become an effective means for timely communication between the central bank and financial institutions, facilitating the implementation of monetary policy. Since 1998, with the transition of the PBOC's monetary policy operations from direct to indirect control, window guidance has become an important tool for transmitting monetary policy. In 2003, the PBOC implemented strict window guidance on commercial bank loans to regulate their loan structure and quantity. In 2004, the PBOC continued selectively advancing window guidance based on industry characteristics. In 2010, the PBOC strengthened window guidance to financial institutions, guiding them to balance the pace of credit expansion, improve credit management systems, and fully leverage the positive impact of credit policy on the national economy. Subsequently, the PBOC has frequently utilized window guidance measures to regulate the flow of credit funds and stock market volatility based on financial institutions' credit structure, stock market fluctuations, and socio-economic conditions, clarifying the central bank's intentions regarding monetary policy and achieving the goals of monetary policy regulation.

(h) Standing Lending Facility

The Standing Lending Facility is an innovative and important monetary policy tool developed by PBOC in recent years. Its primary purpose is to enhance the effectiveness of monetary policy regulation, effectively guard against liquidity risks in the banking system, and strengthen the efficiency of controlling money market interest rates. Objectively, continuous innovation and improvement of liquidity supply and control mechanisms are needed to enhance the ability to cope with short-term liquidity fluctuations, providing necessary liquidity support to maintain and guarantee the normal operation of the financial system. Taking cues from international practices, the PBOC established the Standing Lending Facility at the beginning of 2013. Upon its establishment, it became one of the normal channels for the PBOC to supply liquidity, meeting the longer-term and large-scale liquidity needs of financial institutions. The main targets for the Standing Lending Facility are policy banks and nationwide commercial banks, with a maturity period of 1 to 3 months. The interest rate level is determined based on comprehensive factors such as monetary policy regulation and the need to guide market interest rates. The Standing Lending Facility is typically provided through collateral, with eligible collateral including high credit-rated bond assets and high-quality credit assets. On February 11, 2015, the PBOC announced the nationwide promotion of the Standing Lending Facility to branch institutions, providing short-term liquidity support to eligible small and medium-sized financial institutions. As the goals of the PBOC's monetary policy regulation change, the Standing Lending Facility has evolved into a diversified regulatory tool, consisting of long-term, medium-term, and short-term components, to meet the needs of macroeconomic regulation and promote sustainable social and economic development.

6.2.3 Actively Utilizing Monetary Policy to Address Socioeconomic Fluctuations

The macroeconomic regulation and control system of PBOC is becoming increasingly sophisticated, and its role in maintaining financial stability has been strengthened. Since 1949, the PBOC has been able to respond appropriately to various financial storms based on domestic and international economic situations, earning high reputation both domestically and internationally.

Before the era of economic reform and opening up, the PBOC's functions were primarily focused on "managing funds." However, during various crises, it effectively cooperated with the central government and the State Council to meet the adjustment needs of the economy, preventing a collapse of the national economy. Since the economic reform and opening up, the PBOC has been proactive in innovating and utilizing monetary policy tools to smoothly resolve various economic crises, as shown in Table 6.7.

Monetary policy generally takes the forms of easing, tightening, or a combination of both. Examining the implementation of China's monetary policy from 1979 to the present, it has been predominantly characterized by easing, with tightening policies applied mainly during periods of inflation.

The periods of monetary policy tightening can be roughly divided into the following:

In 1985, with the advancement of the "delegating power and reducing government control" reforms, there was a surge in social demand, leading to upward pressure on overall prices. To curb inflation, the PBOC implemented tightening measures such as collecting loans, reducing new loans, and lowering the growth of monetary supply, stabilizing the rising price trend.

From 1989 to 1991, to address the rapid increase in prices caused by the 1988 price reform, the PBOC prioritized measures to control high prices, aligning with

Table 6.7 The implementation of monetary policy by PBOC since 1979

Time	Monetary policy	Implementation period/year
1979–1984	Easing	6
1985	Tightening	1
1986–1988	Easing	3
1989–1991	Tightening	3
1992-June 1993	Easing	1
July 1993–1997	Tightening	5
1998–2003	Easing	6
First half of 2004–2008	Slightly tight neutral	4
Second half of 2008–2010	Moderately loose	3
2011–2019	Prudent	8

the central government's "rectification and governance" policy. Through tightening monetary policy, the economy quickly returned to normal development.

From July 1993 to 1997, faced with an overheated economy and persistently high prices, the PBOC implemented strict measures of tightening monetary policy, including controlling the scale of credit, significantly raising deposit and loan interest rates, and rectifying financial order. These measures tightened the money supply, enabling a smooth landing of the macroeconomy, overcoming the overheating situation, and achieving a soft landing of economic development.

In the first half of 2004 to 2008, targeting localized economic overheating and rising prices, the PBOC adopted differential reserve requirement policies for financial institutions and moderately lowered the target for monetary supply, thereby suppressing the rapid rise in prices.

During periods of easing monetary policy, notable events include the 1997 Asian financial crisis and the subprime crisis since 2007. During the Asian financial crisis, China's economy quickly entered a period of slow growth, with insufficient effective demand and deflation becoming the main trends since 1998. Against this backdrop, PBOC swiftly adopted a loose monetary policy, lifting the earlier measures controlling loan quotas, enhancing the autonomy of financial institutions in lending, reducing the statutory deposit reserve ratio four times, and beginning in 1997, lowering deposit and loan interest rates for eight consecutive times. Additionally, there was an increased emphasis on open market operations, with timely adjustments to operational directions, fully leveraging the guiding role of credit policies and window guidance. Simultaneously, the Chinese government made it clear to the international community its determination to maintain the stability of the RMB exchange rate, supporting crisis-ridden countries and preventing adverse impacts of the crisis on China's socio-economic conditions. The drawbacks of RMB depreciation outweigh the benefits. Chinese citizens are most concerned about currency depreciation and rising prices. RMB depreciation sends a signal to the public that the Chinese economy is in trouble. Moreover, it can lead to another round of currency depreciation in Southeast Asian countries, particularly impacting the Hong Kong region, causing chaos in financial markets.[19] To address this, the Chinese government implemented a stable exchange rate policy, proactively narrowing the fluctuation range of the RMB exchange rate, and adopting various effective measures to encourage exports and attract foreign investment. In the environment of a loose monetary policy, China quickly overcame the adverse effects of the crisis, successfully maintaining rapid economic growth and securing victory in the defense of the Hong Kong exchange rate.

Since the outbreak of the subprime crisis in 2007, the financial crisis has had a significant impact on China's economy. The export sector suffered severe consequences, overall economic development faced downward pressure, prices shifted from rising to falling, the real estate market remained persistently sluggish, and the

[19] Zhu Mingji. *Speech Records of Zhu Mingji (Volume 3)*, People's Publishing House, 2011: 137–138.

investment growth rate experienced a substantial decline. In response to this situation, PBOC swiftly transitioned from a moderately tight monetary policy to an actively loose one. Starting from October 9, 2008, the PBOC repeatedly lowered the reserve requirement ratio, reduced deposit and loan interest rates, increased the money supply, and expanded the lending scale of financial institutions. "By the end of August 2009, China's money supply had grown by 28.53%, an increase of 10.71 percentage points higher than the end of 2008. Narrow money supply also grew by 27.72%. The growth in the scale of loans was particularly remarkable, with various RMB loans increasing by 8.15 trillion yuan from January to August, a year-on-year increase of 5.04 trillion yuan."[20] Simultaneously, the Chinese government actively responded to international calls, proactively participating in crisis response actions. On one hand, China continuously increased the capital of the International Monetary Fund (IMF), providing emergency funds to the IMF. On the other hand, it effectively addressed requests for financial assistance from the international community, signing eight bilateral currency swap agreements totaling 803.5 billion RMB.[21] Additionally, China actively participated in platforms such as the G20, collaborating with other countries to collectively address the impact of the crisis. Through quantitative easing measures, China quickly recovered from the crisis, making significant contributions to global economic development.

Since 2013, with the rapid rise of internet finance and the shift to a new economic normal, various risks in China's social and economic sectors have gradually surfaced. To avoid regional and systemic financial risks, PBOC, in collaboration with the China Banking Regulatory Commission (CBRC), the China Securities Regulatory Commission (CSRC), and other regulatory bodies, jointly issued the "Guidance on Promoting the Healthy Development of Internet Finance" in July 2015. Subsequently, various regulatory rules in different areas of internet finance were introduced by different regulatory bodies, transforming the previous state of "no entry barriers, no industry standards, and no regulatory rules" in internet finance development. On April 25, 2017, during the 40th collective study session on safeguarding national financial security, Chinese President Xi Jinping emphasized that financial security is an important component of national security and a fundamental basis for stable and healthy economic development. Maintaining financial security is a strategic and fundamental matter related to the overall development of China's economy and society. In this session, President Xi Jinping proposed six measures to strengthen financial stability, providing strong guidance for PBOC to enhance financial supervision and actively use monetary policy to address social and economic crises and prudently handle financial risks. In the 5th National Financial Work Conference held in July 2017 and the 19th National Congress of the Communist Party of China held in October 2017, it was explicitly stated that preventing systemic financial risks would be the bottom line of future financial regulation. In 2018, preventing financial risks became

[20] Li Yang, et al. *60 Years of China's Finance*, China Financial and Economic Publishing House, 2009: 426.

[21] Li De. *Development Process of China's Financial Industry (Volume 2)*, People's Publishing House, 2015: 443.

the main theme of macroeconomic regulation, playing a role in deleveraging the financial sector and serving the real economy. In 2019, preventing risks continued to be one of the government's three major key tasks, with the takeover of Baoshang Bank, a high-risk financial institution, aimed at preventing the spread of risks.

6.2.4 Enhance International Cooperation

While strengthening macroeconomic regulation and maintaining financial stability, PBOC actively enhances cooperation with international and regional financial organizations, as well as central banks of various countries. This is aimed at promoting the improvement of the functions of China's central bank and enhancing the internationalization, influence, and discourse power of China's finance.

A. Joining International and Regional Financial Organizations

Since the reform and opening-up, PBOC has sought to join international and regional financial organizations. At that time, PBOC aimed to restore China's legitimate seats in the International Monetary Fund (IMF) and the World Bank, gradually joining other international financial organizations. This served as a starting point for China's participation in international financial affairs, expressing China's stance in international financial affairs and reflecting the desire of China to participate in international financial cooperation and fulfill international obligations. In early 1980, PBOC, on behalf of China, invited the head of the International Monetary Fund (IMF) to visit China. On March 25, a delegation led by Dunxin from the Asia department of the IMF came to Beijing to negotiate the issue of restoring China's legitimate seat in the IMF. On April 4, 1980, a memorandum was signed between the Chinese side, represented by Wang Weicai, Vice President of the Bank of China and Deputy Director of State Administration of Foreign Exchange, and the head of the delegation, Dunxin. On April 17, 1980, the International Monetary Fund restored the legitimate seat of the People's Republic of China in the organization. On May 15, 1980, the World Bank's board of directors approved the resolution to restore China's legitimate seat in the World Bank. Subsequently, China joined other financial organizations such as the International Development Association (IDA) and the International Financial Corporation (IFC), as shown in Table 6.8.

While joining international financial organizations, China has actively participated in regional financial organizations. In May 1985, China joined ADB, actively participated in the bank's operational activities and decision-making, and strengthened exchanges and cooperation with it. On February 17, 1986, after several rounds of negotiations and discussions with the Asian Development Bank since 1983, China officially became a member of the Asian Development Bank. Subsequently, China successively joined other regional financial organizations, as well as central bank organizations with permanent offices in the Asia–Pacific region. China played an active role in these organizations, further expanding its influence in international and regional financial institutions.

Table 6.8 China's return to or participation in international and regional financial organizations since 1949

Financial organizations	Names of financial organizations	Joining date
International financial organizations	International Monetary Fund (IMF)	April 17, 1980
	The World Bank	May 15, 1980
	Bank for International Settlements	September 9, 1996
	The International Development Association	May 1980
	International Finance Corporation	May 1980
	Basel Committee on Banking Supervision	March 16, 2009
	Financial Stability Board	April 2, 2009
Regional financial organizations	Asian Development Bank	February 17, 1986
	African Development Bank	May 1985
	Organization of the East Asia and Pacific Conference of Central Bank Governors	1992
	Asia-Europe Finance Ministers' Meeting	September 1997
	G20	September 1999
	Southeast African Trade and Development Bank	August 2000
	APEC Finance Ministers' Meeting	October 2001
	West African Development Bank	November 2004
	Islamic Financial Services Board	Became an observer country in the organization in 2004
	Caribbean Development Bank	January 1998
	Inter-American Development Bank	October 2008
	Association of Southeast Asian Nations Central Banks	January 25, 2011
	Organization of Central Banks of Central Asia, Black Sea Region and Balkan Countries	April 2011
	European Bank for Reconstruction and Development	January 15, 2016

(continued)

Table 6.8 (continued)

Financial organizations	Names of financial organizations	Joining date
	SEANZA (South East Asia, New Zealand, and Australia) Central Banks	1987
	"Six-Party Market" Conference with China, the United States, Japan, Australia, Singapore, and Hong Kong	2008
	"Six-Party Governors" Conference with China, Japan, Australia, Malaysia, Thailand, and Hong Kong	2008

B. Strengthening Cooperation with Central Banks of Other Countries

Since Reform and Opening-up, PBOC has intensified its connections and cooperation with central banks of other countries. As of now, PBOC has established close bilateral relations with the central banks of developed countries such as the United States, the United Kingdom, Germany, Japan, Italy, Canada, Australia, and others. It has also developed stable bilateral communication mechanisms with BRICS like Russia, India, South Africa, Brazil, emerging economies like South Korea and Singapore, as well as the central banks of many Asian, African, and Latin American developing countries. By May 2017, PBOC had signed a series of agreements related to investment and more with central banks of over 40 countries or regions, including Venezuela, India, Russia, The Czech Republic, among others. These agreements aimed at consolidating and developing cooperation, strengthening exchanges in financial information, technology, and other aspects. Following the subprime mortgage crisis, PBOC actively collaborated with central banks of other countries to address international financial storms. By early 2019, PBOC had signed bilateral currency swap agreements with central banks from 37 countries or regions, as shown in Table 6.9.

The currency swap agreements signed between PBOC and the mentioned countries or regions have a standard duration of three years, and in most cases, renewal agreements are signed after the expiration. For example, PBOC and the European Central Bank extended their agreement on September 27, 2016, extending the term to September 2019.

PBOC has established representative offices in various regions, including London, New York, Tokyo, Frankfurt, Sydney, etc. These offices are set up to strengthen communication between PBOC and central banks in those regions. The goal is to deepen cooperation in areas such as market research, talent training, cross-border regulation, and foreign exchange fund operations. Additionally, central banks from eight countries or regions, including South Korea, Japan, North Korea, Norway, and Russia, have also set up representative offices in Beijing or Shanghai. This aims

Table 6.9 The first bilateral currency swap agreements signed by PBOC with central banks of other countries (regions)

Signing date	Countries (regions)	Amount/billion Yuan
March 11, 2009	Belarus	200
March 23, 2009	Indonesia	1000
April 2, 2009	Argentina	700
June 9, 2010	Iceland	35
April 18, 2011	New Zealand	250
April 19, 2011	Uzbekistan	7
June 13, 2011	Kazakhstan	70
October 26, 2011	South Korea	3600
November 22, 2011	Hong Kong, China	4000
December 22, 2011	Thailand	700
December 23, 2011	Pakistan	100
January 17, 2012	United Arab Emirates	350
February 8, 2012	Malaysia	1800
February 21, 2012	Turkey	100
March 20, 2012	Mongolia	100
March 22, 2012	Australia	2000
June 26, 2012	Ukraine	150
March 7, 2013	Singapore	3000
March 26, 2013	Brazil	1900
June 22, 2013	United Kingdom	2000
September 9, 2013	Hungary	100
September 12, 2013	Albania	20
October 10, 2013	European Central Bank	3500
July 21, 2014	Switzerland	1500
September 16, 2014	Sri Lanka	100
October 13, 2014	Russia	1500
November 8, 2014	Canada	2000
March 18, 2015	Suriname	10
March 25, 2015	Armenia	10
April 10, 2015	South Africa	300
May 10, 2015	Belarus	70
May 25, 2015	Chile	220
September 3, 2015	Tajikistan	30
May 11, 2016	Morocco	100
June 17, 2016	Serbia	15
December 6, 2016	Egypt	180
April 27, 2018	Nigeria	150

to enhance cooperation with PBOC, facilitating further development in bilateral financial cooperation and economic and trade relations.

C. Expanding International Financial Cooperation

Since the reform and opening-up, PBOC has actively pursued international cooperation in the field of finance. Firstly, it has endeavored to gain support from international or regional financial organizations and institutions, aiming to expand China's international financing channels. After regaining legitimate seats in international financial organizations such as the International Monetary Fund (IMF) and the World Bank, PBOC has strived to secure various concessional funds from these organizations to support domestic economic development. To date, China has received multiple rounds of financial assistance from the IMF. In 1981, China borrowed 450 million Special Drawing Rights (SDRs), approximately $550 million, through the IMF's standby arrangement and 310 million SDRs, approximately $380 million, from the trust fund to offset the then international balance of payments deficit. In 1986, China again borrowed 5.98 billion SDRs, approximately $730 million, from the IMF's standby arrangement to promote China's socio-economic development, and these funds have been fully repaid.[22] As a developing country, China has also obtained significant low-interest concessional loans from the World Bank, totaling approximately $65 billion as of June 30, 2019. Additionally, China has received various concessional loans from regional financial organizations such as the Asian Development Bank. Throughout the process of seeking various forms of financial support, PBOC has also imported advanced technology and management experience from these international or regional financial organizations to enhance the development of China's financial industry.

Secondly, it has drawn on the advanced experiences of foreign central banks to improve the institutional construction of PBOC. PBOC has dispatched personnel to international financial organizations such as the IMF, the World Bank, and central banks of other countries for exchanges on topics like monetary policy, economic hotspots, talent cultivation, institutional construction, and financial supervision. This extensive and systematic discussion aims to enhance the construction of China's central bank system. In terms of financial supervision, China has adopted standards set by the Basel Committee on Banking Supervision. In financial statistics and other areas, China has also adopted various advanced methods and standards internationally. For example, PBOC has formally adopted the Special Data Dissemination Standard (SDDS) established by the IMF. China fully complies with all procedures under SDDS and publishes relevant statistical data in accordance with SDDS standards.

Thirdly, PBOC actively participates in or hosts various international or regional financial conferences during its involvement in various financial organizations. After restoring seats in international financial organizations such as the IMF and the World Bank, PBOC has almost participated in all their activities. Moreover, China has participated in or hosted various meetings of financial organizations such as the G20

[22] People's Bank of China. *Sixty Years of the People's Bank of China (1948–2008)*, China Finance Publishing House, 2008: 80.

summit and the African Development Bank. In May 1989, the 22nd Annual Meeting of the Asian Development Bank was held in Beijing; in November 1997, the 3rd East Asia and Pacific Central Bank Governors' Meeting was hosted in Shanghai; in the same year, the 52nd Annual Meetings of the IMF and World Bank were held in Hong Kong; in May 2007, the African Development Bank Group's Board of Governors' Annual Meetings were hosted by Shanghai; from May 14 to 16, 2015, the 33rd Meeting of the Governors of Central Banks of the Central Asia, Black Sea, and Balkan Regions was hosted by PBOC in Shanghai; on September 13, 2016, China hosted the G20 summit in Hangzhou, and so on. These meetings have significantly enhanced China's financial position and influence in international finance.

Fourthly, China fulfills international obligations to promote international financial cooperation. While receiving substantial financial support from the international community, China actively provides various types of interest-free loans to regional financial organizations such as the Asian Development Bank, African Development Bank, and Caribbean Development Bank (CDB), based on the level of socio-economic development. Additionally, since the 1990s, China has provided significant funds to IMF to support specific projects. In 1994, PBOC provided a loan of 100 million SDRs to the IMF to support debt adjustment in heavily indebted poor countries, and also donated 12 million SDRs to the interest subsidy account for the loan. In 1997, China, within the framework of the IMF, provided a $1 billion loan to the Thai government. In 1999, China donated 13.13 million SDRs to the IMF to continue supporting debt reduction programs in poor countries. In 2005, the Chinese government actively contributed to the IMF's "Post-Conflict and Natural Disaster Emergency Assistance Interest Subsidy Account" to provide aid to affected countries. After the subprime crisis, China proactively provided necessary financial assistance to various countries worldwide. Since the proposal of the "Belt and Road Initiative" by President Xi Jinping in 2013, China has successively contributed to the establishment of regional financial institutions such as the Silk Road Fund and the Asian Infrastructure Investment Bank (AIIB) in Beijing. This initiative aims to assist countries and regions along the "Belt and Road" in building various infrastructure projects. In May 2017, during the Belt and Road Forum for International Cooperation held in Beijing, China added an additional 100 billion Chinese yuan to the Silk Road Fund, playing a significant role in promoting the advancement of the Belt and Road Initiative.

Additionally, PBOC has actively promoted the "going global" initiative for the country's financial industry, systematically bringing in foreign financial institutions. As of 2018, China has fully liberalized its RMB business. According to IMF classification standards for capital accounts (comprising 7 categories and 40 items), China has achieved convertibility in 37 items, accounting for 92.5% of all transaction items, including fully convertible, basically convertible, and partially convertible categories. In the future, China will continue to accelerate the pace of financial industry opening, following a management model that emphasizes consistency between domestic and foreign practices, pre-entry national treatment, and a negative list approach.

Chapter 7
Reform and Development of the Banking Industry

Since the beginning of the reform and opening-up policy, China's banking industry has largely followed the process of reforming the socialist economic system, adapting to the transition from a planned economy to a market economy, and gradually achieving the goals of banking reform. Following the approach of separating allocation and management of funds, the first step was to separate the Agricultural Bank of China(ABC), Bank of China(BOC), Industrial and Commercial Bank of China from the People's Bank of China(ICBC), and the China Constr7uction Bank(CCB) from the Ministry of Finance. These four state-owned specialized banks underwent commercialization reforms and gradually transformed into four state-owned commercial banks.[1] Since 1998, these four state-owned commercial banks have undergone debt shedding, capital injection, financial integration, corporate restructuring, introduction of strategic investors, and listing, becoming state-owned commercial joint-stock banks with relatively sound governance structures. Subsequently, China successively established 14 joint-stock commercial banks such as the Bank of Communications. After the 1990s, a large number of urban commercial banks were established based on urban credit cooperatives. In 1996, rural credit cooperatives were separated from the Agricultural Bank of China, and their operational management systems gradually became independent legal entities through deepening reforms. Subsequently, village and township banks, microfinance companies, and other entities emerged, further strengthening rural financial capabilities. Meanwhile, foreign banks entered China one after another, completely changing the previously single banking system before the reform and opening-up policy, forming a diversified pattern in the banking industry. With the reform and development of the banking industry, their resource allocation functions are increasingly market-oriented, better meeting the needs of China's increasingly diversified economy.

[1] The following text explains that unless otherwise specified, the term "four state-owned commercial banks" refers to Industrial and Commercial Bank of China (ICBC), China Construction Bank (CCB), Agricultural Bank of China (ABC), and Bank of China (BOC).

R. Lan, *The Financial Development of China*, Understanding China,
https://doi.org/10.1007/978-981-97-8273-4_7

7.1 Recovery, Reform and Development of State-owned Banks

The highly centralized and unified financial system, coupled with long-term operations that accumulated inefficiencies, led to the cost of maintaining the function of "managing funds" in the financial system far exceeding its benefits. Against this backdrop, China gradually promoted the reform of the banking system under the inertia of long-term institutional arrangements. In order to reduce the operating costs of the system, the functions of the PBOC were first divided into central bank functions and commercial bank functions. Subsequently, different specialized banks were separated from it to assume corresponding commercial functions, transitioning from a single banking system to a dual banking system where state-owned specialized banks coexist with the PBOC. Since 1984, influenced by the coexistence of policy and commercial businesses, state-owned specialized banks have carried out enterprise reforms, breaking free from constraints such as collective funding and industry restrictions, gradually transitioning towards state-owned commercial banks. Since 1995, in order to improve operational efficiency, state-owned specialized banks have successfully reorganized into state-owned wholly-owned commercial banks. In 2003, state-owned commercial banks began shareholding reforms, improving corporate governance, and gradually transitioning to state-owned controlling shareholders of joint-stock banks. The four state-owned banks have successively gone public, and they continue to improve their corporate governance structures and deepen reforms.

7.1.1 Establishment of State-Owned Specialized Banks

From the beginning of the reform and opening up to 1984 was the period of construction of China's state-owned specialized banks. After the Third Plenary Session of the Eleventh Central Committee of the Communist Party of China established the goal of focusing on economic construction, China began to reform the "highly centralized and unified" economic system, and the socio-economic system quickly moved towards diversification. Under these conditions, the highly centralized and unified financial management system could no longer meet the increasingly diversified needs of economic entities, urgently needing to change the single function of "managing funds" to "adjusting the market." The PBOC responded to this trend by continuously strengthening its macro-financial regulation functions, peeling off commercial banking businesses attached to it, and gradually building a macro-financial system.

In this process, the State Council allocated the commercial banking business separated from the PBOC to the initial four state-owned specialized banks. In March 1979, the Agricultural Bank of China was the first to be separated from the PBOC, directly under the State Council and supervised by the PBOC. Its main task was to be responsible for the former financial business of the PBOC, namely the unified management of funds for agriculture, centralized handling of rural credit, leading rural credit cooperatives, and developing rural financial business. Subsequently, the PBOC successively peeled off foreign exchange, industrial and commercial banking, and other commercial banking functions, setting up the Bank of China and the Industrial and Commercial Bank of China to assume their respective business. At the same time, the China (People's) Construction Bank was also separated from the Ministry of Finance to be responsible for fixed asset investment credit and savings business, as shown in Table 7.1.

After five years of reform and the separation of commercial operations, the establishment of the Industrial and Commercial Bank of China in January 1984 marked the complete separation of commercial operations from the PBOC. The "one-size-fits-all" financial institutional system was completely broken, establishing an independent central bank system and forming a binary banking pattern consisting of the PBOC and four state-owned specialized banks. This marked the true starting point for the development of commercial banks in China, initially forming a macro-financial system.

Since the establishment of the four state-owned specialized banks, their operations were initially not based on the business model of commercial banks but were arranged according to the planned economy's industrial division of labor. They were mainly focused on various designated areas such as rural areas, foreign exchange, basic construction, and industrial and commercial enterprises, providing necessary government fund support for the development of the social economy. Measures such as the allocation and conversion of funds greatly expanded the credit business of

Table 7.1 Establishment of China's state-owned specialized banks

Bank name	Establishment time	Core tasks
Agricultural Bank of China	March 1979	Unified management of agricultural funds, centralized handling of rural credit, leadership of rural credit cooperatives, and development of rural financial services
Bank of China	March 1979	Organization, utilization, accumulation, and management of foreign exchange funds; conducting all foreign exchange business; engaging in international financial activities; serving the socialist modernization construction
China Construction Bank (renamed from China People's Construction Bank in 1996)	January 1983	Supervising fixed asset investment and lending operations, as well as savings business
Industrial and Commercial Bank of Chin	January 1984	Raising funds and utilizing funds in accordance with the country's policies; supporting the development of industrial production and the expansion of commodity circulation; supporting the development of collective, individual, and service industries

state-owned specialized banks. The implementation of measures like fund allocation and conversion significantly expanded the credit business of state-owned specialized banks. "The implementation of fund allocation and conversion led to a rapid increase in the proportion of bank credit in the sources of funds for economic construction. From 1981 to 1992, the proportion of funds from the national budget in the total social fixed asset investment decreased from 28 to 4.3%, while the proportion of domestic loans increased from 12.69 to 27.4%."[2] The practice of banks' credit gradually replacing funds from the national budget transitioned from the previous "unified collection, distribution, storage, and lending" to the management system of "unified planning, hierarchical management, storage and lending linkage, and differential control" in 1980. By 1983, the "full-profit flow system" was implemented within the national specialized banking system, linking various assessments with profit retention. The internal management objectives of risk, cost, and profit were initially established, gradually restoring and expanding financial functions.

At the same time, the establishment of state-owned specialized banks enabled China's banking industry to gradually break away from its previous long-term isolation from the outside world and actively engage with the world. At the beginning of the reform and opening up, China's banking industry only had overseas branches in Hong Kong, Macau, London, and Singapore. On June 3, 1979, the Bank of China opened its branch in Luxembourg, becoming the first overseas branch established by the Bank of China after 1949. Subsequently, Bank of China's branches in New York, representative offices in Paris and Tokyo were established. In September 1984, Bank of China acquired a 50% stake in Banco Tai Fung in Macau for 80 million Macau patacas, marking the beginning of China's banking industry's overseas acquisitions. The internationalization pace of state-owned specialized banks not only provided necessary foreign exchange support for China's economic development but also expanded the overseas business of China's banking industry.

7.1.2 Enterprise Reform of State-Owned Specialized Banks

During the period from 1985 to 1993, it was a stage of enterprise-oriented reform for China's state-owned specialized banks. During this period, the reform of state-owned specialized banks was full of twists and turns. Although the pattern of specialized operation had not been completely broken, there were partial changes to the original framework. Significant progress was made in "delegating power and granting benefits," greatly expanding the scope of independent operation for banks.

Firstly, there was an expansion of the autonomy of state-owned specialized banks. In October 1984, the Third Plenary Session of the Twelfth Central Committee of the CPC issued the "Decision of the Central Committee of the CPC on Economic System Reform," which vigorously promoted the "planned commodity economy," leading to rapid development in the business of state-owned specialized banks. Subsequently,

[2] Yi Gang. *Reflections on Financial Reform in China*, Commercial Press, 2009: 282.

an enterprise-oriented reform was initiated to expand the autonomy of state-owned specialized banks, aiming to push them towards the goal of "independent operation, risk assumption, profit and loss accountability, and self-restraint." In 1985, the state implemented the "allocation and transformation of loans," ceasing to inject capital into state-owned enterprises, and banks became the main channel for managing enterprise working capital. To adapt to this change, the PBOC implemented policies allowing for moderate competition among the four state-owned specialized banks, encouraging and supporting them to compete moderately. This broke the previous "supply-side" operating mode of funds in their respective business areas, improving the operational efficiency, management level, and service quality of specialized banks. Meanwhile, a series of reforms were carried out in the internal management systems of state-owned specialized banks in terms of planning, funds, and finance, promoting the transformation from administrative management to enterprise management. In 1986, the central government attempted to implement a system of chief executive responsibility and target management responsibility for state-owned specialized banks to accelerate the process of enterprise-oriented reform. In December, Deng Xiaoping proposed, "The pace of financial reform needs to be accelerated. Banks should be truly managed as banks. Our banks in the past were currency issuing companies, treasuries, not real banks."[3] According to this requirement, banks were gradually positioned as "special enterprises managing currency." In 1987, a system of "three rates," including the cost rate, comprehensive expense rate, and the ratio of retained profits to supplementary credit funds or insurance turnover funds, was implemented. The authority for business operations, credit fund allocation, interest rate and fee floating, internal institution establishment, profit retention, and staffing and reward-punishment rights for mid-level cadres were all delegated. This significantly broke through the previous financial function of "managing funds" alone, and the responsibilities, rights, and interests of state-owned specialized banks were gradually unified, and their operating mechanisms were further improved, and the responsibility system was initially established.

Since 1988, influenced by changes in the domestic and international economic situation and the need for governments at all levels to utilize state-owned specialized banks and their branches to raise policy-oriented funds for economic construction in the context of fiscal constraints, the pace of enterprise-oriented reform of state-owned specialized banks gradually slowed down. However, starting from 1989, the three-year financial order rectification once again led to the dominance of administrative management practices in the management of state-owned specialized banks, and the reform of state-owned specialized banks entered a stagnant state. In 1992, Deng Xiaoping's Southern Tour once again broke the deadlock of enterprise-oriented reform of state-owned specialized banks, re-establishing the market-oriented orientation of enterprise-oriented reform of state-owned specialized banks. In December 1993, the "Decision of the State Council on Financial System Reform" was issued,

---

[3] Deng Xiaoping. *Selected Works of Deng Xiaoping (Volume Three)*, People's Publishing House, 2008: 193.

clarifying the direction of commercialization reform for state-owned specialized banks.

The second is to gradually break through the credit fund management system of state-owned specialized banks. In 1985, the central government changed the credit management method of "linking deposits and loans, with differential total allocation" implemented in 1980 and implemented nationwide policies such as unified planning, fund allocation, actual loan disbursement, mutual financing, quota management, and loan determination based on deposits. Its core is the principle of "actual loan disbursement based on actual deposits". State-owned specialized banks opened deposit accounts with the People's Bank of China, realizing the separation of currency issuance and credit business, and the separation of credit plans and credit funds management. This initially addressed the problem of state-owned specialized banks relying entirely on the PBOC for credit funds in the past, enabling them to establish economic indicators focusing on fund utilization, expenditure, and profit growth. In January 1986, the State Council promulgated the "Interim Regulations of the People's Republic of China on Banking Management," which specifically included a chapter on specialized banks to regulate their business scope, basic responsibilities, establishment and withdrawal conditions of headquarters and branches, strengthen the management of specialized banks, ensure the healthy development of specialized bank business, and promote and serve the construction of socialist modernization in China.

In 1989, in order to implement the spirit of rectifying financial order and deepening financial reform as laid out in the Third Plenary Session of the Thirteenth Central Committee of the Communist Party of China, the PBOC made certain adjustments to credit fund management. Measures were taken to "strive to increase deposit sources, control the total amount of credit, adjust the structure, ensure key areas, compress general areas, and adjust as appropriate," establish a monitoring system for the total social credit volume, strengthen credit plan management, and implement "quota management based on deposits." The method of setting the highest control quota was established. In March 1994, in response to changes in the socio-economic situation, the PBOC made moderate adjustments to the credit fund management system of state-owned specialized banks and formulated and promulgated the "Interim Measures for the Management of Credit Funds." These measures established the basic principles of "total control, proportional management, classification guidance, and market integration" for credit fund management, implemented strict control over the total volume of monetary credit and the scale of fixed asset loans, and implemented asset-liability ratio management under quota management. By 1998, the PBOC had abolished the control of loan scale, replacing it with a system of proportional management under planned guidance and self-balance, strictly implementing asset-liability ratio management and risk management measures.

Clearly, after this stage of corporatization reform of state-owned specialized banks, various businesses of these banks have seen significant development. A pattern of business cross-competition has emerged among the four specialized banks, with Agricultural Bank expanding into urban areas, Industrial and Commercial Bank reaching rural areas, Bank of China focusing on international markets, and China

Construction Bank penetrating into industrial sectors. This lays necessary institutional foundations for the transformation of state-owned specialized banks into wholly state-owned commercial banks.

7.1.3 Establishment of State-Owned Commercial Banks

The period from 1994 to 2002 marked the transformation of state-owned specialized banks into state-owned commercial banks. During this time, China completely broke the pattern of specialized operations of state-owned specialized banks and achieved a commercial orientation in business operations.

A. Separation of Policy Business and Commercial Business

After the establishment of state-owned specialized banks separate from the People's Bank of China, while the four state-owned specialized banks engaged in commercial operations, they sometimes had to undertake policy-related tasks such as agricultural product procurement. These banks often used this opportunity to attribute various losses in commercial operations to the field of policy lending. At the same time, they vigorously sought re-lending from the People's Bank of China and various financial subsidies to reduce the pressure of their commercial operations. This moral risk and adverse selection behavior severely affected the commercial operating motivation of state-owned specialized banks and increased various adverse losses in bank operations. In this context, to truly transform banks into banks and to comply with the goal of establishing a socialist market economy proposed at the Third Plenary Session of the Fourteenth Central Committee of the Communist Party of China, on December 25, 1993, the State Council issued the "Decision of the State Council on Financial System Reform," which formally proposed the establishment of a financial system dominated by state-owned commercial banks and the strategic transformation from national specialized banks to state-owned commercial banks. In 1994, China established three policy banks including the State Development Bank, China Export–Import Bank, and Agricultural Development Bank of China to undertake policy business of the four state-owned commercial banks.

The establishment of the three policy banks initially separated the policy business and commercial business of state-owned banks and established the system of unified legal persons of state-owned banks. In July 1995, the "Commercial Bank Law of the People's Republic of China" (hereinafter referred to as the "Commercial Bank Law") was promulgated and implemented, which legally stipulated that the four state-owned banks, namely, Industrial and Commercial Bank of China, Agricultural Bank of China, Bank of China, and China Construction Bank, are wholly state-owned commercial banks that operate "independently, bear risks, be responsible for profits and losses, and self-regulate."

B. Institutional Construction of State-Owned Commercial Banks

The "Commercial Bank Law" clarified the institutional conditions for market access, minimum capital requirements, business scope, management supervision, and abolition of state-owned commercial banks. According to this regulation, the four state-owned specialized banks established the direction of transformation into state-owned wholly-owned commercial banks. In 1994, the central government explicitly stated that the self-owned funds[4] of state-owned specialized banks are their capital, which, together with the provision for bad debts and other supplementary capital retained by the banks, constitutes their owner's equity, thus clarifying the capital prerequisite for the transformation of state-owned specialized banks into wholly state-owned commercial banks. Subsequently, in order to strengthen the capital and risk management of state-owned commercial banks, in 1988, the Ministry of Finance promulgated the "Provisional Regulations on the Establishment of Loan Provision Reserves for National Specialized Banks," initiating the classification management of credit assets in the Chinese banking system. In this classification, credit assets are divided into four categories: normal, overdue, stagnant, and bad, based on the loan period. In practice, there were many shortcomings in this method. In response, the People's Bank of China issued the "Notice on Comprehensive Implementation of Five-level Classification of Loans" in 1999. According to this notice, the classification of credit assets shifted from the traditional method to dynamic risk supervision of "five-level classification," dividing loans into five levels: normal, attention, substandard, doubtful, and loss. The "five-level classification" work required the four wholly state-owned commercial banks and policy banks to complete by the end of 1999, while other banking institutions were required to complete it by the end of 2002.

Under the condition of classifying credit assets according to the "five-level classification," the non-performing asset ratio of state-owned wholly-owned commercial banks remained high. "During the Asian financial crisis, although commercial banks reported a non-performing asset ratio of 25%, considering the loan classification standards, accounting standards, financial discipline, etc. at that time, 25% was likely underestimated, and market estimates were basically between 35 and 40%."[5] The high non-performing asset ratio of state-owned commercial banks was even considered "technically bankrupt" by some Western commentators. Thus, reducing the persistently high non-performing asset ratio became a core task for state-owned commercial banks to maintain sustained development and became the key to maintaining financial stability in China. With a high non-performing asset ratio and a capital adequacy ratio that is far from the requirement stipulated in Article 39(1) of "Commercial Bank Law" as shown in Fig. 7.1, there is a considerable gap.

---

[4] The capital of our country's commercial banks had significantly different sources in 1994. Before the reform and opening up, the credit funds were allocated annually by the government; in 1984, the government ceased allocation, and banks began to extract a portion from retained profits as credit funds, also known as self-owned funds.

[5] Zhu Min, Cai Jinqing, Ai Meixia. *The Rise of China's Financial Industry—Challenges and Global Impact*. CITIC Publishing House, Preface, 2010: 30.

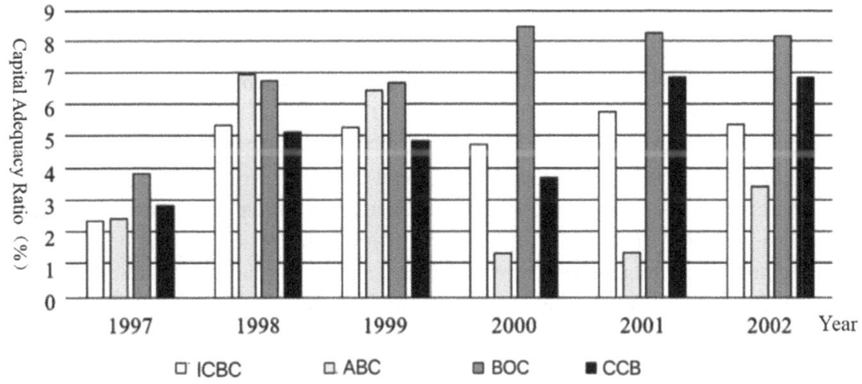

Fig. 7.1 Capital adequacy ratio of China's four major state-owned commercial banks, 1997–2002

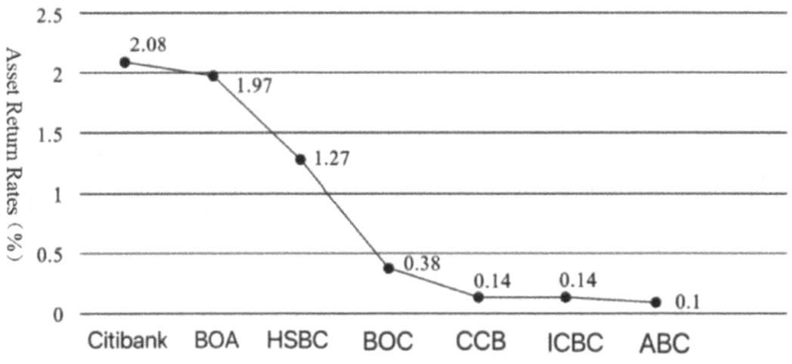

Fig. 7.2 Overview of asset return rates of state-owned commercial banks and large foreign banks in 2003[6]

Clearly, the persistently high non-performing asset ratio and the relatively low capital adequacy ratio of the four state-owned commercial banks significantly hindered their further development. There is a considerable gap in their return on assets (ROA) compared to large foreign banks (see Fig. 7.2), greatly constraining the independence and competitiveness of state-owned commercial banks.

To truly transform the four state-owned specialized banks into wholly state-owned commercial banks in accordance with the objectives of financial reform decisions, they must adhere to the laws of commercial operation and achieve sustainable development of state-owned commercial bank institutions. To this end, the State Council adopted fiscal measures to enhance the profitability of wholly state-owned commercial banks. "In 1997, the Ministry of Finance reduced the corporate income tax rate for state-owned commercial banks from the original 55% (plus an additional 7% adjustment tax) to the general corporate income tax rate of 33%, while appropriately

[6] Compiled based on relevant data from LI Zhihui's *Development and Changes of China's Banking Industry* (Gezhi Publishing House, Shanghai People's Publishing House, 2008: 97).

raising the business tax rate from the original 5–8%."[7] By lowering the excessively high tax rates for banks, profitability of bank operations was significantly improved, and the amount of banks' self-owned funds was proportionally increased. On the other hand, the central government initiated initial financial restructuring based on the high proportion of non-performing assets in the asset structure of the four state-owned commercial banks. At the first national financial work conference held in 1997, the central government clearly stated the establishment of asset management companies to divest non-performing assets from state-owned commercial banks, supplement their capital, abolish loan quotas, and implement asset-liability ratio management and other important reform measures. Following this approach, in 1998, the Chinese government issued special treasury bonds totaling 270 billion yuan to supplement the insufficient capital of the four state-owned commercial banks; in 1999, non-performing assets totaling 1.3939 trillion yuan were divested from the four state-owned commercial banks, and asset management companies such as Huarong, Great Wall, Orient, and Xinda were established to specialize in the disposal of non-performing assets of the four state-owned commercial banks (see Table 7.2).

Through the initial divestiture of non-performing assets from the four state-owned commercial banks, the non-performing asset ratio of state-owned commercial banks improved to some extent. However, constrained by the system and mechanisms, the non-performing asset ratio rebounded quickly, and by 2002, it faced a high level again, greatly restricting the competitiveness of state-owned commercial banks and the progress of their transformation into joint-stock entities, as shown in Fig. 7.3.

Along with the transition to wholly state-owned commercial banks, the four state-owned commercial banks restructured their branch network according to market-oriented principles. They increased the establishment of branches in economically developed regions domestically and significantly reduced the operational institutions in grassroots and economically underdeveloped areas. "From 1998 to 2002, the number of operational institutions of wholly state-owned commercial banks in China decreased by more than one-third, and the number of employees decreased by

Table 7.2 Corresponding institutions for the divestiture of non-performing assets of the four state-owned commercial banks in 1999[8]

Bank name	Corresponding asset management company for non-performing asset divestiture
Industrial and Commercial Bank of China (ICBC)	Huarong asset management corporation
Bank of China	Orient asset management corporation
China Construction Bank (CCB)	Xinda asset management corporation
Agricultural Bank of China (ABC)	Great wall asset management corporation

[7] Li Zhihui. *Development and Changes of China's Banking Industry*. Gezhi Publishing House, Shanghai People's Publishing House, 2008: 97.

[8] Compiled based on relevant data from *China Financial Yearbook* (2003).

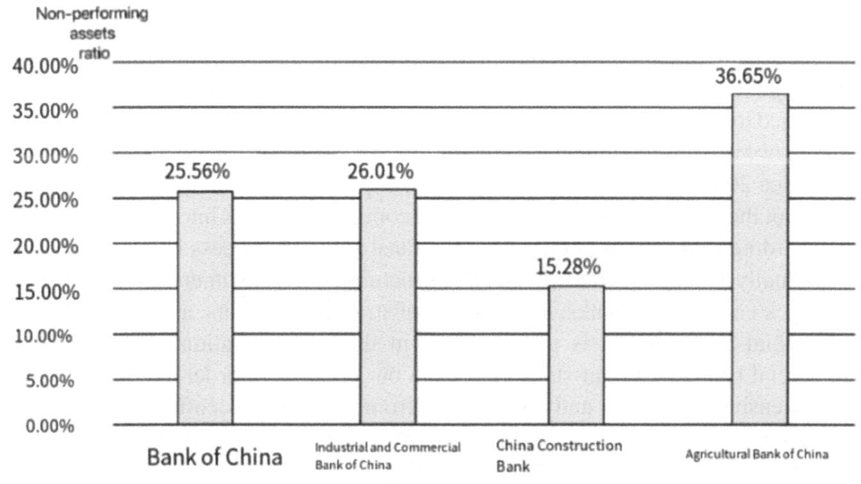

Fig. 7.3 Non-performing asset ratio of the four state-owned commercial banks in 2002[9]

approximately 18%."[10] After the restructuring of institutions, the four state-owned commercial banks gradually embarked on the path of true commercial operation as commercial banks.

7.1.4 Establishment of State-Owned Controlling Shareholding Commercial Banks

The period from 2003 to the present is a time for the transformation of state-owned commercial banks into joint-stock entities and further deepening reforms, as well as for constructing an inclusive financial system. During this period, based on the reform process of state-owned commercial banks, it can be roughly divided into two stages: from 2003 to 2010 was the stage of transforming state-owned commercial banks into joint-stock entities, and from 2011 to the present is a period of further deepening reforms, accelerating informatization, and constructing an inclusive financial system.

A. Transformation of State-Owned Commercial Banks into Joint-Stock Entities

In 2001, China officially joined the WTO. After the five-year transition period ended, China fully opened up RMB and other financial businesses to foreign financial institutions. This inevitably brought new challenges and intense competition to state-owned sole proprietorship commercial banks. Therefore, at the Second National Financial Work Conference convened by the State Council in 2002, it was proposed

[9] Compiled based on relevant data published on the official website of the People's Bank of China.

[10] Li Zhihui. *Development and Changes of China's Banking Industry*. Gezhi Publishing House, Shanghai People's Publishing House, 2008: 96.

to transform state-owned sole proprietorship commercial banks into modern financial enterprises with "clear property rights, well-defined rights and responsibilities, separation of government and enterprises, and scientific management", These enterprises were aimed to have well-structured governance, sound operational mechanisms, clear business objectives, good financial conditions, and strong international competitiveness. Since 2003, state-owned sole proprietorship commercial banks have basically carried out the transformation of state-owned commercial banks into joint-stock entities according to this train of thought. The transformation process is mainly carried out gradually in steps such as financial restructuring, establishment of state-owned joint-stock commercial banks, introduction of strategic investors, and listing.

Financial restructuring is the first link in the transformation of state-owned commercial banks into joint-stock entities in our country. In order to cope with the comprehensive challenges and competition from foreign banks after 2006, as well as to achieve the goal of comprehensive transformation of state-owned commercial banks into joint-stock entities, the central government, in response to the situation where the non-performing assets of state-owned commercial banks have risen again since 2002 and the non-performing loan ratio has reached 24.13%, launched financial restructuring again. In 2003, China established Central Huijin Investment Ltd (hereinafter referred to as Central Huijin) on behalf of the central government to inject $45 billion into Bank of China and China Construction Bank to promote the transformation of state-owned banks. In 2005, Central Huijin again injected $15 billion into Industrial and Commercial Bank of China on behalf of the central government. At the same time, in order to reduce the financial burden of state-owned commercial banks, the central government offset bad debts for state-owned commercial banks conducting joint-stock reform by writing off original capital and returning profits for that year, and again transferred the remaining non-performing assets. Only Bank of China, China Construction Bank, and Industrial and Commercial Bank of China have transferred 1 trillion yuan of non-performing assets. Since the Agricultural Bank of China first proposed the stock reform plan to the State Council in 2004, it has obtained a capital injection equivalent to $130 billion RMB from CIC by November 2008. At the same time, together with the Ministry of Finance, it established a co-management fund and transferred 800 billion yuan of non-performing assets into the co-management fund account to realize the separation of non-performing assets. Through capital injection and non-performing asset separation, the asset quality of the four state-owned commercial banks has been significantly improved, and their capital adequacy ratios have reached the regulatory requirements of 8%, laying a good foundation for subsequent joint-stock reforms and listings.

The second step is to establish state-owned joint-stock commercial banks. The central government's capital injection and other financial restructuring actions for the four state-owned commercial banks have completely changed the situation of poor capital quality in state-owned commercial banks. In 2002, at the Second National Financial Work Conference, it was explicitly stated that to promote the comprehensive reform of state-owned sole proprietorship commercial banks, it is necessary to focus closely on key aspects such as reforming management systems, improving governance structures, transforming operating mechanisms, and enhancing operational performance. The goal was to gradually transform the four state-owned commercial banks into modern state-owned joint-stock commercial banks with sufficient capital, stringent internal controls, secure operations, good service and efficiency, and strong international competitiveness. In accordance with the requirements of the modern enterprise system, the state-owned sole proprietorship commercial banks initiated the joint-stock reform. In 2003, the State Council designated Bank of China and China Construction Bank as the first batch of pilot banks for joint-stock reform, and state-owned banks officially began their joint-stock transformation. In August 2004, Bank of China, controlled solely by the China Investment Corporation, established Bank of China Limited by Shares, marking the beginning of the joint-stock transformation of state-owned sole proprietorship commercial banks, as shown in Table 7.3.

In September 2004, China Construction Bank officially initiated its joint-stock reform. China Construction Bank Limited by Shares was established jointly by Central Huijin, China Jianyin Investment Limited (JIC), Baosteel Group Corporation, State Grid Corporation of China, and China Yangtze Power Corporation. In April 2005, the State Council approved Industrial and Commercial Bank of China to undergo joint-stock reform, which was completed by October. In January 2007, at the Third National Financial Work Conference, it was explicitly stated that Agricultural Bank of China would initiate joint-stock reform based on the principles of "adhering to serving agriculture, rural areas, and farmers, overall restructuring, commercial operation, and listing at the opportune moment." In October 2008, the State Council approved the joint-stock reform plan for Agricultural Bank of China. In November, Central Huijin injected capital into Agricultural Bank of China. In January 2009, Central Huijin, together with the Ministry of Finance, jointly established Agricultural Bank of China Limited by Shares. The establishment of Agricultural Bank of China Limited by Shares marked the completion of the basic joint-stock reform of China's state-owned commercial banks. The transformation into joint-stock limited companies has fundamentally clarified the relationship between state capital and banks, enabling the state to exercise the rights of investors through Central Huijin, limiting liability to the amount of investment, and changing the previous situation where the state bore unlimited liability.

The third step is to introduce strategic investors and improve the equity structure. With the completion of the joint-stock reform of the four state-owned commercial

Table 7.3 Schedule of transformation of four state-owned commercial banks into state-owned sole proprietorship joint-stock commercial banks

Bank name	Transformation date
Bank of China	August 26, 2004
China Construction Bank	September 15, 2004
Industrial and Commercial Bank of China	October 25, 2005
Agricultural Bank of China	January 15, 2009

banks, according to the overall train of thought of the State Council on the joint-stock reform of state-owned commercial banks, "introducing domestic and foreign strategic investors, changing the single equity structure, and achieving diversification of investment entities" is a necessary part of equity reform. By introducing strategic investors, especially foreign ones, capital can be increased, the ownership structure of state-owned commercial banks can be optimized, international advanced management experience can be introduced, and corporate governance can be improved. State-owned joint-stock commercial banks actively carried out the introduction of strategic investors. Based on comprehensive demonstrations and inspections, China Construction Bank, Bank of China, and Industrial and Commercial Bank of China successively completed the introduction of foreign strategic investors, as shown in Table 7.4.

Agricultural Bank of China, based on its own situation, although it had the idea and action of introducing foreign strategic investors after successfully completing the joint-stock reform, did not actually take the action of introducing foreign strategic investors in the practical operation process. Instead, it directly entered the stage of domestic and international listing.

The fourth step is the domestic and international listing of state-owned joint-stock commercial banks. In order to fully utilize the constraints, supervision, and promotion functions of the capital market, and establish a complete set of new market incentives and constraints mechanisms, state-owned joint-stock commercial banks have

Table 7.4 Overview of introduction of foreign strategic investors in state-owned commercial banks

Bank name	Foreign strategic investors	Investment amount (USD)	Ownership percentage (%)
Industrial and Commercial Bank of China	Goldman Sachs Group (USA), Allianz Group (Germany), American Express Company (USA)	$3.78 billion	10
Bank of China	Royal Bank of Scotland (UK)	$3.1 billion	10
	UBS Group (Switzerland)	$500 million	1.6
	Asian Development Bank	$75 million	0.24
	Temasek Holdings (Singapore)	$3.1 billion	10
China Construction Bank	Bank of America (USA)	$2.5 billion	9
	Temasek Holdings (Singapore)	$1.466 billion	5.1

Note Both Bank of China and Industrial and Commercial Bank of China have investments from the National Social Security Fund as strategic investors. The National Social Security Fund invested 10 billion RMB in the former, holding a 3.58% stake, and 18.025 billion RMB in the latter

taken steps to seek domestic and international listings, aiming to further transform their operating mechanisms and truly become entities operating in a market-oriented manner. Subsequently, according to the progress of the overall restructuring of the four state-owned joint-stock commercial banks, from October 2005 to July 2010, all four of China's state-owned joint-stock commercial banks successfully achieved their goals of domestic and international listing, as shown in Table 7.5.

Clearly, through the joint-stock reform and subsequent domestic and international listings, the four state-owned commercial banks have made significant progress in their transformation. This reform has supplemented bank capital, strengthened bank capabilities, improved the operational and managerial concepts of bank employees, established a complete corporate governance structure composed of shareholders' meetings, boards of directors, supervisory boards, and management teams, optimized the corporate governance mechanisms of state-owned joint-stock commercial banks, introduced advanced management experience and technology from abroad, enhanced the level of risk control in banks, and basically achieved the goals of "attracting capital," "attracting intelligence," "attracting standards," and "attracting technology" in the reform of state-owned banks. This lays a solid foundation for the continuous and healthy development of the state-owned banking industry.

B. Comprehensive Development of State-Owned Joint-Stock Commercial Bank

Since 2004, while actively promoting joint-stock reform, state-owned joint-stock commercial banks have also achieved comprehensive development in their business operations. The branch networks of the four state-owned joint-stock commercial banks have expanded to cover all provinces, autonomous regions, and municipalities directly under the central government in China. The knowledge structure of bank employees has been continuously improved, and business operations have expanded to cover all financial services through the establishment of subsidiaries, holdings, and other means.

Table 7.5 Domestic and international listing status of four state-owned commercial banks

Bank name	Listing date	Total financing amount (USD billion)
China Construction Bank	October 2005 (H shares)	169.55
	September 2007 (A shares)	
Bank of China	June 2006 (H shares)	136.77
	July 2006 (A shares)	
Industrial and Commercial Bank of China	October 27, 2006 (H shares and A shares simultaneously)	219.68
Agricultural Bank of China	July 15, 2010 (A shares)	221
	July 16, 2010 (H shares)	

(a) Increase in Asset Size and Strengthening of Strength

Since 2004, the total assets of state-owned commercial banks have experienced rapid growth, increasing from over 15 trillion yuan in 2003 to over 98 trillion yuan in 2018, more than sixfold in 16 years, as shown in Table 7.6.

The absolute value of total assets held by state-owned commercial banks has shown rapid growth. However, their proportion within the entire financial institution sector has exhibited a declining trend, dropping from 54.9% in 2003 to 36.7% in 2018. Over a span of 15 years, this decline amounts to 18.2 percentage points. This illustrates the rapid development of financial diversification in China, gradually changing the monopoly status of state-owned commercial banks that prevailed at the beginning of economic reform and opening-up. Internally within the financial industry, this has led to a diversified competitive landscape, significantly enhancing

Table 7.6 Changes in total assets of state-owned commercial banks and their proportion of total financial institution* assets

Year	Total assets (billion Yuan)	Proportion of total financial institution assets (%)
2003	151,940.6	54.90
2004	169,320.5	53.60
2005	196,579.7	52.50
2006	225,390.4	51.30
2007**	280,070.9	53.20
2008	318,358.0	51.00
2009	400,890.2	50.90
2010	458,814.6	48.70
2011	536,336.0	47.30
2012	600,401.0	44.93
2013	656,005.0	43.34
2014	710,141.0	41.21
2015	781,630.0	39.21
2016	865,982.0	37.29
2017	928,145.0	36.77
2018***	983,534.0	36.70

Note * Financial institutions include policy banks, state-owned commercial banks, joint-stock commercial banks, city commercial banks, rural commercial banks, urban credit cooperatives, rural credit cooperatives, non-bank financial institutions, postal savings institutions, and foreign financial institutions

** After 2007, state-owned commercial banks include Bank of Communications

*** The data for 2018 is sourced from the website of the China Banking and Insurance Regulatory Commission (http://www.cbrc.gov.cn/chinese/newShouDoc/CDF5FDDEDAE14EFEB351CD93140E6554.html)

Data source Compiled based on relevant year data from the official website of the China Banking Regulatory Commission (http://www.cbrc.gov.cn/chinese/home/docViewPage/110009&.current=2)

Table 7.7 Ranking and operating income of five state-owned commercial banks in the fortune global 500 in 2017

Bank name	Fortune global 500 ranking	Operating income (USD million)
Industrial and Commercial Bank of China	22	147,675.1
China Construction Bank	28	135,093.3
Agricultural Bank of China	38	117,274.9
Bank of China	42	113,708.2
Bank of Communications	171	52,989.6

the operational efficiency of financial institutions and the quality of services to the real economy.

The scale of assets of China's state-owned commercial banks has continuously expanded, significantly enhancing their strength and increasing their international influence. In 1995, Bank of China ranked 207th in the Fortune Global 500 list, and by 1999, Industrial and Commercial Bank of China also entered the list, ranking 160th. Subsequently, the positions of state-owned commercial banks in the ranking continued to rise. With the completion of joint-stock reform and listing of the four state-owned commercial banks and the inclusion of Bank of Communications as a large state-owned commercial bank in 2007, these five state-owned commercial banks ranked among the top global banks for several consecutive years following the subprime mortgage crisis. Industrial and Commercial Bank of China maintained its title as the world's largest commercial bank. By 2017, the strength of these five state-owned joint-stock commercial banks continued to lead the global banking industry, as shown in Table 7.7.

In the ranking of core capital of the world's 1000 largest banks by The Banker magazine in the UK, China's four state-owned commercial banks have consistently ranked among the top global banks. In the 2017 ranking, Industrial and Commercial Bank of China, China Construction Bank, Bank of China, and Agricultural Bank of China ranked first, second, fourth, and sixth respectively, maintaining their positions at the forefront of global banking and joining the list of globally systemically important banks. According to the list of globally systemically important banks published by the Financial Stability Board, in 2012, in China, only Bank of China entered the first level of the list, subject to an additional 1% capital buffer requirement. By 2016, all four state-owned commercial banks were included in the list of globally systemically important banks, with Industrial and Commercial Bank of China also listed as a second-tier bank, subject to an additional 1.5% capital buffer requirement.[11]

[11] The research team of the "Jingshan Report". *The Second Half of China's Financial Opening Up*. CITIC Press, 2018: 70.

(b) Deepening Internationalization

On one hand, based on the level of business development, state-owned joint-stock commercial banks have accelerated their expansion into international markets, particularly through establishing branches in foreign countries and in the Hong Kong, Macao, and Taiwan regions of China, as shown in Table 7.8.

Among the countries and regions along "the Belt and Road Initiative", the five state-owned commercial banks have established branches in some of these countries (see Table 7.9), making them the primary financial force from China participating in "the Belt and Road Initiative". However, the number of branches established is relatively small, indicating significant potential for further development.

The strides of state-owned commercial banks in "going global" have increasingly positioned them to play a significant role in China's financial globalization and "the Belt and Road Initiative".

On the other hand, state-owned commercial banks have also intensified their outward-oriented globalization efforts, accelerating the process of mergers, acquisitions, controlling interests, and establishment of subsidiaries in overseas markets as well as in the Hong Kong, Macao, and Taiwan regions.

Bank of China, having separated from the PBOC at the onset of economic reforms, embarked on its "going global" strategy. In September 1984, it acquired a 50% stake in Macau's Tai Fung Bank for 80 million Macau patacas, marking the beginning of its overseas acquisitions. Today, it stands as one of the most internationally diversified Chinese banking institutions.

Industrial and Commercial Bank of China (ICBC) initiated its global expansion with the acquisition of Union Bank of Hong Kong in 1998. By the end of 2017, ICBC had completed 16 overseas acquisitions, spanning across Europe, America, South Africa, Latin America, and other regions. It holds the record for the highest number of overseas acquisitions among Chinese domestic banks. ICBC has established fruitful relationships with 1611 banking institutions in 147 countries and regions worldwide. Its correspondent banks cover over 95% of countries and regions involved in investment and trade with China.

China Construction Bank, mainly focusing on establishing its own branches overseas, accelerated its globalization efforts from the acquisition of Hong Kong's Bank

Table 7.8 Overview of branches established by five state-owned commercial banks in foreign countries and Hong Kong, Macao, and Taiwan Regions of China as of January 2018

Bank name	Number of countries and regions	Number of branches established
Industrial and Commercial Bank of China	45	53
Bank of China	53	92
China Construction Bank	29	38
Agricultural Bank of China	13	16
Bank of Communications	16	21

Table 7.9 Overview of financial institutions established by state-owned commercial banks along the belt and road initiative as of early 2017

Region	Country	Bank of China	Agricultural Bank of China	Industrial and Commercial Bank of China	China Construction Bank	Bank of Communications
South Asia (8 countries)	Bhutan					
	Nepal					
	Afghanistan					
	Bangladesh					
	Pakistan			√		
	India			√		
	Sri Lanka					
	Maldives					
Southeast Asia (11 countries and Mongolia)	Myanmar	√		√		
	Philippines	√				
	Brunei					
	Indonesia	√		√		
	Singapore	√	√	√	√	√
	Malaysia	√		√		
	Vietnam	√	√	√	√	√
	Thailand	√		√		
	Laos	√		√		
	Cambodia	√		√		
	Timor-Leste					
	Mongolia	√				
CIS 5 countries (Central Asia)	Turkmenistan					
CIS 7 countries (Europe)	Kazakhstan	√		√		
	Uzbekistan					
	Kyrgyzstan					
	Tajikistan					
	Georgia					
	Azerbaijan					
	Armenia					
West Asia, North Africa, 17 countries and Greece	Turkey	√		/		
	Iran					
	Syria					

(continued)

Table 7.9 (continued)

Region	Country	Bank of China	Agricultural Bank of China	Industrial and Commercial Bank of China	China Construction Bank	Bank of Communications
	Iraq					
	United Arab Emirates					
	Saudi Arabia			√		
	Qatar			√		
	Bahrain	√				
	Kuwait			√		
	Lebanon					
	Oman					
	Yemen					
	Jordan					
	Israel					
	Palestine					
	Egypt					
	Greece					
	Cyprus					
Central and Eastern Europe, 16 countries	Poland	√		√		
	Czech Republic,	√				
	Slovakia					
	Hungary,	√				
	Slovenia					
	Croatia					
	Romania					
	Bulgaria					
	Serbia					
	Montenegro					
	Macedonia					
	Bosnia and Herzegovina					
	Albania					
	Estonia					
	Lithuania					
	Latvia					

Data source Compiled based on relevant data published by the China Banking Regulatory Commission official website on March 1, 2018)

of East Asia in 2002 and the acquisition of Bank of America (Asia) in 2006. As of now, its overseas institutions span major countries and regions across America, Europe, Asia, Africa, and Oceania, with 16 overseas subsidiaries established.

Agricultural Bank of China, responding to the practical needs of its business development, established wholly-owned subsidiaries in London, UK, and Moscow, Russia, in December 2011 and September 2014, respectively. This move aimed to strengthen its overseas business development, particularly in providing comprehensive services for Chinese enterprises "going global" and foreign enterprises closely connected with China.

Bank of Communications initiated its "going global" strategy relatively later than the other four state-owned commercial banks. In May 2015, it acquired approximately 80% of the shares of BBM Bank in Brazil, marking its entry into overseas acquisitions. Currently, it has established 21 overseas branches and representative offices in 16 countries and regions.

(c) Improvement in Asset Quality but Still Need to Strengthen Risk Awareness

With the increasingly sound institutional development of state-owned commercial banks, there has been a notable improvement in the quality of bank assets, accompanied by a significant increase in capital adequacy ratios and a downward trend in non-performing loan ratios. The changes in capital adequacy ratios and non-performing loan ratios of state-owned commercial banks are shown in Table 7.10.

Since 2003, state-owned commercial banks have significantly improved their asset quality through the disposal of non-performing assets and capital replenishment. Following the outbreak of the subprime mortgage crisis in 2008, the capital adequacy ratio of state-owned commercial banks increased substantially, effectively safeguarding the safety of bank assets. The non-performing loan ratio has gradually declined since 2004, with a significant reduction observed in 2007. Subsequently, the non-performing loan ratio has remained at a relatively low level, but there has been a slight upward trend since 2013. The changes in the non-performing loan ratio of state-owned commercial banks since 2008 are illustrated in Fig. 7.4.

Since 2013, although the non-performing loan ratio has been growing slowly, the underlying risks remain significant. In the years following 2018, the five state-owned commercial banks will undoubtedly align with the spirit of the Fifth National Financial Work Conference held in Beijing in July 2017 and the 19th National Congress of the Communist Party of China. They will strengthen risk prevention and enhance their internal control mechanisms to safeguard against systemic risks and actively serve the real economy.

Since completing their shareholding reforms and listing, state-owned commercial banks have continued to strengthen corporate governance structures, enhance internal governance and institutional development, and improve their ability to prevent risks. Additionally, they have intensified their efforts in bank information technology construction, promoting the development trend of "finance + internet".

Currently, all five state-owned commercial banks have established their own self-service banks, online banking, mobile banking, telephone banking, and other online banking services. They have also developed banking apps, actively integrating the

Table 7.10 Changes in capital adequacy ratio and non-performing loan ratio of state-owned commercial banks

Year	Capital adequacy ratio (%)	Non-performing loan ratio (%)
2004	–	15.57
2005	–	10.49
2006	–	9.22
2007	–	8.05
2008	–	2.81
2009	11.40	1.80
2010	12.20	1.31
2011	12.70	1.00
2012	13.25	0.95
2013	12.19	1.00
2014	14.10	1.23
2015	14.16	1.66
2016	14.23	1.68
2017	14.65	1.53
2018*	15.70	1.41

Note Starting from 2007, the data includes Bank of Communications in addition to the four state-owned commercial banks; before that, it refers only to the four state-owned commercial banks. In the second quarter of 2014, both the four state-owned commercial banks and Bank of Communications adopted advanced capital management methods. The capital adequacy ratio data before 2013 is based on national data and calculated according to the "Commercial Bank Capital Management Measures (Trial)" regulations, which may not be directly comparable to historical data, but still reflects a trend

* Data for 2018 is sourced from the China Banking and Insurance Regulatory Commission website. (http://www.cbrc.gov.cn/chinese/home/docView/2ED43A31B3CA4071A1D76901502E3A7A.html)

Data source Compiled based on relevant annual data from the official website of the China Banking Regulatory Commission

latest information technology into banking services amidst the rapid development of internet finance. The Agricultural Bank of China has widely applied technologies such as facial recognition and voice recognition to its ATMs, while leveraging information technology to reconstruct bank counters, creating centralized "super counters" for all offline transactions. China Construction Bank has collaborated with Huawei to launch "Huawei Pay", while Bank of China has vigorously promoted services such as branch robots, intelligent customer service, facial recognition, anti-money laundering detection, and credit card fraud risk prevention. Industrial and Commercial Bank of China's financial information technology platform leads internationally.

In June 2017, all four state-owned commercial banks established inclusive finance departments and formed strategic partnerships with four internet financial companies, including Alibaba, Tencent, JD.com, and Baidu, to jointly promote the development

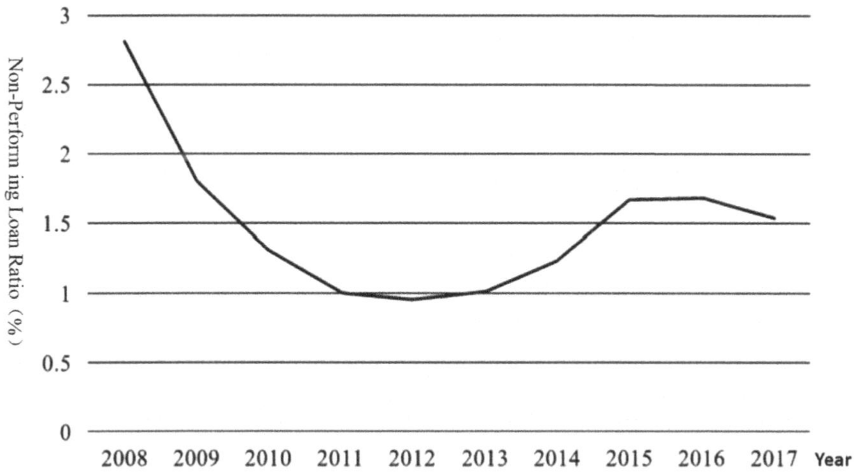

Fig. 7.4 Trends in non-performing loan ratio of state-owned commercial banks since 2008

of financial technology. In June 2018, China Construction Bank established CCB Fintech Co., Ltd., dedicated to software technology, platform operation, financial information services, and other businesses, further deepening the bank's utilization of information technology. During this process, state-owned commercial banks have continuously optimized their physical branch networks according to market-oriented directions. Since 2017, they have been shutting down a batch of sub-branches and community banks in cities like Beijing, Shanghai, and Guangzhou based on business conditions while increasing investments in intelligent development to enhance service efficiency.

7.2 Establishment and Development of Joint-Stock Banks

Since the initiation of reform and opening up, China's economy has increasingly diversified, necessitating more diverse financial institutions to meet the funding needs of a growingly complex range of financing entities. In response to this trend, the Chinese government not only intensified reforms within the financial system but also strengthened the development of financial increments outside the system. In 1987, the establishment of the Bank of Communications in Beijing marked the beginning of the establishment of joint-stock commercial banks. The years from 1987 to 2005 witnessed the widespread establishment of joint-stock commercial banks in China, with a total of 14 being established, forming a nationwide network of joint-stock commercial banks. In 2004, the restructuring and listing of joint-stock commercial banks in China accelerated the pace of informatization and the establishment of an

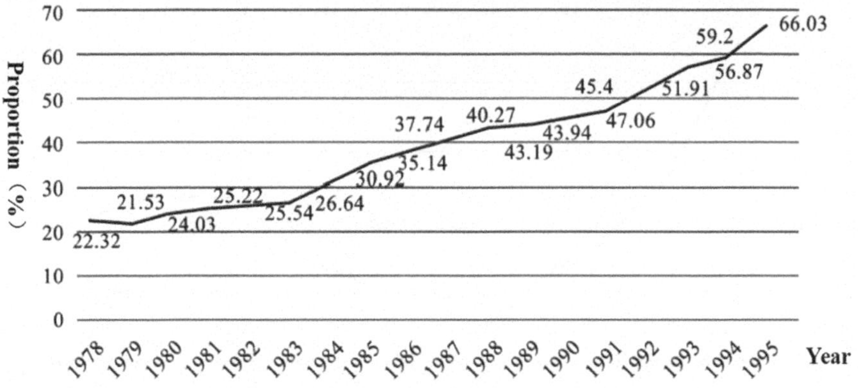

Fig. 7.5 Proportion of output from non-state-owned industries from 1978 to 1995[12]

inclusive financial system. Unlike the initial positioning of state-owned commercial banks, joint-stock banks have always aimed for market-oriented operation and development from the outset.

7.2.1 *Establishment of Joint-Stock Banks*

With the gradual advancement of China's reform and opening up, the Third Plenary Session of the 12th Central Committee of the Communist Party of China in 1984 put forward the concept of a "planned commodity economy", which led to the recognition of various non-state-owned economic components that had previously been heavily suppressed by policies. Consequently, these components experienced rapid development and their share in the national economic output continued to rise. Naturally, there arose a demand for new financial organizations to provide various financial services for them. The proportion of output from non-state-owned industries from 1978 to 1995 is illustrated in Fig. 7.5.

In this context, the demand for financial services from non-state-owned sectors continuously increased, while the supply provided by existing financial institutions in China lagged significantly behind. This situation compelled China to reshape its financial industry and foster diverse forms of finance. In July 1986, the Ministry of Finance restructured the Bank of Communications[13] in a public ownership format, and it was officially established in Beijing in April of the following year, marking the beginning of the nationwide construction of joint-stock banks. Over the next decade,

[12] Compiled based on relevant data from *China's Reform and Development Report (1978–1994): China's Road* (Published by China Financial and Economic Publishing House, 1995).

[13] Bank of Communications, as the first nationwide joint-stock commercial bank, was considered as part of the joint-stock commercial banks until 2007. After that, it was categorized as a state-owned commercial bank.

China successively established 14 joint-stock commercial banks.[14] Additionally, the establishment of Bohai Bank in Tianjin in 2005 brought the total number of joint-stock banks to 14, as shown in Table 7.11.

These nationwide joint-stock commercial banks were established in a manner quite different from specialized state-owned banks, which were separated from commercial operations to build independent central banks. They were established in accordance with the admission conditions stipulated in the Interim Regulations on the Administration of Banks of the People's Republic of China issued in 1986. Their registered capital was quite explicit, following the minimum capital requirements set by the People's Bank of China. Those joint-stock commercial banks established after 1995 were organized according to the provisions of the Commercial Bank Law of the People's Republic of China. Although among the initial shareholders of these joint-stock commercial banks, only China Minsheng Bank was led by private enterprises, while others were led by central or local finance departments, or local state-owned enterprises, their diversified ownership structure broke through the previous monopoly of state ownership in the property rights system, laying the foundation for a more diverse ownership structure. The initial ownership structure of these nationwide joint-stock commercial banks in China is presented in Table 7.12.

In terms of governance structure, these banks initially established a "three meetings and one layer" system, consisting of shareholders' meetings, board of directors, supervisory board, and management. In the layout of bank branches, they broke away from the pattern of state-owned specialized banks based on administrative divisions and instead set up branches based on profitability principles. Regarding banking operations, a market-oriented operational mechanism was preliminarily formed. Subsequently, with the extensive establishment of branches nationwide, these banks significantly improved the regional coverage and service scope of the banking industry, laying a necessary foundation for the formation of a diversified competitive landscape within the banking industry in China. This gradually broke the monopoly of state-owned banks and effectively enhanced the service efficiency of the four state-owned banks, partially meeting the capital supply and demand of different economic entities.

However, after the establishment of these joint-stock commercial banks, they soon encountered the Asian financial crisis in 1997, forcing them to face the impact of market fluctuations. In this crisis, Hainan Development Bank, which had been established for only 2 years and 10 months, was forced to close and liquidate. This event demonstrated that even banks with government shareholders could go bankrupt if they were poorly managed. The collapse of Hainan Development Bank undoubtedly brought significant shocks to China's banking industry. It not only shattered the notion that state-owned banks would not go bankrupt but also provided valuable experience for banking management and risk prevention.

---

[14] Although Hainan Development Bank collapsed and was liquidated in less than three years after its establishment, it is included here mainly because it initially operated as a nationwide joint-stock commercial bank. Hui Shang Bank, formerly known as Bengbu Housing Savings Bank, is not included in this list because it was primarily formed from urban commercial banks and credit cooperatives.

Table 7.11 Overview of China's national joint-stock commercial banks

Bank name	Establishment date	Registered location	Initial capital (in billion yuan)
Bank of Communications	April 1987	Shanghai*****	742.63
China Citic Bank	April 1987	Beijing	467.87
China Merchants Bank	April 1987	Shenzhen	215.77
Ping An Bank*	November 1987	Shenzhen	51.23
Guangdong Development Bank	June 1988	Guangzhou	114.08
Industrial Bank	July 1988	Fuzhou	107.86
China Everbright Bank	April 1992	Beijing	404.35
Huaxia BankOctober 1992	October 1992	Beijing	68.50
Shanghai Pudong Development Bank	January 1993	Shanghai	186.53
Hainan Development Bank**	August 1995	Haikou	16.77
China Minsheng Bank	January 1996	Beijing	283.66
Hengfeng Bank***	October 1987	Jinan	10.00
Zhejiang Bank****	2004	Hangzhou	100.00
Bohai Bank	2005	Tianjin	50.00

Note * Ping An Bank was established in November 1987 and was restructured based on the merger of Shenzhen Development Bank and Fujian Asia Bank in January 2012

** Hainan Development Bank collapsed and went into liquidation 2 years and 10 months after its establishment

*** Hengfeng Bank was formerly known as Yantai Housing Savings Bank

**** Zhejiang Bank was restructured from Zhejiang Commercial Bank, established in Ningbo in 1993, in 2004. After the restructuring, its headquarters were relocated to Hangzhou

***** Initially, the headquarters of Bank of Communications was in Beijing, but shortly after its establishment, it moved to Shanghai. In 2007, it was classified as a state-owned bank in the statistics of the People's Bank of China, alongside the four major state-owned banks (Bank of China, Agricultural Bank of China, Industrial and Commercial Bank of China, and China Construction Bank). After 2007, the number of national joint-stock commercial banks decreased to 12, and the data presented below exclude Bank of Communications, and its related discussions have been included in the section on state-owned commercial banks

7.2.2 Reform and Rapid Development of Joint-Stock Banks

Unlike state-owned commercial banks, while joint-stock commercial banks were being established nationwide, some strictly followed listing rules and successfully went public domestically and internationally, providing experience for subsequent

Table 7.12 Initial ownership structure of nationwide joint-stock commercial banks in China

Name of joint-stock commercial bank main	Shareholding structure
Bank of Communications	The ministry of finance, HSBC, and the entire bank's social security fund council are the top three shareholders, accounting for just under 60%
China CITIC Bank	CITIC group is the major shareholder, with participation from a Spanish foreign bank
China Merchants Bank	China merchants group is the largest shareholder, but there is no actual controlling entity
Ping An Bank	Ping an insurance (group) Company of China, Limited and its holding subsidiaries are the controlling shareholders
Guangdong Development Bank	Guangdong provincial department of finance holds the controlling stake, with participation from 55 other entities including Shandong Liandu, Shanghai Shenhu, and Jiangsu Sugang
Industrial Bank Co., Ltd.	Held by the Fujian Provincial Department of Finance, with participation from multiple enterprises
China Everbright Bank	China Everbright group
Huaxia Bank	Capital iron and steel corporation
Shanghai Pudong Development Bank	Participation from 18 entities including the Shanghai Municipal Bureau of Finance, Shanghai International Trust and Investment Corporation, and Shanghai Jiushi Corporation
Hainan Development Bank	Hainan provincial government holds the majority, with participation from 43 other entities including China North Industries Group Corporation, China Ocean Shipping (Group) Company, and Beijing Capital International Airport
China Minsheng Bank	Established as the first private bank initiated by enterprises such as new hope group, oriental group, China ocean shipping (group) company, and China shipowners mutual assurance association
Hengfeng Bank	Initially initiated by four state-owned commercial banks (Bank of China, Agricultural Bank of China, Industrial and Commercial Bank of China, and China Construction Bank) and other financial enterprises such as China People's Insurance Company
Zhejiang Commercial Bank	22 shareholders, of which 21 are private enterprises
Bohai Bank	Shareholders include Tianjin TEDA Investment Holding Co., Ltd., Standard Chartered Bank (Hong Kong) Limited, China Ocean Shipping (Group) Corporation, China Development Investment Corporation, Baosteel Group Corporation Limited, Tianjin Trust Co., Ltd., and Tianjin Shanghui Investment (Holding) Co., Ltd.

institutional listings in China's banking industry. However, the majority progressed according to the strategic deployment of the State Council after 2002, following the steps of state-owned commercial banks' listings. As of early 2018, only China Guangfa Bank, Hengfeng Bank, and Bohai Bank remained unlisted among the 12 joint-stock banks. During this period, the business of joint-stock commercial banks experienced comprehensive and rapid development, becoming an integral part of China's banking industry. They have played an increasingly important role in activities such as serving the real economy and promoting overall financial reform.

A. Listing of Joint-Stock Banks

The establishment of China's joint-stock commercial banks began with the founding of China's first joint-stock commercial bank, the Bank of Communications, in 1987, which marked the beginning of the establishment and development of joint-stock commercial banks nationwide. Subsequently, the listing of joint-stock commercial banks in China can generally be classified into two categories.

One type involved public subscription at the time of establishment, followed by direct listing. The only national joint-stock commercial bank listed in this manner is Shenzhen Development Bank (referred to as Shenzhen Development). Established on the basis of the reorganization of six credit cooperatives in the Shenzhen Special Economic Zone, Shenzhen Development initially offered RMB ordinary shares to the public through free subscription when the bank was founded in May 1987. Initially, the issuance did not attract much attention or recognition from society, and the shares were mainly subscribed by mobilizing party members and cadres in Shenzhen. In April 1988, the Shenzhen Securities Company was established, and Shenzhen Development became the first bank in the People's Republic of China to have its shares listed and traded, marking the first truly listed bank in China since 1949. In April 1991, Shenzhen Development publicly issued shares to the public and was officially listed on the Shenzhen Stock Exchange, thereby accumulating valuable experience for subsequent domestic bank listings.

The other type involved listing domestically or internationally after establishment and subsequent transformation based on the bank's business development. Shanghai Pudong Development Bank (referred to as Pudong Development), established in 1993, was the second joint-stock commercial bank to be listed. After six years of reform and innovation following its establishment, Pudong Development underwent comprehensive improvements in its capital structure and corporate governance mechanism, leading to a rapid increase in its capital strength. Under these conditions and with the approval of the PBOC and the China Securities Regulatory Commission, it successfully listed on the Shanghai Stock Exchange in 1999, thus initiating the transformation and listing of joint-stock commercial banks. The domestic and international listing status of national joint-stock commercial banks is shown in Table 7.13.

China Minsheng Bank, established in 1996, was the first commercial bank to prepare financial statements according to international standards and was audited by PricewaterhouseCoopers. After rigorous reforms in internal control mechanisms, financial systems, and asset-liability management, China Minsheng Bank's asset quality and capital structure were significantly improved, leading to a successful listing on the Shanghai Stock Exchange in 2000.

China Merchants Bank, after four rounds of capital increases, successfully listed on the Shanghai Stock Exchange in April 2002, becoming the first company in China

Table 7.13 Domestic and international listing status of national joint-stock commercial banks

Types of listing bank	Name	Initial public offering time	Listing situation
Listed at establishment	Ping An Bank*	April 1988	A Shares
Listed after restructuring	Shanghai Pudong Development Bank	September 1999	A Shares
	China Minsheng Bank	December 2000 November 2009	A Shares H Shares
	China Merchants Bank	April 2002, September 2006	A Shares H Shares
	Huaxia Bank	September 2003	A Shares
	Bank of Communications	June 2005 May 2007	H Shares A Shares
	Industrial Bank	February 2007	A Shares
	China CITIC Bank	April 2007	A Shares and H Shares
	China Everbright Bank	August 2010	A Shares
	Zhejiang Commercial Bank	March 2016	H Shares
Not yet listed	China Guangfa Bank	–	–
	Hengfeng Bank	–	–
	Bohai Bank	–	–

Note * Ping An Bank was formed through the merger of Shenzhen Development Bank, established in December 1987, and Ping An Bank (formed through the merger of Shenzhen City Commercial Bank and Fujian Asia Bank) in January 2012, so the listing time here is based on the establishment time of Shenzhen Development Bank

to list using international accounting standards, greatly advancing the normalization of listing procedures in the banking industry.

Hua Xia Bank completed its transformation into a joint-stock commercial bank three years after its establishment in 1995. Through this transformation, Hua Xia Bank significantly improved its capital structure and corporate governance mechanisms, leading to a successful listing on the Shanghai Stock Exchange in 2003.

As the first joint-stock commercial bank established, Bank of Communications began its journey towards public listing in 2004, following the footsteps of state-owned commercial banks. It completed the trilogy of "financial restructuring, introduction of strategic investors, and public listing" successively. In June 2005, it successfully listed on the Hong Kong Stock Exchange (referred to as the HKEx), becoming the first state-controlled bank to complete financial restructuring, the first large-scale commercial bank to introduce overseas strategic investors, and the first mainland commercial bank to be publicly listed overseas. Subsequently, based on the level of banking business development and the improvement of corporate governance structures, China's joint-stock commercial banks began listing both domestically and abroad. As of February 2018, apart from Bank of Communications, only three nationwide joint-stock commercial banks—Hengfeng Bank, Bohai Bank, and China Guangfa Bank—among the remaining 12 joint-stock commercial banks have yet to be listed.

Alongside the successful listings of some joint-stock commercial banks, although there were significant improvements in bank capital structure and asset quality, the changing socio-economic conditions, especially after China's accession to the WTO, brought comprehensive challenges from foreign financial institutions. In order to further improve bank capital structure, enhance corporate governance, or continue seeking domestic and international listings, joint-stock commercial banks in China began actively introducing strategic investors.

In December 1996, China Everbright Bank pioneered the introduction of strategic investors by successfully introducing the Asian Development Bank. Subsequently, the introduction of foreign strategic investors by joint-stock commercial banks can be broadly categorized into three situations. First, after listing, strategic investment partners were successively introduced based on the actual needs of bank development, as seen in the cases of Shanghai Pudong Development Bank, China Minsheng Bank, and Shenzhen Development Bank. Second, during the establishment of banks, foreign strategic investment partners were directly introduced, as in the case of Bohai Bank. When it was established in 2005, it had already brought in Standard Chartered Bank as a foreign strategic investor, making it the first domestic joint-stock commercial bank to introduce foreign strategic investors at the establishment stage. Third, to facilitate joint-stock restructuring and listing, foreign strategic investment partners were introduced before listing, which is the most common practice among China's joint-stock commercial banks. The situation of introducing strategic investors by national joint-stock commercial banks is shown in Table 7.14.

By introducing strategic investment partners, joint-stock commercial banks directly involve these partners, who possess rich management experience, in the bank's operations, business cooperation, risk control, and technological support. This has greatly improved the corporate governance structure and risk control level of joint-stock commercial banks, enhanced their operational capabilities, expanded their international business cooperation scope, and significantly strengthened their influence and competitiveness both domestically and internationally.

B. Rapid Development of Joint-Stock Commercial Banks' Business

With the deepening reform of joint-stock commercial banks, each bank has achieved significant development, with branch networks mainly centered in developed coastal areas. The business scope of most joint-stock commercial banks has expanded to cover various provinces, municipalities, and autonomous regions nationwide, as shown in Table 7.15.

With the rapid expansion of branch networks of joint-stock commercial banks, their businesses have achieved comprehensive development. Currently, leveraging

Table 7.14 Situation of introducing strategic investors by national joint-stock commercial banks

Strategic investor type	Bank name	Introduction time	Strategic investor and their shareholding percentage
Introduced during establishment	Bohai Bank	December 2004	Standard Chartered Bank (Hong Kong) Limited (19.99%)
Introduced during preparation for listing or listing process	Bank of Communications	November 2004	HSBC (19.9%)
	Huaxia Bank	October 2005	Deutsche Bank and Sal. Oppenheim Jr. and Cie. (14%)
	Guangdong Development Bank	February 2006 August 2006	Citibank (20%) IBM Credit (4.74%) Asian Development Bank (0.5%)
	Industrial Bank	December 2003	Hang Seng Bank (15.98%), Singapore Government Investment Corporation (5%), IFC (4%)
	China Everbright Bank	December 1996	Asian Development Bank (3.29%)
	China CITIC Bank	November 2006	Banco Bilbao Vizcaya Argentaria (5%)
	Hengfeng Bank	2008	Oversea-Chinese Banking Corporation (15.4%)
Introduced after listing	Shanghai Pudong Development Bank	September 2003	Citigroup (4.62%)
	Shenzhen Development Bank	May 2004 October 2005	Newbridge Capital (17.89%) GE (7%)
	China Minsheng Bank	July 2004, November 2004	IFC (1.08%) Temasek Holdings (4.55%)
No specific introduction	Zhejiang Commercial Bank	–	Formed from the restructuring of Sino-foreign joint venture banks
	China Merchants Bank	–	Controlled by China Merchants Group

Table 7.15 Deployment of branches of nationwide joint-stock commercial banks before February 2018

Bank name	Number of provinces, autonomous regions, and municipalities directly under the central government covered nationwide
China Merchants Bank	30
China Guangfa Bank	20
Shanghai Pudong Development Bank	31
Industrial Bank	30
Hua Xia Bank	30
China Minsheng Bank	31
Ping An Bank	23
Hengfeng Bank	13
China Everbright Bank	31
China CITIC Bank	20
Zhejiang Commercial Bank	14
Bohai Bank	12

information science and technology such as the internet, they have established intelligent platforms like mobile banking and online banking, providing financial services nationwide. In this process, the total assets of banks have rapidly increased, and their proportion within the entire financial institutions has significantly risen. The changes in the total assets of joint-stock commercial banks and their proportion of total assets in the financial institutions are shown in Table 7.16.

With the expansion of the asset scale of joint-stock commercial banks and the increase in their proportion of total assets among national financial institutions, the strength of banks has significantly strengthened. Their influence domestically and internationally has greatly increased. In 2017, their ranking in the "Top 1000 World Banks" by *The Banker* magazine in the UK is shown in Table 7.17.

In *The Banker* magazine's "Top 1000 World Banks" ranking, 9 nationwide joint-stock commercial banks from China entered the top 100, while the remaining 3 also made it to the top 200. Clearly, joint-stock commercial banks ranked based on core capital have demonstrated vigorous vitality and strong capabilities within a development span ranging from less than 30 years to as short as 12 years. Their expanded asset scale and enhanced strength, coupled with bank restructuring, have led to continuous improvements in their capital adequacy ratios and significant reductions in non-performing loan ratios, as shown in Table 7.18.

Since 2008, the capital adequacy ratio of joint-stock commercial banks has remained stable at around 12%, meeting the requirements of the "Basel Accord" for commercial bank capital adequacy ratios. From 2004 to 2010, the restructuring of joint-stock commercial banks, especially the equity division reform starting in 2005, greatly improved the quality of bank assets, leading to a significant decrease in the non-performing loan ratio.

Table 7.16 Changes in total assets of joint-stock commercial banks and their proportion of total assets in financial institutions*

Year	Total assets (in billions RMB)	Proportion of total assets in financial institutions (%)
2003	38,168.3	13.80
2004	46,972.2	14.90
2005	58,125.2	15.50
2006	71,419.0	16.20
2007**	72,494.0	13.80
2008	88,130.6	14.10
2009	117,849.8	15.00
2010	148,616.9	15.80
2011	183,794.0	16.20
2012	235,271.0	17.61
2013	269,361.0	17.80
2014	313,801.0	18.21
2015	369,880.0	18.55
2016	434,732.0	18.72
2017	449,620.0	17.81
2018***	470,202.0	17.50

Note * Financial institutions include policy banks, state-owned commercial banks, joint-stock commercial banks, city commercial banks, rural commercial banks, urban credit cooperatives, rural credit cooperatives, non-bank financial institutions, postal savings offices, and foreign-funded financial institutions

** Since 2007, joint-stock commercial banks no longer include Bank of Communications, but refer to the remaining 12 banks

*** Data for 2018 is sourced from the website of the China Banking and Insurance Regulatory Commission

Data source Compiled based on relevant year data from the official website of the China Banking Regulatory Commission

Subsequently, especially since 2013, with China's economy entering a new normal, the non-performing loan ratio has increased, indicating that the risks faced by joint-stock commercial banks are continuously growing due to the transformation and upgrading of China's economy. Since 2017, joint-stock commercial banks have experienced an increasing number of violations in wealth management, loans, and other aspects. For example, the Chengdu branch of Shanghai Pudong Development Bank was involved in non-performing loans of 77.5 billion yuan. The impact of such events will undoubtedly promote joint-stock commercial banks to strengthen the construction of standardized operations, internal control systems, information disclosure, and other aspects, in order to resolve financial risks, promote their sustainable development, and return to the essence of serving the real economy. With the continuous strengthening of capital strength, joint-stock commercial banks are expanding their presence both domestically and internationally. In November 1993, China Guangfa

Table 7.17 Ranking of nationwide joint-stock commercial banks in the "top 1000 world banks" by the banker magazine in 2017

Bank name	Ranking
China Merchants Bank	23
China CITIC Bank	25
Shanghai Pudong Development Bank	27
Industrial Bank	28
China Minsheng Bank	29
China Everbright Bank	49
Ping An Bank	59
Hua Xia Bank	67
China Guangfa Bank	93
Zhejiang Commercial Bank	131
Hengfeng Bank	145
Bohai Bank	200

Bank established a branch in Macau, becoming the first joint-stock commercial bank to open a branch overseas, marking the beginning of the globalization of joint-stock commercial banks. The globalization of joint-stock commercial banks is somewhat similar to that of state-owned commercial banks, with both initially establishing branches in Hong Kong, Macao, and Taiwan regions, and later expanding to developed countries in Europe and America, emerging countries, and other developing countries. By the end of 2017, except for Everbright Bank, which had not yet prepared to establish branches overseas and in Hong Kong, Macao, and Taiwan regions, the other 11 nationwide joint-stock commercial banks had begun to establish or had already established overseas branches, and had established relationships with overseas banks, acting as agent banks, etc., playing an increasingly important role in "the Belt and Road Initiative" and the process of globalization. The situation of nationwide joint-stock commercial banks establishing branches overseas and in Hong Kong, Macao, and Taiwan regions by the end of 2017 is shown in Table 7.19.

Meanwhile, during their expansive efforts, joint-stock commercial banks have taken a solid step forward by achieving certain successes in overseas mergers and acquisitions. This has significantly accelerated their globalization process, as illustrated in Table 7.20.

Although the degree of outward globalization of joint-stock commercial banks cannot yet compare with that of state-owned commercial banks, they started later, have fewer overseas mergers and acquisitions, and are not as large in scale. However, sporadic M&A activities also indicate the strategic pursuit of globalization development by joint-stock commercial banks.

Table 7.18 Changes in capital adequacy ratio and non-performing loan ratio of joint-stock commercial banks

Year	Capital adequacy ratio (%)	Non-performing loan ratio (%)
2004		4.94
2005		4.22
2006		2.81
2007		2.15
2008		1.35
2009	11.40	0.95
2010	12.20	0.70
2011	12.70	1.10
2012	13.25	0.99
2013	12.19	1.00
2014	11.23	1.12
2015	11.41	1.53
2016	11.62	1.74
2017	12.26	1.71
2018*	12.76	1.71

Note Before 2006, Bank of Communications was included, while from 2007 onwards, only the 12 joint-stock commercial banks are referred to. In the second quarter of 2014, Bank of Communications and China Merchants Bank adopted the Advanced Approach for capital management, while other banks continued with the previous methods. The capital adequacy ratio for 2013 is based on national data, and the relevant indicators are calculated according to the "Commercial Bank Capital Management Measures (Trial)", so there is no direct comparability with historical data, but it still reflects a trend

* Data for 2018 is sourced from the website of the China Banking and Insurance Regulatory Commission

Data source Compiled based on relevant year data from the official website of the China Banking Regulatory Commission

7.3 Establishment and Development of Urban Commercial Banks

After the reform and opening up, to adapt to the rapid development of urban individual and private economies, China began to establish urban credit cooperatives in 1979 to meet the financing needs of small and medium-sized enterprises and provide funds to local economies. Subsequently, it went through stages such as the comprehensive development of urban credit cooperatives, the restructuring of urban credit cooperatives into urban commercial banks, the restructuring and listing of urban commercial banks, and the rapid advancement towards informatization. Their rapid development, increased capital strength, especially their characteristic positioning of serving regional economies, have played an important role in promoting the development of China's socio-economy.

Table 7.19 Situation of nationwide joint-stock commercial banks establishing branches abroad and in Hong Kong, Macao, and Taiwan regions as of the end of 2017

Bank name	Establishment of branches in overseas and greater China (Hong Kong, Macau, Taiwan) regions
China Merchants Bank	Established branches in Hong Kong, New York, Singapore, Luxembourg, London, Sydney, totaling 6 branches, controlling Yonglong Bank established in Hong Kong
China Guangfa Bank	Established a branch in Macau and an agency in Hong Kong
Shanghai Pudong Development Bank	Established branches in Hong Kong and Singapore, and a representative office in London; established Pudong International
Industrial Bank Co., Ltd.	Established a branch in Hong Kong
Hua Xia Bank	Established representative offices in overseas and Greater China (Hong Kong, Macau, Taiwan) regions
China Minsheng Bank	Established branches in Hong Kong; acquired Tian Shun Securities Group Co., Ltd.
Ping An Bank	Established an agency in Hong Kong
China Everbright Bank	Established branches in Hong Kong and Seoul, and established Guangyin International; branches in Europe and Luxembourg are under construction
China CITIC Bank	Operates China CITIC Bank (International) Limited and CITIC Investment Limited in Hong Kong, with over 40 business outlets in Hong Kong, Macau, New York, Los Angeles, Singapore, and other regions
Zhejiang Merchants Bank	Planning to establish a branch in Hong Kong
Bohai Bank	Established a branch in Hong Kong
Hengfeng Bank	No branches established yet

7.3.1 The Precursor of Urban Commercial Banks—The Stage of Urban Credit Cooperatives

At the beginning of the reform and opening up, there was only the PBOC and some financial institutions attached to it nationwide. Fund allocation was entirely the role of "managing funds" and the cashier. Later, with the rapid development of the social economy across the country, the sole function of "managing funds" could no longer adapt to the actual development of China's diversified economy. In this context, besides separating the commercial functions attached to the PBOC, the central government also accelerated the establishment of urban credit cooperatives.

Since the reform and opening up, various types of economic forms have flourished in cities. In order to provide financial services to urban private, individual, collective

Table 7.20 Overseas mergers and acquisitions of national joint-stock commercial banks

Bank name	M&A date	M&A region	Amount/USD billion	M&A event
China Minsheng Bank	October 2007	United States	3.17	Acquired 9.9% stake in United Bancorp for $317 million. Initially planned to reach 19.9%, but terminated due to the collapse of United Bancorp in 2009, marking China Minsheng Bank's first failed overseas acquisition
China Merchants Bank*	May 2008	Hong Kong, China	46.4	Acquired 53.12% stake in Wing Lung Bank for HK$19.302 billion
China Merchants Bank	October 2008	Hong Kong, China	46.4	Increased its stake in Wing Lung Bank by acquiring 44.7% of shares for HK$17 billion, bringing its total ownership to 97.82%
China CITIC Bank	October 2009	Hong Kong, China	19.05	Acquired 70.32% stake in CITIC International Financial Holdings Limited for HK$14.765 billion
China Merchants Bank	October 2013	Netherlands	0.88	Increased its stake in China Merchants Fund Management Co., Ltd. by 21.6% for €63.6 million
China Merchants Bank	October 2013	Hong Kong, China	0.23	Acquired 50% stake in CMB CNAC for RMB 142 million

Note * China Merchants Bank acquired shares of China Merchants Fund Management Co., Ltd. for the first time in May 2007 by purchasing 10% of its shares from China Electric Financial Co., Ltd., China Huaneng Financial Co., Ltd., China COSCO Financial Co., Ltd., and China Merchants Securities respectively, completing the acquisition with 197.7 million RMB. Therefore, it does not fall under overseas actions

economies, etc., cities across the country began to establish urban credit cooperatives from 1979 to serve the development of local economies. In 1979, Henan Province established the first urban credit cooperative in Zhoukou. In 1983, a large number of collective urban credit cooperatives were piloted in cities such as Shenyang, Changchun, and Zhengzhou. In November 1986, Wenzhou first tried privately-owned urban cooperatives and established Dongfeng Urban Credit Cooperative and Lucheng Urban Credit Cooperative in a joint-stock manner. Subsequently, urban credit cooperatives quickly expanded from first-tier cities to second and third-tier cities, sparking a wave of founding urban credit cooperatives nationwide.

The large-scale establishment of urban credit cooperatives alleviated the tight funds situation in the cities where they were located, partially compensated for the shortcomings of state-owned financial institutions in service, increased the main financial supply entities, and played a certain role in ensuring funds for the orderly advancement of economic reform and opening up in China. Of course, influenced by the fluctuation between the policy of "managing funds" and " ragulating market," the operational management system of urban credit cooperatives was severely interfered with by local governments, with low operational efficiency, a strong planning color in fund allocation, limited capital, and low asset quality, which constrained their due role in promoting local economic development.

In 1992, Deng Xiaoping's Southern Tour broke the debate over "pro-capitalist" and "pro-socialist," and the 14th National Congress of the Communist Party of China established the framework for the development of the market economy. In this context, urban credit cooperatives gradually transformed from a single form to urban credit cooperative unions, and the establishment of urban credit cooperative unions across the country marked the formation of China's urban credit cooperative system. By the eve of the transition of urban credit cooperatives to urban cooperative banks in 1995, China had established more than 5000 urban credit cooperatives. Subsequently, urban credit cooperatives meeting the conditions were successively reorganized into cooperative banks and urban commercial banks. In March 2012, Ningbo Xiangshan County Luye Urban Credit Cooperative was restructured into Ningbo Donghai Bank Co., Ltd., marking the completion of the basic restructuring of urban credit cooperatives in China. Urban credit cooperatives, as a financial institution, exited the historical stage of financial development, but they played a significant role in promoting the development of urban economies during specific periods.

7.3.2 Establishment of Urban Commercial Banks

The large-scale establishment of urban credit cooperatives nationwide, influenced by many factors such as system, mechanism, internal management, and cultural differences, accumulated risks over the long term, bringing enormous impact to local economies. At the end of December 1993, the "Decision of the State Council on Financial System Reform" was issued, which explicitly stated the promotion of the gradual restructuring of urban credit cooperatives into urban cooperative banks. In this context, to resolve local financial risks, effectively integrate urban credit cooperatives, and maintain the stability and sustainable development of urban economies, China began promoting the restructuring of urban credit cooperatives into urban cooperative banks in areas where conditions were ripe starting from 1995.

In 1995, the "Notice of the State Council on the Establishment of Urban Cooperative Banks" was issued, and the PBOC first launched pilot work in 35 cities nationwide to establish urban cooperative banks based on urban credit cooperatives. On June 22, 1995, China's first urban cooperative commercial bank—Shenzhen Urban Cooperative Commercial Bank—was established on the basis of 16 urban credit cooperatives, marking the beginning of the restructuring of urban credit cooperatives. At the end of the same year, Shanghai Bank was restructured on the basis of urban credit cooperatives, becoming the first urban cooperative bank named after a city, greatly advancing the pace of restructuring urban credit cooperatives into urban cooperative banks nationwide. In March 1998, urban cooperative banks were renamed urban commercial banks, marking the transformation of urban cooperative banks into joint-stock banks.

In 2002, Zhejiang Taizhou established the first government non-controlling urban commercial bank—Taizhou Bank—through market-oriented means, enriching the forms of restructuring urban credit cooperatives in China. Subsequently, to accelerate the restructuring of urban credit cooperatives, the PBOC, especially the China Banking Regulatory Commission established in 2003, issued regulations to promote the restructuring of urban credit cooperatives. In November 2005, the China Banking Regulatory Commission, the People's Bank of China, the Ministry of Finance, and the State Administration of Taxation jointly formulated and issued the "Opinions on Further Promoting the Rectification of Urban Credit Cooperatives." These opinions clearly proposed promoting the rectification of urban credit cooperatives and advancing the market withdrawal of revoked and closed urban credit cooperatives. A new wave of restructuring urban credit cooperatives emerged nationwide, and in areas where conditions were ripe, it accelerated the process of jointly establishing joint-stock commercial banks with urban commercial banks and urban credit cooperatives.

At the beginning of the establishment of urban commercial banks, their operations were completely limited to a single city. As the business of urban commercial banks expanded, this development pattern greatly constrained the development space of urban commercial banks, hindered the digestion of non-performing assets, optimized bank resource allocation, controlled risks, and reduced loan concentration. To address this, urban commercial banks, based on the actual situation in various places, basically followed a development path from crossing counties or cities to provinces, then covering the whole country and crossing borders, gradually diverging the setting of their branch institutions. On December 28, 2005, Anhui Province first established a joint-stock commercial bank—Huishang Bank—based on 6 urban commercial banks and 7 urban credit cooperatives. On April 26, 2006, Shanghai Bank established a branch in Ningbo, marking the beginning of urban commercial banks setting up branch institutions across provinces and cities. In April 2012, the wholly foreign-owned Ningbo International Bank was restructured into Ningbo Tongshang Bank, becoming the first wholly foreign-owned bank in China to be restructured into a domestic urban commercial bank. Until now, the forms of restructuring urban commercial banks have become more diverse. They mostly originate from the banks themselves and the actual situations of their cities, adopting methods such as merger and reorganization, acquisition, or self-expansion to achieve scale expansion and business area extension. The expansion of urban commercial banks such as Beijing Bank, Ningbo Bank, and Shanghai Bank has completely surpassed provincial boundaries, greatly advancing the development pace of urban commercial banks in domestic layout.

By the end of 2017, China had established a total of 133 urban commercial banks, and their branch institutions covered all provinces, autonomous regions, and municipalities directly under the central government, playing an extremely important role in promoting the development of local economies.

7.3.3 Reform and Listing of Urban Commercial Banks

With the internal integration of urban commercial banks, the asset scale continues to expand, and asset quality has been effectively improved. Starting from the late 1990s, urban commercial banks began the transformation into joint-stock entities, and thereafter, those urban commercial banks that attracted investment and introduced strategic investors began to seek listings both domestically and internationally. The first urban commercial bank named after its city, Shanghai Bank, attracted international financial institutions such as International Finance Corporation and HSBC Bank as investors in September 1999 and December 2001 respectively, significantly improving the equity structure and enhancing corporate governance mechanisms. After careful preparation, in July 2007, Nanjing Bank and Ningbo Bank were listed on the Shanghai Stock Exchange and Shenzhen Stock Exchange respectively, marking the beginning of domestic listings for urban commercial banks. In September, Beijing Bank successfully went public on the Shanghai Stock Exchange. Following the successful A-share listings of Nanjing, Ningbo, and Beijing Banks, considering the significant market risks, regulatory authorities suspended the approval of domestic urban commercial banks' listing applications for eight consecutive years. In the absence of prospects for domestic listings, starting from 2013, a batch of urban commercial banks such as Chongqing Bank, Huishang Bank, Harbin Bank, and Shengjing Bank turned to seek listings in Hong Kong to overcome the dilemma of being unable to list domestically. Until January 2018, a total of 10 urban commercial banks had successfully listed on the H-share market. In June 2015, Qilu Bank successfully went public, becoming the first urban commercial bank listed on the National Equities Exchange and Quotations (NEEQ), also known as the New Third Board, marking the reopening of domestic listings for urban commercial banks. Subsequently, the pace of urban commercial banks' listings accelerated. As of early 2018, the listing status of some urban commercial banks is shown in Table 7.21.

The orderly restructuring and listing of urban commercial banks have improved the overall capital structure and corporate governance mechanisms of urban commercial banks. The asset scale has shown a rapid upward trend, and by 2018, the total assets of urban commercial banks exceeded 34 trillion yuan, accounting for 12.80% of the total assets of the entire financial institution sector. Since 2004, the total assets of urban commercial banks and their proportion of total financial institution assets are shown in Table 7.22.

Urban commercial banks have rapidly expanded their asset scale, increasing more than 17 times in just 14 years, far outpacing state-owned commercial banks. With the expansion of asset scale, urban commercial banks actively utilize information technology to enhance the quality and efficiency of services to the general public and the real economy. This has significantly contributed to the development of the social economy, with the number of loans increasing year by year.

As the overall strength of urban commercial banks continues to improve, in 2017, two banks, Beijing Bank and Shanghai Bank, entered the top 100 in the "Top 1000 World Banks" list by The Banker magazine, ranked by Tier 1 capital. Six banks

Table 7.21 Listing status of some urban commercial banks as of early 2018

Bank name	Listing date	Listing status
Ningbo Bank	July 2007	A-share
Nanjing Bank	July 2007	A-share
Beijing Bank	September 2007	A-share
Qilu Bank	June 2015	New third board
Guiyang Bank	August 2016	A-share
Jiangsu Bank	August 2016	A-share
Hangzhou Bank	October 2016	A-share
Shanghai Bank	November 2016	A-share
Chongqing Bank	November 2013	H-share
Huishang Bank	November 2013	H-share
Harbin Bank	March 2014	H-share
Shengjing Bank	December 2014	H-share
Jinzhou Bank	December 2015	H-share
Qingdao Bank	December 2015	H-share
Zhengzhou Bank	December 2015	H-share
Zhongyuan Bank	July 2017	H-share
Gansu Bank	January 2018	H-share

including Jiangsu Bank, Nanjing Bank, Huishang Bank, Ningbo Bank, Shengjing Bank, and Tianjin Bank entered the top 200. Seven banks including Jinzhou Bank, Xiamen International Bank, Hangzhou Bank, Harbin Bank, Zhongyuan Bank, Baoshang Bank, and Chongqing Bank entered the top 300. Fifteen banks including Dalian Bank, Chengdu Bank, Guiyang Bank, Guangzhou Bank, Zhengzhou Bank, Jilin Bank, Jiangxi Bank, Suzhou Bank, Changsha Bank, Hebei Bank, Qingdao Bank, Hankou Bank, Dongguan Bank, Lanzhou Bank, and Xi'an Bank entered the top 400. Additionally, 34 other banks entered the top 1000. The number of urban commercial banks entering the top 1000 accounts for nearly half of all urban commercial banks, demonstrating the continuously strengthening capabilities of urban commercial banks.

Meanwhile, their asset quality has also significantly improved, with the capital adequacy ratio steadily increasing and remaining at around 12%. The non-performing loan ratio showed a rapid decline from 2005 to 2011, followed by a slight increase, as shown in Table 7.23.

Since 2013, urban commercial banks have adopted a more rigorous and scientific method for calculating non-performing loan data. Although not directly comparable to pre-2013 figures, the data since 2013 undeniably reflects a slight upward trend in non-performing loans. This indicates an increase in operational risks for urban commercial banks, necessitating effective prevention measures from both regulatory authorities and the banks themselves. On May 24, 2019, Baoshang Bank was taken over by the PBOC and the China Banking and Insurance Regulatory Commission,

Table 7.22 Total assets of urban commercial banks since 2004 and proportion of total financial institution* assets

Year	Total assets (in billions)	Proportion of total financial institution assets (%)
2004	17,056.3	5.40
2005	20,366.9	5.40
2006	25,937.9	5.90
2007	33,404.8	6.40
2008	41,319.7	6.60
2009	56,800.1	7.20
2010	78,525.6	8.30
2011	99,845.0	8.80
2012**	123,469.0	9.24
2013	151,778.0	10.03
2014	180,842.0	10.49
2015	226,802.0	11.38
2016	282,378.0	12.16
2017	317,217.0	12.57
2018***	343,459.0	12.80

Note * Financial institutions include policy banks, state-owned commercial banks, joint-stock commercial banks, urban commercial banks, rural commercial banks, urban credit cooperatives, rural credit cooperatives, non-bank financial institutions, postal savings and remittance bureaus, and foreign financial institutions
** In 2012, Shenzhen Development Bank merged with the original Ping An Bank to become Ping An Bank, but the data has not been adjusted
*** Data for 2018 is sourced from the website of the China Banking and Insurance Regulatory Commission
Data source Compiled based on statistics from relevant years on the website of the China Banking Regulatory Commission

highlighting credit risks within urban commercial banks, though it remains an isolated case.

In response to the rapid development of urban commercial banks, regulatory authorities and the banks themselves have continuously strengthened standardization efforts. On one hand, the PBOC and the China Banking and Insurance Regulatory Commission have enhanced the standardization and management of legal regulations for urban commercial banks. The Commercial Bank Law of the People's Republic of China, enacted in 1995 and revised in 2005, has been pivotal in this regard. Furthermore, various regulatory measures have been continually developed and implemented. The 5th National Financial Work Conference in 2017, as well as the 19th National Congress of the Communist Party of China, both emphasized the need to strengthen financial risk prevention. Regulatory bodies such as the China Banking and Insurance Regulatory Commission have intensified their governance of urban commercial banks' violations and misconduct. For instance, significant fines

Table 7.23 Changes in capital adequacy ratio and non-performing loan ratio of urban commercial banks

Year	Capital adequacy ratio (%)	Non-performing loan ratio (%)
2005		7.73
2006		4.78
2007		3.04
2008		2.33
2009	11.20	1.30
2010	12.20	0.91
2011	12.70	0.60
2012	13.25	0.72
2013	12.19	0.86
2014	12.19	1.16
2015	12.23	1.43
2016	12.42	1.48
2017	12.75	1.52
2018*	12.80	1.79

Note The capital adequacy ratio for 2013 is based on national data, and the relevant indicators of the capital adequacy ratio are calculated according to the results of the "Interim Measures for the Capital Management of Commercial Banks." These data may not be directly comparable to historical data but still reflect a trend

* Data for 2018 is sourced from the website of the China Banking and Insurance Regulatory Commission

Data source Compiled based on statistics from relevant years on the website of the China Banking Regulatory Commission

were imposed on urban commercial banks involved in fraudulent gold cases in Henan Province at the beginning of 2018. On the other hand, in 2013, urban commercial banks established the Urban Commercial Banks Working Committee under the China Banking Association to enhance self-regulation within the industry. The committee aims to promote the stable and sustainable development of urban commercial bank financial institutions by adhering to laws, regulations, and national economic and financial policies. It integrates resources among member units, facilitates communication channels among them, cooperates with relevant departments to protect the legitimate rights and interests of member units, maintains financial market order, improves service levels, enhances core competitiveness, and supports comprehensive and sustainable economic and social development in China. Meanwhile, internal controls within urban commercial banks have been strengthened, including corporate governance and risk prevention mechanisms, to eliminate long-term accumulated risks.

7.4 Reform and Development of Rural Financial Institutions

Since the establishment of the People's Republic of China, the development of rural financial institutions has been continuous, becoming an integral part of China's financial system and playing a significant role in the development of rural areas, farmers, and agriculture. After the reform and opening-up, rural financial institutions experienced comprehensive development. Not only did rural credit cooperatives and the Agricultural Bank of China see significant growth, but rural commercial banks, township banks, and microfinance companies also emerged and grew rapidly. By the third quarter of 2017, the total assets of rural financial institutions had reached 32.36 trillion yuan, accounting for 13.09% of the total assets of the entire financial system. Although rural financial institutions had temporarily served as a "siphon" for urban finance during this period, their role in rural economic development was irreplaceable by any other financial institution.

7.4.1 Restoration and Development of Rural Credit Cooperatives

Before the reform and opening-up, rural credit cooperatives in China had achieved a certain level of development and played a significant role in balancing the financial relationship between urban and rural areas. Despite undergoing several major adjustments in its management system due to its "managing funds" function, rural credit cooperatives remained under the management of the PBOC for the most part, partially fulfilling the role of grassroots institutions of the central bank. After the reform and opening-up, with the separation of the Agricultural Bank of China from the PBOC, rural credit cooperatives were placed under the management of the Agricultural Bank of China. Following this change in the management system, rural credit cooperatives experienced rapid recovery and development. In August 1984, the State Council forwarded the Agricultural Bank of China's "Report on the Management System of Rural Credit Cooperatives," proposing to transform rural credit cooperatives into "autonomously operated, self-financed" cooperative financial organizations. This marked the beginning of the reform of rural credit cooperatives and promoted their rapid development.

The clear positioning of rural credit cooperatives' functions heralded the beginning of their development. Subsequently, by 1993, the number and asset scale of rural credit cooperatives in China had grown significantly. The development of rural credit cooperatives not only significantly promoted the rapid development of agriculture and rural economy but also laid the financial foundation for the rise of township enterprises. However, due to various factors such as unclear positioning in the earlier stage, intervention by local governments, small capital scale, and unclear positioning for "regulating market," the development of rural credit cooperatives was extremely uneven and insufficient. This changed the previously relatively stable and balanced development of urban–rural financial relationships, leading to a trend of segmentation in urban–rural financial relationships. In 1992, China clearly defined the goal of establishing a socialist market economy. In 1993, the Third Plenary Session of the 14th Central Committee of the Communist Party of China proposed accelerating financial system reform, significantly advancing the reform of rural financial institutions.

In accordance with the deployment of the Third Plenary Session of the 14th Central Committee of the Communist Party of China, the "Decision of the State Council on Financial System Reform" was promulgated in December 1993, which clearly proposed, according to the needs of rural commodity economy development, to gradually establish rural cooperative banks based on rural credit cooperatives. Regulations on Rural Cooperative Banks were to be formulated, and rural credit cooperative federations were to be separated from the Agricultural Bank of China and established as joint organizations of grassroots credit cooperatives. Rural cooperative banks were to be established only in counties and below. State-owned commercial banks could invest in rural cooperative banks according to the "Regulations on Rural Cooperative Banks," but could not change the collective cooperative financial nature of rural cooperative banks. In accordance with this requirement, the State Council decided in August 1996 that rural credit cooperatives should be separated from the administrative affiliation with the Agricultural Bank of China and placed under the unified management of the PBOC and provincial federations to promote the transformation of rural credit cooperatives into genuine cooperative financial organizations. Thus, the management system of rural credit cooperatives in China began to follow the principles of cooperative development. In August 1996, the State Council issued the "Decision of the State Council on the Reform of the Rural Financial System," which clearly pointed out that the focus of the reform was to reform the management system of rural credit cooperatives and transform them into genuine cooperative financial organizations.

In 1997, the Asian financial crisis erupted, shifting the focus of the country's financial reform towards risk prevention and accelerating the restructuring of state-owned commercial banks. In 1998, the state enforced mandatory cleanup and rectification of rural cooperative foundations, further affecting the reform of rural credit cooperatives. During this period, although rural credit cooperatives experienced some degree of development, their asset quality was far from optimistic due to historical factors. By 2001, 46% of rural credit cooperatives nationwide were operating at a loss, with 58% having assets that did not cover liabilities.[15] Meanwhile, rural credit cooperatives had deviated from their original purpose of serving members. Under the profit-driven mechanism, they focused more on absorbing funds in rural areas and lending in urban areas, exhibiting a "siphoning effect." Moreover, they had not truly established a democratic management system of "one member, one vote," failing to represent the interests of members or shareholders. In 2001, China formally joined

[15] Li Zhihui. *Development and Transformation of China's Banking Industry*. Gezhi Publishing House and Shanghai People's Publishing House, 2008:154.

the WTO, ushering in comprehensive competition from foreign financial institutions. To ensure that rural credit cooperatives truly serve their members and provide necessary financial support to agriculture, rural areas, and farmers, the central government once again called for reforms of rural credit cooperatives to achieve sustainable development.

In June 2003, the State Council issued the "Pilot Program for Deepening the Reform of Rural Credit Cooperatives." Following the framework of "clarifying property rights, strengthening constraint mechanisms, enhancing service functions, providing appropriate support from the state, and assigning responsibilities to local governments," the pilot reform was initiated in eight provinces and municipalities including Zhejiang, Jiangsu, Shandong, Jiangxi, Jilin, Chongqing, Guizhou, and Shaanxi. In August 2004, the "Opinions on Further Deepening the Pilot Reform of Rural Credit Cooperatives" clarified the direction of market-oriented reform for rural credit cooperatives. With the successful outcomes of the pilot reforms, the State Council expanded the reform of rural credit cooperatives nationwide. By the end of 2006, the reform had been rolled out in 29 provinces and municipalities, and by the end of 2007, the PBOC had issued 165.6 billion yuan of special central bank bills and provided 1.2 billion yuan of special loans to support the transformation of rural credit cooperatives into community and local financial institutions serving agriculture, rural areas, and farmers. Through central funding support policies, the financial condition of rural credit cooperatives improved significantly, their risk resistance capacity increased substantially, and their agricultural credit business level greatly improved.

With the nationwide promotion of the three-tier rural cooperative system, significant progress has been made in the reform of property rights and management systems of rural credit cooperatives. They have not only accumulated a large amount of funds in rural areas and played a significant role in serving agriculture, rural areas, and farmers but also enhanced the strength of rural finance and cultivated a large number of financial professionals serving agriculture, rural areas, and farmers. By 2017, there were 1373 rural credit cooperatives nationwide, with total assets reaching 10 trillion yuan. Their capital quality improved significantly, with a noticeable increase in capital adequacy ratio and a significant decrease in non-performing loan ratio. Meanwhile, the rapid development of rural credit cooperatives has provided necessary financial support for their transformation into rural commercial banks, the improvement of urban–rural financial relations, and the construction of new urban–rural relations.

7.4.2 Establishment and Development of New Rural Financial Institutions

While strengthening the reform of rural credit cooperatives, China encourages and supports the transformation of rural credit cooperatives into commercial banks or cooperative banks in coastal areas and economically developed rural and suburban areas. The approach is to "mature one institution as another develops." In areas where conditions are ripe, small loan companies are established to support existing commercial banks in leading the formation of rural banks, aiming to improve the difficult and costly financing situation in rural areas and expand financial services to cover more people and regions.

A. Establishment of New Rural Financial Institutions

Since 2000, China has initiated both the reform of existing rural financial institutions and the development of new ones. This includes the transformation of rural credit cooperatives into cooperative banks or commercial banks in some provinces and the gradual establishment of small loan companies and village banks.

Firstly, the establishment and development of rural cooperative banks and rural commercial banks. In August 2005, Shanghai established the Shanghai Rural Commercial Bank Co., Ltd. on the basis of rural credit cooperatives, marking the beginning of the transformation of rural credit cooperatives into rural commercial banks. By the end of 2007, 17 rural commercial banks and 113 rural cooperative banks had been established nationwide. In 2013, the pace of constructing cooperative banks and rural commercial banks accelerated. By 2017, 859 rural commercial banks and 71 rural cooperative banks had been established nationwide. Rural credit cooperatives gradually transformed into banks, improving and perfecting their operational mechanisms, optimizing ownership structures, enhancing operational efficiency, expanding branch networks, and initially forming a grassroots rural financial service network covering urban–rural fringe areas and vast rural areas. With the development of new urbanization and the redistribution of the population, some branches of rural commercial banks in suburban and remote mountainous areas have ceased operations due to business contraction. Contrary to the shrinking physical institutions, the networking and intelligence level of rural commercial banks have increased, and the trend of "e-rural commercial banks" has been significantly reinforced.

Secondly, the establishment of new village banks. Village banks are banking financial institutions approved by the China Banking Regulatory Commission according to relevant laws and regulations. They are set up in rural areas by domestic and foreign financial institutions, domestic non-financial corporate entities, and domestic natural persons to mainly provide financial services for local rural economic development. The layout of village banks in China differs from that of state-owned specialized banks; they are entirely developed in a standardized manner. Initially, the China Banking Regulatory Commission issued relevant regulations to standardize the market access conditions, business scope, and regulatory rules of village banks. According to the "Interim Provisions on the Administration of Village Banks" issued by the China Banking Regulatory Commission, the registered capital of village banks set up in prefecture-level cities shall not be less than RMB 50 million, in counties shall not be less than RMB 3 million, and in towns shall not be less than RMB 1 million.

On December 20, 2006, the China Banking Regulatory Commission issued the "Several Opinions on Adjusting and Relaxing the Access Policy of Banking Financial Institutions in Rural Areas to Better Support the Construction of a New Socialist Countryside." The document proposed pilot programs for establishing village banks in rural areas of six provinces and autonomous regions including Hubei, Sichuan, Jilin, Qinghai, Gansu, and Inner Mongolia. Subsequently, the China Banking Regulatory Commission successively issued the "Interim Provisions on the Administration of Village Banks" and the "Guidelines for the Establishment Approval of Village Banks," providing necessary institutional guarantees for the establishment and operation management of village banks while expanding the pilot areas to 31 provinces, municipalities directly under the central government, and autonomous regions. On March 1, 2007, the first three village banks in China were officially opened nationwide. Subsequently, the China Development Bank established the first village bank in Pingliang, Gansu, and HSBC began its layout of village banks in rural areas of Hubei's Suizhou. By the end of 2007, 19 new village banks had been established nationwide. By the end of 2008, 91 village banks had been established, and 57 were established in 2009. Subsequently, the establishment of village banks progressed steadily. By the end of 2013, a total of 1071 village banks had been established nationwide. In 2017, the total number of village banks in China reached 1311, with assets exceeding RMB 1 trillion, playing a significant role in supporting agriculture, serving "three rural issues," and targeted poverty alleviation in their respective regions.

Thirdly, the establishment and development of microfinance companies. According to the deployment of the State Council, China began pilot projects for microfinance companies in five provinces and autonomous regions, including Shanxi, Sichuan, Guizhou, Shaanxi, and Inner Mongolia, starting from 2005. By the end of 2007, seven microfinance companies had been established in these five provinces and autonomous regions. In May 2008, the People's Bank of China and the China Banking Regulatory Commission issued the "Guiding Opinions on Pilot Microfinance Companies," which effectively promoted the development of microfinance companies. In June 2009, the China Banking Regulatory Commission introduced the "Interim Provisions on the Transformation of Microfinance Companies into Village Banks," allowing eligible microfinance companies to be transformed into village banks. Subsequently, while some microfinance companies transformed into banks under suitable conditions, the number of microfinance companies increased rapidly. By the end of 2017, there were 8551 microfinance companies distributed across 31 provinces, municipalities directly under the central government, and autonomous regions, with a paid-up capital of 872 billion yuan and outstanding loans totaling 979.9 billion yuan.

Fourthly, the establishment of agricultural industry funds. In order to promote the development of modern agriculture and introduce diversified funding support, Beijing Agricultural Investment Co., Ltd., Jinshi Investment, Jianyang Trust, and others initiated the establishment of the Beijing Agricultural Industry Investment

Fund in 2009. Subsequently, provinces and municipalities such as Henan, Guangdong, Shandong, Zhejiang, Jilin, and Chongqing successively established agricultural industry funds. In 2012, the first national agricultural industry fund, the China Agricultural Industry Development Fund, was jointly established by the Agricultural Development Bank of China, the Ministry of Finance, CITIC Group, and China Cinda. The establishment of these industry funds has greatly enriched China's modern financial organizations supporting "three rural" issues and promoted the process of urbanization.

Overall, the establishment and development of new rural financial institutions have formed a financial network covering urban–rural fringe areas and vast rural areas across the country in just over a decade. Different from the development path and positioning of state-owned commercial banks, joint-stock commercial banks, and urban commercial banks, they have a clear focus on serving "three rural" issues and still have great expansion potential in rural areas under the strong support of national preferential policies. On January 9, 2018, the China Banking Regulatory Commission issued the "Notice on Carrying Out Pilot Work for Investment Management-type Rural Banks and 'One Bank for Multiple Counties' Rural Banks," launching pilot policies for investment management-type rural banks and "one bank for multiple counties" rural banks nationwide. This move will undoubtedly greatly promote the restructuring of rural financial institutions and play a significant role in bridging the gap in financial inclusion in rural areas, contributing to the construction of an inclusive financial system.

B. Development of New Rural Financial Institutions

Among the types of new rural financial institutions, rural commercial banks are the ones with the strongest financial strength and the most standardized operations. While other new rural financial institutions operate in smaller geographical areas and serve fewer people, they indeed play a certain positive role in benefiting agriculture and serving the rural population. Rural commercial banks have a large number of branches, are organized according to corporate governance, and have clear property rights. By 2018, their total assets exceeded 34 trillion yuan, making them the leaders among current rural financial institutions. After more than a decade of rapid development, the asset quality of rural commercial banks has significantly improved, as shown in Table 7.24.

As seen from the data since 2013, the capital adequacy ratio has generally shown an upward trend. Although the non-performing loan ratio is not high, its trend is increasing, indicating that there are still significant risks in operations. In the future, it is necessary to strengthen the corporate governance mechanism, as well as the construction of ownership structure and internal control mechanisms, to guard against regional and systemic financial risks.

With the strengthening of the capabilities, enlargement of scale, and improvement of mechanisms of rural financial institutions, some rural commercial banks have begun actively seeking listing to supplement their capital and promote further reform and institutional development. In 2010, Chongqing Rural Commercial Bank successfully listed on the Hong Kong Stock Exchange, becoming the first rural commercial

Table 7.24 Asset quality of rural commercial banks

Year	Capital adequacy ratio (%)	Non-performing loan ratio (%)
2013	12.91	1.67
2014	13.81	1.87
2015	13.34	2.48
2016	13.48	2.49
2017	13.30	3.16
2018	13.20	3.96

Note The capital adequacy ratio indicator for 2013 is replaced by the indicator for national commercial banks

Data source Compiled based on relevant information from the official website of the China Banking Regulatory Commission

bank in China to conduct an initial public offering. Subsequently, the listing of rural commercial banks slowed down, and it was not until January 2017 that Jiangyin Bank, Wuxi Bank, Changshu Bank, Wujiang Bank, and Zhangjiagang Bank were listed on the A-share market. In 2018, more than 20 rural commercial banks, including Jiangsu Zijin Rural Commercial Bank, Zhejiang Shaoxing Ruifeng Rural Commercial Bank, Qingdao Rural Commercial Bank, Jiangsu Dafeng Rural Commercial Bank, and Xiamen Rural Commercial Bank, actively prepared for listing, indicating an upcoming wave of listings of rural commercial banks.

Under the impact of high-cost factors such as the internet and information technology, rural financial institutions will inevitably accelerate their "networking" process and vigorously promote the development of internet financial services. Provincial, autonomous region, and municipality federations of rural cooperatives, as well as rural commercial banks, have launched financial services such as mobile payments, internet loans, direct banking, and e-commerce platforms. The internet will bring new development momentum to rural credit cooperatives, rural commercial banks, and other rural financial institutions. In the future, rural financial institutions still have enormous development space, especially in the application of information technology. On the one hand, to solve the "last mile" problem of financial services in rural areas, especially in remote mountainous areas, it is necessary to promote the construction of village convenience stores, self-service stores, and agricultural deposit and withdrawal service points in rural areas. On the other hand, some physical branch offices and other branch institutions may face closure due to constraints such as high costs. In the future, rural financial institutions should deepen reform, transform, strengthen market positioning, actively cultivate qualified rural financial market entities, fully activate rural financial resources, support structural reform of the agricultural supply side, prevent rural funds from being separated from rural areas, guard against the diversion of funds from real to speculative activities, and support them in playing a more proactive role in benefiting agriculture, serving rural areas, and targeted poverty alleviation efforts.

7.5 Other Banking Institutions

In addition to the aforementioned four types of banking institutions, with the increasing diversification of the economy, China's financial functions are becoming more market-oriented. To meet the financial needs of social and economic development, new types of banking institutions continue to emerge. Some are policy banks established to undertake policy-related businesses previously handled by state-owned banks, while others, such as the postal savings system, became independent as the China Postal Savings Bank in 2007. Additionally, private banks gradually emerged after 2013. The emergence of these banking institutions has made China's banking sector more diversified, with their total assets and share of the entire banking industry showing a continuous upward trend, reaching over 53 trillion yuan and 20.11% respectively by 2018. With their growing strength, these institutions are increasingly adapting to the financial needs of different regions, demographics, and enterprises.

7.5.1 Transformation of Policy Banks

The establishment of policy banks in 1994 completely separated commercial and policy businesses, fundamentally changing China's macro-financial system. Since then, Chinese policy banks have continuously reformed in response to the requirements of social and economic development, clarifying their functional positions, business scopes, and strengthening risk control, making significant contributions to social and economic development.

A. Establishment of Three Policy Banks

Before the establishment of policy banks in China in 1994, all policy-related financial businesses were undertaken by the People's Bank of China or state-owned specialized banks that were later separated from it or newly established. The situation where the People's Bank of China or state-owned specialized banks concurrently performed both policy and commercial functions seriously affected the independent exercise of the central bank's responsibilities by the PBOC and the full play of the commercialization functions of state-owned specialized banks. Against this background, the State Council issued the "Decision of the State Council on Financial System Reform" in December 1993, clarifying the direction of the commercialization reform of state-owned commercial banks. In 1994, the State Council decided to establish three policy banks with state capital, and their registered capital and shareholders are as shown in Table 7.25.

The three policy banks, namely China Development Bank, Agricultural Development Bank of China, and China Export–Import Bank, established with state capital in 1994, have undertaken corresponding policy tasks according to the State Council's financial reform plan, as shown in Table 7.26.

Table 7.25 Registered capital and shareholders of chinese policy banks

Bank name	Registered capital (in billions RMB)	Shareholders
China Development Bank	4212.48	Ministry of Finance, China Investment Corporation, Central Huijin Investment Ltd., and National Council for Social Security Fund
Agricultural Development Bank of China	200	Ministry of Finance, etc.
China Export–Import Bank of China	1500	Ministry of Finance, etc.

Table 7.26 Establishment time, funding source, and main functions of Chinese policy banks

Establishment time	Name	Funding source	Main functions
March 1994	National Development Bank	Capital funds allocated by the ministry of finance, key construction fund, national guarantee bonds issued to the public, financial bonds issued to financial institutions	Handling policy loans and discounting business for key national construction projects (including infrastructure and technological reform projects)
April 1994	China Export–Import Bank of China	Special fiscal funds, financial bonds issued to financial institutions	Providing buyer's credit and seller's credit for large-scale electromechanical equipment imports and exports, handling discounting and export credit guarantees for China's banking's complete sets of electromechanical products
November 1994	Agricultural Development Bank of China	Fiscal support for agriculture, deposits from agricultural policy loans, financial bonds issued to financial institutions	Undertaking policy loans for national grain, cotton, and oil reserves, agricultural and sideline products contract acquisition, sales, processing, agricultural development, and other businesses, acting as an agent for the disbursement and supervision of fiscal support funds for agriculture

The establishment of the three policy banks, namely the China Development Bank, the Agricultural Development Bank of China, and the Export–Import Bank of China, indicates the beginning of the separation between policy and commercial operations of state-owned specialized banks in China. These policy banks have gradually assumed the responsibilities previously held by state-owned specialized banks in their respective fields. Subsequently, their roles in China's economic transition have become increasingly important. The China Development Bank has provided substantial financial support in key areas such as infrastructure construction, shantytown renovation, new urbanization, and initiatives like "Going Global" and the "Belt and Road," highlighting the significant role of developmental finance, primarily in long-term investment and financing businesses. The Export–Import Bank of China has supported the export and import of large electromechanical products, complete sets of equipment, and high-tech products, facilitating the overseas expansion of Chinese enterprises and promoting the development of international economic and trade relations, playing a crucial role in international economic and trade cooperation. The Agricultural Development Bank of China has played an irreplaceable role in serving agriculture, particularly in supporting grain, cotton, and oil procurement and reserves, agricultural development, and rural infrastructure construction.

However, these policy banks face some challenges due to changes in domestic and international socioeconomic environments. In particular, issues such as the evaluation of projects not following market rules under government guarantees, the administrative allocation of funds, and unfair competition with commercial banks need urgent reform to clarify their functional positioning, business scope, and risk prevention.

B. Reform of Policy Banks

With the continuous improvement of China's socialist market economy, debates on the functional positioning of policy banks have attracted widespread attention from various sectors of society. In 2001, the State Council established a research group specifically to study the issue of the functional positioning of policy banks. In practice, the business of the three policy banks has been expanded to a certain extent. The Fifth Plenary Session of the Sixteenth Central Committee of the Communist Party of China in October 2005 clearly accelerated the reform of policy finance, focusing on promoting the reform of the China Development Bank. In accordance with the requirements of the modern financial enterprise system, a standardized corporate governance structure was established, commercialized operations were comprehensively promoted, and the main focus was shifted to medium and long-term business, with independent operation, risk-bearing, and self-financing. Following this path of deepening reform, policy banks steadily advanced their reform objectives based on their actual conditions. In 2007, Central Huijin injected an additional $20 billion into the China Development Bank; in December 2008, the China Development Bank Limited Liability Company was established, marking significant progress in the reform of the China Development Bank. At the Third Plenary Session of the Seventeenth Central Committee of the Communist Party of China held in October 2008, the State Council proposed to expand the support of the Agricultural Development Bank of China in agricultural fields, increasing policy finance support for the medium and long-term credit of agricultural development and rural infrastructure construction.

The Third Plenary Session of the Eighteenth Central Committee of the Communist Party of China in 2013 proposed to promote the reform of policy banks. In 2014, the State Council initiated a deepening reform of the three policy banks, focusing on three strategic points: increasing capital reserves, clarifying their functional positioning, business scope, risk control, etc. On April 12, 2015, the State Council approved the comprehensive reform plan for the three policy banks, marking the beginning of the reform of the three policy banks. According to the requirements of the State Council, the three policy banks have deepened their internal reforms to transform into banks with sufficient capital, standardized governance, strict internal control, safe operations, high-quality services, and excellent assets. This reform direction has clarified the positioning of policy banks and delineated their scope of business operations, as shown in Table 7.27.

At the same time, the three policy banks have established their own development requirements based on their actual situations, while adhering to a minimum capital adequacy ratio of 10.5%. The National Development Bank proposed "reasonably supplementing capital and strengthening capital constraint mechanisms", the Bank of China for Import and Export specified "enhancing capital strength and establishing a capital adequacy ratio constraint mechanism", and the China Agricultural Development Bank put forward "establishing a core constraint mechanism based on capital adequacy ratio". In July 2015, the State Administration of Foreign Exchange injected $48 billion into the National Development Bank; in December 2016, the State Council approved the "Articles of Association of the National Development Bank"; in April 2017, the National Development Bank was changed to a joint-stock company. Guided by their respective comprehensive reform plans, the China Agricultural Development Bank and the Bank of China for Import and Export have steadily pursued their reform goals. In November 2017, the China Banking

Table 7.27 Positioning and business scope of policy bank reform

Bank name	Positioning	Business scope
National Development Bank	Developmental finance	Market-oriented operations to support national strategies
China Export–Import Bank of China	Maintaining policy-oriented business as the mainstay	Separate management of policy-oriented and commercial business, supporting foreign trade operations and implementing the "go global" strategy
China Agricultural Development Bank	Strengthening policy functions	Separate management and accounting for policy and proprietary businesses, clarifying responsibilities and risk compensation mechanisms

Regulatory Commission issued the "Supervisory Measures for the National Development Bank", "Supervisory Measures for the Export–Import Bank of China", and "Supervisory Measures for the China Agricultural Development Bank". According to these regulations, they established a "two meetings and one layer" corporate governance structure consisting of a board of directors, a board of supervisors, and senior management, without setting up a shareholders' meeting; additional departmental directors were appointed, emphasizing the role of departmental directors in the board of directors, and implementing an external supervisor system. After 2018, policy banks will inevitably advance their reforms steadily in accordance with the requirements of deepening financial reforms set forth in the 19th National Congress of the Communist Party of China.

C. Development of Policy Bank Business

With the deepening reforms of policy banks, their business development has been greatly enhanced. Firstly, their branch networks basically cover the entire country, and they have made significant progress in "going global" and internationalizing their institutions, as shown in Table 7.28.

Secondly, their capital strength has continued to grow. After 23 years of development, by the third quarter of 2017, the total assets of the three policy banks reached 25.12 trillion yuan, accounting for 9.84% of the total assets of the banking and financial institutions. With a total loan amount of 17.41 trillion yuan, they have played a significant role in China's social and economic development, especially in projects related to the "Going Global" initiative and the "Belt and Road" construction, where their impact has become more pronounced.

Table 7.28 Deployment of domestic and overseas branches of policy banks as of the beginning of 2018

Bank name	Domestic branches	Branches in foreign and Hong Kong, Macao, and Taiwan regions
National Development Bank	37 primary branches and 3 secondary branches in 31 provinces, municipalities, and autonomous regions	Set up a branch in Hong Kong, as well as representative offices in Cairo, Moscow, Rio de Janeiro, Caracas, London, Vientiane, and 6 other locations
China Agricultural Development Bank	Established branches in 31 provinces, municipalities, and autonomous regions	Established branches in 31 provinces, municipalities, and autonomous regions established agency relationships with banks in 26 countries and established close ties with international financial organizations such as the Asia–Pacific rural cooperation organization
China Export–Import Bank of China	29 operational branches in 28 provinces, municipalities, and autonomous regions	Set up a representative office in Hong Kong, branches in Paris, and representative offices in Southeast Africa, St. Petersburg, and Northwest Africa

Thirdly, the influence of policy banks has been increasingly enhanced. These banks not only wield significant influence domestically but also have strong international outreach. China Agricultural Development Bank made it to the *Fortune Global 500* list in 2014, and the National Development Bank followed suit in 2015, highlighting their distinctive influence on the global stage.

7.5.2 Establishment and Development of Postal Savings Bank

At the beginning of the reform and opening up, with rapid economic growth, there was an overheating phenomenon in monetary circulation. In 1986, in order to stabilize the currency, the PBOC collaborated with the Ministry of Posts and Telecommunications to establish postal savings. This aimed to collect idle funds from the society and transfer them to the PBOC. From then until 2007, the Postal Savings Bank operated solely as a non-bank financial institution, apart from attracting savings, without engaging in other banking businesses. Based on the development of postal savings business and to reduce the high interest cost incurred by transferring funds to the PBOC, the Postal Savings Bank separated from the postal system in 2007. After undergoing restructuring and listing, it has become the sixth largest state-owned commercial bank in China, playing a significant role in promoting the development of the economy.

A. Establishment of China Postal Savings Bank

The Third Plenary Session of the Eleventh Central Committee of the Communist Party of China established the policy of prioritizing economic construction, leading to rapid social and economic development. To adapt to this trend, the PBOC expanded the money supply. From 1978 to 1984 alone, the money supply more than doubled, increasing from 21.2 billion yuan to 79.2 billion yuan. The substantial increase in money supply led to economic overheating. In order to stabilize the currency, given the lack of necessary macroeconomic control tools at the nascent stage of establishing the central bank, the PBOC had to contract the money supply through banking institutions, which, however, constrained the pace of economic development. Therefore, in January 1986, with strong support from the State Council, the PBOC and the Ministry of Posts and Telecommunications, acting as the supervising authority and the investment owner respectively, jointly issued the "Agreement on the Establishment of Postal Savings", aiming to absorb savings from the society through the postal system's branches nationwide to transfer them to the PBOC to tighten the money supply. According to the agreement, the Ministry of Posts and Telecommunications first piloted postal savings services in 12 cities including Beijing and Tianjin. By the end of 1986, the "Postal Law of the People's Republic of China" was enacted, explicitly designating postal savings as one of the statutory businesses of postal enterprises. Subsequently, postal savings business rapidly expanded nationwide, and the postal system gradually evolved into a de facto "quasi-banking" system.

When the postal system initially began handling savings business, its task was to help the PBOC absorb excess idle funds from the society, effectively performing open market operations to stabilize the currency. In addition to paying deposit interest according to national regulations, the PBOC paid a fee of 0.22% of the average daily balance per month to the Postal Savings Bank. The Postal Savings Bank earned fixed interest rate differentials without issuing loans to the society. Initially, the amount of savings absorbed by the Postal Savings Bank was relatively small. However, due to the excessively high interest rates provided by the PBOC to the Postal Savings Bank compared to commercial banks' deposits, coupled with the Postal Savings Bank's utilization of its branches distributed nationwide to absorb savings, the amount of savings deposits increased rapidly. By 2000, it had reached 457.8 billion yuan, undoubtedly leading to increasingly heavy interest expenses for the PBOC. In response, since the 1990s, the PBOC has adjusted the interest policy for postal savings transfers several times to gradually align it with the interest policies of other banks in order to reduce interest costs, as shown in Table 7.29.

Meanwhile, as the functions of the PBOC as an independent central bank have become increasingly refined, the objectives of monetary policy have become clearer, and macroeconomic control tools have become more abundant, leading to effective control of money supply. In this context, the continued use of the postal savings

Table 7.29 Changes in the interest policy for postal savings transfers by the People's Bank of China

Year	Interest policy changes
1993	Starting from July 11, 1993, segmented interest calculation was applied to long-term deposits of postal savings transferred to the People's Bank of China. Before the adjustment date, interest was calculated at an annual rate of 10.80%, and after the adjustment date, it was calculated at an annual rate of 12.42%. At the same time, the interest rate for current deposits was adjusted to an annual rate of 3.15%
1996	Starting from May 1996, the deposit interest rate for postal savings transferred to the People's Bank of China was adjusted to 10.53%
1997	Starting from October 1997, the deposit interest rate for postal savings transferred to the People's Bank of China was adjusted to 7.452%
1998	Starting from March 25, 1998, the annual interest rate for postal savings transferred to the People's Bank of China was further reduced to 7.218%
1999	The interest rate for postal savings transferred to the People's Bank of China remained at 5.922% and was adjusted again at the end of 1999
2002	Starting from February 21, 2002, the interest rate for postal savings transferred to the People's Bank of China was reduced by 0.2538 percentage points, from the existing 4.6008–4.347%
2003	Starting from August 1, 2003, for newly added postal savings deposits transferred to the People's Bank of China, interest was calculated at the reserve deposit interest rate of financial institutions, which was 1.89%. For postal savings transferred before August 1, 2003, the existing transfer deposit rate of 4.131% was applied for interest calculation. From August 1, 2003, newly added postal savings deposits were autonomously utilized by postal savings institutions

system by the PBOC to absorb social idle funds is no longer suitable for macroeconomic control needs. Urgent reforms are needed for the postal savings system. Since the reform of the deposit policy of the PBOC in 2003, the new deposits no longer enjoy the stable interest rate differential income. Therefore, by 2004, after postal savings absorbed deposits rose to 800 billion yuan, it had to seek new deposit channels.

The State Council responded to this trend by promoting the reform of both the postal and postal savings institutions. The postal savings were separated from the postal service, and a special postal savings bank was established to handle savings and other financial services. On March 20, 2007, the head office of China Postal Savings Bank was officially established. Subsequently, in accordance with the requirements of corporate reform, China Postal Savings Bank focused on the construction of corporate governance mechanisms and the establishment of branch offices nationwide. After nearly a year of preparation, by the end of 2007, the China Banking Regulatory Commission approved the establishment of 36 primary branches and 20,405 branch offices nationwide for China Postal Savings Bank. In this way, the postal and postal savings systems, which had previously specialized in savings business, were officially separated. China Postal Savings Bank began its path as a state-owned commercial bank, becoming the sixth largest state-owned commercial bank in China.

B. Restructuring and Listing of China Postal Savings Bank

Since the restructuring of postal savings business into China Postal Savings Bank in 2007, following the deployment of banking reforms by the State Council, China Postal Savings Bank has gradually promoted its restructuring and listing according to the steps of the state-owned commercial banks' "restructuring, introduction of strategic investors, and listing" in the shareholding system reform.

Firstly, the functions of China Postal Savings Bank were clarified. China Postal Savings Bank, relying on its extensive branch network, positioned itself in serving communities, small and medium-sized enterprises, and rural areas, dedicated to providing comprehensive financial services to the most dynamic customer groups in China's socio-economic transformation. After more than a decade of development, China Postal Savings Bank has become a leading large-scale retail bank in China. At the same time, China Postal Savings Bank also actively serves large customers and participates in major project construction, playing an increasingly important role in China's economic reform and development.

Secondly, the implementation of the shareholding system reform. When China Postal Savings Bank was established in 2007, China Post Group held exclusive control, and the heads of most provincial, municipal, and autonomous region branches were concurrently members of the party group or members of the party committee of the provincial-level postal companies. Subsequently, after nearly five years of exploration, the China Banking Regulatory Commission approved the shareholding reform plan of China Postal Savings Bank on December 31, 2011; on January 21, 2012, China Postal Savings Bank was officially renamed China Postal Savings Bank Co., Ltd.

Thirdly, the introduction of strategic investors. At the time of the shareholding reform, the assets of Postal Savings Bank exceeded 3.2 trillion yuan, with a loan-to-deposit ratio of less than 20%, a very low non-performing loan ratio, and excellent asset quality. With the implementation of the shareholding system reform of Postal Savings Bank, the loan-to-deposit ratio rapidly increased, and the capital adequacy ratio index showed a significant decline, making it an urgent task for Postal Savings Bank to increase capital and introduce strategic investors. After three years of preparation and investigation, considering factors such as strategic synergy, transaction price, financial strength, and brand influence, China Postal Savings Bank introduced 10 strategic investors in December 2015, including six internationally renowned financial institutions such as UBS Group, JPMorgan Chase, DBS Bank, Canada Pension Plan Investment Board, Temasek, International Finance Corporation, two large state-owned enterprises, China Life and China Telecom, and two Internet leading enterprises, Ant Financial and Tencent. Through this introduction of diversified strategic investors, China Postal Savings Bank raised a total of 45.1 billion yuan in funds, with an issuance ratio of 16.92%, making it the largest single issuance scale in China's financial industry and the largest overall scale in nearly five years since 2015. The introduction of diversified strategic investors greatly enriched the capital of China Postal Savings Bank, completely improved the corporate governance mechanism of China Postal Savings Bank, and improved indicators such as capital adequacy ratio.

Finally, successful listing. With the introduction of strategic investors, China Postal Savings Bank continuously improved its articles of association, rules of shareholders' general meeting, rules of board of directors' meeting, and established a preliminary set of scientific and complete corporate governance system, greatly enhancing the comprehensive strength and competitiveness of China Postal Savings Bank. The capital structure gradually became reasonable, and the corporate governance structure continued to improve, thus forming a more rational "three meetings and one layer." Under these conditions, China Postal Savings Bank successfully listed on the Hong Kong Stock Exchange in September 2016, formally entering the international capital market.

C. Business Development of Postal Savings Bank

The transformation to a shareholding system and listing of Postal Savings Bank greatly improved the bank's governance structure, enhanced operational efficiency, and effectively integrated bank institutions. By 2017, the branch network of Postal Savings Bank covered the entire country, making it the bank with the most extensive branch network in China's financial institutions. With nearly 40,000 business outlets, it served over 500 million individual customers, demonstrating excellent asset quality and significant potential for future development.

In the face of rapid advancements in information technology such as the Internet, the Internet of Things, big data, and artificial intelligence, as well as strong impacts from internet finance, Postal Savings Bank proactively accelerated its informatization process. Currently, it has established a comprehensive electronic banking system that includes online banking, mobile banking, self-service banking, telephone banking, and "micro-banking," forming an interconnected network between electronic channels and physical branches. This integration of offline physical banks with online virtual banks has played a leading role in constructing an inclusive financial system.

The clear positioning of Postal Savings Bank in serving rural areas, agriculture, and small and micro-enterprises provides strong financial support for rural revitalization strategies implemented since the 19th National Congress of the Communist Party of China. The precise positioning of Postal Savings Bank has been fully recognized by the central government. In the past 15 consecutive Central Committee No.1 documents, 12 have mentioned both the pre-restructuring postal savings department and the post-restructuring Postal Savings Bank. The Central Committee No.1 document in 2016 specifically stated support for the establishment of the "agriculture, rural areas, and farmers" financial department by China Postal Savings Bank to build a specialized system to serve agriculture. The 2018 Central Committee No.1 document explicitly stated, "Increase support from China Agricultural Bank and China Postal Savings Bank's agriculture, rural areas, and farmers financial departments for rural revitalization." To implement the requirements of the 2018 Central Committee No.1 document, Postal Savings Bank clearly proposed deepening the institutional mechanism construction of the "agriculture, rural areas, and farmers" financial department, continuously increasing credit funding in key areas for agriculture, actively serving the structural reform of the agricultural supply side, and contributing to the rural revitalization strategy.

Clearly, after restructuring and listing, Postal Savings Bank has significantly strengthened its capital base, rapidly increasing its influence both domestically and internationally. Domestically, Postal Savings Bank has become one of China's six largest state-owned commercial banks. Internationally, according to the "Top 1000 World Banks" ranking by *The Banker* magazine in 2017, Postal Savings Bank ranked 21st in total assets. Additionally, in the "*Fortune Global 500*" ranking, Postal Savings Bank ranked 34th with a revenue of 189.6 billion yuan.

7.5.3 The Rise of Private Banks

With the rapid development of China's economy, existing financial institutions have struggled to meet the demand for capital in society. The issue of "difficulty in obtaining financing" has long been a concern in China. To alleviate the "Macmillan gap" for small and medium-sized enterprises, on June 19, 2013, the State Council executive meeting explicitly encouraged private capital to establish private banks, guiding credit funds to support the real economy. In July, the State Council issued the "Guiding Opinions on Financial Support for Economic Restructuring and Transformation and Upgrading," proposing to "attempt to establish private banks and other financial institutions initiated by private capital at their own risk." With favorable policies in place, a large number of private enterprises became involved in the establishment of private banks. By November 2013, a total of 23 private banks nationwide had obtained pre-approval from the State Administration for Industry and Commerce. Subsequently, after deliberation, the China Banking Regulatory Commission allowed 10 companies to conduct trial operations through designated means. By 2015, five private banks, including WeBank in Qianhai, Jincheng Bank in Tianjin, Minshang Bank in Wenzhou, Webank in Zhejiang, and Huarui Bank in Shanghai, had successively obtained banking licenses, as shown in Table 7.30.

The establishment of the first five private banks has brought a new experience to Chinese enterprises and the public. Unlike traditional banks, they are initiated by private enterprises, have relatively sound corporate governance structures, employ advanced risk control technologies, implement differentiated market positioning and distinctive business operations, and adopt advanced information technology to support banking services and new business models, changing the traditional lending practices of banks. For example, WeBank uses Tencent's social data credit rating scores to issue loans, while Webank leverages Alibaba's big data, especially Ant Financial's technological advantages, to provide financial services to customers. They all operate online without offline branches. The other three private banks

Table 7.30 Basic information of the initial 5 private banks

Private bank name	Initiators	Positioning	Capital (in billion yuan)	Establishment time
WeBank	Tencent, Baiyeyuan, Liye, etc.	Individual savings and loans	30	December 2014
Kincheng Bank of Tianjin	North China, Maigou, etc.	Public deposits and loans	30	April 2015
Wenzhou Minshang Bank	Zhongtai, Huafeng, etc.	Supporting micro and small enterprises, serving rural areas, rooted in communities	20	March 2015
Zhejiang E-Commerce Bank	Ant Microfinance Services Group, Shanghai Fosun Industrial Technology Development Co., Ltd., Wanxiang Agriculture and Animal Husbandry Group Co., Ltd., Ningbo Jinrun Asset Management Co., Ltd., etc.	Micro deposits and loans	40	June 2015
Shanghai Huarui Bank	Shanghai Junyao (Group) Co., Ltd., Shanghai Metersbonwe Fashion and Accessories Co., Ltd., and 10 other private enterprises	Specific regional deposits and loans (trade finance, microfinance, internet finance, etc.	30	May 2015

provide services different from traditional banks based on their own characteristics. In order to strengthen communication and development among private banks, in November 2015, five private banks jointly issued the "China Private Bank Development Convention" in Shanghai, advocating for inclusive development, differentiated development, mutual benefit, and cooperation to promote the development of the social economy.

Since 2016, China's regulatory authorities have successively approved the establishment of the second batch of 12 private banks. By the end of 2017, Chongqing Fumin Bank, Sichuan Xinwang Bank, Hunan Sanxiang Bank, Anhui Xin'an Bank, Fujian Huatong Bank, Wuhan Zhongbang Bank, Beijing Zhongguancun Bank, Jiangsu Suning Bank, Weihai Lanhai Bank, Jilin Yilian Bank, and Liaoning Zhenxing Bank had all been formally approved by the State Council, with the first eight already in operation, greatly enhancing the strength of China's private banks.

Since their opening in 2015, the first batch of five private banks including WeBank have developed rapidly. By the end of 2016, they had all achieved profitability, with total assets reaching 172.07 billion yuan, a non-performing loan ratio of 0.58%, and a capital adequacy ratio of 16.75%, far better than other financial institutions in the same period. In addition to the aforementioned five, a total of 17 private banks have been approved for establishment nationwide, eight of which have already been opened. Their total assets have reached 182.559 billion yuan, an increase of 129.83%[16] from 2016. Their asset quality continues to rank among the top of all financial institutions, with a non-performing loan ratio of 0.53% and a capital adequacy ratio of 24.25% at the end of 2017. Currently, although the asset size of private banks is relatively small, their new business models increasingly conform to the trend of social and economic development, gaining widespread recognition from the public and bringing about a significant "catfish effect" to the development of China's financial industry, driving a wave of innovation in the financial industry. Of course, under the rapidly changing external environment and social economy, the operating modes of these private banks also face relatively high operational risks and will need to continuously strengthen financial risk prevention and control in the future.

7.6 Opening Up of the Banking Industry

Since the reform and opening-up, the Chinese government has been responsive to the diverse development trends in the socio-economic sphere. Beginning in 1979, it gradually loosened the access system for foreign-funded banking institutions. These institutions entered China through two methods: direct establishment and equity participation. Both methods have seen significant development to date. During this period, as foreign-funded banks expanded their presence in China's banking industry,

[16] "First Batch of 5 Private Banks All Profitable, Achieving a Net Profit of 980 Million Yuan Last Year". *People's Daily*, December 26, 2017:10.

the government continuously introduced laws and regulations to regulate their development. By the end of 2017, they had become an integral part of the domestic banking industry, playing an increasingly important role in serving the real economy and facilitating the lives of the people.

7.6.1 *Entry and Standardized Development of Foreign-Funded Banks*

Foreign-funded banks initially entered China by establishing representative offices or branches within the country. After 2006, they transitioned into legal entities in accordance with China's laws and regulations. By 2017, 210 foreign-funded banking institutions had been established in China with total assets exceeding 3 trillion yuan, significantly diversifying the types of banking and financial institutions in China and becoming an important component of the country's financial system.

A. Entry and Initial Development of Foreign-Funded Banks

With the implementation of China's reform and opening-up policy, foreign-funded banks began to enter the Chinese market. In 1979, the Bank of Tokyo-Mitsubishi UFJ was approved to establish a permanent representative office in China. In 1981, the Bank of East Asia from Hong Kong established a branch in Shenzhen, marking the beginning of the presence of foreign and overseas Chinese-funded financial institutions in China. Subsequently, overseas Chinese and foreign-funded financial institutions were introduced and developed, with 528 representative offices established in 25 Chinese cities by 1996.

In line with the gradual entry of foreign and overseas Chinese-funded banks into China, in April 1985, the State Council issued the "Regulations on the Management of Foreign-Funded Banks and Sino-Foreign Joint Venture Banks in Economic Special Zones of the People's Republic of China" to regulate the management of foreign-funded banking institutions. In September 1990, the PBOC issued the "Measures for the Administration of Shanghai Foreign-Funded Financial Institutions and Sino-Foreign Joint Venture Financial Institutions," strengthening the regulation of foreign-funded financial institutions. In April 1994, to strengthen and improve the management of foreign-funded financial institutions, adapt to further opening-up and economic development needs, the PBOC formulated and promulgated the "Regulations on the Management of Foreign-Funded Financial Institutions of the People's Republic of China," stipulating the market access conditions, termination, business scope, and regulatory standards for foreign-funded banks operating in China. This marked the legalization and standardization of the approval and management of foreign-funded financial institutions in China.

In 1996, the PBOC issued the "Interim Measures for the Pilot Management of RMB Business of Foreign-Funded Financial Institutions in Shanghai Pudong," opening up RMB business for foreign-funded banks to serve foreign-funded enterprises and overseas residents, significantly advancing the development of foreign-funded financial institutions in China. In 2001, China joined the WTO, subsequently accelerating the opening-up of the banking industry to overseas institutions. In December, China lifted geographical and object restrictions on foreign-funded banks conducting foreign exchange business within China, allowing them to conduct foreign exchange business for Chinese enterprises and residents. At the same time, China gradually opened up RMB business for foreign-funded banks (Table 7.31).

In late 2001 and early 2002, China successively promulgated the "Regulations of the People's Republic of China on the Administration of Foreign-Funded Financial Institutions (Revised)" and the "Implementation Rules for the Regulations of the People's Republic of China on the Administration of Foreign-Funded Financial Institutions (Revised)." Subsequently, until 2006, in accordance with WTO rules and domestic regulations, China fully opened its domestic market to foreign-funded financial institutions, implementing comprehensive "national treatment." During this period, however, foreign-funded banks entering China still maintained the pattern of only establishing branches. By 2005, a total of 68 foreign-funded banks from 19 countries and regions had set up 170 branches, 24 sub-branches, and 24 legal entities in China, laying the foundation for a preliminary operating network of foreign-funded banks within China.

B. Expansion and Rapid Development of Foreign-Funded Banking Industry

Prior to 2006, foreign-funded banks in China operated in the form of representative offices and branches, lacking independent legal entity status. In November 2006, China promulgated the "Implementation Rules for the Regulations of the People's Republic of China on the Administration of Foreign-Funded Banks," which clarified the market access conditions and implementation details for establishing wholly foreign-owned banks or Sino-foreign joint venture banks in China. It also stipulated that the branches of foreign-funded banks in China would be restructured into wholly foreign-owned banks funded solely by their headquarters, with clear provisions on

Table 7.31 Overview of China's opening-up of RMB business for foreign-funded banks

Time	Opening-up regions
End of 2001	Shanghai, Shenzhen, Tianjin, Dalian
End of 2002	Guangzhou, Qingdao, Zhuhai, Nanjing, Wuhan
End of 2004	Kunming, Beijing, Xiamen, Shenyang, Xi'an
End of 2005	Shantou, Ningbo, Harbin, Changchun, Lanzhou, Yinchuan, Nanning
End of 2006	Geographical and customer restrictions on foreign-funded banks conducting RMB business were lifted at the end of 2006, allowing them to provide RMB services to all customer

the rules to be followed during the restructuring process. In accordance with these rules, China initiated a reform aimed at transitioning foreign-funded banks in China toward a legal entity-oriented model. After more than a year of pilot reforms, foreign-funded banks established in China successfully transitioned from being "branch-led" to being "legal entity-led." Subsequently, through the smooth reform of existing branches and other institutions of foreign-funded banks, the speed of establishment of foreign-funded bank branches in China accelerated. By the end of 2007, a total of 193 banks from 47 countries and regions had set up 242 representative offices in China, including 24 wholly foreign-owned banks, 2 joint venture banks, and 3 wholly foreign-owned financial companies. Additionally, 71 foreign-funded banks from 23 countries and regions had established 117 branches in China.

However, the pace of establishing branch institutions by foreign-funded banks in China gradually slowed down due to global financial crises such as the subprime mortgage crisis and the European debt crisis, although business development continued steadily. By the end of 2015, banks from 15 countries and regions had established 37 wholly foreign-owned banks, 2 joint venture banks, and 1 wholly foreign-owned financial company in China. Additionally, banks from 26 countries and regions had set up 114 branches in China, while banks from 46 countries and regions had established 174 representative offices. Furthermore, 38 foreign-funded legal entity banks and 86 foreign bank branches were authorized to engage in RMB business in China, and 31 foreign-funded legal entity banks and 31 foreign bank branches were authorized to engage in financial derivative transactions in China. Six foreign-funded legal entity banks were authorized to issue RMB financial bonds in China, while four foreign-funded legal entity banks were authorized to operate credit card issuing businesses in China, and one foreign-funded legal entity bank was authorized to operate credit card acquiring businesses in China. Foreign-funded banks had established operational branches in 69 cities across 27 provinces, municipalities, and autonomous regions in China, forming a service network consisting of headquarters, branches, and sub-branches with a certain coverage and market depth, totaling 1044 branches.

As the economies of developed countries in Europe and America, as well as emerging and developing countries, gradually recovered, activities of foreign-funded banks in establishing branch institutions in China resumed. In order to promote the development of business operations of foreign-funded banks in China, the China Banking Regulatory Commission issued the "Notice on Relevant Matters Concerning the Conduct of Partial Business by Foreign-Funded Banks" in March 2017, allowing foreign-funded banks to invest in domestic banking and financial institutions in China to strengthen supervision and management of the establishment of banks by foreign-funded financial institutions in China. With increasingly standardized institutional construction, foreign-funded bank institutions in China have achieved significant development. By the end of November 2017, China had a total of 210 foreign-funded banking financial institutions, including 39 foreign-funded legal entity banks, 17 new-type rural financial institutions with foreign investment, 31 non-banking financial institutions with foreign investment, and 123 foreign bank branches. In addition, there were more than 100 bank institutions with foreign investment.

Table 7.32 Trends in total assets of foreign-funded banks in China since 2007

Year	Change in total assets of foreign-funded banks
2007	1.24
2008	1.37
2009	1.44
2010	1.90
2011	2.34
2012	2.46
2013	2.58
2014	2.81
2015	2.77
2016	3.17
2017	3.24

Data source Compiled based on relevant data from the National Bureau of Statistics website

As foreign-funded bank institutions in China develop slowly and in a regulated manner, their total asset volume has increased rapidly, as shown in Table 7.32.

Over the past decade since the restructuring of foreign-funded bank branch institutions into legal entity banks, the capital scale of foreign-funded banks in China has more than doubled, exerting a certain influence on the development of China's socio-economy. However, their proportion in the total assets of China's banking industry is very low and has shown a continuous downward trend, as shown in Fig. 7.6.

Meanwhile, the asset quality of foreign-funded banks and their branches in China has significantly improved. Data since 2013 shows a considerable increase in capital adequacy ratio and a noticeable decrease in the non-performing loan ratio, as illustrated in Table 7.33.

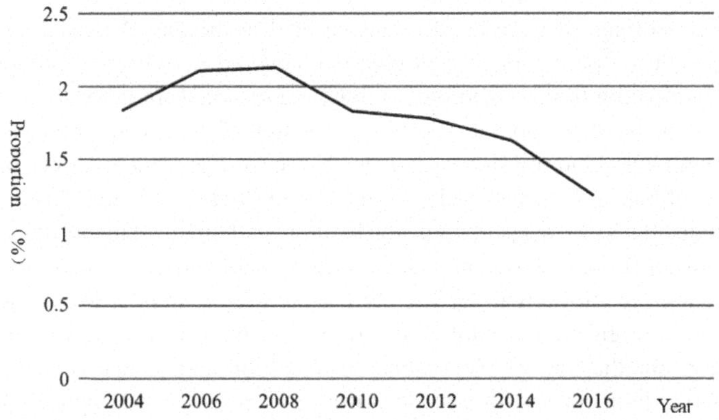

Fig. 7.6 Changes in the proportion of assets of foreign-funded banks to the total assets of the national banking industry

Table 7.33 Asset quality of foreign-funded banks

Year	Capital adequacy ratio (%)	Non-performing loan ratio (%)
2013	12.91	0.51
2014	17.08	0.81
2015	18.48	1.15
2016	18.58	0.93
2017	17.83	0.70
2018	18.40	0.69

Note In 2013, the capital adequacy ratio indicator is replaced with that of national commercial banks, while for other years, the capital adequacy ratio of foreign-funded banks is used
Data source Compiled based on statistics from the official website of the China Banking Regulatory Commission

Compared to various types of banking institutions in China, the capital adequacy ratio and non-performing loan ratio of foreign-funded banks are superior during the same period. Particularly notable is the trend in non-performing loan ratios, where foreign-funded banks show a significant decrease, while Chinese banking institutions have experienced a slight upward trend since 2013. This suggests that foreign-funded banks have more robust risk prevention and internal control mechanisms. As China's financial opening-up deepens, foreign-funded bank institutions are expected to develop more rapidly, playing a more positive role in the transformation of China's socio-economic landscape.

7.6.2 Foreign Financial Institutions' Strategic Investments in the Chinese Banking Industry

In addition to establishing branches or establishing wholly-owned and joint venture banks directly within China, foreign financial institutions can also participate by acquiring stakes in Chinese banking institutions. To compensate for their shortcomings in terms of business networks, RMB funds, and customer information within China and to enhance their competitive strength and influence, foreign financial institutions have cooperated with Chinese financial institutions for a long time. Especially since 1996, foreign financial institutions have seized the opportunity of deepening reforms in China's financial industry to intervene in Chinese financial institutions as strategic investors. In the same year, the Asian Development Bank acquired shares in China Everbright Bank, marking the beginning of foreign financial institutions' investment in Chinese banking institutions.

From 1996 to 2003, foreign financial institutions' investment in Chinese banking institutions did not receive permission from relevant laws and regulations. At this time, the number of foreign financial institutions entering Chinese banking institutions was relatively small and their proportion was not high, representing an initial exploration phase. To regulate the behavior of overseas financial institutions investing in Chinese financial institutions and optimize the capital structure of Chinese financial institutions, after a period of research and exploration, China, with the approval of the State Council, promulgated the "Regulations on Overseas Financial Institutions Investing in Chinese Financial Institutions" in December 2003, which explicitly stipulated the qualifications and shareholding ratios for investing in Chinese financial institutions. Articles 8 and 9 of these regulations clearly stipulate that a single overseas financial institution's shareholding ratio in Chinese financial institutions should not exceed 20%. If the cumulative shareholding ratio of multiple overseas financial institutions in non-listed Chinese financial institutions reaches or exceeds 25%, the supervision and management of that non-listed financial institution will be conducted according to the standards for foreign-funded financial institutions. If the cumulative shareholding ratio of multiple overseas financial institutions in listed Chinese financial institutions reaches or exceeds 25%, the supervision and management of that listed financial institution will still be conducted according to the standards for Chinese financial institutions.

In response to the promotion of China's financial reform at the Second National Financial Work Conference in 2002, Chinese banking institutions began to carry out reforms to become joint-stock companies, with the introduction of strategic investors playing an important role in this process. Against this background, foreign financial institutions accelerated their pace of investment in Chinese state-owned banks, national joint-stock commercial banks, urban commercial banks, rural commercial banks, and other banking institutions. In response to this trend, regulatory authorities such as the China Banking Regulatory Commission strengthened the standardization of foreign financial institutions' investment in Chinese banks. In April 2006, the China Banking Regulatory Commission issued the "Guidelines on Corporate Governance of State-owned Commercial Banks and Related Regulatory Guidelines," which clearly stated in Article 6 the five standards that state-owned commercial banks must follow when introducing strategic investors: (1) the shareholding ratio of strategic investors should generally not be less than 5%; (2) the holding period of strategic investors' equity should be more than 3 years from the delivery date; (3) strategic investors should generally send directors to banks, while experienced strategic investors are encouraged to send senior management personnel to directly disseminate management experience; (4) strategic investors should have rich backgrounds in financial industry management, as well as mature financial management experience, technology, and a willingness to cooperate; and (5) commercial banks with strategic investors should not have more than two state-owned commercial banks as strategic investors. In the same year, in December, the China Banking Regulatory Commission revised the "Implementation Measures for Administrative Licensing Matters of Chinese Commercial Banks," changing the requirement from "qualified overseas strategic investors should be included among the founding shareholders" to "qualified strategic investors should be included among the founding shareholders." In December 2017, with the approval of the State Council, the China Banking Regulatory Commission announced the relaxation of the foreign shareholding ratio restrictions on Chinese banks and financial asset management companies, and for the first time, clarified the consistent implementation of the equity investment ratio rules, thereby significantly promoting the development of foreign financial institutions in China. In March 2018, Premier Li Keqiang explicitly stated in the government work report that the proportion of foreign shares in banks, securities, fund management, futures, and financial asset management companies would be further relaxed or abolished. At the Boao Forum for Asia held in April, Yi Gang, Governor of the People's Bank of China, stated that the proportion of foreign investment in Chinese financial institutions would be implemented within the year, "abolishing the foreign shareholding ratio limits of banks and financial asset management companies, treating domestic and foreign investors equally; allowing foreign banks to simultaneously establish branches and subsidiaries in China … The upper limit on the proportion of foreign shares in securities firms, fund management companies, futures companies, and personal insurance companies will be raised to 51%, and there will be no restrictions after three years."[17] This will undoubtedly accelerate the pace of foreign participation in Chinese financial institutions.

With the increasing standardization of foreign investment in Chinese banks, and the continuous relaxation of regulations on shareholding ratios, business scopes, license quantities, etc., foreign financial institutions have successfully infiltrated five out of the six major state-owned commercial banks (except Agricultural Bank of China), eleven out of twelve nationwide joint-stock commercial banks (except China Merchants Bank), most city commercial banks, and rural commercial banks, actively participating in the establishment of rural banks. Among banking institutions, the investment of foreign financial institutions has become an integral part of the banks, playing a positive role in improving corporate governance, equity structure, risk control capabilities, increasing cooperation with overseas financial institutions, enhancing operational efficiency, and bolstering capital adequacy in Chinese banking institutions. Since 2018, despite factors like the China-US trade war affecting the pace of entry of foreign financial institutions into China, under the policy support of China's continuous deepening reform and opening-up, there still exists enormous space and opportunities for their development in China.

[17] Yi Gang. "Removing the foreign ownership ratio restrictions on banks and financial asset management companies.".

Chapter 8
The Establishment and Development of Non-bank Financial Institutions

Non-bank financial institutions are an important component of China's financial industry. Since the reform and opening up, they have gradually resumed or emerged in the process of financial reform and deepening, in line with the development of the social economy. Now, they have formed a diversified system of non-bank financial institutions, including insurance, securities, trusts, funds, financial leasing, corporate group finance companies, and asset management companies. They play a unique role as bridges and links in supporting the real economy, promoting technological innovation, stimulating consumption and investment, and enriching financial products. They fill in the gaps and deficiencies that banks find difficult to cover in many fields. By the end of 2017, non-bank financial institutions had significantly improved their position in the entire financial system and played an increasingly important role in the social and economic transformation and development.

8.1 Recovery and Development of Insurance Industry

Since the reform and opening up, the recovery and expansion of the People's Insurance Company of China (PICC) Limited marked the beginning of the development of the insurance industry. After 1986, various types of insurance companies were established, breaking the monopoly of PICC and greatly promoting the formation and development of the Chinese insurance market. Since the 1990s, the entry of foreign insurance companies has diversified the main players in the Chinese insurance market. Today, China has formed a fully equipped and diverse insurance market with a wide range of insurance products. Its asset size ranks third globally in the insurance market, playing a crucial role in the development of the social economy and the lives and work of the people.

R. Lan, *The Financial Development of China*, Understanding China,
https://doi.org/10.1007/978-981-97-8273-4_8

8.1.1 Recovery and Development of Insurance Industry

From 1979 to 1995 was a phase of recovery and development for China's insurance industry. Since The Third Plenary Session of the 11th Central Committee of the Communist Party of China, the Chinese insurance industry has gradually recovered in line with the diversified development of the social economy. On April 25, 1979, the PBOC issued "Notice on the Resumption of Domestic Insurance Business and Strengthening of Insurance Institutions", which decided to restore and strengthen the construction of PICC and its branches. Subsequently, the PICC was able to resume its operations and initially restored domestic property insurance business, followed by life insurance business in 1982. Thus, the interrupted domestic insurance business for 20 years was fully recovered. Before 1985, PICC operated as a monopoly in the Chinese insurance market. After that, until the promulgation of the "Insurance Law of the People's Republic of China (hereinafter referred to as "Insurance Law")" in 1995, the development of our country's insurance industry was relatively slow and mainly revolved around various insurance businesses conducted by PICC and banking institutions, with few other insurance companies. An overview of the domestic insurance companies that were restored or established in China from the period of reform and opening up until 1995 is shown in Table 8.1.

The establishment of other insurance companies gradually broke the monopoly of PICC and promoted the development of the insurance business in China. In the Chinese insurance market, a market pattern emerged with PICC, Ping An Insurance Company, and China Pacific Insurance Company being the major players. Meanwhile, foreign insurance companies also began to establish representative offices or branches in China in the 1990s. In 1992, AIA, a subsidiary of American International Group (AIG), established AIA Shanghai Branch in Shanghai. It was the first foreign insurance company granted permission to operate in mainland China and obtained licenses for both life and non-life insurance businesses at its Shanghai office. The establishment of AIA Shanghai Branch introduced insurance marketing methods into China, cultivated the first batch of insurance marketing talents in the Chinese insurance market, and promoted innovation and development in China's domestic insurance industry. In 1994, Tokio Marine and Nichido Fire Insurance Co., Ltd., a Japanese company, was approved to operate a branch in Shanghai, mainly providing insurance services to Japanese companies in China. In 1996, Swiss Reinsurance Company Ltd. established an office in Shanghai, becoming the first foreign company to provide property insurance services in China.

With the increasing number of insurance entities, the Chinese insurance market has shown signs of chaos in an environment lacking comprehensive legal protection. In order to strengthen the standardized development of insurance business, on June 30, 1995, the 14th Session of the Standing Committee of the Eighth National People's Congress adopted the "Insurance Law", which came into effect on October 1 of the same year. The promulgation and implementation of the "Insurance Law"

Table 8.1 Domestic insurance companies established/restored from the period of reform and opening up until 1995

Establishment/recovery year	Insurance company	Remarks
1979	PICC	Established in October 1949; fully restored its domestic operations in 1979 and rapidly established various levels of institutions
1986	Xinjiang Production and Construction Corps Agricultural and Livestock Insurance Company	Renamed as Xinjiang Corps Insurance Company in 1992; Renamed as China United Property Insurance Company in 2002
1986	Ping An Insurance Company (Shenzhen)	Renamed as Ping An Insurance Company of China in 1992; the first joint-stock insurance company in China
1991	CPIC (China Pacific Insurance (Group) Co Ltd.)	Reestablished from the insurance department of Bank of Communications in 1987; Separated and established independently in 1991
1994	TianAn Property Insurance Co., Ltd.	Headquarters in Shanghai
1994	Zhong An Insurance Co., Ltd. (renamed Starr Insurance and Reinsurance Limited)	Headquarters in Shanghai

fundamentally put an end to the fragmented and lawless situation of insurance legislation in China for a long time, becoming an important watershed in the development history of China's insurance industry.

8.1.2 The Restructuring and Steady Development of China's Insurance Industry

The period from 1996 to 2003 was a phase of restructuring and diversification for the Chinese insurance industry.

Firstly, the formation of a diversified insurance landscape. The promulgation and implementation of the "Insurance Law" promoted and regulated the development of the Chinese insurance industry, and also took the first steps towards the segmented restructuring of the insurance sector. In July 1996, in accordance with the requirements of the "Insurance Law" for segmented operations, PICC was reorganized into China People's Insurance Group Company, which included subsidiaries such as

China Life Insurance Company, China Property Insurance Company, China Reinsurance Company, and China Overseas Institutions. This marked the beginning of the era of segmented operations in the Chinese insurance industry. In the same year, the establishment of five joint-stock insurance companies including Taikang Life, Xinhua Life, Huatai Property, Yongan Insurance, and Huatai Insurance, signified the initial formation of a diversified insurance market in China. Subsequently, the number of domestically operated insurance companies with segmented operations significantly increased, greatly strengthening the strength of the Chinese insurance market and promoting increasingly standardized development in the insurance market.

Secondly, foreign insurance companies achieved rapid development in China through more diversified means. During this period, in addition to continuing to establish representative offices or branches in China, foreign insurance companies entered the Chinese market in two ways. One approach was to establish joint venture insurance companies in China through cooperation with Chinese or foreign companies. Most foreign insurance companies chose the joint venture route to enter the Chinese insurance market, while many insurance companies formed alliances with domestic companies in non-insurance sectors to ensure greater freedom in managing their enterprises and determining overall development strategies. In 1996, Manulife-Sinochem Life Insurance Company, in cooperation with China Foreign Economic and Trade Trust Co., Ltd., became the first foreign insurance company to establish a Sino-foreign joint venture insurance company in China. Subsequently, the number of countries and companies establishing joint venture insurance companies in China increased, with participation expanding to a wider range of regions. The investment methods also expanded from initial "Sino-foreign joint ventures" to "foreign-foreign joint ventures," greatly enriching the participants in the Chinese insurance market. Another approach was that some foreign insurance companies entered the Chinese insurance market by introducing strategic investors through domestic insurance companies. Some foreign companies that entered China through this approach before 2005 are shown in Table 8.2.

Thirdly, the establishment of China's insurance regulatory system. With the rapid development of the Chinese insurance industry, the State Council and the central government strengthened their management of the insurance industry. In November 1998, the China Insurance Regulatory Commission (CIRC), directly under the State Council, was established to unify the supervision and management of the national insurance market in accordance with the law, thereby enhancing its regulatory functions for commercial insurance. Subsequently, with the establishment of CIRC branches in various provinces and autonomous regions, a nationwide insurance supervision and management system was formally formed. In February 2001, the Insurance Association of China was established in Beijing, marking the entry of the Chinese insurance industry into a self-regulatory development under supervision. The Insurance Association works in coordination with regulatory authorities to safeguard industry interests, promote industry development, and enhance the insurance industry's ability and efficiency in serving the real economy.

Table 8.2 Partial foreign companies that entered the Chinese insurance market through strategic investment before 2005

Year	Chinese insurance company	Name of foreign company	Investment amount	Ownership percentage (%)
1994	Ping An Insurance Company	Goldman Sachs, Morgan Stanley	\$70 million	15
2000	Xinhua Life Insurance Company	Zurich Insurance Group, International Finance Corporation, Meiji Yasuda Life Insurance Company, ING Groep N.V	\$116.9 million	24.9
2000	Taikang Insurance Company	Swiss Re Life and Pensions, Singapore government Investments, SoftBank Group	\$145 million	24.9
2003	China People's Property Insurance Company	American International Group	\$613.8 million	9.9
2005	China Pacific Life Insurance Company	The Carlyle Group, PCCW Financial Services	\$410 million	24.98

In line with the divisional regulation of the financial industry, China PICC was split into four independent insurance legal entities: China People's Property Insurance Company, China Life Insurance Company, China Reinsurance Company, and Hong Kong Zhongbao Group. Other existing insurance companies also made corresponding institutional and operational adjustments in response to the needs of the segmented regulatory system.

Fourthly, the corporatization reform and listing of state-owned insurance companies. In accordance with the State Council's financial reform plan, state-owned insurance companies accelerated their corporatization reforms. In January 1999, China People's Property Insurance Co., Ltd. was officially renamed PICC, and in March, China Life Insurance Co., Ltd. was renamed China Life Insurance Company. In July 2003, after restructuring, PICC was renamed China Reinsurance (Group) Corporation, and China People's Property Insurance Co., Ltd. and China Re Asset Management Co., Ltd. were established. In November, China People's Property Insurance Co., Ltd. was listed on the Hong Kong Stock Exchange, becoming the first insurance company in the Chinese insurance industry to go public. At the same time, China Life Insurance Company also underwent restructuring and initiated the establishment of China Life Insurance Company Limited, which went public on December 17th and 18th in New York and Hong Kong, making it the largest IPO in the global stock market in 2003.

Fifthly, the steady development of insurance business. The insurance operating models became more diverse, expanding from direct sales and individual intermediaries to include multi-agency agents, brokers, and brokerage firms. The range of insurance products increased from around 130 types in the 1980s, such as property insurance, transportation insurance, agricultural insurance, and simple personal insurance, to over 3,000 varieties, including liability insurance, accidental injury insurance, and credit protection insurance. China has also established an insurance network for export credit insurance that combines policy-based and commercial guarantees. In 1988, China's first export credit insurance company, PICC, was established. In 1992, PICC and China Export–Import Bank jointly handled export credit insurance business, and in 2001, China Export and Credit Insurance Corporation was established. In 2013, China opened up the short-term export credit guarantee business to capable commercial insurance companies. Currently, China Reinsurance (Group) Corporation, Pacific Insurance, Ping An Property and Casualty Insurance, and Dadi Insurance are among the four commercial insurance companies involved in export credit guarantee business. The business model has gradually shifted from policy-based guarantees to a combination of policy-based and commercial guarantees. With the steady development of insurance business, the insurance premium income in China during this period showed a stable growth trend, as shown in Fig. 8.1.

At the same time, the density and depth of China's insurance market also show a similar trend. Insurance depth represents the ratio of premium income to GDP,

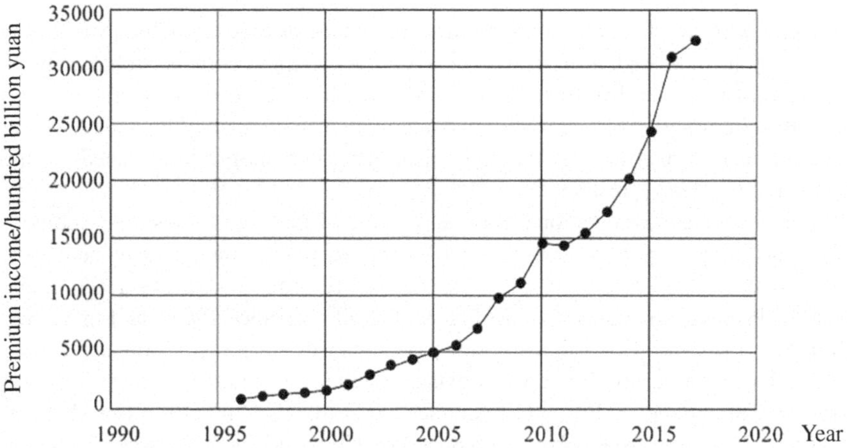

Fig. 8.1 Changes in China's insurance premium income from 1996 to October 2017. *Note* Prior to 2006, it represents insurance premium income, while from 2007 onwards, it represents original insurance premium income (according to the statistical indicators set by the "Enterprise Accounting Standards (2006)", referring to the premium income from original insurance contracts recognized by insurance companies). The original insurance premium income for 2017 only includes the total amount from January to October, while the data for other years represents the full-year figures. *Data Source* Compiled based on relevant year data from the official website of the China Insurance Regulatory Commission

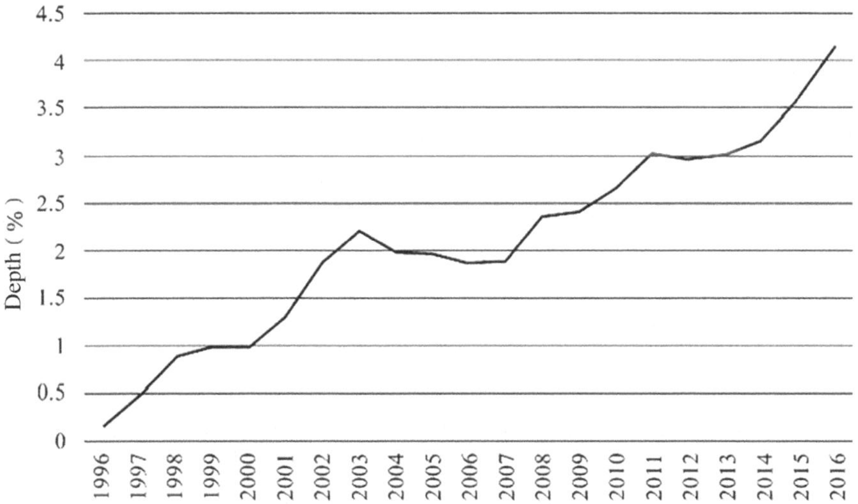

Fig. 8.2 Changes in China's insurance depth from 1996 to 2016. *Data Source* Premium income data from relevant years is sourced from the official website of the China Insurance Regulatory Commission, while GDP data from different years is sourced from the official website of the National Bureau of Statistics. This figure is calculated and compiled based on the data from both sources

while insurance density represents the ratio of premium income to the population. The trends from 1996 to 2016 are shown in Figs. 8.2 and 8.3.

8.1.3 Rapid Development of the Insurance Industry

In 2003, the "One Line, Three Committees" regulatory system was established, and the development of China's financial industry officially entered a segmented operation state. During this period, the insurance industry in China experienced rapid growth, with major insurance companies quickly increasing their strength and expanding their scale. The Chinese insurance market has become an important force in the global insurance market.

Firstly, Chinese insurance companies accelerated their institutional restructuring and listing processes. With the subsequent overseas listings of China Reinsurance (Group) Corporation and China Life Insurance Company, other Chinese insurance companies continuously optimized their equity structure through capital increase, private capital absorption, and foreign investment participation, improving the construction of the 'Three Committees and One Layer' and enhancing corporate governance mechanisms. Based on these foundations, Chinese insurance companies actively expedited the process of going public. As of the end of 2017, except for the

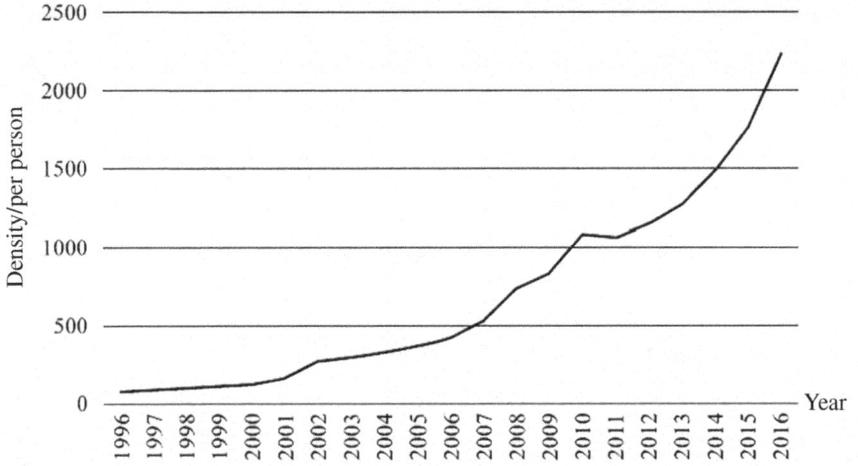

Fig. 8.3 Changes in China's insurance density from 1996 to 2016. *Data Source* Premium income data from relevant years is sourced from the official website of the China Insurance Regulatory Commission, while population data from different years is sourced from the Statistical Yearbook. This figure is calculated and compiled based on the data from both sources

policy-based export credit insurance companies, all other Chinese insurance companies had completed their transformation into joint-stock companies. Eight insurance companies, including Ping An Insurance, China Taiping Insurance, China Life Insurance, Xinhua Life Insurance, China Pacific Insurance, China People's Insurance, China Property and Casualty Insurance, and China Reinsurance, were listed domestically and internationally. Among them, China Life Insurance was jointly listed in New York, Hong Kong, and Shanghai.

Secondly, China has increased the openness of its insurance market. On one hand, Chinese insurance business has gradually opened up. Since China's accession to the WTO in 2001, the opening-up of the Chinese insurance market has been continuously intensified. By November 2004, China had fully lifted the geographical restrictions on the operations of foreign insurance companies, allowing foreign life insurance companies to provide health insurance, group insurance, pension, and annuity services to Chinese and foreign citizens. In 2005, the Chinese insurance industry was fully opened up. Subsequently, newly established insurance businesses in China have continuously followed the pace of openness and opened up to foreign insurance companies. On the other hand, there has been an increasing number of foreign insurance companies establishing their presence in China, with well-known insurance companies from around the world setting up corresponding institutions in the country. In 2003, among the 46 insurance companies listed in the *Fortune Global 500,* 27 of them had already established branches in China. As of October 2017, foreign insurance institutions from 16 countries and regions had set up 57 foreign-funded insurance companies in China, covering various types of insurance including life insurance, property insurance, and asset management. Although the assets of

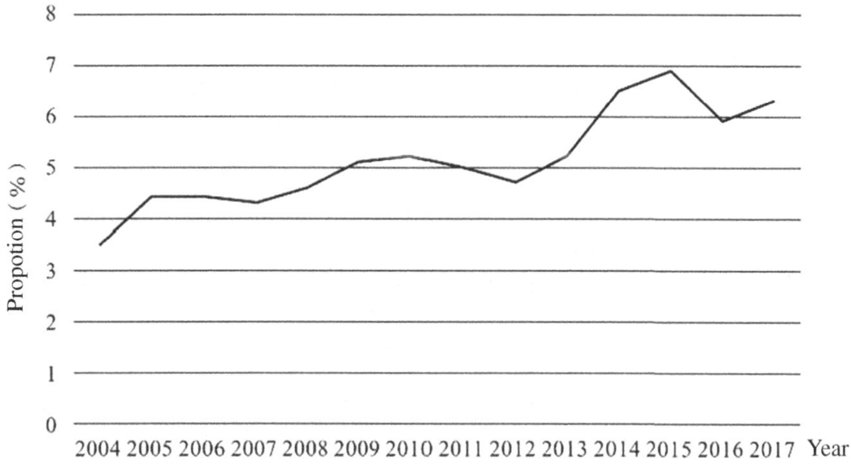

Fig. 8.4 Proportion of foreign-owned insurance in China's insurance industry assets

foreign insurance companies in China have been growing, their proportion in the overall assets of the Chinese insurance industry remains relatively low, as shown in Fig. 8.4. In November 2018, the China Banking and Insurance Regulatory Commission officially approved the establishment of Allianz (China) Insurance Holding Co., Ltd., a subsidiary of Germany's Allianz Group, becoming the first foreign-funded insurance holding company in China. This further promotes the openness of the insurance market.

Thirdly, the internationalization of China's insurance industry has been increasing. Since January 1980, when China Re Group established a liaison office in London, the pace of China's insurance industry "going global" has been growing, with a wider range of operations. Initially, the Chinese insurance industry's "going global" was mainly concentrated in a few countries such as Singapore and the Hong Kong-Macao region. Currently, it has expanded to include countries like the United States, Japan, and European regions. The number of Chinese insurance companies listed overseas has also been increasing. In June 2000, China Pacific Insurance Group Co., Ltd. was listed on the Hong Kong Stock Exchange, marking the beginning of Chinese insurance companies listing overseas. In July 2013, People's Insurance Group of China Co., Ltd. was listed on the Hong Kong Stock Exchange, further accelerating the pace of Chinese insurance companies listing abroad.

At the same time, Chinese insurance companies have diversified their investments overseas. In the early stages of reform and opening-up, Chinese insurance companies mainly established branch offices abroad. However, since the twenty-first century, they have been promoting diversified investments. In July 2013, Ping An Insurance acquired the iconic Lloyd's Building in London for 260 million pounds, marking the first overseas real estate investment by Chinese insurance funds. Anbang Insurance, from 2014 to 2015, completed seven overseas acquisitions, including the acquisition of the Waldorf Astoria Hotel in the United States. In May 2014, Fosun International acquired an 80% stake and voting rights in the largest insurance group in Portugal, Fidelidade, Multicare, and Cares, which accounted for 26% of the domestic insurance market in Portugal. This significantly advanced the globalization process of China's insurance industry. So far, Chinese insurance companies have significantly accelerated their internationalization efforts and diversified their strategies, making them an important force in the international insurance market. In the future, Chinese insurance companies should actively align with major national plans such as the "Belt and Road Initiative" and free trade zone construction, promote the "going global" of insurance enterprises and insurance regulation, make full use of internet technology and continuously innovate their "going global" approaches, and create a new pattern of high-level two-way openness. This will enable them to serve the globalization of the Chinese economy in a more rational manner.

Fourthly, the continuous improvement of China's insurance regulatory system. The supervisory and management agencies, primarily led by the China Insurance Regulatory Commission (CIRC) and its branches in various provinces and cities, have nationwide coverage. By March 2018, when it merged with the China Banking Regulatory Commission (CBRC), the CIRC headquarters had 16 functional departments and two institutions, with 36 insurance regulatory bureaus established in provinces, autonomous regions, directly-administered municipalities, and specifically designated cities, as well as five insurance regulatory sub-bureaus in Suzhou, Yantai, Shantou, Wenzhou, and Tangshan. Under the leadership of the State Council, the functions of the CIRC have become increasingly comprehensive. By March 2018, when it merged with the CBRC, the CIRC had formed a relatively complete set of ten supervisory and management functions (see Table 8.3). This has laid a solid institutional foundation for future reforms in insurance regulation.

Under the unified supervision of the State Council and the CIRC, China has introduced and promulgated a series of laws and regulations, establishing a preliminary legal framework for insurance regulation. In 2001, the "Regulations of the People's Republic of China on Administration of Foreign-Invested Insurance Companies" were formulated and published. In 2006, the "Regulations on Compulsory Traffic Accident Liability Insurance for Motor Vehicles" were formulated and promulgated. In 2008, the "Insurance Law" was revised, which served as an opportunity to strengthen and standardize China's insurance regulatory rules and regulations. In 2012, the "Agricultural Insurance Regulations" were passed. In 2015, a comprehensive revision of the "Insurance Law" was carried out to strengthen the regulation of China's insurance market, promote the healthy and sustainable development of the insurance industry, and control various insurance-related risks within manageable limits. In the future, China will further strengthen and improve the "three-pillar" regulatory system with corporate governance, solvency, and market behavior as its core, establish a comprehensive risk management system, firmly maintain the bottom line of preventing systemic and regional financial risks, and provide strong support for the production and livelihood of the general public.

In response to the trend of mixed operation in the financial sector in China, and to strengthen financial risk prevention, the State Council made a decision to reform the insurance regulatory agencies during the two sessions in 2018. The CIRC and the

Table 8.3 Main functions of the China insurance regulatory commission (CIRC)

① Formulate policies and guidelines for the development of the insurance industry, develop industry development strategies and plans, draft laws, regulations, and industry rules for insurance regulation
② Approve the establishment of insurance companies and their branches, insurance group companies, and insurance holding companies. Collaborate with relevant departments to approve the establishment of insurance asset management companies. Approve the establishment of representative offices of overseas insurance institutions. Approve the establishment of insurance intermediaries such as insurance agencies, insurance brokerage companies, and insurance loss adjustment companies, as well as their branches. Approve domestic insurance institutions and non-insurance institutions to establish insurance institutions overseas. Approve the merger, separation, alteration, and dissolution of insurance institutions, and decide on takeovers and designated receiverships. Participate in and organize the bankruptcy and liquidation of insurance companies
③ Review and approve the qualifications of senior management personnel in various types of insurance institutions. Establish basic qualification standards for insurance practitioners
④ Approve insurance clauses and premium rates for insurance types that are related to public interests, insurance types subject to compulsory insurance by law, and newly developed life insurance types. Implement filing management for insurance clauses and premium rates of other insurance types
⑤ Regulate the solvency and market behavior of insurance companies in accordance with the law. Manage the insurance guarantee fund and regulate insurance deposits. Develop relevant rules and regulations for the use of insurance funds in accordance with laws and national policies on the use of insurance funds, and supervise the use of insurance funds by insurance companies
⑥ Supervise policy-oriented insurance and compulsory insurance operations. Regulate self-insurance and mutual insurance organizations and their business activities. Centralize the management of industry associations such as insurance associations and insurance institutes
⑦ Investigate and penalize illegal and irregular activities such as unfair competition by insurance institutions and insurance practitioners, as well as the operation or disguised operation of insurance businesses by non-insurance institutions
⑧ Regulate insurance institutions established overseas by domestic insurance and non-insurance institutions in accordance with the law
⑨ Establish information technology standards for the insurance industry. Establish an insurance risk assessment, early warning, and monitoring system. Track, analyze, monitor, and predict the operation of the insurance market. Responsible for the unified compilation of national insurance industry data and reports, and publish them in accordance with relevant national regulations
⑩ Handle other matters assigned by the State Council

Source Official website of the China Insurance Regulatory Commission

CBRC were merged to form the China Banking and Insurance Regulatory Commission (CBIRC), with their regulatory and rule-making functions transferred to the People's Bank of China. The newly formed CBIRC will take on more institutional regulatory functions and strengthen micro-prudential insurance supervision.

Fifthly, the development of China's insurance industry has become more orderly and diversified. The development of the insurance industry in China has gradually shifted from a previous "crossing the river by feeling the stones" approach to a more structured development pattern. In 2006, the State Council issued the "Several

Opinions of the State Council on the Reform and Development of the Insurance Industry," which clarified the ideas for the reform and development of the insurance industry. Based on these opinions, the CIRC first released the "Eleventh Five-Year Plan for the Development of the Chinese Insurance Industry" in 2006. In 2011, based on the "Twelfth Five-Year Plan for National Economic and Social Development of the People's Republic of China" and the 2006 "Several Opinions of the State Council on the Reform and Development of the Insurance Industry," the CIRC formulated and issued the "Twelfth Five-Year Plan for the Development of the Chinese Insurance Industry." In 2014, the State Council issued the "Several Opinions on Accelerating the Development of the Modern Insurance Service Industry," which established the important position of the modern insurance service industry in the overall economic and social development and pointed out that "insurance is an important industry in the modern economy and a fundamental means of risk management, as well as an important indicator of social civilization, economic development, and social governance capability." In 2016, the CIRC formulated and published the "Thirteenth Five-Year Plan for the Development of the Insurance Industry in China" in accordance with the "Thirteenth Five-Year Plan for National Economic and Social Development of the People's Republic of China" and the "Several Opinions on Accelerating the Development of the Modern Insurance Service Industry" issued in 2014. This outline clarified the development goals, key tasks, and policy measures for the Chinese insurance industry during the "Thirteenth Five-Year Plan" period (2016–2020). "By 2020, it aims to achieve a national insurance premium income of about 4.5 trillion yuan, an insurance penetration rate of 5%, and an insurance density of 3,500 yuan per capita. The total assets of the insurance industry are expected to reach around 25 trillion yuan."

At the same time, the Chinese insurance industry has achieved comprehensive and rapid development. The number of insurance institutions has steadily increased (see Fig. 8.5), and there has been significant improvement in insurance premium income, insurance density, and penetration. The insurance market in China has continued to expand, surpassing Germany, France, and the United Kingdom in size, and rising from the sixth to the third position globally. The insurance service capabilities in China have greatly enhanced, the insurance ecosystem has significantly improved, and the overall strength of the insurance industry has rapidly grown. In 2003, China Life Insurance entered the *Fortune Global 500* ranking for the first time. In 2006, China Life Insurance became the top life insurance company globally. By 2017, Chinese insurance companies listed in the Fortune Global 500 included Ping An Insurance (ranked 39th), China Life Insurance (ranked 51st), PICC (ranked 114th), Anbang Insurance (ranked 139th), China Pacific Insurance (ranked 252nd), AIA Group (ranked 383rd), China Taiping Insurance (ranked 411th), and Xinhua Life Insurance (ranked 497th). The modernization level of the Chinese insurance industry has been continuously improving. It has evolved from handwritten policies to printed policies, and now to electronic policies. The groundbreaking development of internet insurance has already demonstrated its role in leading the global insurance industry's development trend.

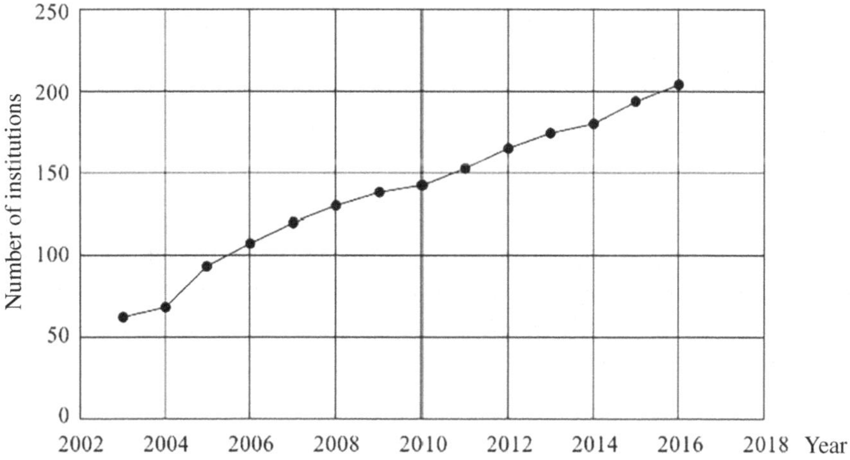

Fig. 8.5 The changes in the number of insurance institutions in China from 2003 to 2016. *Data Source* Compiled based on data from the website of the National Bureau of Statistics

Clearly, the rapid development of the Chinese insurance industry since the reform and opening up is closely related to the transformation of China's financial functions from managing funds' to 'ragulating market'. The rapid development of the economy and society is the necessary foundation for the growth of the Chinese insurance industry. It serves as a 'stabilizer' and 'catalyst' for the development of the economy and society, providing a 'protective umbrella' for the well-being of the people and driving the progress of the Chinese insurance industry. Currently, China is transitioning from being a major player in the insurance industry to becoming a strong insurance nation. In the process of rapid development and growth, the insurance industry needs to continuously leverage its unique functions, innovate in the application of insurance funds, and avoid false and pseudo-innovation that detaches from serving the real economy, ensuring that insurance funds truly serve the overall development of the economy and society. Alongside the financial regulatory system reform in 2018, the China Banking and Insurance Regulatory Commission was officially established on April 8th through the merger of the China Banking Regulatory Commission and the China Insurance Regulatory Commission. This further clarifies regulatory goals, positions, and aims to effectively prevent and resolve financial risks. Efforts are also being made to deepen reforms, promote the opening up of the insurance industry, and guide the industry in improving the quality and effectiveness of services to the real economy, embarking on a new journey from a new starting point.

8.2 The Establishment and Development of Securities Companies

Securities companies are an important carrier in China's capital market and a vital component of financial innovation in China. With the gradual transformation of China's financial functions from "managing funds" to "regulating the market," securities companies initially emerged as institutions engaged in the trading of securities. Subsequently, as the establishment of the Shanghai and Shenzhen stock markets in our country, they evolved into specialized institutions. Today, they have become standardized and significant participants in China's capital market, playing an increasingly important role in the market.

8.2.1 The Emergence and Establishment of Securities Companies

During the period from the beginning of the reform and opening-up policy to the establishment of the stock exchange in 1991, it marked the stage of emergence and initial establishment of securities companies in China. Since the reform and opening-up, China's socio-economic development has been rapid, resulting in a significant increase in demand for capital. Against this backdrop, after a 20-year period without bond issuance, the State Council ended the era by authorizing the Ministry of Finance to resume issuing government bonds in 1981. Initially, government bonds were forcibly marketed through administrative means for a long time without forming a true bond trading market. Subsequently, the emergence of joint-stock companies in places like Shenzhen, Beijing, Shanghai, and the issuance of stocks, corporate bonds, and other securities significantly enriched the variety of trading instruments in the capital market. With the expansion of China's stock market, the increase in investment instruments such as stocks and bonds, as well as the growth of the investor base, there was an urgent need to address the chaos in over-the-counter trading, which demanded the establishment of specialized securities companies. In response to the trend of socio-economic development, Shenzhen was the first to propose the establishment of securities companies to the People's Bank of China. Soon, Shenzhen received a response from the People's Bank of China, agreeing to establish securities companies in the form of units and subsidiaries under the People's Bank. In January 1985, Shenzhen Special Economic Zone Securities Company was established and commenced trial operations, thus marking the beginning of the development of securities companies in China.

At the initial stage of establishment, Shenzhen Special Economic Zone Securities Company had limited understanding of securities business. The company mainly undertook the issuance and circulation of government bonds, and its employees primarily traveled between urban and rural areas to promote government bond sales. As more joint-stock companies emerged in China and the primary and secondary stock markets began to take shape, the agenda gradually included discussions on securities companies representing stock trading. In May 1987, Shenzhen Development Bank publicly issued stocks to the society. Initially, there was no response to the stock offering, so the company had to encourage party members to subscribe first. In April 1988, Shenzhen Special Economic Zone Securities Company began to represent the transfer of Shenzhen Development Bank stocks, and it was only then that stock trading started to attract people's fervent pursuit. This also led to the establishment of a large number of securities companies.

In order to facilitate government bond trading and the development of the securities market, the People's Bank of China and its branches in Shanghai, Beijing, and other cities actively promoted the establishment of securities companies. In 1988, the People's Bank of China approved the establishment of Shanghai International Securities Company, becoming the first joint-stock securities company. From then until the establishment of the Shanghai and Shenzhen stock exchanges, mainland China had formed 43 securities companies. At the same time, the People's Bank of China also authorized some banks and trust companies to engage in securities trading. This laid the foundation for a securities trading pattern where specialized securities companies coexisted with institutions involved in multiple business sectors. To strengthen the regulation of securities trading, the head office of the People's Bank of China formulated and promulgated a series of laws and regulations, including the "Interim Measures for the Supervision and Administration of Securities Companies" in 1990. These measures clearly defined the admission criteria, business scope, and supervision measures for securities companies, establishing a preliminary framework for the regulation and supervision of securities companies. This marked the transition of China's securities companies from disorderly to standardized development.

8.2.2 The Preliminary Development and Consolidation of Securities Companies

From 1992 to 2003, marked the stage of preliminary development and standardization for securities companies in China. The establishment of the Shanghai and Shenzhen stock exchanges greatly facilitated the development of securities companies in China. During this period, the number of securities companies in China increased significantly, with nationwide securities companies being established. The establishment of three major securities companies, Huaxia Securities, Guotai Securities, and Nanfang Securities, in 1992 signified that securities companies in China started to comprehensively engage in underwriting, brokerage, and proprietary trading of securities. The company's branch network also expanded from being limited to a particular region to a nationwide scale. At the beginning of 1992, there were less than 50 securities companies nationwide, but by the end of 2003, "the number increased to 132 securities companies with 3,020 securities branches".[1] The amount of stock underwriting showed a significant upward trend. In 1991, the total amount of underwritten securities was 55.47 billion yuan, while by 2003, the total trading amount of stock funds for only 122 securities companies reached 58,078.36 billion yuan. At the same time, securities companies made significant progress in internationalization. In June 2003, Shanghai-based CITIC Securities became the first qualified foreign institutional investor (QFII) domestic securities investment agent. On July 9 of the same year, UBS completed the first QFII transaction through a dedicated seat at CITIC Securities.

The rapid increase in securities companies led some companies to exceed the compliance boundaries of business operations, extending into investment areas such as industrial enterprises, real estate, and engaging in irregular activities such as underwriting counter bonds and treasury bond repurchases. This resulted in a large number of non-performing assets, laying many hidden risks for the development of securities companies. In response, the State Council Securities Commission and the China Securities Regulatory Commission (CSRC), established in 1992, jointly issued the "Notice on Completely Separating the People's Bank of China from Urban Credit Cooperatives, Securities Companies, and Economic Entities" to promote the separation of banking, securities, and insurance businesses. To strengthen the regulation of securities companies, the regulatory authorities in China subsequently introduced a series of measures to manage the business operations of securities companies. In response to the 1995 "327" Treasury Bond Futures incident,[2] involving the China Economic Development Trust Investment Corporation going long and Shanghai International Securities Company going short, the Ministry of Finance and the CSRC, lacking an effective supervisory mechanism, took administrative measures to suspend treasury bond futures trading, leading to severe consequences and adverse market impacts. This significantly delayed the development of China's capital market. Thereafter, "in order to regulate securities issuance and trading, protect the legitimate rights and interests of investors, maintain social and economic order, and promote the development of socialist market economy" the National People's Congress enacted and promulgated the "Securities Law of the People's Republic of China (hereinafter referred to as the Securities Law) " in December 1998. Article 7 of the "Securities Law" clearly stipulates that "the State Council securities regulatory authority shall exercise centralized and unified supervision and management over the national securities market in accordance with the law. The State Council securities regulatory authority may establish branch offices as necessary to fulfill its supervisory and management responsibilities." Article 6 formally establishes the principle of separate operations: the securities industry, banking industry, trust industry, and insurance industry shall implement separate operations and management, and securities

[1] Li Yang et al. *60 Years of China's Finance*. China Finance and Economic Press, 2009:178.

[2] The "327" Treasury Bond Futures Incident refers to a deliberate speculative event that occurred on February 23, 1995. It involved a showdown between China Economic Development Trust and Investment Corporation, which went long, and Morgan Stanley, which went short, regarding the three-year Treasury bonds issued in 1992 and maturing in June 1995, listed on the Shanghai Stock Exchange.

companies shall be established separately from banks, trust companies, and insurance business institutions, except as otherwise stipulated by the state. This transition from mixed operations to separate operations in securities companies brings about strict classification management, dividing them into comprehensive and brokerage categories based on their types. Meanwhile, the State Council unified China's securities regulatory institutions, with the China Securities Regulatory Commission (CSRC) responsible for the unified supervision of the national securities market and securities operating institutions. In 2001, the CSRC issued a series of laws and regulations, such as the "Regulations on the Management of Securities Companies" and the "Regulations on the Inspection of Securities Companies", which explicitly supervise and manage the behavior of securities companies. In 2003, the CSRC released three ironclad rules against improper operations by securities companies: "strictly prohibiting the misappropriation of customer trading settlement funds, strictly prohibiting the misappropriation of customer entrusted assets, and strictly prohibiting the misappropriation of customer custodied bonds."[3]

With the standardized development of securities companies, some high-quality securities companies began to publicly raise capital and go public during this period. On December 13, 2002, with approval from the China Securities Regulatory Commission, CITIC Securities publicly issued 400 million shares of common A-shares. On January 6, 2003, it was officially listed and traded on the Shanghai Stock Exchange, becoming the first listed securities company in China and greatly advancing the development of China's securities industry. At the same time, as China joined the WTO, Chinese securities companies also embarked on internationalization. On one hand, foreign securities companies accelerated their investments in domestic institutions, promoting the establishment of joint venture securities companies between domestic and foreign securities firms. In 2002, Haitong Securities and France's Lyon Securities jointly established Huayou International Securities Co., Ltd., enhancing the internationalization of domestic securities companies. On the other hand, domestic securities companies accelerated their "going global", with some high-quality securities companies seeking listings at home and abroad.

8.2.3 The Rapid and Regulated Development of Securities Companies

From 2004 to the present, this stage represents the comprehensive governance and regulated development of securities companies in China. Following the adjustment of Chinese securities companies in 2003, the securities market exhibited a sustained downturn from 2003 to 2004. The accumulated risks of securities companies then manifested in a concentrated outbreak, with the exposure of issues at companies like Nanfang and Minfa marking the first occurrence of an industry-wide crisis. In order to fundamentally address the problems of securities companies, the China

[3] Li Yang et al. *60 Years of China's Finance*. China Finance and Economic Press, 2009:178.

Securities Regulatory Commission (CSRC) convened a symposium on the regulated development of securities companies in August 2003, followed by the announcement of the aforementioned "three ironclad rules". In January 2004, the State Council issued the *Opinions on Promoting the Reform, Opening-up, and Stable Development of the Capital Market*, explicitly emphasizing the need to strengthen the supervision of securities companies and promote their regulated operations. This marked the beginning of the comprehensive governance of securities companies in China.

In 2004, the China Securities Regulatory Commission (CSRC) established evaluation criteria for innovative and regulated securities companies. In August, the CSRC held a national symposium on securities regulatory work, deploying and initiating the comprehensive governance of securities companies. At the end of September, the CSRC, in conjunction with other ministries, issued the *Opinions on the Acquisition of Personal Credit Rights and Customer Securities Trading Settlement Funds*. In July 2005, the State Council introduced the *Work Plan for the Comprehensive Governance of Securities Companies*, led by the CSRC and the People's Bank of China, and jointly formed a special working group with the Ministry of Public Security, the Ministry of Finance, the China Banking Regulatory Commission, the Supreme People's Court, and the Legislative Affairs Office of the State Council. The aim was to standardize and rectify China's securities companies, aiming to resolve existing risks by the end of 2007 and lay a solid foundation for their continuous, regulated, and stable development. In August 2005, drawing on foreign experiences, China issued the *Measures for the Administration of Securities Investor Protection Fund* and established the China Securities Investor Protection Fund Co., Ltd., providing protection for the comprehensive governance of securities companies.

Through a comprehensive investigation of risks in securities companies from 2004 to the first half of 2005, by the end of 2006, the various rectification works of securities companies were essentially completed. "Among the 104 securities companies, four companies, including CITIC Securities, had no rectification matters. All 76 companies, including China Securities, completed their rectification. Three companies, such as Huaxi Securities, mostly completed their rectification, with only a few remaining matters to be addressed. Twenty-one restructuring and newly established companies, such as Galaxy Securities, Southwest Securities, and Datong Securities, underwent on-site inspections and acceptance checks and proceeded with relevant procedures, gradually transitioning to routine supervision."[4] Through three years of comprehensive governance, the long-accumulated risks and hazards of securities companies were effectively controlled and resolved. Serious investigations were conducted on illegal securities companies, resulting in the closure of 19 companies (refer to Table 8.4), revocation of licenses for seven companies, revocation of business permits for four companies, and suspension of business operations for 14 companies and nine branches.[5]

[4] Hu Ruyin. *The Development and Transformation of China's Capital Market*. Gezhi Publishing House and Shanghai People's Publishing House, 2008:190.

[5] Hu Ruyin. *The Development and Transformation of China's Capital Market*. Gezhi Publishing House and Shanghai People's Publishing House,2008:193.

Table 8.4 Statistics of securities companies closed during the comprehensive governance period

Company name	Company name
Dapeng securities	Deheng securities
Nanfang securities	Hengxin securities
Asia securities	Wuhan securities
Northern securities	Gansu securities
Hantang securities	Kunlun securities
Company name	Company name
Wuzhou securities	Guangdong securities
Minan securities	Tianqin securities
Minfa securities	Northwest securities
Yunnan securities	Xing'an securities
Tiantong securities	
Nanfang securities	Hengxin securities
Asia securities	Wuhan securities

Source Hu Ruyin, *Development and Transformation of China's Capital Market*, Gezhi Publishing House, Shanghai People's Publishing House, 2008 edition

During the comprehensive rectification period, the China Securities Regulatory Commission (CSRC) and other departments also formulated and promulgated a series of laws and regulations, such as the *Regulations on the Supervision and Administration of Securities Companies*, the *Regulations on the Disposal of Securities Company Risks*, and the *Regulations on Securities Investment Protection*. This initial establishment of the legal framework for Chinese securities companies effectively promoted their standardized development.

With the regulated development of Chinese securities companies, their governance structures have been increasingly optimized, and business innovation has been effectively promoted. Business areas such as Qualified Domestic Institutional Investors (QDI) have expanded significantly. The number of securities companies has steadily increased from 104 in 2006 to 129 as of December 31, 2016. The listing pace of high-quality securities companies has accelerated noticeably. By the end of 2008, only seven securities companies, including Hongyuan Securities, CITIC Securities, Haitong Securities, Changjiang Securities, Guoyuan Securities, Northeast Securities, and Everbright Securities, were listed. As of the third quarter of 2017, the number of securities companies listed in China reached 30, as shown in Table 8.5.

Since the completion of comprehensive rectification in 2007, Chinese securities companies have entered a stage of steady and standardized development. During this period, some securities companies, influenced by the volatility of the Chinese stock market, still engaged in irregular practices to seek high profits. During the 2015 stock market crash, senior executives of CITIC Securities were involved in various irregular practices such as insider trading and leaking insider information, leading to investigations of several individuals and revealing the ZeXi private equity insider

Table 8.5 Statistics of listed securities companies in China as of the third quarter of 2017

Company name	Company name
Shenwan Hongyuan securities	Northeast securities
Guoyuan securities	Guohai securities
GF securities	Changjiang securities
Shanxi securities	Western securities
Guosen securities	CITIC securities
Everbright securities	Southwest securities
Haitong securities	Huaan securities
Orient securities	Pacific securities
CMB securities	Zheshang securities
Guotai Junan	Central china securities
Industrial securities	Soochow securities
Dongxing securities	Huatai securities
Everbright securities	China galaxy securities
Founder securities	First capital securities
China national investment and assurance	Greentown investment

Source 'Industry classification results of listed companies in the third quarter of 2017,' http://www.csrc.gov.cn/pub/newsite/scb/ssgshyfljg/201711/t20171114_326991.html

trading incident. Other securities companies such as Haitong Securities, GF Securities, Founder Securities, and Huatai Securities were also administratively punished by the CSRC for engaging in off-exchange irregular margin trading. Haitong Securities, for example, had its illegal gains of 28.65 million yuan confiscated and was fined 85.96 million yuan.

In order to ensure the standardized development of securities companies, the China Securities Regulatory Commission (CSRC) continuously promulgates corresponding laws and regulations based on changes in the stock market and business innovation by securities companies. In 2015, the 'Securities Law' was revised to ensure the continuous and stable development of securities companies. Against this backdrop, Chinese securities companies have experienced rapid development, with the rise of internet securities and an accelerated pace of internationalization. In October 2015, Pacific Special Acquisition Corp, invested by China Pacific Securities Co., Ltd., successfully listed on the NASDAQ, becoming the first Chinese securities company to be listed in the United States. By the end of 2016, there were already 13 securities companies from China listed in Hong Kong. Meanwhile, the asset quality of securities companies has continuously improved, and their asset scale has significantly increased. By the end of 2016, the total assets, net assets, and net capital of securities companies in China reached 5.79 trillion yuan, 1.64 trillion yuan, and 1.47 trillion yuan, respectively. As of August 2017, nine securities companies, including CITIC Securities, Guotai Junan, Haitong Securities, Huatai Securities, GF Securities, China Merchants Securities, Shenwan Hongyuan Securities, China

Galaxy Securities, and China Securities, had a capital scale exceeding one trillion yuan; among them, four companies had operating income exceeding 10 billion yuan.

According to the spirit of the Fifth National Financial Work Conference and the requirement to 'guard against the systemic financial risks from happening' as stated in the 19th National Congress of the Communist Party of China report, securities companies will strengthen risk supervision while deepening securities company reforms. Alongside the improvement of securities companies' asset quality, the pace of company listings will accelerate, and the level of internationalization will deepen, leading to intensified competition. In the government institutional reform in March 2018, to strengthen supervision and management of securities companies and the securities market, the central government not only retained the China Securities Regulatory Commission but also strengthened its supervisory and management functions.

8.3 The Establishment and Development of Trust Companies

Since 1979, the trust industry in China has undergone a relatively tortuous development process. After five large-scale restructurings in the early stages, by the end of 2017, the total assets controlled by 68 trust companies nationwide had reached 26.28 trillion yuan, making it an important driving force for innovation in China's financial market. Trust companies have played an increasingly important role in supporting social and economic development.

8.3.1 Establishment of Trust Companies

Since the reform and opening up, the reform of the social and economic system has promoted rapid economic development. In response to the needs of the economic situation, the trust industry in China gradually recovered. From then until 1993, it entered the stage of mixed operation for the trust industry in China.

In 1979, Beijing Economic Construction General Corporation was established in Beijing, and Zhejiang Trust and Investment Corporation was established in Zhejiang, marking the beginning of the recovery and development of the trust industry in China. In the same year, China International Trust and Investment Corporation was established in Beijing, signifying the formal start of the recovery and establishment of the trust industry in China. At the same time, the Head Office of the Bank of China established a Trust Consulting Department, which was subsequently restructured into the Bank of China Trust Consulting Company. In June 1980, the State Council issued the "Notice on Promoting Economic Cooperation," clearly stating that banks should pilot various trust businesses, pool funds, and promote joint economic development.

In order to promote the establishment of trust business by banks, the Head Office of the PBOC issued the "Notice on Actively Launching Trust Business" in September 1980, requiring banks to actively establish trust business in areas where conditions permit. Banking institutions and local governments responded positively to the call for establishing trust companies by the central government, leading to a wave of trust company establishments nationwide. By the end of 1982, most provinces and cities across the country had established trust institutions. However, many trust companies that were hastily set up within a short period of time lacked understanding of trust business. As a result, 'many trust products had the name of trust but lacked the essence of trust, or were neither in name nor in essence, mainly used by banks as tools to circumvent credit plan management.'[6] Under such circumstances, there were widespread issues of fund competition, business squeezing, and territorial disputes between trust institutions and banks, which greatly affected the People's Bank of China's goal of controlling the total amount of credit and caused chaotic fund allocation, severely impacting normal economic growth order. In order to maintain a normal financial development order, avoid unnecessary competition, and promote the healthy development of the trust industry, the State Council and the PB0C started a process of cleaning up and rectifying the trust industry in February 1982. By 1999, the Chinese government had conducted five large-scale trust industry restructurings, as shown in Table 8.6.

In February 1982, the State Council began to rectify the fund management of the trust industry, clean up non-bank trust institutions, and strengthen the relationship between banks and trusts. After the initial rectification, the trust industry experienced rapid development in 1984. That year, 15 new trust companies were established, and another 5 trust companies were established in 1985. The rapid development of the trust industry fueled credit expansion, prompting the central government to conduct the second round of rectification in 1985. This round of rectification had a relatively limited impact and failed to curb the rapid increase in the number of trust companies. In 1986, 9 new trust companies were established, followed by the establishment of 11 trust companies in 1987. The trend of rapid increase in trust companies continued in 1988. In response, the central government conducted the third round of rectification for the trust industry in 1988. This round of rectification was more significant, and by 1990, the trust industry was mostly in a state of suspension or semi-suspension. No new trust companies were established, and the excessive establishment of trust companies was completely controlled and improved. The statistics of newly established trust and investment companies in China from 1990 to 1999 are shown in Table 8.7.

After this round of rectification, the number of trust companies was effectively controlled, but issues such as business direction remained unresolved. In response, the central government conducted the fourth large-scale rectification of the trust industry in June 1993. These four rounds of rectification indeed played a role in risk prevention. However, due to the unclear positioning of the trust industry and the lack of clear business direction, the rectification measures only targeted specific

[6] Li Yang et al. *60 Years of China's Finance*. China Finance and Economics Press,2009:112.

Table 8.6 The five reorganizations of trust companies from 1979 to 1999

Time	Reason	Key points of reorganization	Relevant regulations and measures
1982	Illegal fund absorption	Industry cleanup, i.e., clearing non-bank financial trust institutions, stopping local trust businesses, strengthening and coordinating bank-trust relationships	"Notice on Rectifying Domestic Trust Investment Company Business and Strengthening the Management of Funds for Upgrading and Renovation" and other related measures
1985	Credit expansion driven by trust companies	Business cleanup, i.e., stopping the issuance of new trust loans and new trust investments	"Notice on Further Strengthening Bank Loan Inspection Work", "Interim Measures for the Management of Financial Trust Investment Institutions' Funds" and other related measures
1988	Illegal fund absorption and loan issuance by trust companies	Business cleanup and industry cleanup, i.e., during the reorganization period, no new trust institutions or other types of non-bank financial institutions are allowed to be established, and the issuance of trust loans, investments, and interbank lending is stopped | (no specific regulations mentioned)	
1993	Illegal interbank lending, illegal deposit taking, and illegal loan issuance	Separate operations and separate management, i.e., separating the trust industry from the banking industry, cutting off financial relationships between banks and trust companies	"Commercial Bank Law of the People's Republic of China", "Interim Measures for the Asset-Liability Ratio Management of Financial Trust Investment Institutions", "Trust Fund Management Measures" and other related measures
1999	Operational disorder	Standardizing business behavior, i.e., clarifying the trust investment companies' role of "acting on behalf of others and managing finances for others", separating the trust industry from the securities industry, standardizing operations, and classifying and handling	"Notice of the People's Bank of China on the Plan for Rectifying Trust Investment Companies", "Trust Law of the People's Republic of China", "Trust Investment Company Management Measures", "Interim Measures for the Management of Trust Investment Company Fund Trust Business" and other related measures

Table 8.7 Statistics of newly established trust and investment companies in China from 1990 to 1999

Year	Number of newly established trust and investment companies
1990	0
1991	3
1992	2
1993	1
1994	1
1995	1
1996	1
1997	3
1998	1
1999	0

areas. Therefore, there is still a long way to go for the trust industry to truly develop independently. Subsequently, based on the rules of separate operations according to the "Commercial Banking Law of the People's Republic of China", the trust industry and the banking industry were separated, completely cutting off the capital flow between banks and trusts. This marked the beginning of the independent development of the trust industry.

8.3.2 *Rectification and Regulation of the Trust Industry*

In December 1993, the State Council issued the "Decision of the State Council on Financial System Reform". According to this decision, China's trust industry began comprehensive reform, adhering to the rules of segmented operations and regulatory oversight, and first completely uncoupled from banks. By the end of 1996, "168 trust and investment companies wholly owned or controlled by commercial banks were uncoupled and merged, and the number of independent legal entity trust companies nationwide became 244".[7] During this period, trust companies underwent rectification, and the quality of assets significantly improved. In 1994, Shaanxi International Trust and Anxin Trust achieved successful listings. Under the impact of events such as the Asian financial crisis, in 1999, the State Council carried out the fifth large-scale rectification of the trust industry in terms of business and institutions. After the rectification, trust institutions were completely separated from the securities industry, the number of trust investment institutions further decreased, and by the end of 2000, there were only 60 trust institutions nationwide, with total trust assets decreasing to 521.9 billion yuan. However, the quality of trust assets and corporate governance mechanisms improved significantly.

[7] Li Yang et al. *60 Years of China's Finance. China.* Finance and Economic Press, 2009:115.

Subsequently, to strengthen the healthy development of the trust industry, the PBOC issued the "Administrative Measures for Trust and Investment Companies" in January 2001. For the first time, this regulation made clear definitions in areas such as the status, functions, and business scope of trust investment institutions. In October of the same year, to adjust trust relationships, regulate trust behaviors, protect the legitimate rights and interests of trust parties, and promote the healthy development of the trust industry, the National People's Congress enacted the "Trust Law of the People's Republic of China" (hereinafter referred to as the "Trust Law"). Thus, the system clearly defined what constitutes a trust, the establishment, modification, and termination of trusts, trust properties, and various beneficiary relationships, laying down a clear legal status for the development of the trust industry. In 2002, the China Banking Regulatory Commission and the PBOC also promulgated the "Administrative Measures for Trust and Investment Companies" and the "Interim Measures for the Administration of Trust Funds by Trust and Investment Companies," which, together with the "Trust Law," formed the basic legal framework of the trust industry, jointly ensuring its continuous and stable development.

In 2003, the trust industry experienced significant development as the trust system continued to improve. The total assets of China's trust industry reached 257.9 billion yuan. At the same time, the regulatory authority of the trust industry was transferred from the PBOC to the China Banking Regulatory Commission following its establishment. In 2004, the development of the trust industry faced significant challenges due to the downturn in the stock market and tighter macroeconomic controls. Some trust companies deviated from their core trust business and engaged in numerous irregular operations. In 2005, the China Banking Regulatory Commission introduced a series of regulations to address issues such as related-party transactions and information disclosure in trust companies. They also implemented the "Trust Company Rating Method" to incentivize the standardized development of the trust industry. In 2007, in order to bring the trust industry back to its core function, the industry underwent the sixth round of rectification. On March 1st of the same year, the China Banking Regulatory Commission revised and issued the "Regulations on the Administration of Trust Companies" and the "Regulations on the Administration of Collective Trust Plans by Trust Companies." The promulgation and implementation of these regulations was a process of rectifying and reaffirming the development of the trust industry. The term 'investment' was removed from the original term "trust and investment companies," further clarifying the business scope and development direction of trust companies, emphasizing their fundamental nature. Subsequently, the China Banking Regulatory Commission also formulated regulations such as the "Interim Measures for the Administration of Trust Companies' Entrusted Overseas Wealth Management Business" and the "Operational Guidelines for Trust Companies' Private Equity Investment Trust Business" to clarify the positioning of the trust industry and enhance confidence in its development. By the end of 2008, after undergoing re-registration and restructuring, China had basically completed the rectification of the trust industry.

Through rectification, the historical risks and issues accumulated in the trust industry were resolved, and the entire industry transitioned into a professional wealth management institution. Starting from 2008, the trust industry entered a relatively regulated and rapid development trajectory. The number of trust companies significantly increased, reaching 68 companies by 2016, compared to the 30 companies in 2007. The size of trust assets under management continued to expand, reaching 26.28 trillion yuan by the end of 2017, ranking second in terms of asset scale within the financial institution system. Among the 68 companies, CITIC Trust ranked first with assets under management of 1.98 trillion yuan, while Industrial Bank Trust, China Resources Trust, and Huaneng Trust also exceeded one trillion yuan in trust assets. In terms of control entities of trust companies, there has been a shift from the previous monopoly of central and local governments during the early stages of reform and opening up, to a diversified structure involving central and local state-owned enterprises, private enterprises, and foreign strategic investors. The capital structure of Chinese trust companies in 2016 is shown in Table 8.8.

The increasing diversification of capital structure and improvement in asset quality of trust companies has reopened the process of listing for trust companies, which had been interrupted for 24 years. Shandong International Trust (referred to as "Shandong Guoxin") was officially listed and traded on the Hong Kong Stock Exchange in December 2017.

Alongside the increasingly standardized development of trust companies, there have been significant advancements in innovative trust businesses, particularly in areas such as asset securitization, industry funds, family trusts, charitable trusts, and internet trusts. In August 2010, the China Banking Regulatory Commission issued the "Regulations on the Management of Trust Companies' Net Capital," strengthening the risk supervision of trust companies. In 2011, the China Banking Regulatory Commission released the "Notice on Regulating Cooperation in Banking and Trust Wealth Management Business" to further prevent risks in banking and trust wealth management cooperation and promote the healthy development of business cooperation between commercial banks and trust companies.

In December 2014, the China Banking Regulatory Commission and the Ministry of Finance formulated and issued the "Regulations on the Management of Trust Industry Guarantee Funds" to standardize the raising, management, and utilization of trust industry guarantee funds. It aimed to establish a market-oriented risk disposal mechanism, protect the legitimate rights and interests of trust parties, effectively prevent trust industry risks, and promote the sustainable and healthy development of the trust industry. In April 2017, the China Banking Regulatory Commission issued the "Implementation Plan for the Pilot Program of Regulatory Classification of Trust Business" and the "Explanatory Notes on Regulatory Classification of Trust

Table 8.8 Capital structure statistics of Chinese trust companies in 2016

Controlling entity	Number of companies	Proportion (%)
Centrally state-owned	22	32
Locally state-owned	33	49
Privately owned capital	13	19

Business (Trial)," officially launching the pilot reform of regulatory classification for eight major trust businesses, including credit trust, equity trust, standard product trust, interbank trust, property trust, asset securitization trust, public welfare trust, and fiduciary trust. In August, the 'Regulations on Trust Registration Management' were promulgated, and in September, the online registration system was launched, marking the initial establishment of the trust registration system. In November, the "Guiding Opinions on Regulating the Asset Management Business of Financial Institutions (Draft for Solicitation of Comments)" laid the institutional foundation for the future standardized development of trust companies. In response to the rapid growth of banking and trust businesses in recent years, and to promote the standardized and healthy development of such businesses, prevent financial risks, and protect the legitimate rights and interests of investors, the China Banking Regulatory Commission issued the "Notice on Regulating Banking and Trust Businesses" in December 2017. Starting from 2018, value-added tax began to be levied on trust products, which inevitably had a certain delaying impact on the development of the trust industry.

At the Fifth National Financial Work Conference in 2017, it was explicitly stated that the financial sector should return to serving the real economy, deepen reforms, and prevent risks. The report of the 19th National Congress of the Communist Party of China specifically mentioned the importance of "guarding against systemic financial risks". These directions have guided the future development of trust companies towards a more standardized and orderly direction, playing a greater role in the development of the real economy. On April 27, 2018, the People's Bank of China officially issued the "Guiding Opinions on Regulating the Asset Management Business of Financial Institutions", which aimed to regulate the asset management market and prevent financial risks. On July 20, the People's Bank of China, together with the China Banking and Insurance Regulatory Commission and the China Securities Regulatory Commission, issued the "Notice on Further Clarifying Matters concerning the Guiding Opinions on Regulating the Asset Management Business of Financial Institutions", providing direction for the development of the trust industry.

8.4 The Emergence and Development of Other Non-bank Financial Institutions

In addition to insurance, securities, and trust, there are numerous other types of non-bank financial institutions that have emerged, driven by the joint efforts of the government and market entities. These institutions have greatly supplemented the services provided by banking institutions. Some non-bank financial institutions gradually recovered with the progress of reform and opening up, while others emerged as new forms of business models in response to the development of the social economy. Together, they have promoted innovation and development in China's financial industry to meet the financial service needs of different social and economic entities. Due to the variety of other non-bank financial institution types, and considering that some have a relatively short history, the following sections will focus on introducing some influential types to illustrate the diversification and development trends of the financial industry since the transition from "managing funds" to "regulating market".

8.4.1 Financial Companies of Enterprise Groups

Financial companies of enterprise groups are non-bank financial institutions that have emerged along with the reform of large-scale enterprise groups in China, displaying distinct Chinese characteristics. Since the birth of the first financial company of an enterprise group in 1987, after 30 years of development, China's financial companies have covered foundational industries such as energy and power, automobile manufacturing, aerospace, metallurgy, petroleum and chemical industry, coal and steel, military transportation, construction materials, and electronics. They have played an increasingly important role in strengthening centralized management of group funds, improving the efficiency of fund utilization, and reducing financial costs. They have provided strong financial support for the development of China's real economy.

A. The Rise and Initial Development of Financial Companies

From 1985 to 1995, it was the stage of the rise and initial development of financial companies of enterprise groups in China. In 1985, Shenzhen established the Shenzhen Financial Company, which was the first financial company in China. In May 1987, the head office of the PBOC approved the establishment of the Dongfeng Motor Industry Financial Company, pioneering the establishment of compliant financial companies. In the same year, in order to further implement the provisions of the State Council on promoting horizontal economic alliances and deepening enterprise reform to enhance enterprise vitality, the State Commission for Restructuring the Economic System and the State Planning Commission issued the "Several Opinions on Forming and Developing Enterprise Groups". These opinions clearly defined the connotation of enterprise groups, the principles and conditions for forming enterprise groups, and specified that "with the approval of the PBOC, enterprise groups can establish financial companies. Financial companies can internally allocate funds within the group and establish business relationships with banks or other financial institutions. They can also entrust certain specialized banks to handle financial businesses. With approval, group companies can raise funds from society. From the central to local levels, special quotas should be allocated in credit indicators to support the development of enterprise groups."[8] Under the guidance of the "Several Opinions on Forming and Developing Enterprise Groups by the State Commission for

[8] "Several Opinions on Forming and Developing Enterprise Groups by the State Commission for Restructuring the Economic System and the State Planning Commission". http://www.chinalawedu.com/falvfagui/fg21829/31802.shtm.

Table 8.9 Overview of the number of financial companies of enterprise groups, 1987–1995

Year	Number of companies
1987	8
1988	16
1989	16
1990	16
1991	17
1992	27
1993	37
1994	50
1995	58

Restructuring the Economic System and the State Planning Commission", the PBOC approved the establishment of 58 group financial companies by 1995, as shown in Table 8.9.

In April 1988, the National Financial Company Federation was established to strengthen internal business connections and information exchange among financial companies. From 1989 to 1991, the development of group financial companies entered a period of consolidation with no new company establishments, due to the "Notice on Further Cleaning up and Rectifying Financial Companies" issued by the State Council and the "Emergency Notice on Suspending the Approval of Various Types of Financial Institutions" issued by the PBOC. Afterward, group financial companies entered a period of stable development. In January 1991, the Ministry of Finance issued the "Trial Measures for Financial Management of Enterprise Group Financial Companies" to strengthen the financial management of group financial companies. In December 1991, the State Council approved the circulation of a notice from the National Planning Commission, the State Commission for Restructuring the Economic System, and the Office of the State Council on selecting a group of large-scale enterprise groups for pilot programs, greatly promoting the establishment and development of group financial companies. In November 1992, the PBOC, together with the National Planning Commission, the State Commission for Restructuring the Economic System, and the State Council's Economic and Trade Office, issued the "Implementation Measures for the Establishment of Financial Companies in Pilot Enterprise Groups," which standardized the development of enterprise group financial companies at the institutional level and promoted the establishment and growth of these companies. In 1994, the PBOC approved the establishment of the China Financial Company Association to strengthen the self-discipline management of group financial companies.

By 1995, a total of 58 financial companies had been established nationwide. Among them, from November 1990, when the PBOC approved the establishment of the first Sino-foreign joint venture financial company, Shanghai International Financial Corporation Limited, to 1995, a total of four foreign-funded financial companies were established. By 1995, the asset scale of financial companies had reached 75.7

billion yuan, an increase of more than 46 times compared to the 1.6 billion yuan in 1987.

B. Adjustment and Standardized Development of Financial Companies

From 1996 to 2003, it was the stage of adjustment and standardized development of financial companies of enterprise groups in China. During this period, the State Council, the PBOC, the Ministry of Finance, and other government entities successively issued a series of regulations targeting the management of enterprise group financial companies to strengthen their institutional construction and regulate their development. "In order to standardize the business operations of enterprise group financial companies, prevent financial risks, and promote their sound and healthy development", in September 1996, the PBOC issued the "Interim Measures for the Management of Enterprise Group Financial Companies". These measures initially clarified the establishment and changes, business scope, financial accounting, supervision and management, reorganization and takeover, dissolution, and punitive measures in multiple areas of institutional regulations for financial companies. They also specified that foreign-funded enterprise groups are allowed to establish financial companies. In October 1996, the PBOC issued the "Notice on Issues Related to the Establishment and Operation of Finance Companies by Foreign-funded Enterprise Groups," to further regulate the establishment and operation of finance companies by foreign enterprise groups in China. In April 1997, the State Council approved the "Opinions on Deepening the Pilot Work of Large Enterprise Groups" issued by the State Planning Commission, the State Economic and Trade Commission, and the State Commission for Restructuring the Economic System. It pointed out "the importance of deepening the pilot work of large-scale enterprise groups for promoting fundamental changes in the economic system and economic growth models. In accordance with the requirements of establishing a modern enterprise system and improving the entire state-owned economy, the focus was placed on a group of large-scale enterprise groups to facilitate the restructuring and development of a group of enterprises, promote structural adjustments, achieve economies of scale, improve the operational efficiency and effectiveness of state-owned assets, and actively play the backbone role of large-scale enterprise groups in the national economy." The work to develop pilot schemes was required to be completed by June 1998. To this end, the PBOC issued a notice in September 1997 on strengthening the management of funds and other issues related to enterprise group financial companies to promote the standardized development of such companies.

Thereafter, influenced by the high attention given to state-owned enterprise reforms by the central government and the State Council, the PBOC successively introduced a series of policies to encourage the development of financial companies. In June 2000, based on the "Company Law of the People's Republic of China" and the "Law of the People's Republic of China on the People's Bank of China", the PBOC formulated the "Administrative Measures for Enterprise Group Financial Companies" to further establish the systems for the establishment, changes, business operations, supervision, management, and risk prevention of financial companies. In

July 2000, the PBOC issued a notice regarding the implementation of the "Administrative Measures for Enterprise Group Financial Companies." The first article of the notice clearly stipulated that "financial companies established prior to the issuance of these measures should meet the requirements and complete various changes such as capital increase, adjustment of business scope, and amendment of articles of association by June 30, 2001, and complete the replacement of financial licenses. Any business activities not compliant with the measures should be promptly resolved, and the PBOC will conduct inspections on the implementation of the measures by financial companies starting from July 3, 2001."[9] Meanwhile, the PBOC also issued the "Management Regulations for Financial Companies to Enter the National Interbank Money Market and Bond Market," allowing qualified financial companies to apply to become members of the national interbank money market. In December 2000, the PBOC issued the "Approval Procedures for the Establishment of Enterprise Group Financial Companies (Trial)." In April 2003, the China Banking Regulatory Commission was established, and the management of enterprise group financial companies, which was previously under the responsibility of the PBOC, was transferred to the China Banking Regulatory Commission, thereby strengthening the management and standardized development of financial companies.

During this period, as the regulatory framework for financial company management was initially established, Chinese financial companies were undergoing a process of rectification and standardized development. Although the number of financial companies increased from 58 in 1996 to 75 in 2003, the overall number remained relatively stable, as shown in Fig. 8.6. In contrast to the fluctuation in the number of financial companies, their asset size exhibited a rapid growth trend, increasing from 169.3 billion yuan in 1996 to 513.5 billion yuan in 2003. Despite the relatively small increase in the number of companies, their asset strength significantly strengthened.

C. Rapid and Stable Development of Financial Companies

Since 2004, it has been a period of rapid and stable development for financial companies. The establishment of the China Banking Regulatory Commission marked the formal formation of China's financial regulatory system. According to their financial functions, financial companies are now officially supervised and managed by the China Banking Regulatory Commission.

On one hand, the legislation and regulations governing financial companies have been improving. In July 2004, the China Banking Regulatory Commission revised the "Administrative Measures for Enterprise Group Financial Companies." In December 2006, the China Banking Regulatory Commission made the decision to modify the "Administrative Measures for Enterprise Group Financial Companies" to adapt to new trends in the development of financial companies. In the same month, to strengthen off-site supervision of enterprise group financial companies, promote improved risk management and resilience to risks, the China Banking Regulatory

[9] "Notice of the People's Bank of China on Issues Related to the Implementation of the 'Administrative Measures for Enterprise Group Financial Companies'", http://www.fdi.gov.cn/1800000121_23_6818707.html.

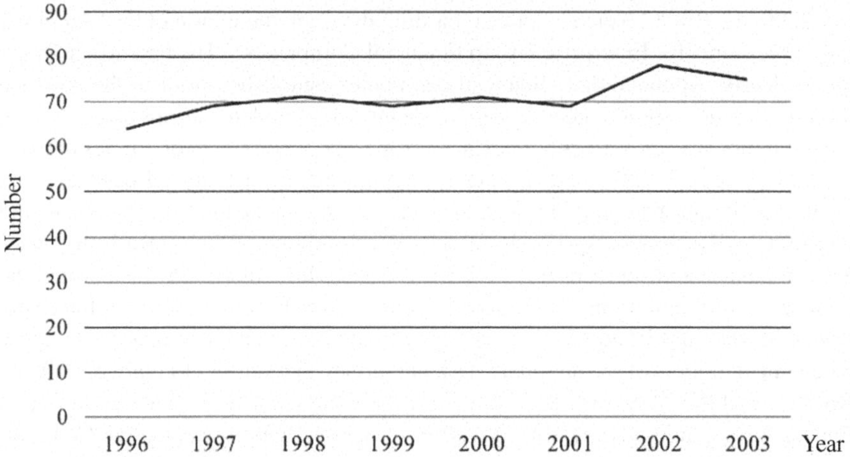

Fig. 8.6 Changes in the number of Chinese enterprise group financial companies from 1996 to 2003

Commission formulated and issued the "Interim Measures for the Assessment of Risk Regulatory Indicators for Enterprise Group Financial Companies." In January 2007, the China Banking Regulatory Commission issued the revised "Operating Procedures for the Application of Establishing Enterprise Group Financial Companies," further standardizing the application process for financial companies to ensure a healthy and orderly market access. In November, to comprehensively assess the risk status of enterprise group financial companies, achieve risk warning, and implement effective classification supervision, the China Banking Regulatory Commission formulated the "Guidelines for Risk Assessment and Classification Supervision of Enterprise Group Financial Companies," which clarified principles of risk assessment and classification supervision for financial companies. Additionally, the China Banking Regulatory Commission has formulated a series of regulations regarding the management of financial company operations, including entrustment business, securities investments, and bond business, to enhance their regulation. Since the 18th National Congress of the Communist Party of China, in order to fully leverage the active role of financial services in the real economy, promote the healthy development of financial companies, and further enhance the management level of central enterprises to achieve the goal of strength and optimization, the State Council, the State-owned Assets Supervision and Administration Commission (SASAC), and the China Banking Regulatory Commission jointly issued the "Guiding Opinions on Further Promoting the Healthy Development of Central Enterprise Financial Companies" in 2014.

On the other hand, with the increasingly standardized financial company management system, financial companies have experienced rapid development. By January 2018, the number of financial companies had reached 245. During this period, not only did domestic financial companies experience rapid development, but foreign

Table 8.10 Statistical table of key risk indicators of financial companies from 2014 to the third quarter of 2017

Time main risk indicators	2014 (%)	2015 (%)	2016 (%)	2017 third quarter (%)
Non-performing asset ratio	0.11	0.05	0.03	0.03
Capital adequacy ratio	21.22	21.19	21.25	22.27
Provision coverage ratio	1215.88	2763.30	3303.79	3722.38
Liquidity ratio	62.34	71.87	64.79	60.35
Interbank borrowing ratio	21.79	22.04	28.40	10.10
Investment ratio	6.58	49.82	30.24	38.24

Data Source Basic Operating Data of Financial Companies

financial companies also made certain progress. Additionally, since August 2006 when foreign enterprises invested in Zhejiang Energy Group Financial Co., Ltd., there has been an accelerated pace of foreign investment in Chinese financial companies, diversifying the capital structure of Chinese financial companies. By the third quarter of 2017, the total assets of Chinese financial companies had reached 7.55 trillion yuan, and the asset quality had significantly improved. The statistical data for the key risk indicators of financial companies from 2014 to the third quarter of 2017 are shown in Table 8.10.

8.4.2 *Financial Leasing Companies*

Since the beginning of reform and opening-up, China has initiated financial reforms. To meet the increasingly diverse economic needs, in July 1981, China Leasing Corporation was registered and established in the State Administration for Industry and Commerce, becoming the first non-bank financial institution and nationwide financial leasing company in China.[10] This marked the beginning of the establishment of financial leasing.

A. Unregulated Development Stage of Financial Leasing Companies

From 1981 to 2000, it was a stage of unregulated development for financial leasing companies in China. During this period, the Chinese government did not enact specific laws and regulations for financial leasing companies, resulting in a relatively

[10] In China, leasing companies are classified into finance leasing companies and financial leasing companies based on differences in regulatory authorities. The former belong to general industrial and commercial enterprises and can be further divided into foreign-funded finance leasing companies and Chinese pilot finance leasing companies, which are managed by the Ministry of Commerce. The latter are managed by the China Banking Regulatory Commission (CBRC) and are considered non-bank financial institutions. In 2017, there were reports of the two types being reorganized and placed under the supervision of the CBRC, but as of June 2019, this had not been realized. Therefore, this section only pertains to financial leasing companies managed by the CBRC.

unregulated development space for these companies. Since the establishment of the first financial leasing company in July 1981 until the early 1990s, financial leasing companies experienced rapid growth. However, some financial leasing companies were involved in irregular related-party transactions with their parent holding companies, leading to chaotic management and serious violations such as lending under the guise of leasing. The promulgation of the "Commercial Bank Law of the People's Republic of China" in 1995 explicitly prohibited commercial banks from engaging in financial leasing business, which intensified the eruption of many accumulated problems faced by financial leasing companies. Four companies, including Hainan International Leasing Co., Ltd., Guangdong International Leasing Co., Ltd., Wuhan International Leasing Co., Ltd., and China Huayang Financial Leasing Co., Ltd., were forced to exit the market. Against this backdrop, the People's Bank of China began to summarize experiences and promulgate specific laws and regulations for the management of financial leasing companies to regulate their development.

B. Standardized Development Stage of Financial Leasing Companies

Since 2000, it has been a period of increasingly standardized development for financial leasing companies in China. In response to the problems faced by financial leasing companies in the previous period, the PBOC announced the "Administrative Measures for Financial Leasing Companies" in June 2000, ending the era of unregulated development of financial leasing companies in China and establishing the legal framework for the financial leasing industry. This measure played a role in regulating financial leasing companies. For the first time, the measures explicitly defined the scope of business operations, functional positioning, safeguard measures for operations and supervision, and market access for financial leasing companies. According to these measures, existing financial leasing companies were required to engage in industry standardization construction, increase capital and expand shareholding to meet the requirement of a registered capital of 500 million yuan. At the same time, the PBOC strengthened on-site inspections and off-site supervision of financial leasing companies, improved the corporate governance structure of financial leasing companies, and implemented operational rectification for several companies, including Sichuan Financial Leasing Company, which did not comply with these measures.

In 2001, China officially joined the WTO. After that, it gradually opened up the financial leasing market to foreign-funded commercial banks and other financial institutions, allowing them to engage in financial leasing services similar to those provided by domestic financial leasing companies. In 2003, the China Banking Regulatory Commission replaced the PBOC as the regulatory body for financial leasing companies. In response to the new development trends in the financial leasing industry, the China Banking Regulatory Commission incorporated the management experience of foreign financial leasing companies and combined it with the domestic reality and national conditions. They applied to the State Council for permission to allow commercial banks to participate in financial leasing business. In 2006, the State Council approved the application from the China Banking Regulatory Commission. To promote the sustainable and healthy development of Chinese financial leasing companies and strengthen the supervision and management of these companies, the China Banking Regulatory Commission revised the "Management Measures for Financial Leasing Companies" which were originally issued in 2000. In March 2007, the China Banking Regulatory Commission issued the revised version of the "Management Measures for Financial Leasing Companies". The newly revised measures further adjusted the institutional framework of financial leasing companies in terms of establishment, changes and termination, business scope, operating rules, and supervision and management. It explicitly stated that only qualified commercial banks, financial leasing companies, large-scale equipment manufacturers, and financial institutions recognized by the China Banking Regulatory Commission can serve as shareholders of newly established financial leasing companies. In accordance with these regulations, starting from 2007, Industrial and Commercial Bank of China, China Construction Bank, Bank of Communications, China Minsheng Bank, and China Merchants Bank successively obtained approval from the China Banking Regulatory Commission to pilot the establishment of financial leasing companies. The access of domestic commercial banks injected new vitality into the development of financial leasing companies, enabling them to grow rapidly. By the end of 2011, the number of financial leasing companies in China reached 18.

With the rapid development of financial leasing companies, the Financial Leasing Professional Committee was established in July 2009 under the China Banking Association to strengthen inter-industry cooperation, encourage orderly competition, and maintain the integrity of financial leasing transactions. Its purpose was to enhance self-discipline and management within the financial leasing industry. In order to promote the development of financing leasing business and further regulate the operational behavior of financial leasing companies, the China Banking Regulatory Commission revised the "Management Measures for Financial Leasing Companies" issued in 2007 and announced the new "Management Measures for Financial Leasing Companies" in March 2014. These measures made certain adjustments to the admission criteria, business scope, operating rules, supervision, and management of financial leasing companies to adapt to the new development trends in the industry. The increasingly improved laws and regulations for financial leasing companies have put China's financial leasing companies on a fast and regulated development track, with some high-quality companies seeking public listings. In July 2016, Guoyin Leasing successfully went public on the Hong Kong Stock Exchange, becoming the first publicly listed financial leasing company in China with a registered capital of 12.6 billion yuan, ranking first among all domestic financial leasing companies. By the end of 2017, the number of financial leasing companies reached 66, with a total registered capital of 193.331 billion yuan. Among the 66 companies, the banking system accounted for 46, holding an absolute control position. Currently, these 66 financial leasing companies are spread across 26 provinces, municipalities, and autonomous regions, with the highest number located in Tianjin, reaching 11. The increasingly regulated development of financial leasing companies has played a certain role in promoting the development of China's social economy and the transformation of its economic structure.

8.4.3 Monetary Brokerage Companies

Monetary brokerage companies originated from the foreign exchange market in the UK over a century ago. In developed Western countries and regions, it has since evolved into a relatively complete industry and become an important part of non-bank financial institutions. In China, however, it started relatively late, and it was not until the year 2000 that China began exploring the possibility and necessity of establishing monetary brokerage companies. After the establishment of the China Banking Regulatory Commission in 2003, China proposed pilot programs to construct the system for monetary brokerage companies in order to adapt to the development needs of the financial market, thus initiating the development of China's monetary brokerage industry.

On August 8, 2005, the China Banking Regulatory Commission announced the "Management Measures for Pilot Monetary Brokerage Companies." These measures defined monetary brokerage companies as "non-bank financial institutions approved to be established within China, specializing in providing brokerage services such as facilitating fund transfers and foreign exchange transactions between financial institutions through electronic technology or other means, and charging commissions for such services." The measures also provided detailed provisions on market access conditions, business scope, supervision and management, as well as legal responsibilities for monetary brokerage companies. In accordance with "Management Measures for Pilot Monetary Brokerage Companies", the China Banking Regulatory Commission approved the establishment of Shanghai International Trust Co., Ltd. and Delibang (Europe) Ltd. to jointly initiate the establishment of Shanghai Guoli Monetary Brokerage Co., Ltd. on December 20, 2005. This marked the establishment of China's monetary brokerage industry, representing another innovation in China's financial organizational system. By the end of 2011, China had established four monetary brokerage companies.

Subsequently, in order to regulate the development of monetary brokerage companies, the Chinese government issued a series of regulations governing the relevant business of these companies. In August 2011, the General Office of the PBOC issued the "Notice on Printing and Distributing the Measures for the Administration of the Financial Urban Area Network of the People's Bank of China (Trial)", which required monetary brokerage companies to connect to the local area network in accordance with the notice to ensure smooth operation of related businesses, facilitate financial information exchange, and ensure network security. In October 2012, the Monetary Brokerage Professional Committee was established under the China Banking Association to strengthen self-regulation and management of monetary brokerage companies. In November 2013, the China Banking Regulatory Commission issued the "Measures for the Qualifications of Directors (Councilors) and Senior Management of Banking Financial Institutions" to improve the qualification management of directors (councilors) and senior management personnel of monetary brokerage companies and other financial institutions, and promote the legal and stable operation of the monetary brokerage and other financial industries. In March 2015, the

Shanghai Stock Exchange issued the "Notice on Matters related to Institutional Investors in the Bond Market of the Shanghai Stock Exchange Receiving Services from Monetary Brokerage Companies", which for the first time clarified the relevant matters regarding institutional investors in the bond market of the Shanghai Stock Exchange entrusting monetary brokerage companies to provide intermediation services for bond transactions, greatly promoting the expansion of business for monetary brokerage companies in the bond market and improving the market liquidity of bonds. In December 2016, the PBOC issued the "Measures for the Administration of Large-sum Transactions and Suspicious Transaction Reports of Financial Institutions," providing a legal basis for regulating the behaviors of currency brokerage companies regarding large-sum transactions and suspicious transaction reporting. In May 2017, the State Administration of Taxation, Ministry of Finance, PBOC, China Banking Regulatory Commission, China Securities Regulatory Commission, and China Insurance Regulatory Commission jointly formulated the "Measures for Due Diligence Investigation of Non-resident Financial Account Tax-related Information," which provides a basis for fulfilling international obligations on automatic exchange of financial account tax-related information and regulating the due diligence investigation behaviors of currency brokerage companies and other financial institutions regarding non-resident financial account tax-related information.

With the increasing standardization of currency brokerage companies in China, well-known foreign currency brokerage companies have set up institutions in China. Shanghai Guoli Currency Brokerage Co., Ltd., Shanghai International Currency Brokerage Co., Ltd., Ping An Lishun International Currency Brokerage Co., Ltd., Zhongcheng Baojiesi Currency Brokerage Co., Ltd., and Tianjin Xintang Currency Brokerage Co., Ltd. have also made significant progress and become important financial intermediaries spanning the currency market, foreign exchange market, and capital market in China, playing an increasingly important role.

8.4.4 Automobile Finance Companies

Automobile finance companies emerged in Western countries such as the United States in the early twentieth century. After World War II, automobile finance companies rapidly developed and became important non-bank financial institutions by the 1970s and 1980s. Before the reform and opening-up, automobile finance companies did not truly emerge in China. It was only after the reform and opening-up that they gradually developed in response to the demands of the social economy, becoming an important financing channel driving China's automobile production, consumption, and leasing.

A. Nascent Development Phase

From the reform and opening-up to 2003, it was the nascent development period of China's automobile finance companies. During this period, China did not establish dedicated automobile finance companies. With the rapid development of China's automobile industry and related sectors, automobile finance businesses emerged in the automobile credit market. However, these related automobile finance services were not provided by specialized financing companies but were led by state-owned commercial banks. During this period, some automobile finance companies emerged, although they were merely in a fledgling status, laying the groundwork for the emergence of future automobile finance companies.

B. Development and Growth Phase

From 2004 to the present, it has been a period of rapid development and growth of China's automobile finance companies. In October 2003, the China Banking Regulatory Commission announced the "Administrative Measures for Automobile Finance Companies," formally allowing non-bank financial institutions to engage in automobile finance services, thus introducing the automobile finance system. On August 8, 2004, Shanghai General Motors Financial Leasing Co., Ltd. was established, marking the birth of China's first automobile finance company. Taking advantage of China's accession to the WTO and the opportunities for liberalizing trade in services, international well-known automobile brands such as Volkswagen, Toyota, Ford, Mercedes-Benz, Dongfeng Peugeot Citroen, Volvo, and Hyundai began to establish corresponding automobile finance companies in China, thus kicking off the rapid development of China's automobile finance companies.

In order to regulate the orderly development of automobile finance companies and address issues such as limited financing methods, narrow profit channels, high credit risks, and multiple approval procedures in automobile finance companies, the China Banking Regulatory Commission revised and officially announced the "Administrative Measures for Automobile Finance Companies" in January 2008, aiming to strengthen the supervision and management of automobile finance companies and promote the healthy development of China's automobile finance business. At the same time, automobile financing leasing business officially became part of the automobile finance company's business, standing alongside retail loans and wholesale loans as the core business of the company, greatly advancing the development of China's automobile finance companies. By the end of 2011, 14 automobile finance companies had been established nationwide, increasing to 25 by July 2016, with total assets reaching 5728.96 billion yuan. During this period, to strengthen the self-discipline management of automobile finance companies, a special Automobile Finance Professional Committee was established under the China Banking Association in June 2014. Since then, the Automobile Finance Professional Committee has compiled an annual "China Automobile Finance Company Industry Development Report" to guide the orderly development of automobile finance companies. In the future, under the supervision and management of the China Banking and Insurance Regulatory Commission and industry self-discipline, the business operations of automobile finance companies will become more standardized, focusing on tasks such as serving the real economy, preventing and controlling financial risks, and deepening financial reforms, promoting the digitization and networking of China's automobile finance companies, and ensuring the continuous and healthy development of the companies.

8.4.5 Consumer Finance Companies

Since the reform and opening-up, along with the annual average high-speed growth of China's economy exceeding 9% for 35 years, the living standards of the vast population have significantly improved, and a certain amount of savings has accumulated. People's lifestyles have shifted towards pursuing higher consumption and better quality. In 2007, the outbreak of the subprime mortgage crisis in the United States quickly impacted China's import and export trade, leading to a downward trend in domestic economic growth. In response, the Chinese government implemented a 4 trillion yuan stimulus package to achieve the goals of "maintaining growth, stabilizing employment, and adjusting the structure." Various levels of government adopted diverse measures to stimulate consumption to enhance its role in driving the economy. In response to the increasing demand from the government and various sectors of society to boost consumption, the China Banking Regulatory Commission began researching the domestic and foreign consumer finance industries from the end of 2007 to demonstrate the necessity and feasibility of developing consumer finance in China. In July 2009, to increase financial support for expanding domestic demand and promoting consumption, the China Banking Regulatory Commission issued the "Trial Measures for the Administration of Consumer Finance Companies." These measures clarified the market access conditions, business scope and rules, supervision, and management of consumer finance companies, laying down the institutional foundation for the establishment of consumer finance companies in China.

According to the "Trial Measures for the Administration of Consumer Finance Companies," with the approval of the State Council, the China Banking Regulatory Commission selected Beijing, Shanghai, Chengdu, and Tianjin to initiate the trial approval of consumer finance companies in four locations. After a year and a half of preparation, on January 6, 2010, the China Banking Regulatory Commission officially approved the establishment of Beiyin Consumer Finance Co., Ltd. by Beijing Bank. In March, Beiyin Consumer Finance Co., Ltd. was officially established, marking the birth of China's first consumer finance company. Subsequently, China Bank and Chengdu Bank as the investment entities established China Bank Consumer Finance Co., Ltd. and Sichuan Jincheng Consumer Finance Co., Ltd., respectively. At the same time, the China Banking Regulatory Commission approved the establishment of JieXin Consumer Finance Co., Ltd., a wholly-owned subsidiary of PPF Group, making it the first wholly foreign-owned consumer finance company in China. After more than two years of development, the four pilot consumer finance companies' total assets reached 4.013 billion yuan by November 2012, and three companies began to make profits.

In order to promote the development of consumer finance companies, in 2013, the China Banking Regulatory Commission promulgated the newly revised "Trial Measures for the Administration of Consumer Finance Companies." The revised measures further clarified and improved the institutional regulations related to the market access conditions and business scope of consumer finance companies. According to its provisions, in September 2013, with the approval of the State

Council, the China Banking Regulatory Commission added 12 new trial cities for consumer finance companies. In June 2015, with the approval of the State Council, China promoted consumer finance companies nationwide. By the end of 2015, the China Banking Regulatory Commission had approved a total of 14 consumer finance companies. From the first establishment to the end of 2015, the average annual number of consumer finance companies was less than 3, demonstrating the cautiousness of the Chinese government in establishing consumer finance companies. From then until April 2017, the pace of approval for consumer finance companies significantly accelerated, with the number of companies increasing. During this period, eight consumer finance companies were approved for establishment, bringing the total number to 22. Starting from 2015, especially in 2017, China strengthened the institutional standardization construction of consumer finance companies. Since 2017, compliant operation has become a necessary condition for market access for consumer finance companies in China, to safeguard the bottom line of "preventing systemic financial risks" mentioned in the report of the 19th National Congress of the Communist Party of China.

Since 2018, under the top-level design of serving the real economy, preventing and controlling financial risks, and deepening financial reforms, the development of China's consumer finance companies will inevitably move towards a more standardized direction, making greater contributions to promoting the improvement of China's consumption level and structural reforms on the supply and demand sides.

Chapter 9
The Establishment and Development of Financial Market

Since the reform and opening up, with the rapid development of social economy, the financial market which was completely suppressed has gradually developed, and a complete financial market system consisting of money market and capital market has been formed so far. During the formation of the financial market, it initially sprouted with the development of social enterprises, and then developed rapidly and disorderly under the strong impetus of local governments to develop the economy. After the "August 10 Incident" in Shenzhen, the financial market gradually transited to the central government's leadership, and gradually shifted to the government-led and market-driven transformation, so far, the degree of marketization has been deepening. Although the development of the financial market has experienced twists and turns, and direct financing has lagged behind indirect financing for a long time, it has become an important force to promote the development of China's real economy, in line with the path of gradual economic development.

9.1 Cultivation and Development of Capital Market

From 1949 to 1978, the central government issued "people-victory convertible bonds" in 1950 and "National Economic Construction Bonds" in 1954–1958. The stock market disappeared with the closure of the stock exchange in 1952 and the socialist transformation of the existing stock companies. Since the reform and opening up, along with the reform of China's social and economic system, the capital market consisting of the bond market and the stock market has gradually emerged and developed, and has become increasingly standardized and market-oriented. By 2017, the size of the stock market ranks second in the world, and the balance of the bond market ranks third in the world, and the process of globalization has been accelerating.

R. Lan, *The Financial Development of China*, Understanding China,
https://doi.org/10.1007/978-981-97-8273-4_9

9.1.1 The Establishment and Development of Stock Market

In the early days of the People's Republic of China, under the new democratic economic system with the state economy as the leader and various economic sectors co-existing, some regions still retained some joint-stock enterprises, and the shares of some large joint-stock enterprises were circulated and transferred within a certain range. Meanwhile, the stock exchanges in Tianjin and Beijing continued to be maintained under the new government. However, with the completion of the socialist transformation of the private industry and commerce in 1953, the joint-stock enterprises were transformed into public–private partnerships and state-owned enterprises, Tianjin Stock Exchange was merged into Tianjin Investment Company, and Beijing Stock Exchange was abolished. After the reform and opening up, with the rise of joint-stock enterprises, China's stock market has been gradually established and developed, and has made obvious progress in standardization and marketization.

A. The Establishment of the Stock Market

After the policy of reform and opening up, in the joint-stock township enterprises and urban small enterprises, the earliest joint-stock economy has sprouted since 1978. In 1980, the agent of Fushun Branch of the People's Bank of China (PBOC) issued shares worth 2.11 million yuan, which started the prelude of China's stock issuance. In November 1982, Shenzhen United Investment Company of Bao'an County launched its initial public offering in Shenzhen. In 1984, the Third Plenary Session of the 12th CPC Central Committee passed the "Decision of the CPC Central Committee on Economic System Reform", and the shareholding system was officially confirmed. Subsequently, Beijing, Shanghai, Guangzhou and other places launched joint-stock pilot. In July 1984, the first joint stock limited company, Beijing Tianqiao Department Store Co., LTD., was established to issue stocks for a period of 3 years; In November of the same year, Shanghai Feilo Acoustics Company issued non-repayable shares to the society, resulting in a true sense of the stock. After that, joint-stock companies developed rapidly in large and medium-sized cities across the country. In December 1986, The State Council promulgated the "Several Regulations on Deepening the Reform of Enterprises and Enhancing the Vitality of Enterprises", which enabled the reform of shareholding system in state-owned enterprises to be carried out rapidly. Accordingly, the pilot of joint-stock enterprises has also been extended from industry to enterprises in the financial industry, commerce, real estate and other industries. The rise of joint-stock enterprises has produced a lot of traded products in China's capital market.

With the rapid development of China's joint-stock enterprises, stock trading activities are gradually formed and institutionalized. In 1986, Jing'an Securities Department of the Trust and Investment Company of the Shanghai Branch of the Industrial and Commercial Bank of China, first listed "Feilo Acoustics" and "Yanzhong Industry" and launched over-the-counter trading, resulting in the secondary market of China's stock trading, initiating the history of China's stock trading. In 1987, the establishment of Shenzhen Special Zone Securities Company promoted the development of China's securities institutions; In 1988, three securities companies, Haitong, Wan'guo and Shenyin, were established successively in Shanghai, which initially formed China's OTC securities trading market. After more than a year of preparation, the Shanghai Stock Exchange was officially opened in December 1990. The Shenzhen Stock Exchange, whose preparations started in 1987, was officially established in July 1991, and since then China's stock market has begun to practice centralized, paperless and networked trading and settlement. At the same time, the national Securities Trading Automated Quotations System (STAQ) established by the Joint Office of Research and Design of Beijing Stock Exchange (later renamed the Research and Design Center of Securities Market of China) was officially put into use in December 1990, and the trading of legal shares began in December 1992. Before and after that, China has established more than 70 local securities trading center; The establishment of "two stock exchanges and one network" has changed the status quo of China's previous stock market, which was scattered, backward and chaotic, and marked the emergence of a centralized stock market.

Before the "August 10 Incident"[1] in 1992, China's stock market mainly developed rapidly under the leadership of local governments. The Shanghai and Shenzhen Stock exchanges were established and managed by the local governments of Shanghai and Shenzhen under the guidance of the local branches of PBOC. At this time, although Shanghai, Shenzhen and other places had formulated a series of rules and regulations to regulate the stock market (see Table 9.1), the stock market was basically in a state of self-evolution, lack of norms or effective supervision, with mainly regional pilot. There were ideological debates on the development of the stock market, and the stock market showed a disorderly development pattern.

Deng Xiaoping's Southern Tour Talks in 1992 politically settled the debate over the development of the securities market. "Are securities and stock markets something good or dangerous? Are they unique to capitalism, and can they be used by socialism? We can not only be permitted to think about those questions, but also, we must try resolutely. If our trial proves to be right after 1 or 2 years, we can popularize it; if wrong, stop. Of course, stop can be fast or slow, but what matters if we leave some room. If we keep this attitude, we may never commit a blunder."[2] After the "August 10 incident" in Shenzhen in 1992, The State Council established the Securities Commission of The State Council and the China Securities Regulatory Commission in October 1992, with then-Vice Premier Zhu Rongji as the director and the leaders of 13 ministries[3] and commissions. The former was in charge of the national securities market and was responsible for the unified management of the

[1] On August 10, 1992, a collective illegal and criminal event was triggered at the Shenzhen Stock Exchange due to a million people scrambling for the lottery draw for the subscription of new stocks.

[2] DENG Xiaoping. *Deng Xiaoping Selected Works (Volume 3)*, People's Publishing House, 2008: 200.

[3] The thirteen ministries and commissions include PBOC, the National Commission for Restructuring the Economic System, the National Development and Reform Commission, the Ministry of Finance, the State Economic and Trade Commission, the Ministry of Supervision, the Supreme People's Court, the Supreme People's Procuratorate, the Ministry of Economic and Trade, the

Table 9.1 Some rules and regulations issued by Shanghai and Shenzhen before the August 10 incident in 1992 to regulate the operation of the stock market

Place	Time	Regulation
Shanghai	Oct. 1984	Interim administrative measures on the issuance of shares
	Jan. 1987	Interim provisions on over-the-counter trading of securities
	Nov. 1990	Measures of Shanghai municipality for the administration of securities trading
	Nov. 1991	Measures of Shanghai municipality for the administration of RMB special stocks
	June. 1992	Provisional provisions of Shanghai municipal Co., LTD
Shenzhen	Oct. 1986	Provisional provisions on the pilot program of state-owned enterprises in Shenzhen special economic zone for demutualization
	May. 1991	Shenzhen interim measures for the administration of stock issuance and trading
	Nov. 1991	Measures of Shenzhen municipality for the administration of RMB special stocks
	Feb. 1992	Provisional provisions of Shenzhen City Co., LTD

national securities market. The latter is the specific executive agency of the former, and is specifically responsible for the supervision of the national securities market. The establishment of the Securities Commission of The State Council and the China Securities Regulatory Commission marked the formation of a unified regulatory system for China's securities market and strengthened the management and supervision of the national securities market. At the same time, China, South, Cathay and other securities limited companies have been established, greatly promoting the development of China's stock market. During this period, the number of listed companies in China's stock market increased from 13 in 1991 to 53 in 1992, and the total market value exceeded 100 billion yuan. Besides A-shares, B-shares were also launched at the end of 1991, showing a rapid rising trend in the stock market.

Of course, in this period, China's stock issuance adopted the way of independent public offering and private pricing. In the design of equity structure, in order to avoid violating the taboo of privatization of state-owned and collective assets, "risking" the loss of state-owned or collective assets, or "shaking" the dominant position of public ownership, at the very beginning China stipulated that state-owned shares and legal person shares would not be listed and circulated. Only public stocks can be traded and circulated in Shanghai and Shenzhen stock exchanges, which leads to the phenomenon of split ownership in China's stock market.

State Administration for Industry and Commerce, the State Administration of Taxation, the State-owned Assets Supervision and Administration Commission, and the State Administration of Foreign Exchange.

B. The Transition of Stock Market from Decentralization to Centralization

From October 1992 to 1999, the development of China's stock market witnessed the transition from decentralized to centralized, local to central stages. Specifically, it is manifested in the following four aspects: First, the management functions of China's stock market were transitioned from the local to the central government. Table 9.2 shows the statistics of the centralization of the management authority of the stock market from 1993 to 1999.

Before 1992, China's stock market was managed by PBOC, local governments and stock exchanges. Since the establishment of the Securities Commission and CSRC in 1997, the management of China's securities market has become a pattern of multi-headed supervision by the Securities Commission, CSRC, PBOC, relevant central ministries and commissions, local governments and stock exchanges. The approval power of relevant stock market, audit power, administrative punishment power, personnel appointment power, legislative power, etc. were also centralized

Table 9.2 Statistical table of the centralization of administrative authority of the stock market from 1993 to 1999

Year	Key events of centralization
July, 1993	According to the "interim measures for the administration of stock exchanges", stock exchanges shall be administered by the local governments and supervised by the China securities regulatory commission. The general manager of the exchange shall be nominated by the local government jointly with the China securities regulatory commission (CSRC), appointed by the board of directors, and reported to the securities commission for the record
Nov, 1993	The securities commission of the state council shall be responsible for the pilot work of the futures market, and the CSRC shall execute it
Mar, 1995	According to "the institutional formulation plan of the china securities regulatory commission," CSRC has been established as a public institution directly under the state council at the vice-ministerial level, and is the regulatory executive agency of the securities commission of the state council
July, 1995	According to "the 1995 decisions on the arrangement of work of securities and futures," the chairmen and vice-chairmen and vice-presidents of the stock exchanges and futures exchanges are nominated by the CSRC and recommended to the general assembly or board of directors of the exchanges or futures exchanges after consultation with the local governments
Aug, 1997	The Shanghai and Shenzhen stock exchanges are under the management of CSRC
Nov, 1997	Rationalize the securities management system, exercise vertical leadership over local securities regulatory departments, and transfer securities-operating institutions supervised by PBOC to CSRC. The chief and deputy general managers of the exchange shall be appointed and removed by CSRC
Apr, 1998	The securities commission of the state council was merged with CSRC, and the CSRC was designated as a ministerial-level institution directly under the state council
July, 1999	"The securities law of the People's Republic of China" was implemented to ensure the administrative status of CSRC in the management of exchanges by way of law

in the relevant ministries of the central government, and fully centralized in CSRC by 1999. While taking over the securities regulators across the country, the CSRC set up securities regulators in nine cities, including Tianjin, Shenyang, Shanghai, Ji'nan, Wuhan, Guangzhou, Shenzhen, Chengdu and Xi'an; CSRC offices were set in Beijing and Chongqing; and offices of securities regulatory commissioner were set in 25 provinces, autonomous regions and cities under the planned independent listing. In July 1999, all agencies were listed and the vertical leadership system of CSRC was established.

Second, the institutionalization of the stock market has been accelerated. In addition to the formulation and promulgation of various specific stock market norms, laws and regulations, the promulgation of the "Securities Law of the People's Republic of China" in 1998 and its amendment in 2005 have greatly improved the quality of China's stock market and made the development of China's capital market more standardized and legalized. During this period, although China's stock market has experienced many drastic fluctuations, with the improvement of the stock market level and issuance system, the stock trading market has obviously matured.

Third, the local securities trading institutions concentrated in moving in Shanghai and Shenzhen exchange. More than 70 local securities trading centers established around 1992 were merged into the Shanghai and Shenzhen trading markets by 1993. STAQ and the National Electronic Trading System (NET), launched in Beijing in April 1993, were shut down in September 1999; At the same time, over-the-counter markets that existed in various places were also cleaned up and closed. In this way, China's securities market quickly realized the transformation from decentralized to nation-wide centralized trading market.

The fourth is the transformation of stock issuance from social independent offering to unified issuance management. From the perspective of the access, pricing and distribution of stock issuance, it has obviously changed from disorder to centralized and unified management by the government. Table 9.3 shows the changes of China's stock issuance system before 1999.

Of course, in the process of centralized management of China's stock market from the local to the central government, China's stock market has achieved rapid development, as shown in Table 9.4.

At this stage, China's stock market has achieved rapid development, and the types of stocks have increased correspondingly. In 1992, The State Council allowed Shanghai and Shenzhen to issue "Renminbi special shares" (B-shares). Shares issued on the B stock market were restricted to foreign investors until February 2001, after which they were opened to domestic investors. In July 1992, The State Council approved the listing of state-owned enterprises in Hong Kong (H-shares). In July of the following year, Tsingtao Beer successfully issued H-shares on the Hong Kong Stock Exchange, becoming the first mainland enterprise listed overseas.

During this period, China's stock market experienced great ups and downs, there were 5 bull markets and 5 bear markets in just 7 years; Moreover, market manipulation and insider trading are rampant, and there are incidents such as the arrears of major shareholders of Monkey King Group and Ji'nan Qingqi, and the hollowing of listed companies by major shareholders such as Daqing Lianyi, which seriously affected the

Table 9.3 Changes of China's stock issuance system before 1999

Issuance system	Issuance style
Access management on issuing body	Before October 1992, stock issuance was basically non-public, with the audit chaotic
	From 1993 to 1995, it was the quota management under the audit system
	From 1996 to 2000, it was indicator management under the audit system
Issuance pricing	Before the establishment of the Shanghai and Shenzhen Stock exchanges, it was a stage of pricing that there was no system to follow, with private placement
	Stage of public offering of fixed price (1991–1998)*
Allocation of new shares	Before 1990 was the stage of independent decision to offer shares to the society
	1991–1993 was period of subscription certificate**
	1994 was period of advance full-payment and proportional placing
	1994–1995 was the period of bidding issuance
	1995–1997 was the period of online pricing lottery

Notes *During the period from June 1994 to January 1995, four companies, Ha Suibao, Qinghai Sanpu, Xiahua Electronics, and Qiongjinpan, attempted to issue stocks with pricing through online bidding

**The subscription certificate (form) method went through three stages: limited issuance of subscription certificates (1991–1992), unlimited issuance of subscription certificates (1992), and unlimited issuance of subscription forms linked to savings deposits (1993)

Table 9.4 Statistical table of listed companies, total market value and number of accounts in China's stock market from 1992 to 1999

Year	Number of listed companies	Total market value/100 million yuan	Number of accounts opened/ ten thousand households
1992	53	1048	216.65
1993	183	3531	835.17
1994	291	3691	1107.76
1995	323	3474	1294.19
1996	530	9842	2422.08
1997	745	17,529	3480.26
1998	851	19,506	4259.88
1999	949	26,471	4481.19

Source Based on "the relevant data of China securities and futures statistical yearbook"

"open, fair and just" development of China's stock market. In the context of economic development, some systems regulating the stock market had not been effectively implemented, and there was a lack of necessary institutional constraints in many key areas, which led to the characteristics of "gambling market" in China's stock market during this period. Obviously, "Due to the lack of dividend system, delisting mechanism, short-selling mechanism, as well as the existence of the phenomenon of 'shell resources', the hollowing out of major shareholders and government protection, the stock market has gradually formed a kind of investment concept that does not pay attention to the intrinsic value of stocks but more investment speculation, forming a strong market speculation atmosphere."[4]

C. The Standardization and Marketization of the Stock Market

Before 1998, as the stock market management authority was transferred to the central government, the administrative color was extremely thick, and the stock market appeared a phenomenon of "chaos when given freedom and stagnation when controlled". In 1998, the Chinese government enacted the Securities Law of the People's Republic of China, which clarified the legal status of the China Securities Regulatory Commission as the main body in charge of China's stock market, thus kicking off the prelude of the transformation of China's stock market to standardization and marketization.

First, the issuance system of stock market is becoming increasingly standardized and market-oriented. Although the unification of the issuance system of China's stock market in the early stage created a relatively favorable social and economic environment for the development of the stock market, the administrative examination and approval system, which emphasized management and neglected supervision, undoubtedly generated a lot of rent-seeking space in the process of stock issuance. Only in the period of indicator management under the examination and approval system, according to the people in industry estimates, at this stage, the public-relation cost of each enterprise for stock issuance was from 0.5 to 30 billion yuan, which became a warm bed for breeding corruption.[5] At the same time, the quality of newly listed companies had been weakened, resulting in the strange phenomenon of "no risk" in China's new stock market. After that, the issuance system showed a trend of increasingly standardized and market-oriented development, as shown in Table 9.5.

Since 2008, the China Securities Regulatory Commission (CSRC) has promulgated a series of regulations such as the Interim Measures for the Securities Issuance and Listing Sponsor System and the Measures for the Management of Securities Issuance and Underwriting to strengthen the institutionalization of stock issuance. With the expansion and diversification of the stock market, CSRC promulgated the revised Administrative Measures on Securities Issuance and Underwriting in September 2017. In accordance with the notice of The State Council on further

[4] HU Ruyin. *Development and Changes of China's Capital Market*, Truth and Wisdom Press, Shanghai People's Publishing House, 2008: 78.

[5] HU Ruyin. *Development and Changes of China's Capital Market*, Truth and Wisdom Press, Shanghai People's Publishing House, 2008: 99–100.

Table 9.5 Changes of China's stock issuing system since 2000

Issuance system	Issuance ways
Issuance access	From 2001 to 2004 was a channel system under the audit system
	It has been a sponsor system under the audit system since 2004
Issuance pricing	It was online bidding in 2001
	2002 was auction system and placing new shares at market value
	2006 was IPO inquiry system + online pricing
	2009 was to improve the sponsor restraint mechanism, optimize online issuance
	2012 was book-building mechanism and placing at market value, but subject to full advance payment
Apportionment of shares	Since 1998, online lottery has been combined with offline placement, and "green shoes" and "callback" mechanisms were also introduced

cleaning up the departmental rules and normative documents involved in the "release and management service", CSRC announced and implemented a batch of new regulations such as the "Measures for the Management of the Securities Issuance and Listing Sponsor System" in November 2017.

In terms of stock issuance access, although the audit system was still adopted, the review speed of new shares had been accelerated in terms of specific practices. As of June 2017, the number of listed companies in China reached 3297, 245 more than that at the end of 2016, an increase of 7.43%; In 2018, Foxconn was approved and approved for stock issuance in just 36 days, setting a record for the fastest IPO (listing) in China's A-stock market. The review of new shares was increasingly following a standardized process, but the transition and transformation to the registration system was bumpy. In February 2014, the State Council approved "the Plan for the Reform of the Registered Capital Registration System", and in December 2015, the Standing Committee of the National People's Congress passed "The Decision of the Standing Committee of the National People's Congress on authorizing the State Council to Adjust and Apply the Relevant Provisions of the Securities Law of the People's Republic of China in Implementing the Reform of the Stock Issuance Registration System". It intended to adjust the relevant provisions of the Securities Law of the People's Republic of China on the approval system for public stock offerings in the public offering of stocks listed on the Shanghai and Shenzhen stock markets, implemented a registration system, and the transitional implementation period was 2 years, but before the expiration of the authorization period in February 2018, CSRC made an explanation on the "Decision on Extending the Authorization of the State Council to Adjust the Application of the Relevant Provisions of 'the Securities Law of the People's Republic of China' in the implementation of the reform of the Stock Issuance Registration System (Draft)", and once again extended the implementation time of the registration system; At the same time, in order to improve the quality of IPO, in March 2018, CSRC set strict profit targets for companies applying for listing, but made an exception for "unicorn" companies. In the 2019 government work report,

China clearly put forward the task of "establishing a science and technology innovation board and piloting a registration system", thus promoting the implementation of the ever-lengthening registration system and deepening the reform of the stock market access system. On April 2, the Shanghai Stock Exchange officially launched the registration system of the science and technology innovation board. At this time, although "the Securities Law" had not been amended, there were no legal obstacles to the implementation of the registration system. In the issuance pricing, China still adopts the inquiry system, but basically use the highest P/E ratio to determine the price of new shares. In the distribution of new shares, the way of placement is more diverse, and the degree of marketization is deepening.

Obviously, although there are still many shortcomings in the field of stock issuance, such as non-residents have not been allowed to issue stock securities in the country, its system has been further standardized, and China's stock market has become more efficient and competitive, and its quality has been greatly improved.

The second was to promote the reform of non-tradable shares and realize the unified circulation and trading of all stocks on the stock market. At the beginning of the implementation of the non-tradable share structure in China, the state-owned shares and legal person shares that had long occupied 2/3 of the total stock market could not be listed and circulated. The behavior of non-tradable shares had resulted in the distortion and conflict of interests of different types of shareholders, and led to many bad phenomena in China's stock market, such as unfair dividend distribution, hollowing of listed companies by major shareholders, frequent connected-transactions of listed companies, and impulsion of equity financing of listed companies. As a result, stock prices failed to reflect market supply and demand, distorting stock price signals, and the stock market became a "casino", thus unable to become a barometer of the economy. To this end, the Chinese government began to weigh the reform of non-tradable shares in the late 1990s. In September 1999, the Fourth Plenary Session of the 15th CPC Central Committee adopted "the Decision on Several Major Issues concerning the Reform and Development of State-owned Enterprises", in which it was clearly stated that some state-owned listed companies with good reputation and great development potential should be selected and some state-owned shares should be appropriately reduced without affecting the state holding. According to this decision, the China Securities Regulatory Commission established the way to allocate state-owned shares to reduce state-owned shares, and approved Guizhou Tire and Jialing China to pilot in December, but the trial failed due to insufficient preparation. In June 2001, The State Council issued "the Interim Measures for the Administration of Reducing State-owned Shares to raise social security Funds", Article 5 of which stipulates "The reduction of state-owned shares mainly adopts the way of issuing state-owned shares. When a company limited by shares owned by the State (including a company listed overseas) issues shares to public investors for the first time or additional shares, the state-owned shares shall be sold at 10% of the a mount raised; If a Co., Ltd has been established for less than 3 years, the state shares to be sold shall be transferred to the National Council for Social Security Fund by means of transfer, and it shall entrust the company to sell them in one or several batches at the time of public offering. All proceeds from the sale of the stock of state-owned shares shall be handed over to the national social security fund." A subsequent trial to reduce state-owned shares also failed.

Based on the experience of the failures of the trial above, the Chinese government initiated detailed preparatory work such as social discussion and high-level research. Under these conditions, "The State Council issued Several Opinions on Promoting the Reform, Opening Up and Stable Development of the Capital Market" in January 2004, pointing out that "with the goal of expanding direct financing, improving the modern market system, and giving greater play to the basic role of the market in resource allocation, building a transparent and efficient capital market with a reasonable structure, sound mechanism, complete functions and safe operation." Make sure "actively yet prudently solve the problem of non-tradable shares; regulate the transfer of non-tradable shares of listed companies to prevent the loss of state-owned assets. Steadily solve the circulation problem of the shares of listed companies that cannot be listed and circulated." In April 2005, "Notice on Issues Related to the Pilot Reform of Non-tradable Shares in Listed Companies" was promulgated, which officially kicked off the prelude of the reform of non-tradable shares in China's securities market. In May, four listed companies, Sany Heavy Industry, Zijiang Enterprise, Tsinghua Tongfang and Jinniu Energy, first launched the pilot reform of non-tradable shares. In September, CSRC issued the "Administrative Measures for the Reform of Non-tradable Shares in Listed Companies", marking that the reform of non-tradable shares was rolled out from the pilot to all enterprises with non-tradable shares. Later, in order to cooperate with the reform of non-tradable shares, various government entities involved in the stock market in China introduced corresponding favorable measures, as shown in Table 9.6.

In this way, under a series of favorable policy measures and stimulation, and following market rules, enterprises involved in the equity division reform, in practice, fully respected the interests of major stakeholders. By December 2006, "a total of 1,301 listed companies in the Shanghai and Shenzhen stock markets had completed or entered the stock reform program, accounting for 98% of the companies that should

Table 9.6 Main measures for the reform of non-tradable shares in 2005

Date	Issuer	Policy
June, 12	CSRC	Notice on issues related to the increase of public shares held by the controlling shareholders of listed companies implementing the reform of non-tradable shares
June, 13	Ministry of finance, state administration of taxation	Notice on issues of tax policy related to the pilot reform of non-tradable shares
July, 18	Shanghai and Shenzhen stock exchanges	Interim measures for the administration of warrant business
Aug, 23	CSRC, state-owned assets supervision and administration commission (SASAC), ministry of finance, PBOC, ministry of commerce	Guiding opinions on reform of non-tradable shares of listed companies

undergo the reform; only 40 listed companies had not entered the stock reform program,"[6] essentially achieving the goal of equity division reform. This allowed for the simultaneous trading and circulation of all types of stocks in the stock market.

Third, the information disclosure system of the stock market is becoming more and more perfect and standardized. Before the establishment of the Shanghai and Shenzhen Stock exchanges, there was almost no disclosure of relevant information about the joint-stock companies traded on the Chinese stock market, and their status was closely related to the private placement of stock offerings. After the establishment of the Shanghai Stock Exchange, Shenhua Holdings, Yuyuan Mall, Feilo Shares, Feilo Acoustics, Guangdian Electronics, Zhejiang Phoenix Chemical, Airen Shares, Yanzhong Industry and other "Old Eight Shares" circulated on "the Shanghai Securities News" on June 10, 1991, the first collective disclosure of annual reports. Meanwhile, companies listed on the Shenzhen Stock Exchange also disclosed relevant information, which opened the prelude of information disclosure of listed companies in China's stock market. In June 1992, the promulgation of "the Accounting System for Pilot Shareholding Enterprises" marked that the information disclosure of listed companies in China had entered a period of institutionalization. In 1995, CSRC introduced "the Content and Format of the Annual Report", which was modified on the basis of the 1994 annual report, so that the information disclosure of listed companies in China was increasingly standardized. Later, according to the information disclosure of listed companies in the stock market, the information is not timely, incomplete, poor authenticity, and no high degree of fairness, CSRC continued to increase the pace of institutionalization. So far, China has built a relatively complete institutional framework of compulsory and voluntary combination in the information disclosure system, which is composed of basic national securities laws, special laws and administrative regulations on securities, relevant departmental rules and industry self-discipline rules on exchanges. Of course, in order to ensure the timely, complete, true and fair information disclosure, under the leadership of CSRC, China has established a set of information disclosure supervision system composed of CSRC, its local offices, and stock exchanges. By March 2018, it had formed a nationwide supervision and management network consisting of 21 functional departments, one inspection team and three centers within the CSRC headquarters, 36 securities regulatory bureaus in provinces, autonomous regions, municipalities directly under the central government and cities separately listed in the plan, as well as the offices of the Shanghai and Shenzhen securities Regulatory Commissioners.

So far, there are still many deficiencies in the listed companies and stock trading in China's stock market. Every year, a large number of listed companies are punished for illegal information disclosure, and only in the first eight months of 2017, the number of companies and individuals in violation cases reached 80. The Financial Stability Board, established in 2017, further strengthened the liaison between various regulatory bodies and played a clear supervisory communication role. CSRC keep pace with the times to follow up the establishment of relevant systems and regulatory systems

[6] HU Ruyin. *Development and Changes of China's Capital Market*, Truth and Wisdom Press, Shanghai People's Publishing House, 2008: 146.

to ensure the fairness and transparency of the stock market and protect the rights and interests of investors from being harmed. In the reform of state institutions in March 2018, CSRC was still retained, which shows the Chinese government's determination to increase the proportion of direct financing and strengthen the management of financial markets.

Fourth, the governance of listed companies is deepened and the proportion of investment institutionalization is increased. With the increasing marketization of the securities market, under the guidance of "the Enterprise Law of the People's Republic of China" and other laws and regulations, the governance mechanism of listed companies has been continuously improved, and a structure consisting of the general meeting of shareholders, the board of directors, the board of supervisors and the management has been established.

The construction of a diversified investor system has begun to take shape, and the proportion of institutional investment is increasing. In 2003, the Qualified Foreign Institutional Investor (QFII) pilot was launched, and Swiss Bank and Nomura Securities became the first foreign institutional investors permitted to invest in the domestic stock market. After a 3-year trial period, China promulgated and implemented "the Measures for the Administration of Domestic Securities Investment by Qualified Foreign Institutional Investors" in August 2006. In 2007, China approved 52 overseas QFII investments worth 30 billion US dollars; Since then, China has accelerated the development of overseas QFII, and by January 25, 2017, China has approved 276 overseas QFII qualifications, with a total cumulative investment quota of 87.309 billion US dollars. In December 2011, the Securities Commission of China, PBOC and the State Administration of Foreign Exchange jointly issued "the Pilot Measures for Domestic Securities Investment by RMB Qualified Foreign Institutional Investors of Fund Management Companies and Securities Companies", allowing qualified fund companies and securities companies to conduct pilot RMB Qualified Foreign Institutional Investor (RQFII) business. By 2017, more than 180 companies have obtained the RQFII business qualification, with an investment amount of more than 500 billion yuan. At the same time, a large number of institutional investors such as insurance, social security funds, and enterprise annuity have entered the stock market, which has greatly improved the investor structure of China's stock market and significantly improved the unbalanced development of various investors. By 2017, although the number of retail investors in China still occupies an absolute advantage, the proportion of individual investors in the circulation market value has shown a significant decline, while the proportion of the shareholding market value of various institutional investors in the circulation market value has steadily increased, reaching 63%. The changes in the investor structure of China's stock market since 2006 are shown in Table 9.7.

Among various institutional investors such as QFII, RQFII, insurance companies, finance companies, securities investment funds, fund management companies, enterprise annuity, brokerage self-management, brokerage collective financial management, social security funds, trust companies, Sunshine private equity, and banks, institutional investors show diversified characteristics through the development and differentiation in recent years. But the share of institutional investors in the stock

Table 9.7 Changes in the investor structure of China's stock market since 2006 (unit: %)

Year	Individual investor	General corporate	Institutional investor
2006	70	25	5
2007	59	29	12
2008	55	23	22
2009	39	14	47
2010	36	13	51
2011	33	13	54
2012	34	12	54
2013	37	11	52
2014	37	10	53
2015	42	7	51
2016	40	7	53
2017	32	5	63

market has changed to some extent. By 2017, insurance companies had surpassed public funds to become the most important force among institutional investors in China's stock market.

Fifth, the administrative color of the stock market management has weakened, and the degree of marketization has deepened. Before 2009, regulators could not only intervene in the pricing of new shares in the primary market, but also determine the rhythm of new shares, and the color of "policy market" was extremely obvious. In June 2009, CSRC issued "the Guiding Opinions on Further Reform and Improvement of the New Share Issuance System", which for the first time started the market-oriented reform of the new share issuance system in China's stock market. After the in-depth reform in recent years, the primary market has basically achieved marketization, but after the stock market crash in June 2015, the administrative color seems to have strengthened. In the secondary market, with a series of institutional construction, the color of administration has also been significantly reduced, and the degree of marketization has been greatly deepened.

With the increasing standardization and marketization of China's stock market, China's stock market has achieved great development. Although the Shenzhen and Shanghai composite indexes have experienced huge fluctuations for many times, they have shown a trend of wave-like uplift as a whole (see Table 9.8). By 2017, the size of China's stock market ranked second in the world, and the Shanghai and Shenzhen Stock exchanges ranked fourth and sixth in the world's top ten exchanges respectively. In the stock market, the number of listed companies increased significantly, from 949 in 1999 to 3552 in 2017. The structure of the industry is increasingly optimized, and the varieties of trading are increasing. The varieties traded on Shanghai and Shenzhen stock markets have covered the four categories of stocks, bonds, funds and derivatives, and Shanghai Stock Exchange and the Shenzhen Stock Exchange have become stock exchanges with relatively complete market structure in the world.

In 2001, the Securities Association of China established the agency share transfer system. In 2006, the non-listed joint-stock enterprises in Zhongguancun High-tech Park were initially listed in the agency share transfer system, which greatly expanded the function of the agency share transfer system. In 2004, Shenzhen Stock Exchange launched the small and medium-sized enterprises section, and the number of listed stocks increased from 8 to 822 by the end of 2016. On October 31, 2009, China officially launched the Growth Enterprise Market (GEM), which increased from 36 in that year to 570 by the end of 2016, so far China has basically formed a multi-level and multi-functional capital market system. At present, Shanghai and Shenzhen Stock exchanges have a trading system and basic communication facilities that can support the efficient and stable operation of the securities market, and a self-regulatory system with remarkable efficiency to ensure the orderly operation of the securities market.

With the rapid development and increasing standardization of China's capital market, the opening degree of the capital market is expanding day by day.

On the one hand, the opening of the domestic capital market to overseas has deepened. In addition to the above-mentioned QFII and other active participation

Table 9.8 Fluctuation table of Shanghai and Shenzhen composite index since 1997

Year	Shanghai composite index (close)	Shenzhen composite index (close)
1997	1194.1	381.3
1998	1146.7	343.4
1999	1366.6	402.2
2000	2073.5	635.7
2001	1646.0	475.9
2002	1357.7	388.8
2003	1497.0	378.6
2004	1266.5	315.8
2005	1161.1	278.8
2006	2675.5	550.6
2007	5261.6	1447.0
2008	1820.8	553.3
2009	3277.1	1201.3
2010	2808.1	1290.9
2011	2199.4	866.7
2012	2269.1	881.2
2013	2116.0	1057.7
2014	3234.7	1415.2
2015	3539.2	2308.9
2016	3103.6	1969.1
2017	3307.17	1899.34

Source From the relevant data of the website of the National Bureau of Statistics

in the domestic stock market and other activities, on November 14, 2014, CRSC, the Ministry of Finance and the State Administration of Taxation jointly issued the "Shanghai–Hong Kong Stock Connect" Pilot Program and the tax policy of QFII and other participation, and CRSC officially approved the stock trading of the "Shanghai–Hong Kong Stock Connect" on November 17. In August 2016, The State Council approved "Shenzhen–Hong Kong Stock Connect Implementation Plan", in September, Shenzhen Stock Exchange adopted "Shenzhen–Hong Kong Stock Connect Operational Guidelines", and in December, the "Shenzhen–Hong Kong Stock Connect" was officially opened, deepening the institutional construction of the management system of foreign investor relations and of the exchanges themselves, improving the all-round service for foreign investors, and strengthening cross-border regulatory cooperation. In June 2017, Morningstar, Inc. incorporated China's A-shares into the Morgan Stanley Capital International Index, which greatly promoted the internationalization of China's capital market.

On the other hand, domestic institutions and individuals have also accelerated the pace of "going out" and actively participated in overseas capital market activities. While promoting the orderly participation of various institutional investors in the domestic stock market, CSRC also actively promotes the participation of domestic institutions and individuals in the overseas stock market. In February 2007, the Bank of China issued the first qualified Domestic Institutional Investor (QDII) product—the Bank of China U.S. Dollar (BOC Dollar).

In July, CSRC promulgated the "Proposed Regulations for the Management of Overseas Securities Investment by Qualified Domestic Institutional Investors", which strongly promoted QDII's participation in overseas securities and other investment activities; By 2017, QDII's investment activities had covered 35 countries and regions. In August 2007, the State Administration of Foreign Exchange issued "the Pilot Program for Domestic Individuals to Invest directly in Overseas Securities Markets". Bank of China Tianjin Branch actively promoted the business of domestic individuals investing in Hong Kong stocks (QDII2), known as the "through-train to Hong Kong Stocks". However, under the influence of the subprime crisis and other factors, the investment activities were postponed. In 2013, the central government relaunched the "through-train to Hong Kong Stocks", but it has yet to be fully operational. The Fifth National Financial Work Conference in July 2017 and the Report of the 19th National Congress of the Communist Party of China in October pointed out that China will further expand the development of financial markets. The 2018 Government Work report further clarified that China will vigorously promote the opening of the financial market in the future and the Shanghai–London Stock Connect was officially launched in London on June 17, 2019.

9.1.2 The Rise and Development of Bond Market

The bond market is an important part of China's financial market. In the first 20 years of reform and opening up, China went through a period without any public debt, and naturally there was no bond market. In 1981, our country resumed the bond issue, which opened the prelude of the development of our bond market. Since then, in order to meet the needs of rapid social and economic development, the bond market has diversified, bond varieties have become more diverse, issuers have increased, transaction clearing technology has improved, and the issuance scale has continued to expand. By 2017, China's bond market has grown into a huge market with a balance of more than 70 trillion yuan, and the balance of the bond market ranks third in the world and second in Asia.

A. Formation and Development Process of Bond Market

At the beginning of reform and opening up, in the face of persistent fiscal deficits in 1979 and 1980, The State Council decided to issue national bonds once a year in 1981, ending China's 20-year "debt-free era" and gradually restoring the national bond issuance market. In July 1981, the Ministry of Finance issued 4.9 billion yuan of Treasury bills for the first time. The following July, the Treasury issued Treasury bills to individuals. At the beginning, China adopted administrative distribution to issue national debt, focusing on government workers and employees of state-owned enterprises, with party members and cadres taking the lead, salary withholding or even mandatory apportion to ensure the completion of national debt issuance targets. In 1982, China International Trust and Investment Corporation issued 10 billion Japanese yen financial bonds in Japan. In 1984, corporate bonds were also issued in some places, which greatly enriched the variety of bonds. In 1988, the government tried to use the counters of commercial banks and China Postal Savings to issue national bonds to the public, and initially formed a primary market of national bonds. At the same time, the Ministry of Finance reported the "Pilot Implementation Plan for Opening the Treasury Bill Transfer Market" in March 1988, which successively allowed the Treasury bill to be circulated and transferred in two batches in 61 cities across the country, thus laying the foundation for the development of the secondary market of Treasury bonds.

In 1990, China gradually opened up the national debt trading market, and in 1991, it changed the issuance mode to underwriting syndicate for government bond subscription and underwriting composed of financial institutions, which promoted the development of the secondary market of national debt. In 1992, the government changed the issuance of Treasury bonds from once a year to twice a year, and the spot Treasury bonds began to enter the exchange for public trading. In the same year, Wuhan National Debt Trading Center was established, which greatly promoted the development of China's national debt market. In December 1992, Shanghai Stock Exchange launched 12 varieties of 1992 3- and 5-year national debt futures standard contracts with 4 delivery months, including 3, 6, 9 and 12 months, thus opening the curtain of the development of national debt futures market. In 1993, the government bond futures began to be piloted in Shanghai Stock Exchange, and the first-level dealer system was introduced in the government bond market. In 1995, all the trading bodies of national debt were transferred to the exchange market. After the "327" Government Bond Futures Incident, China temporarily closed the existing national debt futures market and carried out mandatory rectification. In 1996, the Shanghai and

Shenzhen Stock exchanges issued a large number of bookkeeping Treasury bonds and carried out repurchase transactions of Treasury bonds, and the bond market system of the exchanges took shape and moved toward full marketization. At this time, "the issuance of national debt has realized the transition from offtake underwriting to open bidding, and a market-oriented issuance model of 'base offtake, differential bidding, competitive pricing, and balance distribution' has been initially established. The issuance method of national debt has also changed from physical vouchers to paperless electronic bookkeeping, and the secondary market transaction of national debt has also adopted an electronic way, which has greatly reduced the issuance cost and transaction cost."[7]

In 1997, under the conditions of overheated stock market and separate operation of the financial industry, PBOC required commercial banks to withdraw from the stock exchange bond market and set up the national inter-bank bond market at the same time, thus forming two separate bond markets in the bond market. Bank institutions are not allowed to participate in the exchange bond market, and the exchange bond market can only be participated by funds and brokerages, and funds and brokerages can participate in the inter-bank bond market. Naturally, the trading volume of the exchange bond market shrank significantly before 2007, showing a trend of marginalization. The inter-bank bond market has developed rapidly with the participation of many institutions. On November 8, 2004, China Minsheng Bank successfully issued 5.8 billion RMB subordinated bonds through the interbank bond market, which greatly expanded the channels for commercial banks to supplement their capital. China Minsheng Bank also became the first commercial bank in China to successfully issue subordinated bonds through private placement in the national interbank bond market. In order to activate the quotation of the bond market and improve the liquidity of the bond market, China introduced the system of market maker in the inter-bank bond market in 2004. Since then, China's bond market has developed steadily, with a significant increase in both issuance and trading volume.

In 2008, under the influence of the subprime crisis, the government took strong stimulus measures of 4 trillion yuan to stabilize growth, ensure employment, adjust the structure and other policy objectives, resulting in a substantial expansion of bond issuance and trading volume. In 2010, CSRC, PBOC and the China Banking Regulatory Commission (CBRC) jointly issued "the Notice on Issues Related to the Participation of Listed Commercial Banks in the Bond Trading Pilot Program on the Stock Exchanges", which effectively promoted the interconnection between the two bond markets and improved the operation efficiency of the bond market. After that, in order to promote the orderly standardization of bond issuance, China has continuously increased the standardization of the bond market to ensure the stable issuance of various types of bonds and ensure the sustainable development of the bond market.

In 2013, along with Chinese economy enters the new normal, economic growth is shifting from high speed to the medium–high speed; economic driving force from

[7] People's Bank of China. *Sixty Years of the People's Bank of China (1948–2008)*, China Finance Publishing House, 2008: 76.

the inputs to innovation and efficiency. In response to this change of social economy, China's bond market has accelerated the innovation and development, the breadth and depth of continuous expansion, and product innovation continues to promote the construction of the system. In this context, the varieties of China's bond market continue to increase, and the trading volume shows considerable fluctuations under the influence of economic transformation, as shown in Table 9.9.

In 2013, the trading volume of the two major trading market entities in China's bond market fell significantly, but soon affected by the steady growth of the economy after the speed change, the trading volume rose rapidly, providing the necessary financial support for the development of the real economy.

With the standardization and continuous development of China's bond market, the internationalization of China's bond market is also increasing, and the number of overseas participants is increasing, which has effectively attracted overseas countries and regions to issue bonds in China's bond market. In 2007, China's first RMB bond landed in Hong Kong, that is, "dim sum bond". In July 2015, PBOC opened the interbank bond market to foreign central banks, international financial institutions and sovereign wealth funds. On May 16, 2017, PBOC and the Hong Kong Monetary Authority (HKMA) jointly announced "the Bond Connect Program" between Hong Kong and the Mainland. On June 21, PBOC issued "the Interim Measures for the Administration of Cooperation on Bond Market Connectivity between the Mainland and Hong Kong". The Shanghai Headquarters of PBOC, the National Interbank Lending Center, the Interbank Market Clearing House Co., LTD., and the Central Government Bond Registration Co., Ltd. issued corresponding detailed rules on filing guidelines, trading rules and settlement rules respectively. On July 2, PBOC issued "the Joint Announcement of the Hong Kong Monetary Authority of the People's Bank of China"; On July 3, the "Bond Connect" and "Northbound Connect" were officially put into operation, and the "Southbound Connect" was introduced to the market. In

Table 9.9 Changes in trading volume of the bond market in China (unit: trillion yuan)

Year	Trading volume of interbank bond market	Trading volume of exchange bond
2008	37.1	0.2123
2009	47.3	0.2085
2010	64.0	0.1662
2011	63.6	0.1253
2012	75.2	0.0886
2013	41.6	0.0804
2014	40.36	2.81
2015	86.7	3.4
2016	127.1	5.3
2017	102.8	5.5

Source Monetary policy implementation report for the fourth quarter of the calendar year since 2008

March 2018, Zhou Xiaochuan, governor of PBOC, answered the journalist's question about the "Southbound Connect" during the two sessions and pointed out that "in fact, if the 'southbound' bond market is opened, it is not difficult, and I think it can be done at any time as long as there is demand."[8] On March 23, Bloomberg gradually added Chinese bonds to the Bloomberg Barclays Global Aggregate Bond Index; Citibank also announced that onshore Chinese bonds are eligible for inclusion in Citibank's related emerging market and regional government bond indices. These have greatly improved the degree of the two-way opening of China's bond market.

B. Types of Bond Markets

With the continuous expansion of bond market and the increasing diversification of social and economic needs, the types of bond market in our country are gradually increasing, and bond market is increasingly becoming an important financing place in our country's financial market, which greatly supplements the insufficiency of indirect finance.

Before the establishment of China's inter-bank bond market in 1997, the types of bonds traded in the bond market were mainly national bonds, enterprise bonds issued in 1984 and a very small amount of financial bonds. From 1997 to 2004, with the deepening of commercialization reform of state-owned banks and the opening of shareholding reform, the issuance of financial bonds increased significantly, and the types of transactions in the bond market gradually concentrated on national bonds and financial bonds. During this period, the average annual bond issuance from 1998 to 2001 was about 400 billion yuan, and there was a substantial increase in issuance after 2002 (see Table 9.10). In 2003, in order to strengthen the construction of control measures of monetary policy, PBOC began to issue central bank bills as an important tool of open market operations to control the money supply. Different from foreign countries, China's central bank bills are not traded in the bill market, but are more circulated in the bond market to supplement the shortage of national debt in the open market operation of the central bank.

In 2004, the types of bond market in China increased greatly. On the one hand, financial institutions issue subordinated bonds in the inter-bank bond market to supplement their subsidiary capital; On the other hand, it began to introduce non-financial bonds such as short-term financing bonds and long-term corporate bonds. In 2005, the International Finance Corporation and the Asian Development Bank issued renminbi-denominated bonds in China, known as "panda bonds". In 2006, in the issuance of financial bonds, China innovatively launched mixed capital bonds of commercial banks, which further broadened the channels for commercial banks to replenish capital and enriched the varieties of financial bonds in the bond market. In April 2008, PBOC issued "Measures for the Management of Debt Financing Instruments for Non-Financial Enterprises in the Inter-Bank Bond Market". According to the measures, China's bond market for the first time issued medium-term notes of 7 companies registered by the inter-bank bond market dealers association. In this way,

---

[8] "Zhou Xiaochuan Talks About 'Southbound Trading': As Long as There Is Demand, We Can Do It at Any Time", http://ent.chinanews.com/cj/shipin/cns/2018/03-09/news759905.shtml.

Table 9.10 Various types of bond issuance in China's bond market (unit: 100 million yuan)

Year	Bond variety				
	National debt	Local government bond	Financial bond	Corporate credit bond	International agency bond
2001	4884	–	2590	147	–
2002	5934	–	3075	325	–
2003	6280	–	4520	358	–
2004	6924	–	5009	327	–
2005	7042	–	7188	2047	21.3
2006	8883	–	9635.8	3938	8.7
2007	7637	–	11,913	5059	–
2008	8558	–	11,797	8723	–
2009	17,927	–	14,524	16,629	–
2010	19,778	–	14,123	16,812	–
2011	17,100	–	23,492	23,103	–
2012	16,154	–	26,202	37,365	–
2013	20,230	–	26,310	36,699	–
2014	21,747*	–	36,552	51,516	–
2015	21,058	38,351	102,095	67,205	115
2016	30,658	60,428	182,152	82,242	412
2017	39,932	43,581	258,056	56,352	573

Note Financial bonds include financial bonds of China Development Bank, policy financial bonds, ordinary bonds of commercial banks, subordinated bonds of commercial banks, mixed capital bonds of commercial banks, bonds of securities companies, inter-bank certificates of deposit, etc. Corporate credit bonds include non-financial corporate debt financing instruments, enterprise bonds and corporate bonds, convertible bonds, separable bonds, small and medium-sized enterprise private debt, etc.

*Before 2014 treasury bonds include local government bonds issued by the Ministry of Finance

Source Collated according to relevant data in the fourth quarter monetary policy implementation report of previous years

a complete non-financial bond system consisting of short, medium and long-term corporate bonds has been formed in China's bond market.

In November 2009, the national interbank bond market received an innovative development and for the first time, a collective note set up by the Association of Interbank Bond Market Dealers was issued on the national interbank Bond Market. Collection notes are debt financial instruments that are issued by means of unified product design, unified denomination, unified credit promotion and unified registration, and agree to repay the principal and interest within a certain period of time. Although the collection notes of small and medium-sized enterprises play a certain role in resolving the financing problem of small and medium-sized enterprises, they are very difficult to issue due to high interest rate, issuance cost, poor liquidity and other factors. Later, although the introduction of the bill issuance guarantees from "China Bond Credit Promotion Investment Co., LTD" greatly reduced the above difficulties, yet so far, the issuance is still small, the small and medium-sized enterprises financing difficulties cannot really be solved. Therefore, in December 2010, China's bond market innovatively launched ultra-short-term financing bonds to broaden corporate financing channels and meet the diversified investment needs of investors.

In November 2011, PBOC issued the "Notice on Relevant Matters Concerning Local Governments in Pilot Provinces (Cities) Issuing Bonds on the National Interbank Bond Market." According to the requirements of this notice, local governments in Shanghai, Shenzhen, as well as Zhejiang and Guangdong provinces, started pilot programs for issuing bonds independently. This changed the previous practice of bond issuance being handled by the Ministry of Finance, marking the beginning of local governments issuing bonds independently and expanding the variety of trading instruments in the bond market.

With the increasing variety of bond market, the bond market has formed a complete bond type consisting of national debt, local government bonds, financial bonds, corporate credit bonds, international institution bonds, etc. Each main bond type is subdivided into different sub-categories, covering various types of short, medium and long term in times of time, which basically conforms to the needs of social and economic diversification. Of course, the issuance of different types of bonds in different years is affected by the degree of economic development.

With the increasingly complex of social economy, on the basis of continuously standardizing the bond market, China will increase the innovation of bond types to meet the needs of social and economic development, expand the financing channels of different economic entities, and meet the financing needs of different entities.

C. Participants of Bond Market

The participation in China's bond market has continuously expanded with the development of the market. Before 1988, bonds in China were mainly distributed to administrative, corporate, and individual entities through political mobilization and administrative methods under government guidance. In 1988, some commercial banks and China Postal Savings counters began to participate in bond trading, selling and trading bonds to the public. In 1992, securities exchanges officially participated in spot bond trading, forming the initial on-exchange trading participants. In 1994, securities exchanges introduced bond futures trading, greatly stimulating the growth of bond trading volume. After the "3·27" bond futures incident, the State Council closed the bond futures market of the exchanges and officially halted all over-the-counter bond trading activities, making the securities exchanges the only legal participants in the bond market. At this time, the participants in the securities exchange bond market included banks, securities firms, funds, and other financial institutions.

In 1997, the Asian financial crisis broke out, and China established a financial industry segregation system. Under this constraint, PBOC required all banks to withdraw from the exchange bond market and established the interbank bond market. Consequently, in the exchange bond market, the participants included securities firms, funds, and other institutions, while banks were prohibited from entering.

In 2007, corporate credit bonds made a breakthrough in the exchange bond market, and the market quickly incorporated insurance companies, social security funds, trust companies, rural credit cooperatives, large enterprise institutions, and other entities, greatly expanding the participants in the exchange bond market. Currently, the exchange bond market mainly consists of two types of participants: securities firms and other institutions with exchange membership qualifications, which can engage in bond brokerage or proprietary businesses in the exchange market, and other qualified institutions that can apply for dedicated bond seats to engage in bond business. Investors who meet certain conditions can only entrust exchange bond market members to conduct bond trading. Trading in the exchange bond market is conducted through continuous bidding, while the custody and settlement of bonds are handled by the designated Chinese securities registration and settlement institution appointed by the exchange.

When the national interbank bond market was established in 1997, PBOC allowed only domestic banking institutions to participate. In 1998, PBOC approved foreign banks and insurance companies to join the interbank bond market. In 1999, the participants of the interbank bond market were further extended to rural credit cooperatives, investment funds and securities companies. After that, with the continuous emergence of various kinds of financial organizations in our country, the participants in the bond market have naturally expanded to various types of financial institutions at home and abroad. Table 9.11 shows the changes in the access of participants in the interbank bond market.

There are two types of participants in the inter-bank bond market: one is the market members who can directly trade; the second is non-market members who can only trade indirectly through bond settlement correspondent banks. Participants in

Table 9.11 Changes in the access of participants in the interbank bond market

Year	Participants in the inter-bank bond market
1997	State-owned commercial banks, joint-stock commercial banks, urban cooperative banks
1998	Foreign banks, insurance companies, etc
1999	Rural credit cooperatives, investment funds, securities companies
2000	Financial company, financial leasing company
2001	Small and medium-sized financial institutions entered the market through bond agents
2002	Non-financial legal persons such as enterprises entered the market through bond settlement agents
2005	International development institutions such as the International Finance Corporation and the Asian Development Bank, as well as the Pan-Asian Fund and the Asian Bond Fund
2010	Foreign central banks or monetary authorities, Renminbi clearing banks in Hong Kong and Macao, and overseas participating banks in Renminbi settlement of cross-border trade
2013	Qualified foreign institutional investors, Renminbi qualified foreign institutional investors
2015	International financial institutions, sovereign wealth funds
2016	Medium and long-term institutional investors such as pension funds

the interbank bond market are required to place their bonds in custody at the Central Government Bond Depository and Clearing Co., LTD., rely on the private network platform of the interbank lending center for bond trading, and clear and transfer funds through the electronic clearing system of PBOC.

At the same time, China has gradually liberalized the right of non-financial institutions and financial institutions overseas to issue Renminbi bonds in the interbank bond market. In 2005, international development institutions such as the International Finance Corporation and the Asian Development Bank were allowed to issue Renminbi bonds in the interbank bond market, marking the beginning of international development institutions' access to the interbank bond market to issue Renminbi bonds. In 2013, Daimler AG issued 5 billion yuan of debt financing instruments in the interbank bond market, marking the opening of channels for foreign non-financial institutions to enter Renminbi bond financing. In 2015, The Hongkong and Shanghai Banking Corporation Limited (HSBC) and Bank of China (Hong Kong) Limited were allowed to issue Renminbi bonds in the interbank bond market, indicating that international commercial banks have become the main issuers in the interbank bond market. In 2016, the Canadian province of BC and South Korea completed the registration of 9 billion yuan of Renminbi bonds, indicating that the interbank bond market has further expanded to foreign governments. In 2016, China opened its interbank bond market to all foreign financial institutions, and by 2017, various overseas issuers had issued Renminbi bonds totaling more than 80 billion yuan.

9.2 The Cultivation and Development of Money Market

The money market is a general term for the short-term financing market of less than 1 year, which consists of inter-bank lending market, bond repurchase market, bill market, money market fund, gold market, short-term bond market, foreign exchange market, short-term credit market and many other sub-markets. Since the reform and opening up, the sub-markets in the money market have not developed simultaneously, but have gradually developed according to the actual development of social economy. Market participants continue to increase, product types are increasingly rich, and the transaction scale is expanding. Although there are twists and turns during this period, the overall trend of rapid development is still promoting the sustainable and healthy development of China's social economy.

9.2.1 Interbank Lending Market

The interbank lending market is a place for commercial banks to adjust their surplus and shortage positions, allowing the efficient utilization of excess reserves in the financial system. The interbank lending market is the earliest, fastest-growing, and largest market in China's money market. It started in 1984, and the implementation of the "actual loan, actual deposit" credit fund management system in 1985 promoted the formation of the interbank lending market. In 1986, several major cities such as Wuhan, Guangzhou, Xi'an, and Shenyang established interbank lending networks, leading to the rapid development of the interbank lending market in China.

From 1992 to the first half of 1993, the interbank lending market in China experienced a chaotic state. The number of interbank lending intermediary institutions nationwide reached 1,170, and the amount of irregular lending exceeded 150 billion yuan by May 1993, seriously affecting the normal operational order of the interbank lending market. In order to regulate the development of the interbank lending market in an orderly manner, PBOC began to rectify the interbank lending order and collect irregular lending funds in June 1993. After a period of effective governance, the "Four Stoppings" were basically achieved, namely, stopping new violations, stopping lending to non-financial and non-banking financial institutions, stopping lending business of interbank lending intermediary institutions below the provincial level, and stopping the injection of funds into banks' self-operated entities.[9] Through effective regulation and rectification, a unified national interbank lending market was initially established and operated by January 1996. Subsequently, the restrictions on interbank lending rates were lifted, and market-oriented rates were implemented. Following the requirements of the segregated supervision system, funds were prohibited from flowing into the capital market, and self-operated businesses of lending institutions were halted. In 1998, PBOC approved commercial banks to authorize their branches to join the national interbank lending market. In the same year, foreign banks operating Renminbi business in Shanghai Pudong were allowed to enter the national interbank lending market. The participants in the lending market expanded from domestic banks to foreign bank institutions, as well as non-bank financial institutions such as insurance companies, financial asset management companies, and trust companies. This marked the complete establishment of a unified, open, competitive, and strictly regulated national interbank lending market in China.

Since 1998, the lending volume in China's interbank lending market has shown explosive growth. By 2008, the transaction volume had exceeded 15 trillion yuan. In order to further develop the money market, regulate interbank lending transactions, prevent interbank lending risks, and protect the legitimate rights and interests of all parties involved in interbank lending, PBOC formulated and issued the "Interbank Lending Management Measures" in August 2007. These measures specify the admission subjects and conditions, transaction and settlement, risk management, information disclosure rules, supervision and management, and legal responsibilities in the interbank lending market, greatly promoting the institutional development of China's interbank lending market. Since 2007, influenced by factors such as the subprime crisis, China's interbank lending market has shown rapid development. By February 2018, the interbank Renminbi market had a total transaction volume of 55.41 trillion yuan through lending, treasury bonds, and repurchase agreements,

[9] People's Bank of China. *Sixty Years of the People's Bank of China (1948–2008)*, China Finance Publishing House, 2008: 75.

Table 9.12 Changes in the average daily turnover of China's interbank lending market since 2008

Year	Annual daily turnover/trillion yuan
2007	0.4088
2008	0.5111
2009	0.6240
2010	0.7180
2011	0.7861
2012	1.06
2013	0.9412
2014	1.21
2015	2.44
2016	3.28
2017	3.18

Source Financial statistics report since 2008 calendar year, http://www.pbc.gov.cn/diaochatongjisi/116219/116225/mdex.html

with an average daily turnover of 3.26 trillion yuan, representing a 22.2% increase compared to the same period of the previous year, as shown in Table 9.12.

The standardized development of China's inter-bank lending market and the expanding scale of lending have played a great role in promoting the stability of China's financial market and the rapid development of the real economy.

9.2.2 Bond Repurchase Market

The bond repurchase market is an important part of short-term fund financing, serving as a link between the money market and the capital market. With the recovery of bond businesses such as government bonds since the reforms and opening-up, the bond repurchase market in China has gradually developed. The earliest bond repurchase transactions can be traced back to July 1991 when the Securities Trading Automated Quotations System (STAQ) piloted bond repurchase transactions to enhance the liquidity of off-exchange bond market. Subsequently, securities exchanges across the country introduced bond repurchase transactions. Initially, the main purpose of launching bond repurchase transactions was to obtain funds from individuals or extract funds from commercial banks, escaping the control of PBOC's credit scale. This promoted the rapid expansion of bond businesses, and by 1994, the scale of repurchase transactions reached 300 billion yuan. Against this backdrop, the market risks of bond repurchase transactions became increasingly apparent. In response, PBOC carried out rectification of bond repurchase transactions in August 1995, completely curbing off-exchange repurchase transactions and consolidating all bond repurchase transactions in the Shanghai Stock Exchange, thus forming a nationally unified bond repurchase trading market.

After 1995, although China initially established the principle of separate financial operation, commercial banks were still allowed to participate in bond repurchase transactions in the exchange bond market to extract funds for investment in the stock market, which led to financial chaos. In response, China carried out another rectification of the bond repurchase market in 1997, forcing commercial banks to withdraw from the exchange bond market and establishing a national interbank bond market for bond transactions. As a result, China had two parallel bond repurchase markets. Similar to the aforementioned bond market, initially, the participants in the interbank bond repurchase market were limited to banking institutions. With the expansion of the business, the participants gradually expanded to include non-banking financial institutions such as insurance companies, funds, and non-financial enterprises. At the same time, the bond repurchase market showed a trend towards short-term transactions, gradually focusing on repurchase transactions within 7 days, returning to the functions of the money market. Through bond repurchase transactions, the participants mainly achieved the goals of liquidity management, yield generation, and risk balancing.

Under the mutual promotion of the exchange bond repurchase market and the interbank bond repurchase market, China's bond repurchase business has achieved significant development, and the volume of bond repurchase transactions has been increasing year by year (see Table 9.13), becoming an important component of fund financing in China's money market.

As can be seen from Table 9.13, the trading volume of the two parallel markets in China's bond repurchase market is very different. The inter-bank bond repurchase market has always occupied the main position of the bond repurchase market, and the exchange bond repurchase market has achieved rapid development since 2011, and by 2017, it has occupied nearly 1/3 of the bond repurchase transaction volume. The two jointly promote the development of China's bond repurchase market business.

9.2.3 The Bill Market

The bill market is an important venue for short-term fund financing, and with the development of the socio-economy, its financing function in the financial market has become increasingly prominent, making it an integral part of the money market. In the early years of the establishment of the People's Republic of China, the bill market, which had achieved significant development during the past, was completely interrupted through socialist transformation movements. Subsequently, China entered a long period without a bill market.

After the reforms and opening-up, with the gradual recovery and development of commercial credit, China gradually developed a bill acceptance and discount market based on commercial bills. In 1981, China carried out a pilot project for local commercial acceptance and discount of bills in the Yangpu district and Huangpu district of Shanghai. The Xuhui district office and the Tianchang County branch in Anhui province conducted a pilot project for inter-provincial acceptance and discount

Table 9.13 Changes in China's bond repurchase transaction volume (unit: trillions of yuan)

Year	Inter-bank bond repurchases transaction volume	Exchange bond repurchase transaction volume
2000	1.58	–
2001	4.01	–
2002	10.19	–
2003	11.72	–
2004	9.44	4.41
2005	15.9	1.45
2006	26.59	1.78
2007	44.8	1.83
2008	58.1	2.4
2009	70.3	3.6
2010	87.6	6.59
2011	99.5	20
2012	141.7	34.6
2013	158.2	66
2014	224.4	90.72
2015	457.8	128.2
2016	601.3	233.6
2017	616.4	260.2

Source Based on the quarterly monetary policy implementation reports since 2000, http://www.pbc.gov.cn/zhengcehuobisi/125207/125227/index.html

of bank drafts. In 1982, PBOC expanded the bill discounting business further through the approval of "The Report on the Restoration of Bill Acceptance and Discount Business". "The Provisional Measures for Commercial Draft Acceptance and Discount" formulated by PBOC in 1984 promoted acceptance and discount services nationwide. However, due to factors such as irregular behavior by market participants, there were occurrences of misconduct, where some criminals, banks, and a minority of enterprises used commercial bill acceptance and discount to obtain or defraud funds. In response, PBOC suspended the nascent bill acceptance and discount market. In May 1993, PBOC issued the "Commercial Draft Measures," which brought systemic reforms to the bill market. After gradually resolving settlement issues in the bill market, bill discounting and rediscounting were able to develop to a certain extent.

In May 1995, the Standing Committee of the National People's Congress issued the "People's Republic of China Negotiable Instruments Law" (hereinafter referred to as the "Negotiable Instruments Law"), which officially came into effect on January 1, 1996. The "Negotiable Instruments Law" defines the concept of negotiable instruments and specifies that negotiable instruments mainly refer to drafts, promissory notes, and checks, significantly promoting the development of bill acceptance and discount markets. In 1997, PBOC successively issued the "Implementation Measures for Bill Management", "Provisional Measures for Rediscounting by Head Offices of State-owned Commercial Banks", and "Management Measures for Commercial Draft Acceptance, Discounting, and Rediscounting". In 1998, PBOC issued a notice on "Improving and Perfecting the Management of Rediscount Business". The introduction of these laws and regulations regulated the development of China's bill market and also facilitated the construction and development of bill markets in key cities such as Shanghai, Tianjin, Chongqing, Dalian, and Nanjing, which are financial centers with strong radiating power, promoting the formation of regional markets in China's bill market.

In 2000, China's first specialized bill agency, the Bill Business Department of Industrial and Commercial Bank of China (ICBC), was established in Shanghai, marking the beginning of a professionalized, scaled-up, and standardized development period for China's commercial bank bill business. The bill market showed a rapid growth trend. Subsequently, Bank of China and Construction Bank of China (CBC) also established "bill centers" and "bill discount windows" to engage in bill trading activities. In June 2003, China officially launched the Chinese Bills Network as a unified service platform that laid necessary foundations for the development of the national bill market. In November of the same year, ICBC released its "ICBC Bill Price Index", greatly promoting centralized trading in our country's bill market. In July 2005, following approval from the China Securities Regulatory Commission (CSRC), Agricultural Bank of China (ABC) opened its Bill Business Department in Shanghai as the second specialized bill agency nationwide, further driving forward construction efforts for such agencies in our country. In September, to regulate operational procedures for negotiable instruments and strengthen risk management, "the Notice of PBOC on Issues Related to Improving the System of Negotiable Instruments Business" was officially released. In November 2006, PBOC published "Guidelines on Promoting Commercial Acceptance Draft Businesses' Development", encouraging innovation within our country's bills business sector. In June 2007, PBOC introduced check image exchange system nationwide, leading to a relatively stable phase in our country's bills market development. During this period, China's bills business experienced rapid growth with transaction volumes increasing year by year as shown in Fig. 9.1.

The rapid development of the bill market business urgently needs to strengthen information communication and improve business operation efficiency. In October 2009, the electronic commercial bill system constructed and managed by PBOC was officially put into operation, marking the entry of China's bill market into the electronic phase. Subsequently, influenced by the loose monetary policy environment, bill business has shown a significant increase. In 2013, China's economic growth slowed down, and it began to transition from high-speed to high-quality development, with funds undergoing a change from "real to virtual". Under the premise of stable economic growth, structural adjustment, and prevention of financial risks, China has strengthened the institutionalized management of bill issuance, discounting, rediscounting, and other business activities in the bill market.

In December 2015, the General Office of the China Banking Regulatory Commission (CBRC) issued "A Notice on Risk Warnings in Bill Business", clearly listing

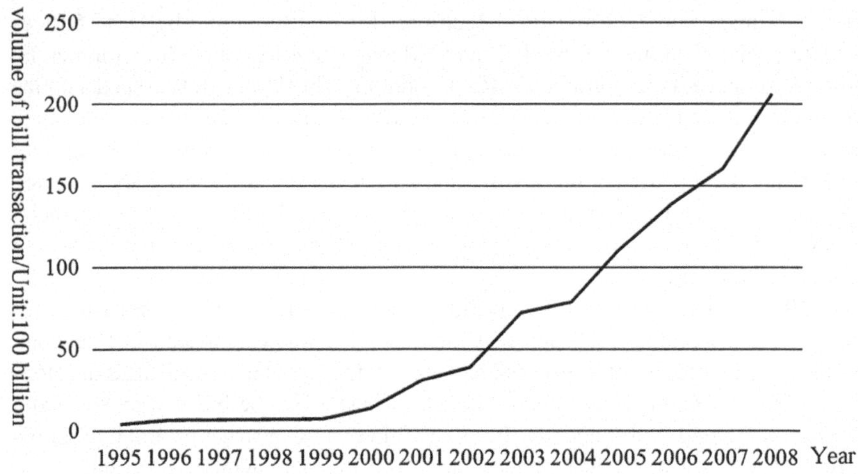

Fig. 9.1 Changes in the volume of bill transactions in China from 1995 to 2008[10]

seven major irregularities and two prohibited activities. In April 2016, PBOC and the CBRC jointly issued "A Notice on Strengthening the Supervision of Bill Business and Promoting the Healthy Development of the Bill Market", strictly regulating inter-bank account management, effectively preventing and controlling bill business risks, and promoting the healthy and orderly development of the bill market. In September 2016, PBOC issued "A Notice on Regulating and Promoting the Development of Electronic Commercial Bill Business", gradually promoting the standardized development of electronic commercial bill business. In November 2016, the General Office of PBOC issued "A Notice on Preparing for the Access of Bill Trading Platforms", regulating the phased content and testing arrangements of bill trading platforms. In December 2016, PBOC issued the "Bill Trading Management Measures", which clarified bill trading rules, provided an opportunity for commercial banks to standardize bill business development, gradually formed an intensive market organization form with legal persons as participating entities, improved the risk control capabilities of market participants, and promoted the healthy development of the bill market.

In December 2016, the Shanghai Bill Exchange officially opened, ushering in a new era of standardized on-exchange trading in the Chinese bill market. This marked the beginning of comprehensive electronization, diversification of participating entities, and centralized trading in the Chinese bill business, which will have a profound impact on the development of the bill market, money market, and the entire financial market. After the establishment of the bill exchange, a series of rules were issued, including "Shanghai Bill Exchange Bill Trading Rules", "Shanghai Bill Exchange Paper Commercial Bill Business Operation Procedures", and "Shanghai Bill Exchange Bill Registration Custody Clearing and Settlement Business Rules" to regulate bill trading activities.

[10] Created based on relevant data from the official website of the People's Bank of China.

Table 9.14 Bill issuance and discounting in China from 2009 to 2017 (unit: trillions of yuan)

Year	Cumulative amount of commercial bills issued	Accumulated discount amount
2009	10.3	23.2
2010	12.2	26.9
2011	15.1	25.0
2012	17.9	31.6
2013	20.3	45.7
2014	22.1	60.7
2015	22.4	102.1
2016	18.1	84.5
2017	17.0	40.3

Source Compiled according to the monetary policy implementation report for the fourth quarter of every calendar year since 2009, http://www.pbc.gov.cn/zhengcehuobisi/125207/125227/index.html

Under relatively loose monetary policies and increasingly standardized bill trading conditions, China's bill market business has achieved stable and continuous development. However, after reaching its peak in terms of bill issuance and discounting amounts in 2015, these figures gradually declined, as shown in Table 9.14.

9.2.4 Money Market Funds

Compared to developed countries like Europe and America, China's money market funds (MMF) are a relatively new phenomenon in the money market. They emerged more than 30 years after the development of MMFs in Europe and America. By the end of 2002, Chinese fund companies began seeking to introduce money market funds to the market. In March 2003, China Merchants Fund attempted to hide money market funds under its Antai series of funds in preparation for market launch. However, their initial activities did not receive approval from the China Securities Regulatory Commission (CSRC). Subsequently, China Merchants Fund, Huaxia Fund, and Bosera Funds, after six months of careful preparation, obtained recognition from the CSRC in December 2003, and their products were successively introduced to the market (see Table 9.15). This marked the formal emergence of China's money market funds.

From the issuance of the first batch of money market funds, they were all limited by the policies at that time and were not directly named as money market funds. Instead, they were issued as cash funds, representing the early stage of development for money market funds. Afterwards, four fund management companies including Changxin, Taixin, Huaxia, and Nanfang successively introduced their varieties of money market funds to the market. At this point, China had a total of seven fund management companies that issued seven money market fund products. However, these products

Table 9.15 Issuance of the first money market funds in China

Fund company	Name of money market fund	Time to market
Hua'an fund company	Hua'an cash Fuli investment fund	14 December 2003
China merchants fund management company	China merchants cash appreciation fund	15 December 15 2003
Bosera funds company	Bosera cash income fund	16 December 16 2003

were not formally named as money market funds, but rather transitional products in the development stage of quasi-money market funds in China.

In August 2004, CSRC and PBOC jointly issued the "Interim Measures for the Administration of Money Market Funds." This regulation was the first governing rule for money market funds in China, which standardized the naming, investment types, and residual maturity of money market funds, promoting the formal development stage of money market funds in the country. In the fourth quarter of the same year, Nuo'an Fund Management Company, in accordance with the "Interim Measures for the Administration of Money Market Funds", launched the first fund product named "Money Market Fund" in China's money market. Subsequently, Galaxy Asset Management and HFT Investment Management Companies introduced the Galaxy Yin Fu Money Market Fund and HFT Money Market Fund, respectively. This accelerated the development of money market funds in China. The total changes in China's money market funds since 2003 are shown in Table 9.16.

Subsequently, the variety of money market funds and the number of management companies increased, and the scale of issuance continued to expand. In order to regulate the development of money market fund business, CSRC successively issued a series of regulations, such as the "Special Provisions on Information Disclosure of Money Market Funds," the "Notice on Relevant Issues of Investment in Money Market Funds," the "Notice on Seeking Opinions on Further Broadening the Investment Scope of Money Market Funds," the "Notice on Issues Related to the Investment of Money Market Funds in Short-term Financing Bills", and the "Notice on Issues Related to the Investment of Money Market Funds in Bank Deposits." These regulations greatly promoted the standardized and legal development of money market

Table 9.16 Overview of changes in the total amount of China's money market funds since 2003 (unit: 100 million yuan)

Year	Total amount of money market funds
2003	3.31
2004	610.82
2005	1867.90
2006	794.88
2007	1110.46
2008	3891.74
2009	1643.25

fund business and the operations of various fund management companies, better protecting the legitimate rights and interests of money market fund investors.

With the rapid development of China's socio-economy, money market fund management institutions have responded to this trend by continuously strengthening institutional construction and expanding the operational space of money market funds. Starting from 2011, the regulatory authorities in China abolished the upper limit rule that restricted money market funds from investing more than 30% in negotiated deposits. The yield of money market funds has continued to surpass the interest rates of 1-year fixed-term deposits during the same period. In 2013, as China's economy entered a new normal, especially after the collaboration between Yu'E Bao and Tianhong Fund, money market funds experienced explosive growth. Innovative products emerged one after another, greatly enriching the variety of money market funds in China and becoming an important channel for the general public's wealth management. In order to regulate the operational behavior of money market funds and curb risks in innovation, in December 2015, the CSRC, in conjunction with PBOC, jointly issued the "Administrative Measures for the Management of Money Market Funds," which standardized the fundraising, operations, and related activities of money market funds, protecting the legitimate rights and interests of investors and relevant parties, and greatly promoting the development of money market funds.

With the increasingly standardized management of money market funds in China, they have not only gradually become important institutional investors, investment forces, and investment tools in the country's securities market, but also an important force in stabilizing the stock market. The total issuance of money market funds has shown an upward trend year by year, and the variety of money market funds has continued to increase, reaching 587 by 2017. Money market funds have played an increasingly important role in the development of China's real economy.

9.2.5 The Gold Market

After the establishment of the People's Republic of China, strict control was imposed on the circulation of gold, prohibiting private buying and selling of gold and silver. Gold mining companies were required to sell all their gold to PBOC, which would then allocate gold to authorized entities. In June 1983, the State Council issued the "Regulations of the People's Republic of China on Gold and Silver Management", which continued the policy of "unified management, centralized purchase, and allocation of gold and silver". It stated that "all units and individuals within the territory of the People's Republic of China shall not use gold and silver as a unit of measurement, and private buying, selling, lending, and mortgaging of gold and silver are prohibited". It also mentioned that "the acquisition of gold and silver shall be uniformly handled by the People's Bank of China. Without permission or authorization from the People's Bank of China, no units or individuals are allowed to acquire gold and silver." With the rapid development of the Chinese economy and the increasing demand for gold, the planned control approach was no longer suitable for the new situation. In August 2000, the Shanghai branch of PBOC approved Shanghai Lao Feng Xiang Profiles & Gifts Company to engage in the business of buying and redeeming old gold jewelry, making it the first commercial enterprise in China to pilot the business of freely exchanging gold. This marked the beginning of the market-oriented development of the gold market.

In the 10th Five-Year Plan, the Chinese government set clear goals for establishing a gold market. In 2001, PBOC officially announced the cancellation of the planned management system of gold "centralized purchase and allocation," and gold market trading began to enter a market-oriented track. In October 2002, the Shanghai Gold Exchange was established, marking the comprehensive opening of the Chinese gold market. The gold exchange operates on a membership basis, and over the past 20 years, its participants have expanded from initial banking institutions and gold and precious metals production and operation enterprises to financial members, foreign members, comprehensive members, and proprietary members. The exchange has also become the largest tangible market for global gold spot trading, with various products covering spot, futures, and derivatives of gold and silver. Meanwhile, the over-the-counter gold market of commercial banks and the gold futures market of the Shanghai Futures Exchange gradually developed. In 2003, Bank of China piloted the trading of "paper gold" under the name of "Gold Accumulation Program" in Shanghai, which quickly expanded to other large commercial banks. The over-the-counter gold market mainly engages in gold credit, gold management, and gold investment businesses and has now integrated various gold businesses regulated by PBOC. In January 2008, the Shanghai Futures Exchange officially launched gold futures contracts, greatly promoting the deepening development of the gold market. Since 2009, the trading volume of gold in China has rapidly increased, with significant fluctuations in gold trading prices, as shown in Table 9.17.

With the increasing formation and development of China's gold market, the Chinese government actively promotes the deepening development of trading markets and mechanisms, and strengthens the standardized construction of gold trading. In 2010, PBOC, together with the National Development and Reform Commission, CBRC, and other units, jointly issued the "Several Opinions on Promoting the Development of the Gold Market", which played a positive role in promoting the development of the gold market, strengthening regulatory oversight, and protecting investors' interests. In 2011, the international gold prices experienced a rapid increase, which increased the risks in our country's gold market. In response, PBOC strengthened the management of gold trading and issued the "Shanghai Gold Exchange Business Supervision and Management Rules". At the same time, several government departments jointly issued the "Notice on Strengthening the Management of Gold Exchange or Platforms Engaging in Gold Business Transactions", to crack down on illegal gold trading and gold derivative trading platforms, ensuring the stable development of our country's gold market. In 2012, the Chinese government introduced interbank gold inquiry trading, which significantly improved the liquidity of the gold market, perfected the trading mechanisms, and further deepened market functions. Afterward, in the interbank gold inquiry trading,

Table 9.17 Cumulative trading volume and annual weighted average price changes in the Chinese gold market

Year	Cumulative trading volume/ten thousand tons	Annual weighted average price (yuan/gram)
2009	0.47	215
2010	0.61	265.8
2011	0.74	327.5
2012	0.64	339.81
2013	1.16	278.6
2014	1.85	249.51
2015	3.41	222.86
2016	4.87	263.9
2017	5.43	273

Source Compiled according to the monetary policy implementation report for the fourth quarter of every calendar year since 2009, http://www.pbc.gov.cn/zhengcehuobisi/125207/125227/index.html

China successively introduced various trading instruments such as gold forwards and swaps, providing market participants with more diversified risk management tools. The Shanghai Gold Exchange extended the trading hours and implemented Friday night trading. In 2014, the Shanghai Gold Exchange established a market-making system and launched gold inquiry options business, expanding the participation of market entities. It also established an international business segment within the Shanghai Free Trade Zone, steadily advancing the internationalization process of the gold market. In 2016, China standardized the bank's account gold business and implemented the centralized pricing mechanism for gold in Chinese yuan, further improving the price formation mechanism of the Renminbi gold market and promoting the stable and rapid development of gold market operations.

Chapter 10
The Revolution of Foreign Exchange Management System and the Development of Foreign Exchange Market

Since the beginning of the reform and opening up, with the rapid development of China's socio-economy, the existing foreign exchange management system has become inadequate to meet the demands of the new socio-economic situation. In response to the trend of economic development, the Chinese government separated the foreign exchange management agency from the People's Bank of China (PBOC) and established the State Administration of Foreign Exchange (SAFE). Foreign exchange management gradually shifted from government intervention to market regulation. During this period, the Chinese foreign exchange market began to take shape, fostering a positive interaction among various market participants in the financial sector, thereby contributing to the healthy and sustainable development of China's economy in areas such as foreign trade and investment.

10.1 Revolution of the Foreign Exchange Management System

The reform of China's foreign exchange management system began with the establishment of SAFE, followed by gradual reforms of related management mechanisms based on the degree of demand for foreign exchange, in order to adapt to the reform and development of the socio-economic system. By 2019, China had established a diversified management mechanism centered around SAFE. This mechanism enables timely decision-making on foreign exchange policies that are suitable for China's socio-economic development and changes in the international economic situation, in response to fluctuations in the domestic and global economic environment.

R. Lan, *The Financial Development of China*, Understanding China,
https://doi.org/10.1007/978-981-97-8273-4_10

10.1.1 Revolution of the Specialized Foreign Exchange Management Institutes

Before the reform and opening-up, China's foreign exchange management relied on the Bank of China, which was a subsidiary of PBOC. Except for remittances from overseas Chinese and foreign exchange activities conducted by branches of the Bank of China abroad, other foreign exchange management efforts faced significant setbacks. The amount of foreign exchange dwindled, with the national foreign exchange reserves reaching only 167 million US dollars by 1978, which was insufficient to meet the demands of socio-economic development. Against this backdrop, the central government promptly adjusted its foreign exchange management policies. It encouraged tourism activities to attract foreign exchange and established SAFE in March 1979. The Administration shared offices with the Bank of China and was managed by the Bank of China. The establishment of SAFE marked the beginning of the reform of China's foreign exchange management system, leading to the normalization of foreign exchange management in China. Subsequently, based on changes in the socio-economic situation and the level of foreign exchange demand, the Chinese government continuously adjusted the main bodies and authorities of foreign exchange management institutions. Since the reform and opening-up, the changes in foreign exchange management institutions are as shown in Table 10.1.

In August 1982, SAFE separated from the Bank of China and was placed under the management of PBOC, strengthening its foreign exchange management functions. In June 1988, although SAFE was still managed by PBOC, its authority was elevated to that of a bureau-level institution directly under the State Council. In December 1989, SAFE was upgraded to a deputy-ministerial-level institution and placed under the supervision of PBOC. The branch offices of SAFE and the branches of PBOC throughout the country shared offices. From then until 2017, SAFE was directly

Table 10.1 Revolution of foreign exchange management institutes since the reform and opening-up

Time	Revolution	Management institutes
March, 1979	SAFE was set up	SAFE is co-located with the Bank of China, which acts as an escrow agent for the Bank of China
August, 1982	SAFE was separated from Bank of China	Escrowed by PBOC
September, 1983	SAFE	Exercising foreign exchange management functions under the leadership of PBOC
June, 1988	SAFE was a bureau-level institution directly under the State Council of China	Escrowed by PBOC
December, 1989	SAFE has been upgraded to the vice-ministerial level	Administered by PBOC under one roof; branches of the State Administration of Foreign Exchange are co-located with branches of PBOC at their locations

Table 10.2 All directors of SAFE

Name	Serving time
Bu Ming	1979–1982.5
Tang Gengyao	1988–1990.12
Yin Jieyan	1990.12–1994.1
Zhu Xiaohua	1994.1–1995.9
Zhou Xiaochuan	1995.9–1998.4
Wu Xiaoling	1998.4–1998.10
Li Fuxiang	1998.10–2000.5
Wu Xiaoling	2000.5–2001.4
Guo Shuqing	2001.4–2003.3
Hu Xiaodong	2003.3–2009.7
Yi Gang	2009.7–2016.1
Pan Gongsheng	2016.1–Now

under the State Council and its operations were managed by PBOC, but it was not a subordinate agency. The head of SAFE was generally concurrently held by a vice governor of PBOC. The former directors of SAFE are listed in Table 10.2.

SAFE consists of 8 functional departments (offices) and Party committees, including the General Department (Department of Policies and Regulations), the Department of International Payments, the Department of Current Account Management, the Department of Capital Account Management, the Department of Management and Inspection, the Department of Reserve Management, the Department of Personnel (Department of Internal Audit), the Department of Science and Technology, and 4 public institutions including the Central Foreign Exchange Business Center, the Foreign Exchange Business Data Monitoring Center, the Department Service Center, and the magazine press of China Forex. SAFE established branch bureaus (foreign exchange management departments) in each province, autonomous region, municipality directly under the Central Government and some sub-provincial cities, central branch bureaus in some prefectures (cities) and branch bureaus in some counties (cities). These agencies are co-located with PBOC's local agencies. As a result, a set of top-down vertical management agencies was formed nationwide, and its functions were adjusted accordingly with the changes in social and economic development. By 2018, the basic functions of SAFE were mainly the followings: (1) To study and propose policy recommendations on the reform of the foreign exchange management system and the prevention of balance of payments risks and the promotion of balance of payments; to study the gradual promotion of RMB capital account convertibility, cultivate and develop the foreign exchange market policy measures, and provide PBOC with recommendations and basis for the formulation of RMB exchange rate policy. (2) Participate in drafting relevant laws and regulations and departmental regulations on foreign exchange management, and issue normative documents related to the performance of its duties. (3) Responsible for the balance of payments, external debt statistics and monitoring, the release of relevant information in accordance with regulations, and undertake the work related to the monitoring of cross-border capital flows. (4) Responsible for the supervision and management of the national foreign exchange market; assume the responsibility for the supervision and management of foreign exchange settlement and sale business; cultivate and develop the foreign exchange market. (5) Responsible for supervising and checking the authenticity and legality of current account foreign exchange payments and receipts in accordance with the law; responsible for implementing foreign exchange management of capital items in accordance with the law and continuously improving the management in accordance with the process of convertibility of RMB capital items; regulating the management of domestic and foreign exchange accounts. (6) Responsible for the implementation of foreign exchange supervision and inspection in accordance with the law, and the imposition of penalties for violations of foreign exchange management. (7) Assume responsibility for the management of the country's foreign exchange reserves, gold reserves and other foreign exchange assets. (8) Draw up and implement development plans and standards and norms for foreign exchange management information technology, and share supervisory information with relevant management departments in accordance with the law. (9) Participate in relevant international financial activities. (10) Undertake other matters assigned by the State Council and PBOC.

10.1.2 The Revolution of Foreign Exchange Management System

As mentioned earlier, during the period of "managing fund" in China, a single exchange rate system was adopted. During this period, the state maintained balance of payments through directive planning and administrative measures such as "balancing income with expenditure" where all foreign exchange income had to be sold to the state, and foreign exchange was allocated according to a planned distribution. China rarely borrowed foreign debt and did not accept foreign investment. The exchange rate of the Chinese yuan was merely used as an accounting tool, and there was no foreign exchange market in China. After the reform and opening up, in accordance with the fundamental requirements of social and economic development and economic system reform, China decided to reform its foreign exchange system in August 1979. Subsequently, China's foreign exchange management system has gradually shifted towards reducing directive planning and fostering and enhancing the role of market mechanisms in foreign exchange resource allocation. After more than 40 years of effort, China has established a foreign exchange management system that adapts to the requirements of a socialist market economy. During this period, China's foreign exchange management system has gone through several stages roughly as follows.

A. A Dual Exchange Rate Management System Coexisting with Both Planned and Market Mechanisms

After the reform and opening-up, as part of the reform of the foreign trade system to stimulate the enthusiasm of export enterprises to earn foreign exchange and ensure the concentrated use of limited foreign exchange resources for national economic construction, the State Council issued the "Regulations on Vigorously Developing Measures to Increase Foreign Exchange Income from Foreign Trade" on August 13, 1979. This regulation clarified the implementation of the foreign exchange retention system in China and, based on this, formulated and promulgated the "Trial Measures for Retaining Foreign Exchange for Export Commodities." Thus, the foreign exchange retention system began to be implemented in 1979, promoting both trade and non-trade foreign exchange retention methods while managing and balancing foreign exchange centrally by the state and ensuring priority use. This practice of allowing export-oriented enterprises to retain a certain proportion of their foreign exchange earnings and permitting units holding retained foreign exchange to transfer excess foreign exchange quotas to units in need significantly boosted the enthusiasm of export-oriented enterprises and facilitated rapid development in foreign trade. Under these conditions, a dual exchange rate system, consisting of official and adjustment market rates, existed in the initial foreign exchange market in China. Therefore, besides announcing the official exchange rate of the renminbi, the state also had to establish a trade internal settlement rate to meet the settlement needs of import and export trade and related expenses. As a result, a de facto dual exchange rate system was established in China. It was not until January 1, 1985, when China officially abolished the trade internal settlement rate, that the coexistence of the official exchange rate and the adjustment market rate began to transition towards the coexistence of the official exchange rate and the market-clearing rate.

The dual exchange rate system played a positive role in promoting export earnings, balancing foreign exchange receipts and payments for foreign-invested enterprises, and regulating currency circulation by the central bank. In early 1992, to meet the demand for renminbi settlement in border areas during the process of opening up, China approved 13 border cities such as Heihe to conduct small-scale border trade settlement activities. As the reform and opening-up continued to deepen, the drawbacks of the dual-track system of the renminbi exchange rate, with both official and adjustment market rates, gradually became apparent. The coexistence of multiple exchange rates led to disorder in the foreign exchange adjustment market, fueled speculation, and the existence of a long-term foreign exchange black market was extremely detrimental to the stability of the renminbi exchange rate and the credibility of RMB. It was imperative to reform and adjust it to meet the further development needs of the social economy.

B. Establishment of a Market-Oriented Foreign Exchange Management System

In November 1993, the "Decision of the Central Committee of the Communist Party of China on Establishing a Socialist Market Economic System" clearly proposed to "reform the foreign exchange management system, establish a floating exchange rate system based on market supply and demand, and a unified and standardized foreign exchange market, gradually making the renminbi a convertible currency." On December 28 of the same year, PBOC issued an announcement on "Further Reforming the Foreign Exchange Management System," stipulating that the official and adjustment exchange rates of the renminbi would be merged from January 1, 1994. At the beginning of 1994, China carried out a major reform of the foreign exchange system, abolishing the foreign exchange retention system, implementing a bank-based exchange settlement system, adopting a single, managed floating exchange rate system based on market supply and demand, and establishing a unified and standardized foreign exchange market. After the successful integration of the renminbi exchange rate system, PBOC determined the exchange rate of 1 US dollar to 8.7 RMB yuan. Subsequently, further improvements were made to the foreign exchange management system. In 1996, all restrictions on routine international payments and transfers were completely lifted, achieving full convertibility of the renminbi's current account. In the same year, the "Foreign Exchange Administration Regulations of the People's Republic of China" were promulgated and implemented, clarifying the basic principles and systems of China's foreign exchange management in law and providing specific regulations for financial institutions engaged in foreign exchange business. In 1997, the Asian financial crisis broke out. China, considering its own situation and the international economic environment, made a commitment not to devalue the renminbi. It adhered to this commitment with a responsible stance, creating a favorable social and economic environment and order for Asian countries to emerge from the crisis.

During the height of the Asian financial crisis, the Chinese government not only firmly ensured the stability of RMB exchange rate system and gradually pushed forward reforms of the exchange rate system but also established currency swap mechanisms with neighboring countries to help them jointly cope with the crisis. When necessary, China provided corresponding foreign exchange support to these countries. In November 1997, China held the first National Financial Work Conference, strengthening the top-level design in the financial sector. This changed the relatively scattered and short-term financial adjustment behaviors of the past, strengthened financial risk prevention, and prevented speculative attacks on external currencies. In terms of the foreign exchange system, China adopted a "fixed exchange rate regime pegged to a single currency," effectively preventing the influence of external currencies. It also provided full support to the Hong Kong Monetary Authority, successfully repelling multiple speculative attacks led by international speculators such as Soros, and smoothly weathered the Asian financial crisis. Through the operation of the foreign exchange market mechanism during this period, China established a good international image in the foreign exchange market, winning widespread praise from the international community and laying a solid foundation for subsequent reforms of China's foreign exchange management system.

C. Gradual Establishment of a Market-Oriented Foreign Exchange Management System

Since joining the WTO at the end of 2001, China has rapidly integrated into the global economy, further expanded its opening up to the outside world, maintained a continuous large trade surplus, and rapidly increased its foreign exchange reserves. This led to a significant increase in the proportion of foreign exchange deposits, putting increasing pressure on PBOC to offset these deposits. Trade frictions also increased year by year. Against this backdrop, China responded to the challenges of the new situation by deepening the reform of the foreign exchange management system, which effectively promoted the facilitation of trade and investment, steadily promoted the opening up of the capital account, strengthened the management of cross-border capital flows, improved the monitoring of international balance of payments, and enhanced the management of foreign exchange reserves. In 2001, PBOC explicitly set the goal of standardizing, professionalizing, and internationalizing the management of foreign exchange reserves, establishing an investment benchmark management model and risk management framework, and improving the institutional mechanisms for the management of large-scale foreign exchange reserves, gradually diluting the "fixed exchange rate regime pegged to a single currency" implemented during the Asian financial crisis. In 2002, China allowed neighboring countries such as Vietnam to settle border trade transactions in their own currencies with the renminbi. In 2004, China officially launched cross-border renminbi businesses in Hong Kong and Macau.

On 21 July 2005, PBOC issued an announcement on the reform of the RMB exchange rate market formation mechanism, announcing the implementation of a managed floating exchange rate system based on market supply and demand and adjusted by reference to "a basket of currencies". The RMB exchange rate is no longer stuck to a single US dollar and the exchange rate formation mechanism is more flexible. As a result, the RMB exchange rate floats in both directions, with increased flexibility and a more pronounced linkage with major international currencies. Since then, China has continued to improve the managed floating exchange rate system in accordance with the principles of provocativeness, controllability and gradualness. Under this system, the Foreign Exchange Centre publishes daily mid-rates for the RMB against the USD, JPY, EUR and HKD.

Under the market-based exchange rate formation mechanism, it became more convenient for enterprises and individuals to hold and use foreign exchange. In terms of foreign exchange management, China gradually abandoned the mandatory buying and selling of foreign exchange and implemented a voluntary trading system. With the gradual relaxation of foreign exchange positions in the interbank market, the management approach shifted from "easy inflow and strict outflow" to "easy outflow and strict inflow," gradually establishing a system framework for balanced management of capital flows in both directions. In August 2008, the State Council issued a revised version of the "Regulations of the People's Republic of China on Foreign Exchange Administration," officially establishing a balanced regulatory approach and canceling the mandatory buying and selling of foreign exchange at the administrative regulation level while strengthening the monitoring of cross-border capital flows. In 2008, the US subprime mortgage crisis triggered a global financial crisis. China promptly initiated crisis response measures, making efforts to prepare emergency plans for the reversal of international payments, actively preventing financial risks, ensuring the overall security of foreign exchange reserve assets, and withstanding the strong impact from the international financial crisis. In this context, Zhou Xiaochuan, then Governor of PBOC, proposed reforming the existing international monetary system by using Special Drawing Rights (SDRs) to replace currencies issued by sovereign states. Although this idea may not be practical at present, it underscores the harm of the dollar-based system established in the early 1970s and the need for improvement. Against this backdrop, the Chinese government promoted bilateral or multilateral currency swaps to reduce dependence on the US dollar and stabilize the RMB exchange rate system.

Since 2009, in response to the increasingly complex cross-border capital flows, growing scale, and rapidly increasing demand for facilitation among market entities, China has further standardized the individual foreign exchange purchase and sale system. It revised the "Assessment Measures for the Implementation of Foreign Exchange Management Regulations by Banks" to enhance the compliance management of banks in foreign exchange. At the same time, China has accelerated the transformation of foreign exchange management concepts and methods, proposing the "Five Transformations": shifting from emphasis on approval to emphasis on monitoring and analysis, from emphasis on pre-event supervision to emphasis on post-event management, from emphasis on behavior management to emphasis on entity management, from the "presumption of guilt" to the "presumption of innocence", and from the "positive list" (only activities explicitly authorized by law are allowed) to the "negative list" (activities are allowed unless explicitly prohibited by law). After a period of preparation and promotion, significant progress has been made in the transformation of the foreign exchange management system's concepts and methods. In 2012, the use of the renminbi expanded to the field of cross-border direct investment; in 2013, efforts were made to promote the reform of foreign exchange facilitation systems, supporting the development of cross-border e-commerce and Internet finance by launching pilot projects for cross-border e-commerce forex payments in cities such as Shanghai. Steady progress has been made in making the renminbi convertible under the capital account to enhance the efficiency of cross-border capital allocation. In 2016, PBOC established a self-discipline platform for foreign exchange business banks, effectively organizing 14 core member banks to sign the "Banking Industry Convention on Foreign Exchange Business Operation", smoothly completing the construction of a provincial-level self-discipline mechanism for the national foreign exchange market, and improving the transmission mechanism of foreign exchange policies. Since the end of 2016, facing the trend of a significant decline in foreign exchange reserves, SAFE and PBOC have continuously strengthened the management of foreign exchange. By early 2018, they had partially reversed the trend of capital outflows, stabilizing foreign exchange reserves and laying a necessary economic foundation to address financial risks. On March

23, 2018, U.S. President Trump signed a $60 billion tariff document against China, increasing the risk of a trade war and significantly impacting China's exchange rate system. In July, the U.S. officially imposed a 25% tariff on $34 billion worth of Chinese goods, initiating a trade war that had a huge impact on China's foreign exchange system. In response, China has strengthened the construction of the foreign exchange management system to guard against exchange rate risks, while continuing to deepen the opening up of the foreign exchange field by gradually relaxing controls over capital projects.

10.2 The Formation and Development of Foreign Exchange Market

Before the reform and opening-up, foreign exchange transactions in China were strictly controlled and managed by the state, and there was no substantive foreign exchange market. The exchange rate went through three different stages according to the needs of social and economic development at different times. Before 1952, it was a single floating exchange rate system; from 1953 to 1972, it was a single fixed exchange rate system; and from 1973 to 1980, it was a single floating exchange rate system based on a "basket of currencies." Since the reform and opening-up, with the rapid development of China's social and economic progress, the previously relatively single exchange rate system could no longer meet the needs of the new social and economic situation. In response to this situation, the Chinese government has promoted the reform of the exchange rate system, facilitating the gradual formation and improvement of the foreign exchange market to cater to the diversified needs in areas such as foreign trade and investment. The variety of trading products and the diversity of participating entities in the foreign exchange market have jointly promoted the development and prosperity of China's foreign exchange market.

10.2.1 Revolution of Foreign Exchange Market

In 1973, the United States terminated the fixed exchange rate between the US dollar and gold, leading to the gradual formation of the international foreign exchange market, which has since become the largest financial trading market in the world. China's foreign exchange market has developed gradually in tandem with the pace of reform and opening-up. It has undergone a complex process of transition from an officially controlled foreign exchange allocation to a dual-track adjustment market and then to a unified foreign exchange market. After more than 40 years of development, the trend toward marketization in China's foreign exchange market has become increasingly apparent.

A. Formation and Development of Foreign Exchange Adjustment Market

With the transition from a unified foreign exchange management system to a dual-track foreign exchange system, China formulated and promulgated the "Interim Plan for Foreign Exchange Adjustment" in October 1980. According to this plan, the Bank of China began to experiment with foreign exchange adjustment services in 12 coastal open cities such as Beijing and Shanghai starting from October 1980. State-owned and collective enterprises were allowed to participate in the adjustment using retained foreign exchange quotas, paying for the use of foreign exchange adjustment rights. This marked the initial formation of China's foreign exchange adjustment market. In November 1985, the first foreign exchange adjustment center was established in the Shenzhen Special Economic Zone. Subsequently, foreign exchange adjustment centers were established nationwide to handle quotas and foreign exchange adjustment for local Chinese-funded enterprises and joint ventures. The introduction of a fair bidding market model made the foreign exchange adjustment market more standardized and transparent. With a significant increase in foreign exchange adjustment volume in 1985, the foreign exchange adjustment prices showed a certain degree of change. "...After 1985, the foreign exchange adjustment prices can be truly considered as another type of 'exchange rate,' and the formal establishment of the dual-track exchange rate system, where both the official exchange rate and the foreign exchange adjustment prices coexist, occurred."[1]

In 1986, China's foreign exchange allocation business was transferred from the Bank of China to SAFE, marking the beginning of a new stage in the development of China's foreign exchange allocation market. In October of the same year, the State Council issued the "Regulations on Encouraging Foreign Investment," allowing foreign-invested enterprises to participate in foreign exchange allocation business in economic special zones and coastal open cities. However, they were not permitted to participate in the foreign exchange allocation business of state-owned and collectively-owned enterprises. At the same time, SAFE raised the foreign exchange allocation prices, allowing negotiations between buyers and sellers for foreign exchange allocation in economic special zones and Hainan Province. With the increasing volume of foreign exchange allocation business, the scope of foreign exchange allocation expanded to provinces, autonomous regions, municipalities directly under the central government, and separately planned cities.

In March 1988, SAFE formulated and issued the "Regulations on Foreign Exchange Allocation," effectively promoting the development of foreign exchange allocation business. To adapt to this trend, SAFE established a national foreign exchange allocation center in Beijing to handle foreign exchange allocation business between provinces, municipalities, and central government departments, marking the formation of a unified national foreign exchange allocation market in China. In September 1988, the Shanghai Foreign Exchange Allocation Center was established as the first public foreign exchange allocation market in China. Subsequently, public foreign exchange allocation markets were established in Fuzhou, Shenzhen, Xiamen,

[1] YI Gang. *Reflections on China's Financial Reform*, The Commercial Press, 2009: 218.

Beijing, and Nanjing. By the end of 1993, a total of 108 foreign exchange allocation centers and 18 foreign exchange allocation markets had been established nationwide, greatly promoting the development of China's foreign exchange allocation market. The volume of foreign exchange transactions increased significantly (see Table 10.3), laying a solid foundation for the convergence of exchange rates.

Meanwhile, the fluctuations in the exchange rate of the US dollar against the Chinese yuan showed a trend of depreciation, as depicted in Fig. 10.1.

B. Establishment and Development of Unified Foreign Exchange Market

In order to meet the requirements of establishing a socialist market economy, China accelerated the reform and construction of the foreign exchange market starting from 1994. After the merger of the official exchange rate and the adjustment rate of the renminbi in 1994, the weighted average price of 18 open foreign exchange markets determined on December 31, 1993, was officially adopted, marking the formal operation of China's unified interbank foreign exchange trading market. In April 1994, the

Table 10.3 Overview of national foreign exchange trading volume from 1988 to 1993

Year	Foreign exchange trading volume/100 million US dollars
1988	62.6
1989	85.7
1990	131.6
1991	204.5
1992	251.0
1993	237.6

Data source Qi Qun. Development and Innovation of China's Money Market, Law Press, 2012

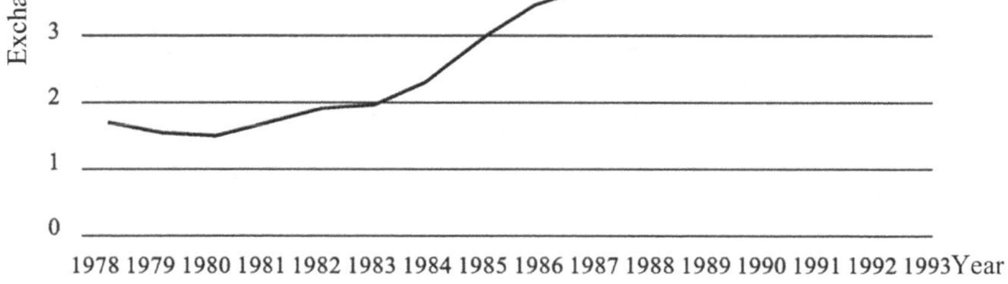

Fig. 10.1 Dynamics of USD to RMB exchange rate changes from 1978 to 1993

Foreign Exchange Trading Center (FETC) officially began operations. Leveraging computer networking with sub-centers and adjustment centers scattered across the country, designated banks conducted transactions through appointed traders recognized by FETC, forming market rates. Meanwhile, the trading entities in the foreign exchange market continued to expand according to the development needs of the business. In 1994, only Chinese-funded enterprises, institutions, and groups were allowed to settle foreign exchange through banks. By June 1996, PBOC issued the "Regulations on Settlement, Sale, and Payment of Foreign Exchange," explicitly incorporating foreign-invested enterprises into the interbank settlement and sale system. The development of the unified interbank foreign exchange market not only provided a platform for PBOC to intervene in the foreign exchange market when necessary but also laid the foundation for market-based adjustments in the foreign exchange system. Accordingly, the central bank set a certain range for exchange rate fluctuations based on the actual economic development of China, aiming to maintain the stability of the renminbi exchange rate. In response to the impact of the 1997 Asian financial crisis, China once again adopted a "pegged single currency fixed exchange rate system," effectively preventing external currency shocks and smoothly weathering the regional currency crisis. With China's formal accession to the WTO in 2001, FETC accelerated its technological innovation and integration with international standards. By 2003, FETC had developed into a comprehensive service platform for "trading, information, and supervision" in China's foreign exchange market.

After a series of reforms and adjustments in the foreign exchange market, from the merger of exchange rates in 1994 to 2005, the exchange rate of the US dollar against the Chinese yuan remained relatively stable in China's foreign exchange market, as shown in Fig. 10.2.

On July 21, 2005, PBOC initiated the market-oriented reform of the RMB exchange rate formation mechanism, transitioning from the policy of pegging solely

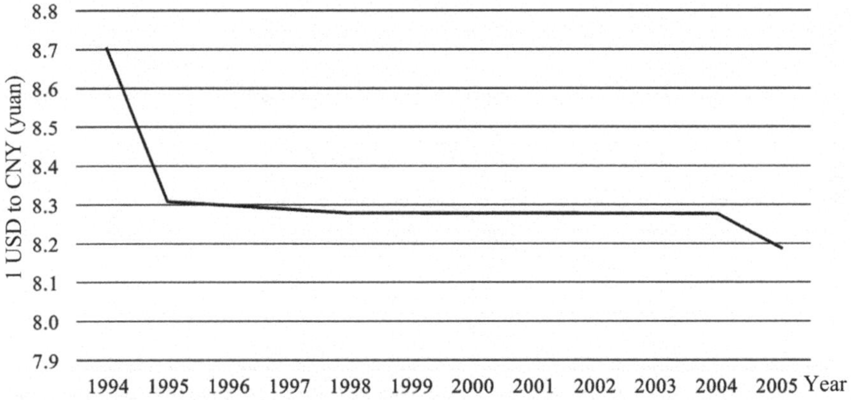

Fig. 10.2 The trend of the mid-point exchange rate of 1 US dollar to Chinese yuan from 1994 to 2005

to the US dollar to a managed floating exchange rate policy based on market supply and demand, with reference to a "basket of currencies." This reform allowed for minor fluctuations in the exchange rate. On the day of the reform, the exchange rate of the US dollar against the Chinese yuan rose by 1.9%, from 8.27 to 8.11 yuan. By the end of the year, China Foreign Exchange Trading Center adopted the "Reuters Trading System" as a new generation of electronic trading system for foreign exchange, which greatly promoted the development of the interbank foreign exchange market, significantly enhancing the transparency and efficiency of China's foreign exchange market, and further improving the mechanism for the formation of the RMB exchange rate. At the end of 2006, with the rapid increase in China's foreign exchange reserves, PBOC proposed the significant policy of "hiding foreign exchange reserves among the people," effectively advancing the development of the RMB exchange rate towards full convertibility. On January 11, 2007, the RMB against the US dollar broke through the 7.80 mark, exceeding the Hong Kong dollar for the first time since 1994. At the same time, some non-US dollar currencies were included in the RMB exchange rate basket, encouraging the use of non-public foreign exchange. In January 2007, the South Korean won was included, and the weight of the euro increased significantly. By May 2008, the weight of the euro had nearly approached that of the US dollar, in response to the impact of international capital flows.

With the spread of the international financial crisis to China, the quantitative easing policy in the United States and the European debt crisis have had a significant impact on China. The RMB exchange rate faced substantial appreciation pressure, and the weight of the US dollar in the RMB exchange rate basket began to rise significantly, essentially returning to the situation where the RMB exchange rate was pegged to the US dollar. In 2009, to avoid exchange rate risks and reduce exchange losses, the State Council approved a pilot program for cross-border trade settlement in Renminbi for 365 enterprises in Shanghai, Guangzhou, Shenzhen, Zhuhai, and Dongguan. In June 2010, with the approval of the State Council, the pilot cities for cross-border Renminbi settlement were expanded to 20 provinces, autonomous regions, and municipalities directly under the central government, and the scope extended from Hong Kong, Macao, and ASEAN to all countries and regions. At the same time, PBOC reformed the mechanism for determining the RMB exchange rate to enhance its flexibility. This reform was not a one-time revaluation adjustment but rather a dynamic management and adjustment of the RMB exchange rate fluctuation based on market supply and demand and referencing a basket of currencies within the announced fluctuation range of the foreign exchange market. In August 2011, PBOC expanded the scope of domestic areas for cross-border Renminbi settlement nationwide. On April 16, 2012, PBOC increased the floating range of the RMB against the US dollar in the interbank spot foreign exchange market from 0.5 to 1%. Subsequently, the RMB exchange rate entered a slow appreciation zone, as shown in Fig. 10.3.

In August 2012, China comprehensively promoted the reform of the goods trade management system, abolishing transaction-by-transaction verification and adjusting the customs clearance process, significantly enhancing the efficiency of foreign

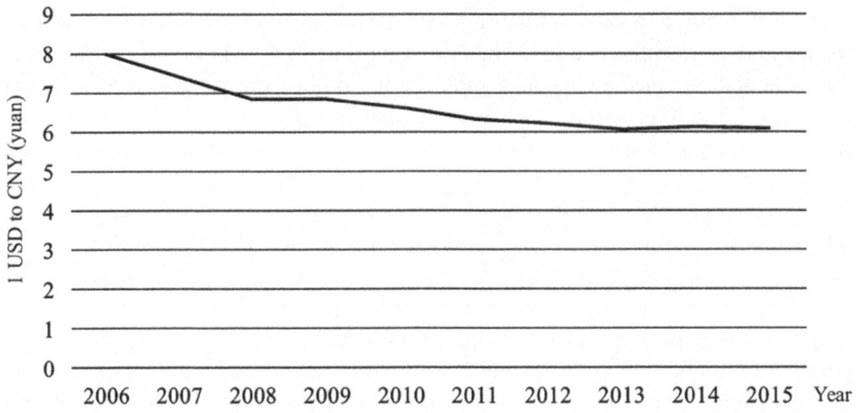

Fig. 10.3 The changes in the central parity rate of the US dollar against the Chinese yuan from 2006 to August 2015

exchange receipts. At the same time, the management of foreign direct investment in foreign exchange was simplified, essentially achieving convertibility for direct investment. In 2014, PBOC increased the floating range of the Renminbi against the US dollar in the interbank spot foreign exchange market from 1 to 2%, and abolished the management of the spread between banks' buying and selling prices for customers' US dollars, greatly enhancing the marketization of the foreign exchange market.

On August 11, 2015, PBOC announced an adjustment to the RMB against the US dollar exchange rate quoting system, where market makers would refer to the previous day's closing rate in the interbank foreign exchange market and provide the mid-point rate to the China Foreign Exchange Trade System. This adjustment made the RMB to USD mid-point rate mechanism more market-oriented, reflecting the current supply and demand dynamics of the foreign exchange market more accurately. The "8·11" exchange rate reform marked the end of the long-standing unilateral RMB appreciation mode, transitioning to a more flexible two-way floating exchange rate. In February 2016, PBOC clarified the mechanism for the RMB to USD mid-point rate quoting, which incorporated changes in the basket of currencies alongside the closing price, enhancing the rules, transparency, and marketization of the exchange rate formation mechanism. Subsequently, the depreciation trend of the RMB against the USD began to slow down, and from 2016 to May 2017, there was a significant appreciation, with the USD reaching almost 7 RMB at one point. In response, in May 2017, PBOC introduced a counter-cyclical factor in the RMB exchange rate to hedge against pro-cyclical movements in the foreign exchange market, preventing potential "herd effects" and enhancing the market-oriented fluctuation of the RMB exchange rate. As a result, the trend of the USD against the RMB started to decrease, reaching 6.579 RMB on October 15, 2017. By February 14, 2018, the USD against the RMB showed a significant increase trend, breaking through 6.27 RMB. According to the Monetary Policy Report for the fourth quarter of 2017 released by PBOC, it was

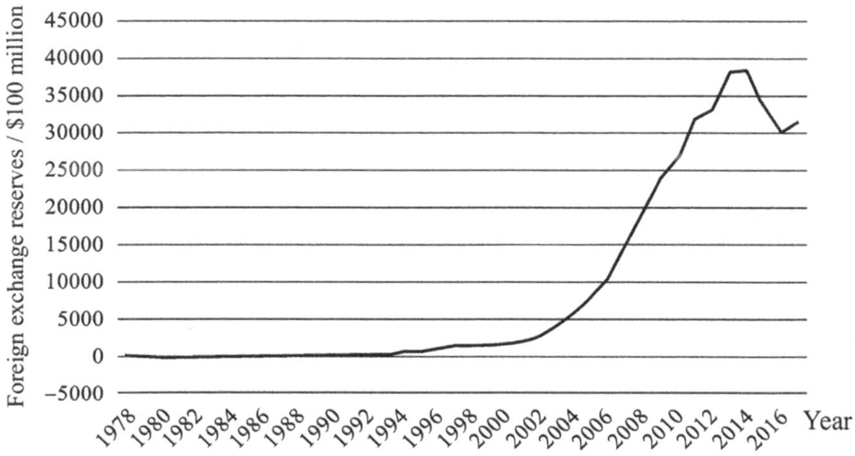

Fig. 10.4 The fluctuation trend of China's foreign exchange reserves from 1978 to 2017[3]

clearly stated that the bank had essentially withdrawn from the normal intervention mechanism and would further deepen the reform of the RMB exchange rate formation mechanism, improve the managed floating exchange rate system based on market supply and demand, reference to a basket of currencies for adjustment, and increase the market-driven determination of the exchange rate. This aimed to enhance the two-way floating flexibility of the RMB exchange rate and maintain its basic stability at a reasonable and balanced level.[2] Since July 2018, influenced by the China-US trade war, the RMB against the USD has shown a depreciation trend, increasing the exchange rate risk.

Obviously, after over 40 years of exploration, China's foreign exchange market has increasingly adapted to the needs of social and economic development, complementing the free trade mechanism. The administrative intervention has gradually diminished, while market-driven fluctuations and formation mechanisms have strengthened. During this period, influenced by fluctuations in China's foreign exchange reserves (see Fig. 10.4), the government still intervenes in the foreign exchange market when there are significant fluctuations in reserves. For example, since 2015, due to substantial decreases in China's foreign exchange reserves, PBOC significantly strengthened administrative interventions in the foreign exchange market in 2017 to prevent excessive fluctuations in reserves.

[2] China's Monetary Policy Implementation Report for the Fourth Quarter of 2017: http://www.pbc.gov.cn/goutongjiaoliu/113456/113469/3484662/index. html.

[3] Compiled based on data from the official website of SAFE of China since 1978.

10.2.2 *The Diversity of Foreign Exchange Trading Instruments and Participants*

Since the reform and opening up, as China's foreign exchange market gradually took shape, the variety of trading instruments in the market has increased, and the participants have become more diverse. The gap between the domestic foreign exchange market and the international foreign exchange market has been narrowing, playing a more significant role in the development of China's foreign trade and economic relations.

A. Foreign Exchange Market Trading Instruments

Before the reform and opening up, China predominantly pursued a balanced budget policy and avoided both domestic and foreign debts. Consequently, the variety of foreign exchange trading instruments was limited, with the focus primarily on meeting domestic demand and concentrating on currency exchange transactions. Subsequently, constrained by the reform process of the foreign exchange management system, the evolution of trading instruments in China's foreign exchange market can be broadly categorized into the following developmental stages.

From 1978 to 1984, the variety of foreign exchange trading instruments remained largely unchanged. During this period, China continued the practice of centralized allocation of foreign exchange by the central authorities, determining the exchange rates based on the midpoint of the US dollar and Deutsche Mark groups. The available foreign exchange varieties were mainly concentrated in a few types such as the US dollar and Hong Kong dollar, and there was no nationwide foreign exchange market established at this time.

From 1985 to 1994, with the formation and development of the foreign exchange adjustment market, the variety of foreign exchange trading instruments in China's foreign exchange market increased. However, influenced by long-term planning thinking, spot foreign exchange transactions remained the main form, mainly focusing on the buying and selling of the Chinese yuan against the US dollar and Hong Kong dollar. The types available for trading were limited. Regarding transactions between foreign currencies, domestic banks had not yet established formal trading platforms, and transactions needed to be completed through overseas banks.

From 1995 to 2005, the number of trading instruments in China's foreign exchange market increased slowly. With the establishment of the interbank foreign exchange market, the scope of transactions in China's foreign exchange market continued to expand, and the variety of trading instruments increased significantly. Constrained by the fixed exchange rate system pegged to the US dollar, members of the interbank foreign exchange market did not need to bear the risk of exchange rate fluctuations, and product trading was mainly concentrated in spot trading instruments. However, forward foreign exchange transactions had already begun to emerge in the domestic bank counter market. In 1997, Bank of China began to handle forward exchange transactions based on the principle of actual demand for current account transactions and designated capital and financial projects. Subsequently, other major banks such as Industrial and Commercial Bank of China, Agricultural Bank of China, China Construction Bank, Bank of Communications, China Merchants Bank, and China CITIC Bank also started offering this service. In terms of spot trading, by 2005, two major categories had been formed: transactions between RMB and foreign currencies, and transactions between foreign currencies. The latter no longer required the involvement of overseas banks and could be completed in the interbank foreign exchange market. Moreover, more foreign currencies were included in China's foreign exchange trading market, enriching the variety of tradable foreign currencies with the inclusion of currencies such as the Japanese yen and the Euro.

Since 2005, China's foreign exchange market has witnessed a significant increase in trading instruments. The foreign exchange reform in 2005 greatly promoted the development of China's foreign exchange trading market. Up to now, China's foreign exchange market has formed four types of foreign exchange trading instruments: spot trading, forward trading, swap trading, and foreign exchange options innovation. In terms of spot foreign exchange trading, the range of currencies for RMB exchange with foreign currencies has been further expanded. As of March 2018, a total of 24 currencies, including the US dollar, Japanese yen, and Euro, are available for enterprises, individuals, and interbank transactions for buying and selling foreign exchange. Meanwhile, complete services are provided for interbank transactions, bank counters, and the "Forex Reserve" platform. Their weights in the currency basket referencing RMB exchange rate are shown in Table 10.4.

In terms of forward foreign exchange trading, PBOC continuously expanded the interbank forward exchange settlement and sale services, introducing term varieties such as 1 week (1 W), 1 month (1 M), 3 months (3 M), 6 months (6 M), 9 months (9 M), and 1 year (1 Y). In the bank counter market, China offers two types of forward trading, fixed delivery date and spot trading, which essentially meet the needs of individuals and businesses. However, among the four types of trading varieties, forward trading has the smallest trading volume.

In terms of foreign exchange swap trading, on April 24, 2006, the domestic interbank foreign exchange market officially launched RMB foreign exchange swap transactions. Since then, this business has been continuously expanded, with a significant increase in transaction volume. By early 2018, swap transactions accounted for the largest share among the four types of trading varieties. PBOC also utilizes currency swaps as a monetary policy tool, significantly expanding the scope of open market operations to mitigate interest rate and exchange rate risks.

Regarding foreign exchange options trading, PBOC approved the launch of foreign exchange options trading in the interbank foreign exchange market in January 2011. On April 1 of the same year, RMB foreign exchange options trading was officially introduced in the interbank RMB foreign exchange market. On December 1 of the same year, the State Administration of Foreign Exchange opened the "RMB Foreign Exchange Options Portfolio" business. Subsequently, the foreign exchange options trading business continued to develop, and by January 2018, RMB-denominated foreign exchange transactions had experienced rapid growth, as shown in Table 10.5.

Table 10.4 Weightings of the "a basket of currency" referenced in the renminbi exchange rate index as of the beginning of 2018

Currency	Weight
USD	0.2240
EUR	0.1634
JPY	0.1153
HKD	0.0428
GBP	0.0316
AUD	0.0440
NZD	0.0044
SGD	0.0321
CHF	0.0171
CAD	0.0215
MYR	0.0375
RUB	0.0263
THB	0.0291
ZAR	0.0178
KRW	0.1077
AED	0.0187
SAR	0.0199
HUF	0.0031
PLN	0.0066
DKK	0.0040
SEK	0.0052
NOK	0.0027
TRY	0.0083
MXN	0.0169

B. Participants in the Foreign Exchange Market

Before 1984, there was no strictly defined foreign exchange market in China. The limited foreign exchange and trading business was mainly handled by the Bank of China, and there were no bank counter foreign exchange retail services for enterprises and individuals. Subsequently, with the emergence of China's foreign exchange adjustment market, the participants in China's foreign exchange market gradually increased.

In 1985, the Trust Department of the Shanghai Branch of the Bank of China pioneered the domestic corporate foreign exchange quota adjustment business. In early 1986, this business was transferred to the Shanghai Branch of SAFE. In November, the Shanghai Branch of SAFE began handling foreign exchange adjustment business between foreign enterprises. At the beginning of 1988, local foreign exchange adjustment business was established in coastal provinces where foreign exchange was scarce, operated by the branches of PBOC. Subsequently, with the

Table 10.5 Foreign exchange market trading volume in China, January 2018

Trading instruments	Trading volume/billion yuan
• Spot	54,319
Bank customer market	18,377
Interbank foreign exchange market	35,942
• Forward market	3588
Bank customer market	2946
Interbank foreign exchange market	642
• Foreign exchange and currency swaps	83,625
Bank customer market	463
Interbank foreign exchange market	83,162
• Options	4022
Bank customer market	1204
Interbank foreign exchange market	2818
• Total	145,554
Therein: Bank customer market	22,990
Interbank foreign exchange market	122,564
• Therein: spot	54,319
Foreign exchange and currency swaps	83,625
Options	4021
Forward market	3588

Data source Foreign exchange trading situation in China 2018

establishment of foreign exchange trading centers and adjustment markets, enterprises gradually became the main participants in China's foreign exchange adjustment market, with banks acting as brokers. All foreign exchange transactions had to be approved by SAFE based on the sequence of foreign exchange adjustment use quotas before they could be adjusted. Foreign exchange adjustment could only be allocated by the state to central ministries and commissions, as well as provinces, autonomous regions, and municipalities according to the plan. It could not be uniformly allocated nationwide. The decentralized foreign exchange adjustment markets across the country were also organized based on administrative regions. If there was a shortage of foreign exchange in a certain region, it could not be adjusted nationwide. Even if enterprises selling foreign exchange had quotas for retained foreign exchange, the enterprises buying foreign exchange quotas might not necessarily receive the actual amount of foreign currency they needed in a timely manner.[4] At that time, the foreign exchange adjustment market operated on a membership system, only allowing member trading and accepting non-member entrusted foreign exchange transactions. Clearly, the main participants in the foreign exchange market

[4] QI Qun. *Development and Innovation of China's Money Market*, Law Press, 2012: 93.

were considered from the perspectives of earning and using foreign exchange, without involving aspects such as hedging foreign exchange risks.

With the reform of the foreign exchange management system in 1994, China abolished the previous system of foreign exchange retention and surrender, and implemented the system of banks conducting foreign exchange transactions with enterprises. A nationwide unified and standardized interbank foreign exchange market was established. On April 4th, the interbank foreign exchange market officially commenced operation, marking a shift from the previous practice where enterprises were the main players in the foreign exchange adjustment market to banks becoming the main participants in China's foreign exchange market. FETC served as the intermediary institution for interbank foreign exchange transactions, connecting decentralized centers across the country. Through reform and development, the participants in China's foreign exchange market gradually expanded, primarily through bank counters, interbank foreign exchange markets, and FX trading platforms (individual foreign exchange spot trading markets). Bank counters mainly catered to RMB and foreign currency transactions for non-financial institutions and individuals, and the number of banks providing such services has increased and expanded to various types of banking institutions across China. The interbank foreign exchange market served transactions between financial institutions and operates under a membership system, covering state-owned banks, joint-stock commercial banks, and policy banks entirely, and partially covering city commercial banks, foreign banks, rural credit cooperatives, non-bank financial institutions, as well as a few non-financial institutions like China National Chemical Corporation (ChemChina) and Huawei. The number of participants in financial derivative products in the foreign exchange market has gradually increased with the development of the economy, as shown in Table 10.6.

With the expansion of operations, PBOC and SAFE approved the participation of overseas financial institutions such as the National Bank of Austria, the Bank of Greece, the Central Bank of Jordan, the National Bank of Pakistan, the Central Bank

Table 10.6 Changes in the number of members in China's foreign exchange market since 2011 (unit: institutions)

Year	Spot market	Forward market	Foreign exchange swap	Currency swap	Option market
2011	318	73	71	–	27
2012	353	79	79	–	31
2013	405	88	87	80	33
2014	465	98	97	84	39
2015	518	123	123	99	61
2016	582	154	154	127	84
2017	645	194	192	163	116

Data source Compiled from the quarterly monetary policy implementation reports since 2011, http://www.pbc.gov.cn/zhengcehuobisi/125207/125227/index.html

of Iraq, the Central Bank of Malaysia, the Reserve Bank of India, the Bank of Korea, the Monetary Authority of Singapore, the Bank of Indonesia, the Bank of Thailand, the Reserve Bank of Australia, the National Bank of Hungary, and the Hong Kong Monetary Authority in China's interbank foreign exchange transactions, thereby greatly promoting the openness of China's foreign exchange market. The Foreign Exchange Trading System is a tool for banks to accept commissions from individual customers to engage in foreign exchange trading; individuals cannot directly engage in foreign exchange trading and can only buy and sell foreign exchange through designated banks to obtain arbitrage profits.

As the degree of internationalization of RMB continues to increase and the level of openness of the foreign exchange market expands, PBOC and SAFE will undoubtedly permit more eligible financial institutions, non-financial institutions, individuals, etc., to participate in foreign exchange market transactions.

Chapter 11
The Rise and Standardized Development of Internet Finance

In 2013, the rapid development of internet finance in China gave rise to the "Catfish Effect" in the country's financial sector, triggering a wave of innovation in the industry. It expanded the scope of financial services, extended the financial industry chain, and rapidly enhanced the competitiveness of China's financial industry. However, the emergence of internet finance on the basis of the "three nos" (no entry threshold, no industry standards, no relevant regulatory controls) also brought significant risks. Incidents such as defaults, disappearances, and fraud became rampant, affecting and disrupting the normal development order of China's financial industry and harming the rights of numerous investors. In response, regulatory bodies such as the People's Bank of China (PBOC) continuously explored measures to regulate the development of internet finance. They introduced various measures to lay the foundation for the increasingly standardized and healthy development of internet finance.

11.1 Development of Internet Finance

Originating from developed countries, internet finance had been introduced to China early on, and various models of internet finance were established in response. However, it wasn't until 2013 that China's internet finance exhibited a rapid development trend. As of now, China's internet finance has taken a leading position over other countries in terms of overall scale and across multiple sectors. The development of China's internet finance is increasingly integrated into the practical development of the social economy, serving the growth of the real economy.

R. Lan, *The Financial Development of China*, Understanding China,
https://doi.org/10.1007/978-981-97-8273-4_11

11.1.1 Background of the Rise of Internet Finance

The initial stages of China's internet finance, much like developed countries, originated from the informatization of modern finance. However, it wasn't until the penetration of non-financial industries into the financial sector that China's internet finance drew attention from various sectors of society. It became a core driving force for financial innovation and the construction of an inclusive financial system. While the emergence of pure internet finance reflects some aspects of emulation from developed countries, its rise and rapid development are more attributable to China's unique economic ecosystem and socio-economic conditions.

A. Service Blind Spots in Modern Finance

As mentioned earlier, financial organizations in China have achieved significant development, forming a relatively complete financial system to date. However, influenced by long-term financial repression, the degree of development of financial organizations is not high, financial markets lack refinement, financial services are limited, there are few financial products, and the coverage of financial institutions is small. There are many obvious blind spots in financial services. The "Pareto Principle" is showing an expanding trend without limits, urgently requiring new financial organizations and technologies to meet or fill various gaps left by modern financial organizations.

Firstly, there are temporal and spatial blind spots in financial services. Modern financial organizations such as banks, insurance, and securities have limitations in terms of working hours, making it difficult to meet financial needs beyond regular working hours or those requiring substantial amounts. Spatially, the coverage of financial organization branches is limited, and vast rural and economically underdeveloped areas often cannot access necessary formal financial services. In the 1990s, during the commercialization reform of state-owned banks in China, state-owned commercial banks massively withdrew from rural financial markets. From the early 1999 to the end of 2002, the net reduction in personnel at the Industrial and Commercial Bank of China (ICBC) was 161,600, and during the same period, the net reduction in the number of branches of the Agricultural Bank of China (ABC) was 19,200. Subsequently, influenced by the level of economic development, state-owned commercial banks reestablished branches in rural areas, but their role was often not injecting funds into rural areas. Instead, they absorbed deposits in rural and economically backward areas, transferring funds to regions with better economic development, such as cities. Although informal finance and traditional financial organizations are less restricted by time factors and can generally respond to needs promptly, their spatial service coverage is extremely limited. Regarding clients, they are often confined to certain familiar groups and cannot cover all industries and the general population. In terms of funds, the amounts are usually small and often cannot meet the requirements of the target groups. Regarding interest rates, the rates charged by these financial organizations are generally higher than the interest rates set by the government, easily leading to social events.

Secondly, there are blind spots in the clientele of financial services. Due to the underdevelopment of the financial market and a relatively limited range of financing methods, direct financing accounts for a very low proportion, with indirect financing through financial organizations like banks being the main source of financing in China. "Banks have always played a dominant role in China's financial system, and the allocation of social funds is mainly through indirect financing.... In 2007, direct financing through forms such as government bonds, corporate bonds, and stocks accounted for 21.3% of the total social financing."[1] The proportion of direct financing subsequently fluctuated significantly due to factors such as the subprime crisis, reaching only 16% by 2012. Indirect financing through banks became the main way for the allocation of social funds. In terms of fund allocation, funds from financial organizations such as banks mainly flow to state-owned enterprises, collective enterprises, large and medium-sized private enterprises, and specific objects supported by policies, showing significant imbalances in the allocation of financial resources. From 2000 to 2007, in China's non-state-owned manufacturing industry, enterprises with total sales and employment numbers exceeding 90% of the industry's total were those with a scale below 20 million yuan. However, only 20% of these enterprises obtained bank loans. In terms of actual interest rates, state-owned enterprises only needed to pay a financing rate of 1.6%, while private enterprises had to pay a fund usage rate as high as 5.4%.[2] "Micro and small enterprises account for the absolute majority of market entities. As of the end of 2013, the total number of various types of enterprises nationwide was 15.2784 million, of which micro and small enterprises accounted for 11.6987 million, or 76.57% of the total number of enterprises."[3] "Small and micro enterprises create final product and service values equivalent to 60% of the total Gross Domestic Product (GDP), contribute 50% of the national tax revenue, complete 65% of invention patents, and develop more than 80% of new products."[4] However, these small and micro enterprises, which play a crucial role in the Chinese economy, are unable to access corresponding services from modern finance. The preference of modern financial organizations for specific sectors, groups, and policy-focused objects naturally makes it difficult for them to cater to small and micro enterprises and the low-to middle-income population. Consequently, there are evident blind spots in financial services in terms of clientele.

Thirdly, there are operational service challenges for modern financial organizations. With the rapid development of the socio-economic environment, the acceleration of people's lifestyles, and the fast flow of social information, there are numerous new demands for fund circulation. People require shortened financing times and

---

[1] ZHANG Jie. *Performance of China's Rural Financial System Adjustment: A Perspective of Financial Demand*, Renmin University of China Press, 2007: 7.

[2] LIU Xiaoxuan, ZHOU Xiaoyan. "An Examination of the Allocation Relationship Between Financial Resources and the Real Economy—Also on the Causes of Economic Structural Imbalance", Financial Research, 2011, Issue 2.

[3] State Administration for Industry and Commerce. "Report on the Development of Small and Micro Enterprises Nationwide".

[4] WANG Liangliang. *Development of Internet Finance: A Study on the Impact on Traditional Financial Industry*, China Financial Publishing House, 2016: 116.

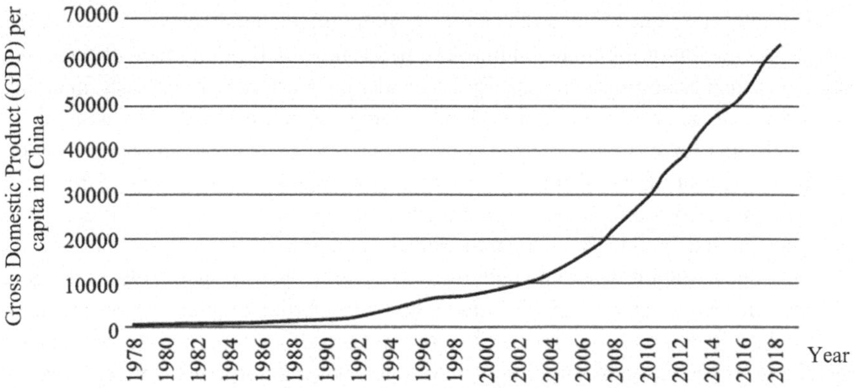

Fig. 11.1 Changes in China's per capita GDP from 1978 to 2018[5]

simplified procedures. The financing procedures of modern financial organizations are complex, requiring various proofs and application forms. In some cases, fund seekers may even need to rely on personal connections to provide a certain percentage of kickbacks for financing. On the other hand, banks, driven by the need for fund security, may require fund seekers to have certain assets as collateral or individuals with certain assets to provide guarantees. Such complex procedures and lengthy processes naturally increase the costs for fund seekers in terms of time and other aspects, making it difficult for many people in need of funds to obtain necessary financial services from modern financial organizations.

B. A Financial Service Blind Spot Arising from the Increase in People's Income

Since the reform and opening up, China's economy has maintained a high-speed growth for 35 years, with an average annual growth rate exceeding 9%. China's GDP increased from 367.87 billion yuan in 1978 to 90.03 trillion yuan in 2018. Per capita GDP in China rose from 385 yuan in 1978 to 64,643.5 yuan in 2018. The changes inper capita GDP in China from 1978 to 2017 are shown in Fig. 11.1.

With the significant increase in China's per capita GDP, household savings in China surpassed 10 trillion yuan in September 2003, reached 20 trillion yuan in August 2008, exceeded 30 trillion yuan in December 2010, and reached 40 trillion yuan in January 2013. Faced with rapidly growing household deposits, the Chinese government proposed in 2007 to allow the general public to enjoy wealth-based returns. However, the existing wealth preservation and appreciation measures in the financial industry are significantly asymmetric to the financial management needs of the general public. On one hand, the interest income from bank deposits is very low, making it difficult to ensure the acquisition of wealth-based returns for the general public. On the other hand, the diverse financial management provided by modern finance faces extremely high financial management thresholds, excluding the vast

[5] According to the data from the website of the National Bureau of Statistics of the People's Republic of China over the years.

majority of the public from the scope of existing financial management, preventing a growing number of people with financial management needs from obtaining necessary investment and financial management services. "The investment channels for residents in our country are relatively narrow, with low returns. The interest rate on bank time deposits is basically between 3 and 5%, while the return on bank wealth management products is basically between 4 and 8%. Trust product returns are slightly higher, but the required initial capital is relatively large."[6] In such a context, the financial management needs of middle- and low-income people urgently require new financial service organizations and technologies to meet them.

C. The Potential for Financial Breakthroughs Triggered by the Development of Information Technology

Since the mid-twentieth century, breakthrough developments in information technologies such as the Internet, Internet of Things, big data, cloud computing, blockchain, artificial intelligence, and more have completely transformed the ways of communication between different regions. In theory, they have addressed the issue of asymmetry in financial information, enabling a significant enhancement of modern investment methods, which were previously reliant on manual operations, property collateral, and pledging. The interactions, once confined to tangible spaces, are gradually shifting towards more diverse trends in virtual spaces. Simultaneously, the cross-border operation of the financial industry through information technology has become possible, greatly improving the existing financial service methods, scope, and concepts. Specific aspects include the following.

Firstly, it completely resolves the temporal and spatial constraints between financial supply and demand. With the increasing popularity of personal computers, smartphones, the emergence and promotion of the Internet and cloud space, and especially the advancement of financial informatization since the 1990s, the temporal and spatial limitations between financial supply and demand have gradually dissolved. At the same time, the evolution of tools such as big data and cloud computing has, to a certain extent, overcome the hard constraints of information asymmetry between existing financial organizations and financial demand subjects. Financial organizations can rely on various data left by increasingly developed social networks, search engines, online shopping, the Internet of Things, and more to predict the credibility and preferences of the demanders. This greatly changes the past ways of assessing the honesty of demanders based on the amount of assets, etc.

Secondly, the development of virtual network spaces under mobile communication-internet technology. The transition from wired to wireless communication, rapid updates in technologies such as smartphones and mobile computers, better cater to the trend of personalized development for the public. The development of Internet technology "has changed the business operations of enterprises, making every aspect of production, distribution, exchange, and consumption dependent on network support. Whether it is the coordination and configuration of internal

---

[6] CHEN Yong. *Research Report on China's Internet Finance (2015)*, China Economic Publishing House, 2015: 160.

resources or the acquisition and integration of external information, the network provides a convenient and effective platform."[7] The virtual platform provided by the network, combined with the connectivity of technologies such as mobile communication, significantly expands the space for human interactions. It breaks the situation of relying on tangible spaces with physical characteristics in the past, providing necessary conditions for modern finance to reduce costs related to manual labor and physical locations while extending the effective space for financial services.

Thirdly, the development of technologies such as social networks, search engines, big data (including small data), cloud computing, and biometric recognition has improved the situation of information asymmetry and the imperfect credit system. Various social networks, e-commerce platforms, and other platforms developed based on the internet and communication technologies have allowed for the preservation of various types of previously unstructured texts and behavioral data that couldn't be retained before. The development of storage technologies in various cloud formats has allowed various types of small and big data to be formed. Massive amounts of data deeply cover relationships between people, emotions, and experiences of different groups, presenting in a more three-dimensional and vivid collection of data. In addition to the accumulated data from traditional financial institutions, telecoms, and industrial and commercial enterprises, companies like Alibaba, Tencent, JD.com, Baidu, etc., have experienced explosive growth in data. Leveraging search engines, cloud computing, and other methods, they integrate and refine scattered data, transforming it into various useful resources. This provides necessary technological support for credit investigations, personalized customization, and predictions of consumption preferences for different groups and companies. Currently, PBOC's credit system has reached a considerable scale. The establishment of the Hundred Credit Information Co., Ltd., recognized by PBOC in February 2018, has significantly promoted the construction of China's credit system, creating conditions for resolving the issue of information asymmetry in existing financial activities.

Fourthly, the development of Internet of Things, Artificial Intelligence, and their combination with the internet make everything possible. The development of internet technology, driven by the spirit of "openness, equality, collaboration, and sharing," has completely transformed the ways of information sharing and interaction through the "Internet+" approach, causing disruptive impacts on traditional industries. The construction of the Internet of Things on the basis of the internet utilizes communication technology to connect sensors, controllers, machines, personnel, and objects in new ways, achieving connections between people and things, and things with things. Following agreed protocols, it facilitates information exchange and communication, realizing the intelligent identification, positioning, tracking, monitoring, and management of objects. The development of the Internet of Things not only achieves sharing but also brings about personalization, interactivity, and entertainment.

[7] CHEN Huihui. *Research on Technological Innovation and Competitive Strategy in Network Externality Markets*. Economic Management Press, 2015: 1.

Clearly, with the development of the above technologies, industry boundaries are becoming increasingly blurred, and the boundaries between online and offline financial services are also becoming unclear. As the integration between technology and finance becomes more harmonious, traditional deposit and payment methods will be changed. Technology companies, leveraging their keen sense of market opportunities, have designed and provided products and services that replace existing financial organizations such as banks, insurance, and securities. Currently, large technology companies including Baidu, Tencent, Sina, NetEase, and Toutiao, as well as e-commerce enterprises or platforms like Alibaba, JD.com, Meituan, and Didi, are actively promoting the rise of internet finance in China.

11.1.2 Overview of the Development of Internet Finance[8]

Under the combined influence of the aforementioned factors, China's internet finance experienced a period of dormancy for a long time and rapidly rose in 2013. By 2018, China's internet finance had already surpassed international levels in areas such as third-party payments (online payments), online lending, blockchain, and more. The increasing standardization of internet finance, coupled with the construction of an inclusive financial system driven by it, to some extent alleviated "difficult financing" and partially addressed the issue of "expensive financing".

A. Development Status of Internet Finance

Internet finance initially originated from the informatization of modern financial organizations. In the late 1980s and 1990s, some pure internet finance emerged in developed countries such as the UK and the US, involving non-financial industries engaging in financial operations. This formed various models in addition to the "finance + internet" model. The earliest occurrences of various models of pure internet finance are shown in Table 11.1.

Although these pure internet finance models quickly spread to China after emerging in developed countries in Europe and the United States, and corresponding models were established in China, before 2013, except for a certain level of development in internet payments, other models did not generate significant social responses. The occurrence of pure internet finance models in China is shown in Table 11.2.

Since 2013, China's economic growth rate has shifted from high-speed to medium–high-speed, entering a new normal of economic development. Issues accumulated during the long period of high-speed growth have become more pronounced. Particularly in the financial sector, the "McMillan gap" faced by small and medium-sized enterprises has become increasingly severe. The problem of "difficulty in financing" in areas lacking modern financial coverage, such as suburban and rural

[8] LAN Rixu. "Reflections on the Impact of the Development of the Internet Finance Industry on China's Industrial Restructuring," *Research on Industry and the History of Science and Technology*, 2017, Issue 2.

Table 11.1 Statistics on the earliest occurrences of various models in pure internet finance

Internet financial models	Name	Year of origin	Country of origin
P2P	Zopa	2005	United Kingdom
Crowdfunding	ArtistShare	2001	The United States
Online payment	PayPal	1999	The United States
Internet insurance	InsWeb	1995	The United States
Internet banking	SFNB	1995	The United States
Internet securities	E* TRADE	1982	The United States
Internet wealth management	Mint	2007	The United States

Table 11.2 Statistics on the occurrence of pure internet financial models in China

Internet finance name	Internet finance company or product name	First appearance time
Internet payment	PayEase	1999
P2P	CreditEase	June, 2005
Crowdfunding	Demohour	April, 2011
Pure internet bank	Qianhai WeBank	January 18, 2015
Internet insurance	Zhong'an Online Property Insurance Company*	February, 2013
Internet securities	China Huarong Trust Investment Corporation Zhanjiang Branch**	1997
Internet wealth management	Alibaba's Yu'E Bao	2013

Note *The first third-party insurance website in China appeared in 1997, named China insurance information network. In March 2000, the e-commerce insurance website "Wang Xian Wang" introduced the first online insurance purchasing function. The true emergence of an Internet insurance company should be attributed to Zhong'an Online Property Insurance Company
**China was the first country to implement the use of microcomputer local area networks to process the core business of stock exchanges

regions, has become more prominent. Many people, having experienced long-term economic growth, have accumulated some wealth. However, to gain wealth returns, they must confront the high financial thresholds and low interest yields of bank deposits. Against this backdrop, "...leveraging information technology, on one hand, has led the informatization of modern financial organizations, promoting the internetization of finance. On the other hand, the existing financial blind spots and the current state of 'difficulty in financing' have driven various information technologies into the financial field, leading to the internetization of finance."[9] In 2013, the innovative act of Alibaba's Yu'E Bao, a product developed in collaboration with Tianhong Fund, marked the explosive growth of China's pure internet financial business. From June 2013 when Yu'E Bao was introduced to February 26, 2014, its user base reached 81

[9] LAN Rixu. Changes in Financial Organizations at Home and Abroad: A Perspective Based on Market-Technology-Organization, Social Sciences Academic Press, 2016: 203.

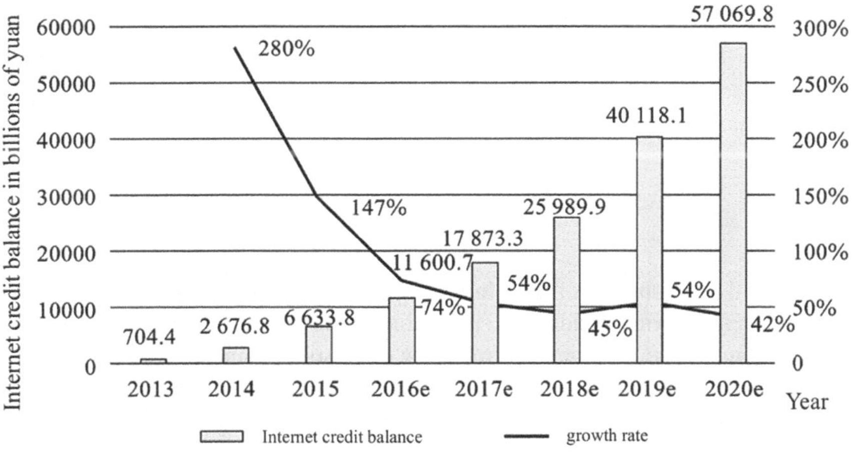

Fig. 11.2 Changes in China's internet credit growth rate and credit balance since 2013[10]

million, with funds exceeding 5 trillion yuan. The user base surpassed the effective number of accounts in the Shanghai and Shenzhen stock markets, which had a development history of 23 years, in just over half a year. Tianhong Fund, partnering with Yu'E Bao, quickly rose from an unknown small fund company to a leader in the fund industry in a little over half a year. The behavior of Yu'E Bao quickly triggered the "Catfish Effect" across various sectors. The explosive growth of money market funds has surged, reaching 5 trillion yuan by June 2017, presenting a significant challenge to the banking industry. In 2012, Alibaba's Jack Ma, Tencent's Pony Ma, and Ping An's Ma Mingzhe jointly proposed the establishment of "Zhong'an Online Property Insurance Co., Ltd." which was approved by the China Insurance Regulatory Commission (CIRC) In February 2013, marking the beginning of the development of internet insurance. The joint venture of these three influential figures in the business world, engaging in insurance, created a sensation in the financial industry. Pure internet financial models centered around P2P lending and crowdfunding rapidly rose, and internet credit, as shown in Fig. 11.2, has grown rapidly since 2013.

Six models, including internet payments, online lending, equity crowdfunding, internet insurance, internet wealth management, and internet consumer finance, all experienced explosive development. By early 2016, there were 270 companies with internet payment licenses, 2959 P2P platforms, and 338 crowdfunding platforms with 186 focused on equity crowdfunding. By the end of 2016, the four major internet finance giants centered around "BATJ" (Baidu Finance, Ant Financial, Tencent, JD Finance) not only penetrated almost all financial business areas, obtained necessary financial licenses, but also surpassed any modern financial organization in terms of funds and user numbers (For instance, the valuation of China's largest bank, Industrial and Commercial Bank of China, was 47.8 billion USD in 2017 with 215 million online banking users) (see Table 11.3).

[10] The data is sourced from iResearch Institute.

Table 11.3 Estimated valuation and number of verified users for "BATJ" at the end of 2016

Name	Strength valuation/USD (billion)	Number of verified users (million)
Baidu finance	–	90
Ant financial	75	500
Tencent	30	400
JD finance	46.65	100

The rapid development of pure Internet financial enterprises has not only filled many financial service blind spots, promoting a wave of financial innovation but has also changed the development trajectory of existing financial enterprises. It has accelerated the pace of online and informational transformation for existing financial enterprises, showcasing a trend of rapid convergence between the two. As of June 2017, four state-owned commercial banks and the four Internet giants have initiated collaborations: China Construction Bank with Alibaba, Industrial and Commercial Bank of China with JD.com, Agricultural Bank of China with Baidu, and Bank of China with Tencent. These collaborations aim to achieve new breakthroughs in financial technology. Additionally, all four state-owned commercial banks have established inclusive finance service departments in June, significantly advancing the construction of China's inclusive finance system.

Looking at the rise of Internet finance in China, its size and scale have surpassed those of any developed country within a short period. To a certain extent and within a certain scope, it has overcome various issues related to financial blind spots caused by long-term economic development and the limitations of modern finance. However, factors such as insufficient market refinement in the financial sector and significant differences in the development levels of existing financial institutions have resulted in relatively high service costs for financial services provided to middle and lower-income individuals and small and medium-sized enterprises. This situation falls short of completely addressing the issues of "difficulty in financing" and "expensive financing." Despite the impact of Internet finance on the modern financial system, existing financial institutions have quickly absorbed many conveniences and advantages brought by pure Internet finance, leading to their integration with pure Internet finance. This integration has given rise to innovative formats that lower service costs, enhance service efficiency, and cover financial blind spots. A notable example is how banks, leveraging online platforms, have established numerous low-interest lending channels. The emergence of "bottom-line" pure Internet financial companies and the widespread development of supply chain finance and consumer finance have significantly propelled the deepening development of China's financial industry. In the field of information technology application and certain technological innovations related to Internet finance, China has surpassed developed countries, possessing international competitiveness. Thus, China has entered a new stage of "Chinese creation" in the field of Internet finance.

B. Regulatory Development of Internet Finance

The development of China's Internet finance industry initially took place under the conditions of the "three nos". Its rapid growth has had a significant impact on China's modern financial industry, existing regulatory methods, and institutions, while also bringing profound effects to various other sectors in society. This has led to the emergence of numerous new business models. The "Double Innovation" (mass entrepreneurship and innovation) policy promoted by the State Council has facilitated a wave of innovation in China's economic development. However, lacking necessary entry thresholds, industry standards, and legal norms, the development of Internet finance itself has brought about various issues. Some Internet finance companies are of uneven quality, engaging in illegal and irregular activities under the guise of Internet finance. Large-scale events such as mass defaults, runs, closures, and cleanups have occurred, impacting the normal operations of China's financial industry and harming the interests of investors and consumers.

In this context, the development of Internet finance in China has sparked widespread debates in society. Represented by views from figures like Jack Ma, there is a belief that "if banks do not change, then we will change banks," questioning whether Internet finance will overturn traditional finance and turn banks into "dinosaurs of the twenty-first century." On the other hand, commentators like Niu Wenxin, Chief Commentator of CCTV Finance Channel, argue that products like Yu'E Bao are "vampires," significantly increasing the operating costs of the real economy and suggesting that they should be banned. The State Council and various government departments at different levels generally acknowledge the development trend of Internet finance. They believe that, under prudent and innovative regulation, Internet finance should be given certain space for innovation and development. Plans for the innovative development of Internet finance have been included in the State Council government work reports since 2014 (see Table 11.4). This reflects the government's approach of openness, tolerance, gradual regulation, departing from the "one-size-fits-all" management style prevalent in the 1980s and 1990s.

Table 11.4 Content related to internet finance in the government work reports of the state council from 2014 to 2018

Year	Content related to internet finance
2014	Promoting the healthy development of internet finance and improving the coordination mechanism of financial regulation
2015	The rise of internet finance has emerged as a new force, promoting the healthy development of internet finance
2016	Regulating the development of internet finance
2017	be highly vigilant against the accumulated risks of internet finance and other related areas
2018	Strengthen financial supervision, coordinate comprehensively, improve the supervision of shadow banking, internet finance, financial holding companies, and further enhance financial regulatory measures

Certainly, PBOC has not completely allowed the unrestricted development of Internet finance. Instead, it has implemented different regulatory measures based on the actual development status of various areas or models within Internet finance. For the early and deeply penetrated third-party payment sector, the PBOC took formal regulatory actions by issuing the "Administrative Measures for Non-Financial Institutions Providing Payment Services" in June 2010. According to the regulations, non-financial institutions providing payment services are required to obtain a payment business license. September 1, 2011, was the final deadline for third-party payment institutions to obtain licenses. Payment enterprises that failed to obtain the license by this date were not allowed to continue engaging in payment services. Subsequently, based on the actual situations of enterprises, PBOC issued payment licenses to 271 companies. During this period, PBOC also rectified and reorganized payment enterprises that did not meet regulatory requirements. As of September 1, 2017, 24 companies had their payment licenses revoked, and other non-compliant companies were fined or subjected to other penalties. Additionally, for unlicensed and unauthorized payment enterprises, the "Measures for Investigating and Dealing with Unlicensed and Unauthorized Operations" came into effect on October 1, 2017, to regulate the healthy and continuous development of the third-party payment industry. In 2016, the Chinese government proposed establishing a unified non-bank payment institution network payment clearing platform (referred to as NetsUnion). In early 2017, it received approval from the State Administration for Industry and Commerce. On June 30, NetsUnion officially started to allow payment institutions to connect, with Tencent's Financial Cloud being the first to connect, and other payment institutions connecting after a 1-year transition period. The establishment of NetsUnion provided payment institutions with a unified fund clearing service, corrected violations by payment institutions engaged in cross-bank clearing business, changed the current situation where payment institutions had multiple connections with banks to conduct business, supported payment institutions in one-point access platform transactions, saved connection costs, improved clearing efficiency, and facilitated real-time monitoring of the flow of social funds by regulatory authorities to ensure the safety of customer funds. Simultaneously, NetsUnion accelerated the formulation of unified QR code payment standards to address the relative chaos in QR code standards among payment enterprises. Through these robust measures, the Internet payment industry achieved regulated and orderly development.

For other areas or models within Internet finance, based on continuous tracking and investigation, PBOC, along with the China Banking Regulatory Commission (CBRC), China Securities Regulatory Commission (CSRC), Ministry of Public Security, Ministry of Industry and Information Technology, Ministry of Finance, State Administration for Industry and Commerce, Legislative Affairs Office of the State Council, and the Cyberspace Administration of China, jointly issued the "Guiding Opinions on Promoting the Healthy Development of Internet Finance" on July 18, 2015. This document defined the concept of Internet finance and specified the regulatory authorities responsible for overseeing each model (refer to Table 11.5).

Table 11.5 Regulatory attribution of internet finance models

Internet finance models	Regulatory attribution of internet financial models
Internet payment	PBOC
Peer-to-peer lending (P2P) and microfinance	CBRC
Internet trust and internet consumer finance	
Equity crowdfunding	CSRC
Internet fund sales	
Internet insurance	China insurance regulatory commission (CIRC)

Subsequently, various regions nationwide formulated and issued different types of regulatory rules in accordance with regulatory requirements. National regulatory authorities responsible for various aspects of Internet finance also successively introduced detailed nationwide regulatory guidelines, as shown in Table 11.6.

Meanwhile, the China Internet Finance Association, jointly established by PBOC, CBRC, Payment and Clearing Association of China, CSRC, and others, was founded in Shanghai on March 25, 2016. Subsequently, it introduced a series of documents, including the "Charter of the China Internet Finance Association," "Self-Discipline Convention for Members of the China Internet Finance Association," "Initiative for the Healthy Development of the Internet Finance Industry," "Management Measures for Members of the China Internet Finance Association," and "Management Measures for Self-Discipline and Punishment of the China Internet Finance Association," to regulate the development of Internet finance. At the same time, various levels of financial regulatory authorities in China conducted normative rectification for different models of Internet finance, providing them with a certain transition period. During this period, the licensing system was implemented for online small-scale lending. By May 26, 2017, China had established 129 online small-scale lending companies, with 127 of them obtaining official licenses, and the remaining two had been filed with local regulatory authorities.

Faced with the indiscriminate nature of Internet financial enterprises and the increasing trend of risks, the government work report during the two sessions in 2017 departed from the previous encouraging approach and explicitly warned about the risks of Internet finance. In July, the Fifth National Financial Work Conference

Table 11.6 Regulatory rules for different models of internet finance in China

Time	Regulatory rules for internet finance models
December 2014	Draft for solicitation of opinions on administrative measures for private equity crowdfunding financing (Trial)
July 2015	Interim measures for the supervision of internet insurance business
August 2015	Notice on special inspections of institutions conducting equity financing activities through the internet
August 2016	Interim measures for the management of business activities of online lending information intermediaries

was held, where President Xi Jinping proposed strengthening financial regulation, transforming the regulatory approach from prudent supervision to functional and behavioral supervision, and ensuring that finance returns to its essence of serving the real economy. The 19th National Congress of the Communist Party of China in October emphasized "guarding against the occurrence of systemic financial risks." In December 2017, the leading group office for the special rectification of Internet financial risks and the special rectification of P2P online lending risks officially issued a "Notice on Standardizing and Rectifying the Cash Loan Business," specifying coordinated regulation and launching cleanup and rectification of online small-scale lending. The government work report in 2018 explicitly stated the need to strengthen regulation and improve the regulatory system for Internet finance. In response, PBOC, CBRC, CSRC, and CIRC successively enhanced supervision and management of various models of Internet finance to promote its sustainable development.

Clearly, experiencing rapid development over the past 3 years since 2013, starting from July 2015, China's Internet finance industry entered a stage of standardized development, promoting the convergence and healthy development of the "finance + internet" and "internet + finance" models. During this period, companies engaged in "internet + finance," such as Ant Finance and JD Finance, have increasingly clarified their positioning, shifting their development focus from fintech to tech-based finance. While maintaining various financial licenses, they are returning various financial services to traditional financial institutions like banks. These companies are providing a variety of intelligent tech services to financial institutions.

11.1.3 Characteristics of Internet Finance

The rise and rapid development of Internet finance undoubtedly bring new impetus to the development of China's financial industry. In comparison with traditional finance, it is evident that the essence of Internet finance, while still financial in nature, possesses distinctive features.

A. Blurred Industry Boundaries

Before the emergence of Internet finance, within the Chinese traditional financial industry—under the regulatory framework of segmented operations and supervision—the boundaries between financial organizations and financial markets were clear-cut. The financial industry had minimal intersections with other sectors in society, apart from activities like fund transfers. However, the emergence of various models in Internet finance and the continuous evolution of new models have disrupted the established order of traditional finance, altering the operational models and regulatory methods of the original financial industry. This has progressively blurred the boundaries between different financial businesses, shattered the separation of financial industry operations from other sectors, leading Xie Ping to describe Internet finance as a third financial operating mechanism that is distinct from both indirect financing by commercial banks and direct financing through capital markets. It is often referred to as the "Internet direct financing market" or "Internet financial model".[11] Internet finance not only blurs the boundaries between various financing systems within the financial industry but also, through technological means, connects various financial business contents. Utilizing licensing methods, it operates in the form of financial groups engaging in nearly all financial businesses, providing all financial products. It pursues mixed operations, forming a complete financial ecosystem within the enterprise. Moreover, it bridges the gap between finance and other industries and markets. Although the existing models of Internet finance were incorporated into the regulatory framework in July 2015, its mixed operational approach has made it challenging for regulatory authorities to adapt. Therefore, during the 5th National Financial Work Conference in July 2017, Xi Jinping explicitly emphasized the need to strengthen financial regulation, making the prevention of systemic financial risks the bottom line. This involves accelerating the construction of relevant laws and regulations, improving the governance structure of financial institutions, enhancing the construction of macro-prudential management systems, and placing greater emphasis on behavioral supervision.[12] Clearly, the cross-industry operations of Internet finance have completely blurred the existing boundaries within the financial industry, accelerated integration with the real economy, and driven the transformation of China's financial regulatory approach. Subsequently, the establishment of the Financial Stability and Development Committee and the reform of financial regulatory institutions in March 2018 have responded to the increasing demand for blurred boundaries in financial development, gradually transitioning towards a mixed-ownership structure in regulatory systems, and driving the formation of a "large central bank" pattern.

B. Lower Transaction Costs

In the context of the convergence of new technologies with the financial industry, Internet finance has eliminated the temporal and spatial constraints and numerous service blind spots present in traditional finance. It caters to the broader demands of the general public and gradually achieves the goal of reducing transaction costs. Whether it is indirect financing institutions like banks or direct financing channels such as securities and bonds, high transaction costs exist, mainly including the profits, taxes, and salaries of financial institutions. For instance, in 2011, the profits of national banks and securities firms were approximately 1.1 trillion yuan, tax revenue was about 500 billion yuan, and employee salaries amounted to 1 trillion yuan.[13] At the same time, these institutions are unable to cover various social strata and industries, which often poses significant challenges to the supervision of the financial industry. The advent of modern information technology has significantly

[11] XIE Ping, ZOU Chuanwei. "A Study on Internet Financial Models," *Financial Research*. 2012, Issue 12.

[12] "Xi Jinping Emphasizes Serving the Real Economy, Preventing Financial Risks, Deepening Financial Reforms, and Promoting the Healthy Development of the Economy and Finance in a National Financial Work Conference".

[13] XIE Ping, ZOU Chuanwei. "A Study on Internet Financial Models," *Financial Research*. 2012, Issue 12.

reduced the degree of information asymmetry and uncertainty in modern finance, partially alleviating the dilemma of serving specific entities. Leveraging new information technologies such as search engines, big data, social networks, and cloud computing, Internet finance has greatly reduced transaction costs. In this model, the degree of information asymmetry in the market is extremely low, and the costs for parties involved in transactions, such as matching funds, terms, space, and risk sharing, are very low. Intermediaries like banks, securities firms, and exchanges play no role in this process. Issuance, trading of loans, stocks, bonds, and payments are conducted directly online, making Internet finance highly efficient and approaching a state of no financial intermediaries.[14] This is something that traditional and modern finance cannot achieve.

C. Inclusive Finance

The service blind spots and financial constraints in modern finance have created many gaps in China's financial service supply. In an effort to address these gaps, modern finance in China, under the leadership of government departments such as PBOC, has attempted to construct an inclusive finance model. However, based on their specific actions, the inclusive finance initiatives by modern finance have largely remained in the area of institutional outreach rather than truly achieving inclusive finance. Leveraging information technology, Internet finance incorporates the spirit of the "open, equal, collaborative, and sharing" ethos of the internet, making it more innovative. Through technologies like big data and cloud computing, it reduces information asymmetry, allowing those ignored by modern finance, such as lower-income populations, small and micro-enterprises, economically disadvantaged and remote areas, to access necessary financial services. In contrast to the banking sector's financial services, which tend to follow the "Pareto Principle" where 20% of customers receive 80% of the services, Internet finance targets a larger proportion of the "long tail," specifically the 80% of small and micro customers. The financial needs of these small and micro customers are often small and personalized, underserved by the traditional financial system. Internet finance, with its inherent advantages, efficiently caters to the personalized needs of users.[15] In its use of information technology, Internet finance gradually changes the transaction methods of modern finance, with institutions exhibiting characteristics of dematerialization and business detachment. This transformation influences people's financial habits, making Internet finance more accessible to the general public. It truly demonstrates inclusivity towards the broader society, ensuring that individuals with financial service needs can obtain corresponding financial services at their cost, significantly promoting the construction of China's inclusive finance system.

[14] XIE Ping, ZOU Chuanwei. "A Study on Internet Financial Models," *Financial Research*. 2012, Issue 12.

[15] LUO Mingxiong, TANG Ying, LIU Yong. *Internet Finance*, China Financial and Economic Publishing House, 2013: 6.

D. Optimized Capital Allocation and Efficiency of Services

The emergence of new forms of Internet finance in China has brought about a transformative change in the landscape of financial business models. While its financial essence—capital circulation, payments, wealth management, information intermediation, risk pricing, and others—has not fundamentally changed, Internet finance has significantly improved the quality and efficiency of financial services and capital allocation by integrating the latest information technology into the financial industry. Traditional modern financial institutions, such as banks, securities, and insurance companies, continuously incorporate new technologies into the financial sector for long-term financial innovation. This enhances the efficiency of capital allocation across different time and space dimensions. However, their practices tend to favor the "Pareto Principle," specifically the 20% highlighted in the principle. In contrast, Internet finance operates differently, echoing Jack Ma's observation that "China's financial industry, especially the banking sector, serves 20% of customers. What I see is that 80% of businesses are not served."[16] Leveraging internet, big data, cloud computing, blockchain, and other information science and technology, Internet finance reduces the frequency of occurrences of information asymmetry and uncertainty. It significantly expands the population benefiting from financial services, thereby improving the efficiency of capital allocation. Payments are also made more efficient and convenient through these technological advancements.

11.2 The Model of Internet Finance

Since the rise of China's Internet finance in 2013, its model has been continuously innovated, showing an increasingly rich and diversified trend. However, from the carrier of each model of Internet finance, it is composed of nothing more than "finance + Internet" and "Internet + finance", and each model is further refined into several sub-models according to the connotation of financial services provided. Of course, with the repositioning of finance and technology, the above two models show different trends in function.

11.2.1 Finance + Internet

The Internet-based mode of finance means that existing financial institutions or quasi-financial institutions (third-party payment institutions with financial licenses, etc.) rely on information technologies such as the Internet, big data, cloud computing, and social networks to improve the efficiency of financial functions such as payment, financing and investment, financial management, consulting services, and risk pricing

[16] "MA Yun: The Financial Industry Needs Disruptors," *People's Daily*, June 21, 2013.

to meet the financial needs of society. Gradually resolve the financial problems caused by economic development and solve the service dilemma in the original financial organizations. According to this connotation, the Internet of finance can be further refined into the following sub-models.

First, the Internet securities model. Internet securities means that existing securities companies use Internet technology to build an online platform to provide investors with a full range of securities business services such as product introduction, information release, research, transaction, risk control, account management, etc., to provide investors with diversified products, efficient service quality, and reduce the transaction threshold. In order to achieve efficient, convenient, low-cost investment across time and space. The development of Internet securities in China has roughly gone through the stages of securities companies setting up websites, online offline business, and financial supermarkets with securities as the core, providing investors with comprehensive or personalized securities business services. The development of Internet securities in China has roughly gone through stages such as the establishment of securities company websites, the online transformation of offline businesses, and the securities-centered financial supermarket, providing comprehensive or personalized securities business services to investors.

Compared with developed countries' Internet securities, China's Internet securities development still has certain gaps. On the one hand, this is due to the relatively lagging development of China's securities companies and securities markets, which still lag behind indirect financing such as banks. In 2013, it accounted for less than 15% of China's total financing. On the other hand, in China's Shanghai and Shenzhen stock markets, state-owned enterprises dominate the listed companies, and there are not many tradable varieties, resulting in higher risks and a relatively low proportion in the entire economy. In terms of the internetization of securities companies, although China's Internet securities started early, the China Huarong Trust Investment Company Zhanjiang Branch launched the multimedia public information network online trading system as early as 1997, leading foreign countries in aspects such as the use of microcomputer LAN in exchange core business systems and the paperless issuance, trading, and settlement process. However, in the field of internet securities, it has not yet reached the level of economies of scale and scope seen in developed countries. Of course, the internet securities model guided by securities companies has gradually extended to information technology companies such as e-commerce participating in the securities business field. However, these information technology companies, due to the lack of securities licenses, cannot issue securities products and can only stay in the value transmission link of securities product agency sales and wealth management period, without truly penetrating the value creation link in the securities field. Since 2013, with the impact of pure internet finance, the networkization of China's securities companies has made great progress, entering a new field of technological innovation and providing investors with comprehensive securities services.

The second is the internet insurance model. Internet insurance refers to insurance companies providing insurance products and services to customers through the internet and other information technologies, enabling online consultation, account opening, planning, underwriting, policy issuance, settlement of claim, and other insurance operations, completing the sale and service of insurance products, and transferring premiums to insurance companies through banks or third-party payment institutions. The development of this model initially involved insurance companies setting up websites to introduce and promote insurance business and products. Subsequently, its functions expanded continuously, leading to the current development of a virtualized, direct, electronic, and transparent insurance supermarket model. Customers can obtain all insurance-related services from internet insurance, and insurance companies can even conduct big data and small data analysis based on the data left by customers online to provide personalized insurance products and other services to a wide range of customers. Since the establishment of China Insurance Information Website (CIIW) in November 1997 and the issuance of the first internet insurance policy by Xinhua Life Insurance Company in December of the same year, until the "Three MA Selling Insurance"[17] phenomenon in 2013, all insurance companies set up their own websites, creating a comprehensive internet insurance model. Similar to internet securities, some e-commerce and information companies have also entered certain businesses in internet insurance. However, they are unable to truly issue insurance products and can only engage in insurance-related activities such as agency sales.

The third is the internet banking, mobile banking, phone banking, unmanned banking, and other models. Internet banking, mobile banking, and others are the utilization of internet and mobile communication technologies by the banking industry to move payment, settlement, credit, and wealth management, and other credit intermediary services from offline to online, providing credit intermediary services to individuals and companies. The integration of the banking industry with the internet and other information technologies has progressed in sync with the development of these technologies. It has evolved from computer-assisted banking to electronic banking, online banking, and the increasingly popular mobile banking. Banks continuously invest in and apply information technology, expanding into non-traditional banking areas such as e-commerce and mobile payments. This helps consolidate and expand the relationship between banks and customers in terms of deposits, loans, remittances, and other business activities, leading to a rapid improvement in the efficiency of the entire socio-economic activities. Currently, "the internet and banking have moved beyond the initial stage of external technological application, initiating the penetration and integration of core business, by satisfying customer needs and creating additional customer demands, providing customers with comprehensive, multidimensional services".[18] The banking industry leverages internet, mobile communication, artificial intelligence, and other technologies to enhance the customer credit service experience and level. In the face of competition from e-commerce and information technology companies, banks have also expanded into fields such as e-commerce, showcasing a growing trend of integration between

[17] "Three MA" refers to Alibaba's Jack MA, Ping An's MA Mingzhe and Tencent's MA Huateng who jointly set up Zhong'an Online property insurance company.

[18] YAO Wenping. *Internet Finance: The Coming New Financial Era.* Citic Press, 2014: 155.

financial supermarkets and e-commerce. With the integration of finance and the internet spirit of "equality, openness, collaboration, and sharing", this model has the potential to form a relatively complete financial ecosystem, enabling customers to access comprehensive financial services and other social services they require.

Internet banking and mobile banking are widely used in China's internet finance. As mentioned earlier, due to the limited coverage of existing financial institutions, many rural areas and even urban fringe areas are unable to access necessary financial services from banks and other financial organizations. At the same time, obtaining necessary financial support from banks involves tedious procedures and hard constraints such as guarantees, pledges, and collateral, making it impossible for low-and-middle-income individuals to receive regular financial services from banks. Internet banking, mobile banking, and other services developed "through technology such as the internet and communication have managed to lower management and operational costs by eliminating physical branches, and the cost savings have been used to increase the unit returns or market share of existing businesses. They have attracted users through offering high-interest deposit accounts or low-interest loans".[19] So far, China's banking industry has made significant progress in this regard, reaching into the bottom of society, rural areas, and remote regions. In urban areas, existing bank branches are increasingly providing smart services, and even in April 2018, unmanned banking services emerged as a brand-new offering.

The fourth is the internet finance sales model. Internet finance sales refers to financial institutions such as funds and trusts using the internet and other information technologies to create online platforms for the sale of financial products. This model serves as a link and bridge between customers and financial institutions. "On the one hand, financial institutions sell financial products to customers through internet financial sales platforms; on the other hand, internet financial sales platforms directly reflect customer demands and investment preferences."[20] Clearly, financial institutions still dominate this model, but they leverage internet and information technologies to reduce transaction costs and tap into customers' potential financial needs. Currently, this model has given rise to third-party payment institutions due to the involvement of fund transfers in financial product sales and various goods. By October 2013, China had already licensed 250 payment institutions as third-party payment providers with quasi-financial institutional characteristics. Even after regulatory reforms in 2017, there were still 247 third-party payment institutions. The development trend of internet sales models gradually breaks the segmented operation pattern of China's financial industry, weakens the barriers between traditional financial institutions, and presents a trend towards mixed development.

[19] YAO Wenping. *Internet Finance: The Coming New Financial Era.* Citic Press, 2014: 159.

[20] YAO Wenping. *Internet Finance: The Coming New Financial Era.* Citic Press, 2014: 81.

11.2.2 Internet + Finance

The Internet financialization model refers to the cross-border expansion of business operations in the financial sector by e-commerce and information technology companies. It also includes independent financial services such as payment processing, financial investment, wealth management, information consulting, and risk pricing conducted by information technology companies. These initiatives aim to meet the financial supply and demand functions of the socio-economic system. Based on the operational differences observed in practice, Internet financialization can be further divided into the following sub-models.

The first is the Internet or online financing model (online lending). Internet financing refers to the use of platforms constructed through information technology, such as the Internet, to achieve information exchange without relying on intermediaries such as banks, securities, and trusts. This model significantly broadens the audience for financial supply and demand, allowing individuals and entities that have difficulties accessing financial services through traditional channels, such as the lower-middle class, small and micro enterprises, rural and remote areas, to obtain necessary financial services. It also helps reduce information asymmetry prevalent in traditional finance. Due to the long-term impact of financial repression on China's financial industry, existing financial institutions are unable to meet the high demand for small-scale social borrowing and cannot accommodate informal finance. Additionally, interest rate controls prevent the general public from earning higher interest returns. Therefore, the emergence of the Internet financing model perfectly caters to the financing needs of the masses, leading to an explosive growth in Internet financing. The most typical examples of this model are peer-to-peer lending (P2P) and crowdfunding.

P2P, which stands for peer-to-peer lending, is a model where individuals or organizations borrow and lend funds through independent third-party online platforms. Although originating from developed countries, this model has seen deeper development in mainland China. However, there are significant differences in development between different regions. Cities like Beijing, Shanghai, Hangzhou, Shenzhen, and Guangzhou have surpassed any foreign country or region in many aspects of development. By early October 2013, there were already over 500 P2P platforms, exhibiting a trend of rapid expansion. By January 2016, this number had grown to 3944. However, due to factors such as the domestic credit system, degree of interest rate liberalization, and regulatory framework, the operation of P2P lending in China still differs significantly from that in foreign countries. China has introduced more online-offline integration and guarantees to comply with regulatory guidelines, with only a small number of P2P platforms serving as information platforms. As a result, P2P lending is prone to pitfalls such as fund pooling, illegal fundraising, and illegal fundraising, leading to a phenomenon of both rapid growth and mass closures. In December 2015, "the Draft Regulations for P2P Lending" were released for public consultation. In early 2016, "the Special Campaign for Risk Control of P2P Online Lending" was announced, with a 1-year plan for completion. However, in 2017, an additional year of transition time was granted based on the actual situation of online lending, aiming to regulate its development. In 2018, the China Banking and Insurance Regulatory Commission (CBIRC) extended the deadline by another year based on the progress of online lending regulation in different regions to ensure compliant development. At the same time, specific industry access regulations were established, categorizing platforms into compliant, reforming, merging, and exiting categories based on their operational status. Through comprehensive regulation, the goal is to achieve full coverage management and risk prevention for P2P lending.

Crowdfunding is a financing method that involves raising funds from the public or specific individuals through online platforms such as the internet for personal or business activities or projects. Crowdfunding projects are diverse, and different platforms have their own focuses. Since its creation in the United States, crowdfunding has experienced rapid development worldwide, surpassing 1500 platforms by June 2013. Since 2011, crowdfunding models in China have witnessed rapid growth, with nearly 500 crowdfunding platforms by the end of 2015. Compared to foreign countries, crowdfunding operations in China are relatively limited. Based on the current legal environment in China, most crowdfunding platforms (such as Demohour, Dreamore, Tmeng, Emie, etc.) adopt a reward-based model. Only a few crowdfunding platforms (such as Dajiatou, Angels Union, and Venture Capital Investment Circle) cautiously explore and attempt equity crowdfunding based on China's legal environment.[21] The lack of clear definitions, especially for equity crowdfunding, has led to chaos in this field. As a response, the China Securities Regulatory Commission (CSRC) initiated regulation and standardization of crowdfunding platforms in August 2015, subsequently releasing corresponding crowdfunding management rules to clarify the essence of crowdfunding and its operational rules, guiding its compliant development.

The second financing model is internet wealth management. Internet wealth management refers to activities conducted through online platforms created by information technology such as the internet and mobile communication for the purpose of providing financial information, products introduction, consultation, sales, planning, and servicing. Due to restrictions such as financial licenses, these platforms are generally unable to provide financial products themselves. They primarily serve as intermediaries in the introduction and sales of financial products issued by modern financial institutions such as funds, trusts, securities, and insurance using internet technology. Clearly, based on the services provided by internet wealth management, online platforms can be roughly categorized into three types: tool-based, advisory-based, and transaction-based. Unlike developed countries where internet wealth management platforms primarily offer financial planning services to the general public, China's domestic wealth management platforms have developed to some extent. There are small-scale, independent online wealth management institutions such as Wacai, Tongbanjie, and Cunzhe. However, "in an environment where commercial integrity is relatively lacking, it is difficult for clients to truly trust a

[21] LUO Mingxiong, TANG Ying, LIU Yong. *Internet Finance*, China Financial and Economic Publishing House, 2013: 185.

communication method that can only be conducted through the internet or phone."[22] Therefore, the third-party wealth management model is still in its infancy and has not yet become the preferred wealth management method for the public. People are more inclined towards internet wealth management models like Yu'E Bao and the internet-based financial model with its offline transaction channels. In the future, the internet wealth management model will demonstrate a rapid development trend as a result of the fast-paced and diversified demands of the general public in wealth management.

The third model is the internet payment model. Internet payment refers to a convenient payment method created by e-commerce and information technology companies that take advantage of their own information technology capabilities and address the high costs associated with traditional financial institutions' payment services, using bank cards as carriers. In the initial stage of development, this model still relies on bank cards and accounts for payment. However, with technological advancements, these payment methods are gradually transitioning to independent modes, thereby reducing transaction costs. Subsequently, companies like Alibaba, Tencent, Baidu, and others have leveraged this and utilized the large balance amounts in customer payments to develop various wealth management products. They have integrated funds, trusts, insurance, securities, and other modern financial institutions to transform their services into wealth management offerings, breaking through many limitations of traditional financial organizations in wealth management (such as entry quotas and redemption periods). This has led to the convergence of different financial services under the internet finance model.

The fourth model is the pure online banking model. This model involves the establishment of banks through information networks such as the internet. These types of online banks belong to the category of pure online banking (mentioned later in the text). They operate entirely online, relying solely on the internet for banking services without physical branches. Hence, they are also referred to as "banks without banks". "The latest technologies such as telephone banking, ATMs, personal computers, and the internet enable banks to provide convenient financial services to customers within a geographic area without the need for physical branches. These advanced transmission systems allow customers to deposit money, apply for loans, express financial needs, access the latest account information, and, in some cases, directly communicate with bank representatives without having to visit traditional bank branches".[23] Clearly, customers are not restricted by internet access methods (PC, PDA, mobile, etc.) or geographical limitations. As long as they can access the internet, regardless of their location, they can securely and conveniently manage their assets and enjoy various financial services provided by banks. Online banks, operating on the internet as a platform, are not limited by geographical boundaries, physical branches, or business hours. They can provide various banking services such as deposits, loans, settlements, payments, and wealth management through the

[22] YAO Wenping. *Internet Finance: The Coming New Financial Era*. Citic Press, 2014.

[23] JAMES W. Brock, *Industrial Structure in the United States*, China Renmin University Press, 2011: 343.

internet at any time and from anywhere, even through a mobile internet terminal. Since online banks do not have physical branches, they save significant operational costs and personnel expenses. In 2013, Alibaba proposed to establish an online bank. In July 2014, Shenzhen Qianhai WeBank was approved, and it announced its establishment on October 22nd. Its official website was launched on December 28th, and it officially started operating on January 26th, 2015. Afterwards, Alibaba's MYbank, Baidu's Baixin Bank, and other online banks started to open, marking a period of rapid development for online banking in China.

Apart from the aforementioned models, internet finance in China also made significant progress in digital currencies. In 2014, PBOC established the Digital Currency Research Institute to accelerate research on digital currencies, promote their development, and adapt to the opportunities brought by information technology. Currently, PBOC has made great strides in the development and research of sovereign digital currencies. At the same time, the Chinese government has strengthened the regulation of virtual currencies. On September 4th, 2017, PBOC, together with the Cyberspace Administration of China, Ministry of Industry and Information Technology, State Administration for Industry and Commerce, China Banking Regulatory Commission (CBRC), China Securities Regulatory Commission (CSRC), and China Insurance Regulatory Commission (CIRC), jointly issued the announcement "Concerning the Prevention of Risks Associated with Token Offerings". It explicitly stated that token offerings, including initial coin offerings (ICO), are essentially unapproved illegal public fundraising activities, and it required an immediate cessation of all token offering and fundraising activities. Organizations and individuals that have completed token offering fundraising should make arrangements for refunds and so on. In the future, with the gradual introduction of digital currency and the increasing popularity of network payment, China's currency field will show the development trend of "cashless society".

11.3 The Impact of Internet Finance

China's Internet finance originated from the informationization of modern finance, but what really stirred the financial industry was the pure Internet finance model that rose in 2013. The rapid rise of pure Internet finance has not only caused a wave of financial innovation, enriched financial products, but also brought a direct major impact on the modern financial industry, is or has changed their business, philosophy and mode of operation. The two-way and integrated development of modern financial informatization and pure Internet finance has changed the previously closed space of financial development, blurred the boundary between the industry and the market, and presented a trend of open development, jointly promoted the in-depth reform and development of China's financial industry, and enhanced the core competitiveness of China's financial industry. At the same time, the rise of Internet finance and its practices have also brought indirect impacts on China's social and economic development, and brought many beneficial impacts on economic structure upgrading and industrial structure transformation.

11.3.1 The Influence of Internet Finance on Modern Finance

Since the rise of Internet finance in 2013, it has not only expanded the scope of China's financial industry and formed a new business philosophy, but also had a major impact and influence on the development of China's existing financial industry. This impact obviously has the meaning of impact-reaction, which greatly promotes the integration of modern financial informatization and pure Internet finance, and improves the efficiency of financial services to society.

A. Impact and Expand the Original Financial Business

The development of Internet finance in China has greatly impacted the business structure and operation activities of the existing financial industry. Specifically, there are two aspects as follows: on the one hand, it impacts the original financial business activities and affects their earnings. At present, although modern finance such as banking, securities and insurance still occupies a dominant position in financial services such as deposit, credit, settlement, financial management, information consultation and risk pricing, these industries have been strongly impacted by Internet finance. In the deposit field, since the birth of Yu'e Bao and various Internet financial "Bao" (means "treasure"), its high yield, fast speed and low threshold enable funds to flow out of banks, securities and other institutions, greatly reducing the amount of bank deposits. The flow of funds to those "Baos" enables them to negotiate with the bank on the deposit of large amounts of funds, raises the interest rate of funds deposit, increases the cost of banks, and once triggered disputes about "funds idling" and "Yu'ebao is a vampire". It has brought a strong impact on banks and securities. Under the conditions of China's deposit interest rate liberalization and loan interest rate liberalization,[24] the deposit and loan spreads have been further narrowed, completely changing the era when banks relied on deposit and loan spreads to obtain huge profits in the past. This behavior of those "Baos" has forced modern financial organizations such as banks not to pay attention to the business model and

[24] China's interest rate reform is moving towards marketization. In 1993, it was established that "non-bank institutions first, then banks; First foreign exchange, then local currency; Large amount first, then small amount; Loan first, then deposit "sequence; By 2008, except for the deposit and loan interest rates of commercial banks, the prices of bonds, trusts and foreign exchange were basically market-based. Before 2013, the People's Bank of China set an interest rate benchmark, and on July 20 of the same year, the People's Bank of China abolished the floor of 0.7 times the lending rate of financial institutions. On October 23, 2015, the People's Bank of China cancelled the floating ceiling of the interest rate of time deposits over 1 year of commercial banks; In 2018, the People's Bank of China promoted the reform of interest rate liberalization, announced in April that it would release the self-discipline agreement of the deposit interest rate ceiling of commercial banks, and the interest rate benchmark would be merged with the market-oriented interest rate, but it had not been opened until June 2019.

respond to the competition of the "Baos". In the banking industry, there began to be a phenomenon of launching financial products similar to Yu'e Bao. By February 27, 2014, seven banks, including Minsheng Bank, PBOC, Ping An Bank, Guangdong Development Bank, Bank of Communications, Industrial and Commercial Bank of China and Shanghai Pudong Development Bank, had launched financial products similar to Yu'ebao.

"In the field of credit, complex and cumbersome procedures, coupled with high costs caused by reliance on manual and physical branches, have led modern financial organizations to develop a characteristic of favoring the rich and neglecting the poor. This makes it difficult for them to meet the financing needs of small and micro enterprises, lower-middle-class people, rural areas, and underdeveloped economic regions. With the help of information technologies such as the Internet, big data, cloud computing, blockchain, and artificial intelligence, Internet finance has basically overcome the above characteristics of modern finance. Online lending, pure Internet banking, micro-lending, Ant Financial, and Jingdong industry chain finance, which are the main bodies of P2P and crowdfunding, provide funds for various financing needs.

Crowdfunding raised over 20 billion yuan in 2016; P2P loan balance exceeded one trillion yuan by 2017; pure internet banks like WeChat Pay provided loans exceeding hundreds of billions yuan in 2016. In the future, their lending will continue to grow rapidly and will to some extent change the lending pattern in modern finance. Therefore, modern financial organizations such as banks continuously establish institutions such as small-scale credit departments and inclusive finance business units to respond to challenges from internet finance.

In the field of financial management, the scope of financial management carried out by modern financial organizations is mainly concentrated in the field of financial investment behavior and consulting. In China's financial services, the banking sector dominates. In 2005, banking institutions began to carry out financial services. By the end of 2017, a total of 562 banking institutions had obtained financial services qualifications, with 93,500 financial products and 29.54 trillion yuan of stock funds. From the perspective of these financial services, they generally have the characteristics of high threshold, large quota, inflexiability to realize cash, "hegemonization" of agreement regulation and control, and complex procedures; According to regulatory requirements, customers who buy bank wealth management products for the first time must go to the business outlet for risk tolerance assessment, and the starting amount of the first purchase of products must reach 50,000 yuan. In this way, the vast majority of people are excluded from the scope of financial management, and many customers are deeply harmed by the "overlord" clause and fall into the financial trap. With the increasing of people's income, obtaining wealth income has become their urgent need. Internet finance uses information technology to provide financial products with no threshold, no limit and no time agreement (T + 0), which basically solves the financial service problems existing in modern finance, provides corresponding financial channels for different income groups, changes the situation of customers' dependence on financial organizations in the past, and makes customers gradually independent. In 2013, after the birth of Yu'e Bao, within less than half a year, its users exceeded the number of valid accounts of the Shanghai and Shenzhen stock markets with a 23-year history of development. Such a rapid development trend of Internet finance fully conforms to the different financial characteristics of the public, promotes the rapid development of China's financial management field, and enables people of different strata to get different degrees of sense of acquisition from wealth investment. Now, most people are not willing to stay in the bank as a deposit after their salary, but to switch to various types of Internet financial products with both liquidity and profitability. In the face of the impact from the Internet finance, modern financial organizations have made corresponding changes, gradually changing the past kind of "pick and choose" mentality, but also use information technology to expand downward, showing more "civilian" trend. In the field of payment channels, since the establishment of the first third-party payment enterprise in China in 1999, it has changed the mode of modern finance that one account at a time, cross-institution and remote withdrawal fees are higher, and you can walk around the world with the help of mobile phones without carrying more cash. So that in 2017, the Internet finance with Alibaba as the main body put forward the concept of "cashless society". In the face of this trend, Internet finance does not yet pose a "disruptive" threat to traditional large banks, as the government says private banks will likely focus more on innovative financial products. State-owned commercial banks can also use their legal power and monopoly power to reduce the business capabilities of competitors. In response to the explosive growth of Internet finance companies, some banks have set limits on the amount of transfer payments their customers can make, such as Yu'e Bao and Wantong. In March 2014, PBOC and regulators also suspended Tencent and Alibaba's online credit card and QR code scanning payment services in an effort to contain the fallout from the rapid growth of the Internet finance industry. In 2017, PBOC and others proposed the establishment of the Internet connection, requiring all third-party payment enterprises to cut into the payment channels of the Internet connection, breaking the pattern of Internet finance domination, triggering financial infrastructure changes. Mobile payment has become one of the so-called "new four great inventions"[25] in China today, and modern finance must also adapt to this changing trend. In the field of information consulting, although China's modern financial organizations have built their own consulting system, they prefer VIP customers more than the aforementioned business development in the financial field, which is of no substantive significance to the vast majority of people. Internet finance is completely different, they make full use of network technology to carry out a wide range of information consulting services, according to the needs of different customers to provide corresponding services, to lay the foundation for the deep cultivation of financial and other fields of business. Influenced by the impact of Internet finance, the modern financial industry has gradually changed the past model and adopted a relatively flexible way to provide different consulting services for different customers to meet the financial needs of different income groups. In terms of risk pricing, modern finance mostly relies on the physical form of people

[25] Mobile payment, high-speed rail, bike-sharing and online shopping are considered China's four new inventions, according to an online survey.

and property, and uses modern financial theory and other simulation to determine the risk preference, so as to determine the price of financial assets. Internet financing relies on big data or small data, social networks, cloud computing, blockchain and other information technologies to speculate the preferences of individuals and enterprises, so as to judge their degree of risk, and then determine their risk pricing of financial needs, which completely changes the practice of judging financial asset prices based on physical form, and greatly reduces the cost in the field of risk pricing. It expands the scope of financial transactions and improves the efficiency of financial transactions.

On the other hand, it has expanded the depth and breadth of existing financial application information technology. Modern finance has been undergoing informatization since the 1950s, achieving internet-based finance according to different stages of demand. However, before the rise of internet finance, modern financial informatization mainly used information technology as an auxiliary means for business development. With the rapid development of internet finance, the application of information technology gradually shifted from being an auxiliary tool to network virtualized office work. Currently, with mature applications such as big data, cloud computing, and artificial intelligence (AI), the network process driven by internet finance has transformed into comprehensive intelligence. In response to this trend in development needs, modern finance has deepened its use of information technology in the financial field.

In June 2017, China Agricultural Bank promoted "face-recognition cash withdrawal" technology throughout its branches based on pilot testing results, achieving intelligent transformation where customers can withdraw money from ATMs without using a bank card. In September 2017, Lanzhou Bank collaborated with Alipay and WeChat Pay to innovate by allowing funds from these payment platforms to be directly withdrawn as cash at their ATMs; thus creating a channel between internet payments and traditional banks. China Construction Bank launched a new type of branch called "unmanned bank" in Shanghai in April 2018 where customers can conduct various financial transactions on-site or remotely through networks without assistance from tellers or lobby managers. At the same time, modern finance not only established its own institutions for innovative applications of information technology but also accelerated establishing fintech subsidiaries to promote technological application and innovation in the financial sector.

Since the establishment of Industrial Bank's financial technology subsidiary in 2015, Ping An, China Merchants Bank, Everbright Bank, Construction Bank, Minsheng Bank and other six banks have successively established their own financial technology subsidiaries by deepening the integration of finance and technology.

B. Innovating the Existing Financial Management Concept

Banking, securities, insurance and other modern financial industry in order to resolve uncertainty and information asymmetry, there is a strong fundamental dependence on material. In the process of operation, they need to rely on property as collateral, pledge, guarantee or direct cash transactions to safeguard their asset protection rights. During their operations, they need to rely on collateralization or direct cash transactions with physical assets to safeguard their asset rights. To achieve this reliance on physical assets, they have developed a relatively complex evaluation and review process. This achieves the goal of protecting asset security but undoubtedly increases their operational costs. Obviously, under the concept of modern finance based on physical guarantees and according to cost–benefit principles in operation, they naturally prefer objects with economic strength, certain scale and policy support while excluding financing needs from lower-middle class individuals, rural areas with small-scale dispersed financial demands or small- and micro-enterprises without economic strength. As a result, modern finance increasingly exhibits aristocratic characteristics in practice that strongly favor the top 20% defined by "Pareto Principle". Internet finance gradually resolves the physically-oriented financial service concept through information science and technology. By utilizing big data analysis tools like cloud computing etc., internet finance reconstructs trust structures between fund suppliers and demanders while resolving information asymmetry issues between them; thus inherently possessing inclusive features.

By utilizing artificial intelligence, internet finance has significantly reduced the labor intensity in financial services, improved work efficiency, reconstructed business processes, enriched customer service methods, controlled business risks, and innovated business models. Clearly, the application of information technology in internet finance has greatly enhanced fund allocation efficiency and fund security, gradually changing the current situation where modern finance is heavily constrained by physical assets and returning to the essence of serving the real economy and prioritizing people.

C. Affecting the Original Financial Mode of Operation

Before the rise of Internet finance, although the degree of modern financial informatization in China has made great progress, they basically use physical outlets to open up space for business and provide the vast majority of financial services manually. The degree of green finance is extremely low, the level of financial services is not high, the efficiency is low, and the phenomenon of queuing is extremely serious, which often leads to customer dissatisfaction. Traditional operating methods of banks, securities firms, insurance companies and other modern financial organizations resulted in high costs related to physical branches as well as operations and channels; manual operation methods and rigid institutional mechanisms consumed a significant amount of time cost for various financial transactions. In this context, modern finance underwent reforms such as process reengineering around the 1990s to reduce service links and lower operating costs but achieved less than satisfactory results due to lack of strong competitors; moreover information technology applications were often regarded merely as auxiliary means for human work.

With the rise of internet finance in China, they have completely changed the operating mode of modern finance by relying on information technology. The previous manual-based and physical branch-dependent operations quickly shifted to virtual spaces online, resulting in a rapid increase in operational efficiency and completely changing the long waiting time that were previously experienced. In this competitive environment, a disruptive concept of "banks don't change, we change banks" has emerged. This forces modern financial organizations such as banks, securities firms, and insurance companies to strengthen their construction of internet finance platforms and improve the functionality of their information service platforms to achieve further innovation in marketing channels.

Under the strong stimulation of internet finance, banks, securities firms, insurance companies, and other modern financial organizations have basically achieved offline business online transformation and green operation methods. They have established intelligent service systems primarily through Apps as carriers. People can now complete almost all financial services online, completely changing the traditional way of queuing for transactions at various financial institutions' physical branches. As a result, these branches began to appear unpatronized.

The rapid development of internet finance has brought comprehensive impact to existing financial branches, making the gradual closure of high-cost branch institutions an inevitable trend for future development. As of the fourth quarter of 2017, banks have closed nearly 400 community outlets and agencies, which also brings opportunities for further deepening reforms in modern finance, thus achieving Pareto improvement in the financial system under information technology development.

D. Reshaping the Ecological Environment of Modern Finance

After 1949, the financial industry gradually transitioned from a diversified form with "public–private partnership" as a mandatory institutional change to a unified system, making it dependent on fiscal resources for a long period of time. After the reform and opening up, with rapid socio-economic development, China's financial industry has shown a rapid and diversified development trend again. However, constrained by inertia thinking, it is still a highly monopolistic industry. They clearly lack strong external competitors and enjoy high monopoly profits with insufficient competitive pressure. Currently, although they have made some improvements in industry mechanisms and access standards under environmental pressures, there are still many obstacles for private capital to enter existing financial sectors under conditions such as national credit replacing industry credit and "too big to fail". The existing financial system is also unable to provide necessary financial services for all members of society; on the contrary, they continuously raise barriers such as service quality requirements and access thresholds using their monopoly advantages.

In this context, the Internet thinking originated in the original financial industry has rapidly spread to the Internet industry and third-party institutions involved in financial business, making Internet finance show a trend of rapid growth. In practice, they have integrated the Internet spirit of "openness, equality, collaboration, and sharing" into Internet finance, and gradually brought the lower and middle class people and micro, small and medium-sized enterprises who have long been excluded from modern financial services into the service scope of Internet finance, reflecting the inclusive value-added concept of increasing people's wealth income. At the same time, it has also, to some extent, gradually included areas that have long existed and are difficult to monitor, such as private finance, into Internet finance. The emergence and development of new forms of Internet finance have broken the previous financial ecology in which the supply side, demand side, infrastructure, supervision and other four parties are relatively isolated. With the help of network platforms, various subjects have narrowed the distance between each other, reduced the intermediary, granted many rights to customers, and paid more attention to customer experience, which naturally caters to the needs of the public. It solves many problems that traditional finance cannot solve. "Internet financial business has the characteristics of small, fast and convenient, so it has significant inclusiveness, solving many problems that the traditional financial system cannot be well solved, and the traditional financial system permeates, promotes and complements each other, and jointly constitutes a broad financial system."[26] Obviously, the improvement of the financial ecological environment caused by the development of Internet finance provides a new financial ecological environment with innovation, competition, equality, inclusiveness and openness as the connotation of modern finance, reflecting the development trend of scientific and technological finance, green finance and inclusive finance.

11.3.2 The Reference of Internet Finance to Social and Economic Development

China's Internet finance has been developing rapidly since 2013, and has been leading the world in the fields of online payment and online lending. Although the development of Internet finance is very short, its rapid development in practice and many practices that change the original development pattern of China's finance, as well as the way it deals with the government and the market, technology imitation and innovation can undoubtedly provide useful reference for China's social economy today, especially for the core link of economic restructuring—the transformation of industrial structure.

A. The Wave of Innovation and the "Catfish Effect" Formed in the Rise of Internet Finance Industry

Innovation is the recombination of production factors. According to the innovation theory of Joseph Alois Schumpeter, the innovation process consists of five steps: product innovation, technological innovation, market innovation, resource allocation innovation and organizational innovation.[27] From the perspective of the development process of China's Internet finance, we can clearly see that the development of Internet finance industry in China is the introduction of technology from abroad and began to imitate, and then set up different Internet finance models, but in a long period of time before 2013, it did not cause much response in China. In 2013, the success of Yu'e Bao aroused the attention of all sectors of society, which quickly triggered

[26] Promoting Innovation and Preventing Risks to Promote the Healthy and Sustainable Development of Internet Finance. http://www.pcac.org.cn/index,php/dongtai/list_details/ids/281/id/57/cid/184/topicid/4.html.

[27] Joseph Schumpeter. *The Theory of Economic Development—An Inquiry into Profits, Capital, Interest, and the Business Cycle*. The Commercial Press, 2000.

the infiltration of relevant industries with information technology companies as the main body into the financial field, forming a grand cross-border operation. Internet finance broke the characteristics of modern finance's being elite and aristocratic, quickly penetrated into the long tail of 80% of the "20–80 law" and triggered the long tail effect, divided a large number of deposits from modern finance, and basically took over the middle and lower customers. Although the market share is small, its number is growing rapidly, and it soon triggered a "catfish effect" in the financial industry. The future of finance has two major opportunities, one is the financial Internet, the financial industry to the Internet; The second is Internet finance, pure layman leadership, in fact, many industry innovation is triggered by laymen."[28] The "subversive" competition from pure Internet finance has forced original financial organizations such as banks, insurance, securities, funds, and trusts to respond and join in the innovation of "finance + Internet". Securities and insurance are born with the genes of the Internet and will soon be upgraded to the level of Internet finance. Banks have set up various banking "treasure", and entities have upgraded to Internet financial platforms. As a result, a wave of innovation in China's financial field has been aroused, and the original unbalanced pattern of financial distribution has been changed in a very short time. This situation may make China's Internet finance industry have core competitiveness and narrow the gap in financial competition with developed countries.

The innovation wave and the "catalyst effect" triggered by the rise of internet finance have changed the long-standing situation of "suppression" and relative backwardness in China's financial sector. The emerging financial new forms and strong competitiveness have provided a strong demonstration effect for the situation of lacking core technologies that is commonly faced in the adjustment of China's social and economic structure and industrial structure upgrading. In the adjustment of the industrial structure dominated by manufacturing, we can adopt an active and proactive attitude, as the Ministry of Commerce has done in its "Made in China" advertising campaigns globally, to absorb advanced technologies and management experiences from overseas countries to drive the transformation of China's industrial structure. With the support of the State Council's "innovation and entrepreneurship" policy, we can cultivate the "waves" of innovation in economic structure adjustment and stir the "catfish" of innovation in traditional industries, ultimately achieving the upgrading of industrial structure and transformation of production methods.

B. The Extension of the Industrial Chain Formed in the Rise of Internet Finance and the Enhancement of Added Value

Before the rise of Internet finance, China's original financial system, under long-term "suppression", not only maintained its elite and aristocratic characteristics, but was limited to 20% of the "20–80 law" group, accounting for 80% of the middle and lower classes of people, absolute advantages of small and medium-sized enterprises, suburbs and rural areas, basically unable to get the necessary services of

[28] MA Yun. "Financial industry needs disruptors", *People's Daily*, June 21, 2013, 10th edition.

modern financial organizations. Modern financial organizations serve more state-owned enterprises, specific industries and specific objects determined by government policies. Since the reform and opening up, "the expansion of the boundary of public financial property rights has strengthened the ability of the state to control financial resources, so that it can use these financial resources to replace the rapidly declining fiscal capacity to support economic growth within the system".[29] The emergence and rapid development of Internet finance has broken the service boundaries of the original financial industry. It focuses more on the blind area of long-term economic development and modern financial services, such as the blind area of time, space and object that cannot be covered by modern financial organizations mentioned above. The service objects involved in the Internet finance industry cover all groups of people, all kinds of enterprises, and all kinds of regions, showing the characteristics of inclusive finance, which greatly expands the industrial chain of China's financial services, and the service objects completely break through specific industries, specific regions, and specific groups. With the help of modern information technologies such as the Internet, big data and cloud computing, the situation of information asymmetry in China's financial industry has been changed, transaction costs in financial services have been reduced, and the efficiency of financial services has been improved. At the same time, various financial products that were previously born in modern finance have gradually become external, turning the design, production, allocation and sales of the entire financial product into an industrial chain.

The extension of the industrial chain and the increase of added value caused by the development of Internet finance have broken the original service boundaries of the financial industry and formed a trend of cross-border service, which has generated a great driving force for the adjustment of industrial structure under the new normal. The adjustment of China's industrial structure not only needs to rely on innovation, but also needs to integrate the original industries according to the actual situation of China's manufacturing industry and the rising cost of various factors, so as to enhance the added value of China's manufacturing industry in the global industrial chain. This approach is the best way for those industries that do not have core technologies and brands to transform and upgrade. In the process of increasing the added value, we will gradually cultivate core technologies and well-known brands in order to ultimately achieve the goal of industrial structure adjustment.

C. Two-Way Development and Integration of Internet Finance

From the very beginning, China's Internet finance has shown a two-way development trend. The "Internet + finance" approach demonstrated by pure Internet finance has penetrated into various fields of the original financial industry in a short period of time, breaking the boundary between direct financing and indirect financing, the real economy and the financial market, and showing the power of "Internet+". It has brought unprecedented impact to all walks of life in society. "The network has also changed the way enterprises operate. The production, distribution, exchange

[29] LI Zhihui. *The Development and Change of China's Banking Industry*. Gezhi Publishing House, Shanghai People's Publishing House, 2008.

and consumption of enterprises cannot be separated from the support of the network. Whether it is the coordination and allocation of internal resources or the acquisition and integration of external information, the network provides a convenient and effective platform for them."[30] The original financial organizations such as banks, insurance and securities continue to move forward on the basis of informatization, and the scope and degree of "finance + Internet" have been greatly expanded and improved, basically covering various models involved in pure Internet finance, forming many group financial organizations such as Ant Financial and Jingdong Finance that have obtained financial licenses. At present, the two-way development of Internet finance has begun to show a trend of integration, becoming a frontier in the current Chinese financial field, with the trend of restructuring China's financial system and structure. The two-way and integration of the Internet financial development reflects the points and trend in development of the industry. At present, China's economic restructuring needs to be based on the situation of different industries and different regions, to conduct a panoramic survey, comprehensive integration, and selectively improve the industrial structure. The structural adjustment of China's economy is very different from that of developed countries since the 1950s. Developed countries have a relatively complete industrial chain, and the phenomenon of "hollowing out" of the industry has appeared in the differentiation of the outward transfer, while many industries in China do not have core technologies, brands and other elements, and only carry out processing and production according to foreign order requirements. If the industrial transfer of developed countries and regions is followed, China will inevitably have the phenomenon of "collapse" of industries or regional industries, which will seriously affect employment and social stability. For this, we can use the two-way way of horizontal and vertical extension of the industry to achieve industrial integration and retain the higher value-added part of the industrial chain. In the process of integration to form economies of scale and scope of the economy of the industry, through the integration trend between the upstream and downstream industries, in order to eventually form an industrial group with its own advantages, to achieve regional economic structure adjustment and upgrading.

D. Appropriate Space for Policy Support in the Development of Internet Finance

When Chinese internet finance experienced an explosive growth at the beginning, although all models were fully developed, the entire industry was in a state of "three noes" (no laws, no regulations, no supervision), which led to a mixed quality of internet finance enterprises. A significant number of businesses were founded with some form of deception, leading to a constant stream of illegal deposit-taking, illegal fundraising, online pyramid schemes, money laundering, deceptive lending, forming a fund pool for self-funding, and other events. Meanwhile, the rise of Yu'ebao sparked a huge debate in society, and even saw calls for its abolition, with some comparing Yu'ebao and similar products to vampires.

---

[30] CHEN Huihui. *Research on Technological Innovation and Competitive Strategy in Network Externality Market*. Economic Management Press, 2015: 1.

However, the Chinese government has not resorted to banning them, but has given them ample room to innovate and develop. This point is not only mentioned in the report of the two sessions, but is also expressed more clearly in the "Guiding Opinions on Promoting the Healthy Development of Internet Finance" issued on July 18, 2015. The opinion states that "Internet finance is a new thing and emerging business model. We should formulate moderately relaxed regulatory policies to leave room for innovation in Internet finance". After a period of exploration, PBOC, in conjunction with relevant departments, incorporated various models of Internet finance into the relevant regulatory bodies of the existing financial management system, and conducted surveys across the country by each regulatory body. Subsequently, detailed regulatory guidelines were issued one after another, and a special rectification campaign was launched in April 2016. In October, the State Council issued the "Implementation Plan for the Special Rectification of Internet Finance Risks", launching a special rectification campaign on Internet finance and giving Internet finance-related models and operators 1 year of transition time to comply with the guidelines and rectification requirements. In 2017, in response to the new phenomena and forms of Internet finance, the rectification work on Internet finance took a differentiated approach to different models, extending the overall rectification period to June 2018. In 2018, under the bottom-line thinking of preventing financial risks, the rectification time was again extended. In this way, the phenomenon of "one-size-fits-all" administrative intervention was avoided, giving Internet finance a self-adjusting and innovative development space.

In the relationship between government and market, China has been wavering between "managing funds" and "regulating the market" from the reform and opening up to 1993, resulting in the dilemma of "chaos when given freedom and stagnation when controlled" in financial development. In terms of the policy approach to the development of Internet finance, the relationship between the two has clearly shown a greater emphasis on marketization and legalization, with less administrative intervention. The government's effective handling of the relationship between government and market in the development of Internet finance has great reference value for China's current industrial structure adjustment.

In terms of the relationship between the government and the market, China has been vacillating between "managing funds" and "regulating the market" from the reform and opening up to 1993, resulting in the dilemma of "chaos when given freedom and stagnation when controlled" in the financial development. In terms of the attitude towards the development of Internet finance, the policy ideas reflected in the relationship between the two obviously emphasize more marketization and legalization, and less administrative intervention. The government's effective handling of the relationship between the government and the market in the development of the Internet finance industry has great reference space for the current adjustment of China's industrial structure. After all, the adjustment of a country's industrial structure involves a wide range of areas and is difficult to complete in a short period of time. In this regard, China needs to be fully aware of this point at the policy level in the process of industrial structure adjustment. Many policy measures formed in the process of economic structure adjustment should also conform to the characteristics of China's industrial structure, which is dominated by manufacturing, with few core technologies and shortage of brands, and gradually promote the upgrading of industrial mix and structure. Finally, China will achieve the goal of industrial structure transformation and upgrading in a relatively stable and sustainable socio-economic environment.

Concluding Remarks

Through a review and summary of the 70 years of financial development in China, we can see that the development of China's financial industry, although it has gone through a fairly tortuous process, has become increasingly in line with the national situation and market laws, and has returned to its essence of serving the real economy. In the future development of China's financial industry, it must draw lessons from the past 70 years of experience and avoid "a familiar regression," so that the financial industry can truly serve the development of social and economic affairs and form a virtuous cycle; at the same time, it must handle the relationship between financial supervision and innovation, adhering to the principle of guarding against systemic financial risks, actively promoting financial innovation, and occupying the high ground of financial innovation. Currently, China's booming internet finance has greatly promoted the development and innovation of financial services, narrowed the gap in financial industry development between China and developed countries, and led in third-party payment and online lending in international level. However, in the future development of China's financial industry, we still need to pay attention to the following issues based on the past development experience.

First, the orderly promotion of the development trend of financial mixed industry. Since the financial sector was divided into different industries in 1995 and the "One Bank, Three Commissions" system was established in 2003, China's financial industry has officially entered the era of sectoral supervision and operation. After more than a decade of development, China's financial industry and financial system construction have made great progress. The rapid development of the financial industry, especially the rise of internet finance since 2013, has quickly broken the scope of specialized operations and blurred the boundaries between the market and institutions, leading to a high degree of integration among various financial forms and functions, forming a de facto integrated operation trend. However, in terms of the system, China has not yet fully clarified this trend, thus bringing many inconveniences to the development of various financial forms and forming many gray areas, which are prone to become the epicenters of future financial risks. The establishment of the Financial Stability Board in 2017 and the merger of the China Banking

R. Lan, *The Financial Development of China*, Understanding China,
https://doi.org/10.1007/978-981-97-8273-4

Regulatory Commission and the China Insurance Regulatory Commission, the reorganization of financial functions, and the personnel integration between the People's Bank of China and the China Banking and Insurance Regulatory Commission have undoubtedly restructured China's financial regulatory model and initially conformed to the trend of financial integration. In the future, we should still actively promote and deepen financial reform, follow the laws of market development, conform to the trend of financial integration, accelerate the construction of financial systems, and ensure the healthy and sustainable development of China's finance.

The second is the construction of inclusive finance and returning to the "original intention" of serving the real economy. The essence of finance is to serve the real economy, and "de-reality" is prone to trigger regional or systemic risks. Before the reform and opening up, the formation of the "managing funds" mechanism, although it suppressed the development of financial functions and businesses, was actually in line with the needs of capital-poor countries to promote modernization construction. It effectively achieved the concentration of dispersed capital and promoted the orderly development of heavy industry in a harsh domestic and international environment. During this period, affected by abnormal interventions such as political movements, the "managing funds" function tended towards extremism, greatly distorting the development of the financial industry. At the beginning of the reform and opening up, China adapted to the trend of diversified social and economic development and promoted the transformation of "manage funds" to "adjust the market." In the first 15 years, deeply influenced by the planned economic system, China's financial functions swung back and forth between "managing funds" and "regulating market", leading to the development disorder of "chaos when given freedom and stagnation when controlled" in the development of finance. Later, with the establishment of the socialist market economic system, China's financial development increasingly conformed to the trend of marketization, partially improved the relationship between finance and the economy, and provided the necessary financial basis for the long-term high-speed development of the economy. In 2013, China's economy entered a new normal phase, with economic growth transitioning from high-speed to medium–high-speed and shifting from quantity-oriented to quality-oriented. The hidden contradictions that had been concealed by the long-term high-speed economic growth were gradually revealed, and the supply–demand blind spots in the financial field were exposed. The infiltration of information technology into the financial field led to the rise of internet finance, and the rapid development of inclusive finance, tech finance, and green finance to some extent alleviated the "difficulty in accessing financing" situation. Modern financial organizations such as banks, securities, and insurance will further adapt to this trend, with their branches being lowered, and they will work together with pure internet finance models to promote the deepening development of inclusive finance in China, so that all entities that need financial services can obtain the necessary financial services based on their prices. The construction of an inclusive finance system will not only become an important topic in China's financial development in the coming years, but will also increasingly drive financial development back to its "original intention" of serving the real economy. Third, the positive interaction between China's financial regulation and innovation. Finance is the core of social economy, and the financial crisis is an important source of economic fluctuations. "Financial security is an important component of national security and an important foundation for the stable and healthy development of the economy. ... Finance is lively, the economy is lively; finance is stable, the economy is stable."[1] However, financial risks cannot be eradicated completely, as Schumpeter said, "There is no remedy that can permanently prevent the large-scale economic and social processes in which the status, lifestyle, cultural values and ideals of business enterprises and individuals, etc., sink to the scale of society and ultimately disappear."[2] But by studying crises and summarizing past development experiences with effective integration of current national conditions, taking proactive regulatory measures can have a significant effect in preventing and reducing the harmful effects of crises. However, if regulation is excessive, it will suppress financial innovation and distort the development of finance. This was experienced many times in the 70-year development process of China's finance, where we have gone to extremes in the relationship between financial innovation and regulation, and fallen into financial development dilemmas. In the future, in order to effectively address the relationship between regulation and innovation, we must learn from the experience of "managing funds" extremization and the experience of "chaos when given freedom and stagnation when controlled" in regulating the market, and effectively maintain the positive interaction between financial regulation and innovation in promoting financial development, and prevent extreme behavior. Currently, in China's approach to the innovation and regulation of internet finance, the relationship between the two has been effectively managed, giving emerging financial forms a certain space for innovative development and time, effectively promoting financial development while promptly promoting the reform of financial regulatory systems and mechanisms and orderly resolving various risks in financial development. In the future, according to the deployment of the Fifth National Financial Work Conference and the financial layout target in the report of the 19th CPC National Congress, we must continuously strengthen financial supervision and deepen the reform of financial supervision systems and mechanisms to guard against systemic financial risks, while giving financial development moderate innovative space to occupy the technological high ground in financial development and lead the global financial development trend.

Fourth, continuously expand the degree of China's financial openness. Since the reform and opening up, China's finance has increasingly integrated into globalization. Foreign financial institutions have entered the domestic financial market in an orderly manner and have become an important part of China's financial industry. The pace of China's financial organizations "going out" has become faster and faster, and their financial strength has continued to grow, significantly improving their international competitiveness. The scale and technical application level of internet finance are at the international leading level, and the fields of online payment and online lending are beginning to lead the global financial development. In 1996, China fully achieved

[1] XI Jinping: *Do a Good job in Financial Work and Maintain Financial Security.*

[2] Joseph Schumpeter, *The Theory of Economic Development: An Examination of Profit, Capital, Credit, Interest, and the Business Cycle*, The Commercial Press, 2000, pp. 282–283.

the convertibility of the RMB for the current account; the degree of opening up for the capital account has also been deepening, and it has been fully opened in most areas to date, while the remaining areas are being opened in an orderly manner. In 2009, the first pilot of cross-border trade RMB settlement in Shanghai has been promoted to the nationwide "Belt and Road" initiative, which has greatly promoted the internationalization process of China's RMB. In the future, with the continuous improvement of China's financial openness, China will be more and more widely involved in the governance of global finance, and Chinese elements in the financial field will become more and more.

Fifth is the continuous drive of China's financial industry by the reform of the existing financial system and the expansion of new financial products. Since 1949, the development of China's financial industry has been deeply explored around the two parts of existing reform and new expansion. The reform of the existing financial system has been the main line of China's financial development for 70 years. Before the reform and opening up, China's financial system underwent a transformation from a diversified financial institution to a unified People's Bank of China, with financial functions going to the extreme of "managing funds." After the reform and opening up, the commercial and policy functions of the People's Bank of China gradually evolved into a diversified financial system dominated by state-owned financial organizations, and then the orderly reform around state-owned financial organizations was launched, which has developed into a commercial financial organization system with an improving governance structure, becoming the driving force for China's rapid social and economic development. The expansion of new financial products is the crystallization of China's increasingly diversified economic trend. Since the rapid development of China's economy since the reform and opening up, the financial supply and demand have been in a dilemma, and new financial organizations have been emerging continuously. The financial market has grown from scratch, and a diversified and multi-tiered financial system has been established. They work together with the reform of the existing financial system to promote the deep development of China's financial industry. In the future, China's financial industry will continue to develop in a sustained manner through both the reform of the existing system and the expansion of new areas. Therefore, China still needs to handle the relationship between the two properly to promote the healthy and sustainable development of the financial industry in a more harmonious way.

Sixth, be cautious in handling the role of the market and the government in China's financial development. In the 70 years of China's financial development since 1949, if the relationship between the market and the government is not handled properly, financial development will certainly experience a relatively tortuous process, even restricting economic development; if the relationship is properly handled, finance will show a rapid development trend, playing a greater role in promoting economic development. Before the reform and opening up, the market function was basically suppressed, and the financial function was highly concentrated on "managing funds". From the reform and opening up to the present in 1995, China's financial function has fluctuated between "managing funds" and "regulating the market", sometimes with a stronger market role, sometimes with a stronger government role, always trying to find a balance between the two, but with financial development constantly constrained and not smooth. With the clear definition of the "regulating market" function, China's financial industry entered a period of rapid development. In 1997, the First National Financial Work Conference was held, which effectively played the top-level design role of the government in financial development and further offset the market's shortcomings in promoting financial development, thus accelerating the development of finance. In the future, China needs to further clarify the decisive role of the market in resource allocation, and the government needs to play a greater role to promote the sustainable and healthy development of China's finance.

Postscript

On the occasion of the 70th anniversary of the founding of the People's Republic of China, reviewing and summarizing the development of China's financial industry holds significant theoretical and practical value for its future development. The 70-year development of finance in China is extremely extensive, and each part or stage could form a book or a series of works. Clearly, presenting such a complex and lengthy financial evolution in a single work is an extremely challenging task. Building on existing research, this book takes a unique approach and strives to discuss the complex 70-year development process of finance from the perspective of the evolution of financial functions, dividing it into four stages for analysis. After clarifying and summarizing the changes in financial development, it concludes that the initial establishment of the financial system in the early days of the People's Republic of China continued the practices of various revolutionary bases during the war period, meeting the needs of economic development through state-owned or collective funds and issuing currency. Until the establishment of the 'fund management' function in 1978, the financial system catered to the goal of domestic modernization but was disrupted by various political movements, severely affecting the performance of financial functions and hindering its role in serving the real economy. After the reform and opening-up, the financial function oscillated between "fund management" and "market regulation," representing a crucial aspect of China's gradual economic reform. Attempts were made to explore a unique path for China's financial development, but in practice, it fell into the dilemma of intervention or non-intervention. The clear positioning of "market regulation" is more in line with the development needs of China's socio-economy. The first National Financial Work Conference held in 1997 significantly elevated the top-level design thinking of financial development, promoting a positive interaction between China's finance and the real economy. Subsequently, the National Financial Work Conference held every 5 years undoubtedly provided a clear direction for the reform of China's finance.

This book, as part of the "Research Series on the Economic and Social Development of the People's Republic of China," is edited by Associate Director Wu Li from the Contemporary China Research Institute. It is included in the "13th Five-Year Plan" national key book publishing project. Since the initiation of the

R. Lan, *The Financial Development of China*, Understanding China,
https://doi.org/10.1007/978-981-97-8273-4

publishing project by Huazhong University of Science and Technology Press in 2016, through multiple discussions in Beijing, Tai'an, and other places, the structure and content of the manuscript gradually took shape. During this period, the author successfully applied for the 2017 project of the National Social Science Fund with the title "Research on the Development of China's Financial Development: 1949–2019." Subsequently, through data collection, organization, and the process of simultaneous writing, lecturing, and discussing, the author completed the manuscript titled "Research on the Development of China's Financial Industry." This book is one of the midterm achievements of the National Social Science Fund's general project and has received support from the first batch of the Education Ministry's national university "double leading" teachers' party branch secretary's studio—the Economic History Department Teachers' Party Branch Secretary's Studio at the Central University of Finance and Economics School of Economics. It is also one of the key achievements commemorating the 70th anniversary of the founding of the People's Republic of China by the studio. The content of this book was systematically taught to master's and doctoral students at Central University of Finance and Economics in 2016. Later, at the invitation of Professor Yan Hongzhong from the School of Economics at Shanghai University of Finance and Economics, the author lectured at the Economic History Forum of Shanghai University of Finance and Economics. Some content was also presented at the Fourth "Economics and History" Academic Seminar of Renmin University of China. It can be said that this book is a crystallization of the "mutual learning through teaching" and small-scale teaching discussions.

This book closely examines the 70-year development of China's financial industry and the changes in economic development. From the perspective of financial functions, it outlines a general framework of financial transformation, providing a platform for future research and practical discussions. At the same time, it hopes to serve as a starting point for seeking advice from colleagues. If the content of this book captures your interest or resonates with you, contributing to your thoughtful research, it would bring great satisfaction to the author. Due to various constraints, there may be shortcomings in the book, and the author sincerely invites readers to offer valuable feedback. The author's email is galenlan@126.com.

The writing of this book has received assistance from many individuals. Mr. Wu Li, Deputy Director of the Institute of Contemporary China Studies, provided comprehensive guidance throughout the entire process, from the title and structure to the final manuscript formation. Gratitude to Mr. Wu cannot be adequately expressed in words. During the writing process, I also received substantial assistance from Professor Yao Sui of the School of Finance at Central University of Finance and Economics, Professor Li Tao, Associate Professor Gu Weiyu, Professor Gao Wei, Associate Professor Fu Lin, and Associate Professor Xiao Xiang from the School of Economics, Associate Professor Xiao Xiang from the School of Marxism at CUEB, Professor He Ping from Renmin University of China, Professor Chen Zhengping from Tsinghua University, Professor Xiao Guoliang and Professor Zhou Jianbo from Peking University, Researcher Zhao Xuejun, Researcher Dong Zhikai, Researcher Peng Xinchun, Researcher Wei Mingkong, and Researcher Sui Fuming from the

Institute of Economics at the Chinese Academy of Social Sciences, Researcher Gao Chaoqun and Researcher Huang Yingwei from the Editorial Department of "Research on Chinese Economic History," Researcher Zheng Yougui, Researcher Wang Ruifang, Associate Researcher Duan Juan, and Dr. Guo Xuhong from the Institute of Contemporary China Studies, Professor Su Shaozhi from Zhongnan University of Economics and Law, Professor Yan Hongzhong, Professor Li Nan, and Professor Du Xuncheng from Shanghai University of Finance and Economics, Professor Wu Jingping, Professor Zhu Yingui, and Professor Zhang Xule from Fudan University, Researcher He Shuijin from the Shanghai Academy of Social Sciences, Professor Wang Yuru and Associate Professor Gong Guan from Nankai University, Associate Professor Shen Xiaoyong from Beijing Institute of Technology, and many others.

Special thanks to the caring and support of my parents, wife, brothers, and other relatives both materially and spiritually. It is their concern and affection that relieved my worries, allowing me to concentrate on writing and successfully completing this book on time.

References

1. People's Bank of China. 2008. *Sixty years of the People's Bank of China (1948–2008)*. China Finance Publishing House.
2. Yang, Xitian, et al. 2002. *General history of Chinese finance (volume 6): the period of the People's Republic of China*. China Finance Publishing House.
3. Li, Yang, et al. 2009. *60 years of China's finance*. China Financial and Economic Publishing House.
4. Li, De. 2015. *Development process of China's financial industry (volume 2)*. People's Publishing House.
5. Lan, Rixu. 2016. *Changes in financial organizations at home and abroad: a perspective based on market-technology-organization*. Social Sciences Academic Press.
6. Li, Zhihui. 2008. *The development and changes of China's banking industry*. Truth & Wisdom Press, Shanghai People's Publishing House.
7. Hu, Ruyin. 2008. *Development and changes of China's capital market*. Truth & Wisdom Press, Shanghai People's Publishing House.
8. Shang, Ming. 1999. *50 years of finance of China*. China Finance and Economics Press.
9. Shang, Ming, Li Chen, Chengming Wang. 1993. *Chronicle of financial events in the People's Republic of China*. China Financial Publishing House.
10. Chinese Academy of Social Sciences, Central Archives. 2011. *1958–1965 economic archives of the People's Republic of China: finance volume*. China Financial and Economic Press.
11. Xu, Shuxin. 2018. *Outline of the monetary history of the Chinese revolutionary base areas*. China Finance Press.
12. Du, Xuncheng. 2002. *The system, functions, and changes of Shanghai finance: 1897–1997*. Shanghai People's Publishing House.
13. Yao, Sui. 2007. *A history of Chinese finance*. Higher Education Press.
14. Jiang, Hongye. 1991. *The history of local banks in China*. Hunan Publishing House.
15. Hong, Jia Guan. 2001. *History of Chinese finance*. Southwest University of Finance and Economics Press.
16. Chen, Yun. 2005. Four essays on finance and economy (March or April 1944)—July 1956. *Party Literature* 3.
17. Financial Research Institute of the People's Bank of China. 1983. *Collected works of Cao Jurong*. China Financial Publishing House.
18. Zhang, Jie. 2007. *Performance of China's rural financial system adjustment: a perspective of financial demand*. Renmin University of China Press.
19. Yi, Gang. 2009. *Reflections on China's financial reform*. The Commercial Press.
20. Qi, Qun. 2012. *Development and innovation of China's money market*. Law Press.
21. Yang, Peixin. 1982. *China's finance*. People's Publishing House.
22. Central Compilation and Translation Bureau of the CPC Central Committee. 2005. Collected works of Chen Yun (volume two). *Central Compilation and Translation Press*.

R. Lan, *The Financial Development of China*, Understanding China,
https://doi.org/10.1007/978-981-97-8273-4

23. Su, Ning. 2007. *China financial statistics (1949–2005)*. China Financial Press.
24. Wu, Li. 2010. *Economic history of the People's Republic of China*. China Times Economic Press.
25. Yang, Decai. 2009. *New perspectives on Chinese economic history (1949–2009)*. Economic Science Press.
26. Lan, Rixu. 2017. Reflections on the impact of the development of the internet finance industry on China's industrial restructuring. *Research on Industry and the History of Science and Technology* 2.
27. Lan, Rixu. 2017. Financial changes and characteristics in China: based on the perspective of financial function changes. *Journal of Hebei Normal University* 6.
28. Xie, Ping, Chuanwei, Zou. 2012. A study on internet financial models. *Financial Research* 12.
29. Zhang, Xiaojun, Yue, Ma. 2016. *Understanding Chinese finance*. Chemical Industry Press.
30. Yao, Wenping. 2014. *Internet finance: the coming new financial era*. Citic Press.
31. Chen, Huihui. 2015. *Research on technological innovation and competitive strategy in network externality markets*. Economic Management Press.
32. Wang, Liangliang. 2016. *Development of internet finance: a study on the impact on traditional financial industry*. China Financial Publishing House.
33. Zhang, Jianhua. 2010. *Financial system of China*. China Financial Publishing House.
34. Xi, Jinping. 2017. Secure a decisive victory in building a moderately prosperous society in all respects and strive for the great success of socialism with Chinese characteristics for a new era—report at the 19th national congress of the communist party of China.
35. Deng, Xiaoping. 2008. *Deng Xiaoping selected works (volume 2)*. People's Publishing House.
36. Zhu, Min, Jinqing, Cai, Meixia, Ai. 2010. *The rise of China's financial industry—challenges and global impact*. CITIC Publishing House.
37. Cao, Yuanzheng. 2018. *Great power and great finance: 40 years of financial system reform in China*. Guangdong Economic Publishing House.
38. "Jingshan Report". 2018. *The second half of China's financial opening up*. CITIC Press.
39. Joseph, Schumpeter. 2000. *Economic development theory: an inquiry into profits, capital, credit, interest, and the business cycle*. Translated by He Wei, Yi Jiaxiang, Zhang Junkuo, and others. The Commercial Press.
40. Laurent, Brafman, Röesky, Thomas. 2009. *The great transformation of the Chinese economy*. Translated by Fang Ying, Zhao Yang, and others. Gezhi Publishing House, Shanghai People's Publishing House.
41. Brock, James W. 2011. *Industrial structure in the United States*. China Renmin University Press.

SPRINGER NATURE

GPSR Compliance

The European Union's (EU) General Product Safety Regulation (GPSR) is a set of rules that requires consumer products to be safe and our obligations to ensure this.

If you have any concerns about our products, you can contact us on ProductSafety@springernature.com

In case Publisher is established outside the EU, the EU authorized representative is:

Springer Nature Customer Service Center GmbH
Europaplatz 3
69115 Heidelberg, Germany

The manufacturer's authorised representative in the EU is Springer Nature Customer Service Centre GmbH, Europaplatz 3, 69115 Heidelberg, Germany. If you have any concerns regarding our products, please contact ProductSafety@springernature.com

Printed and bound by CPI Group (UK) Ltd, Croydon, CR0 4YY
06/10/2026
02228482-0002